International Adjudication on Trial

INTERNATIONAL ECONOMIC LAW

The *International Economic Law* series, established by the late Professor John H. Jackson, addresses a range of issues in international economic law, which includes international trade law, international investment law, and the global financial order. The Series aims to encourage interest in the broad contours of international economic law, heightening awareness of its significance across the globe, as well as its continuous interactions with other areas. The Series editors encourage quality submissions from a wide range of perspectives, including doctrinal, theoretical, empirical, and interdisciplinary. Novel and cutting-edge research is particularly welcome, as are contributions from both emerging and established scholars from around the world.

ALSO PUBLISHED IN THIS SERIES

China's International Investment Strategy
Bilateral, Regional, and Global Law and Policy
Edited by Julien Chaisse

Emissions Trading Schemes under International Economic Law
James Munro

The Trade Policy Review Mechanism
A Critical Analysis
Mathias Kende

Mega-Regional Trade Agreements: CETA, TTIP, and TiSA
New Orientations for EU External Economic Relations
Edited by Stefan Griller, Walter Obwexer, and Erich Vranes

Small and Medium-Sized Enterprises in International Economic Law
Edited by Thilo Rensmann

Domestic Law in International Investment Arbitration
Jarrod Hepburn

Treaty Shopping in International Investment Law
Jorun Baumgartner

International Adjudication on Trial

The Effectiveness of the WTO Dispute Settlement System

SIVAN SHLOMO AGON

OXFORD
UNIVERSITY PRESS

OXFORD
UNIVERSITY PRESS

Great Clarendon Street, Oxford, OX2 6DP,
United Kingdom

Oxford University Press is a department of the University of Oxford. It furthers the University's objective of excellence in research, scholarship, and education by publishing worldwide. Oxford is a registered trade mark of Oxford University Press in the UK and in certain other countries

First Edition published in 2019

Impression: 1

Published in the United States of America by Oxford University Press
198 Madison Avenue, New York, NY 10016, United States of America

British Library Cataloguing in Publication Data

Data available

Library of Congress Control Number: 2019941481

ISBN 978–0–19–878896–6

Printed and bound by
CPI Group (UK) Ltd, Croydon, CR0 4YY

To my parents

Series Editor's Preface

For around two decades, the dispute settlement system of the World Trade Organization (WTO) was characterized as the 'jewel in the crown' of the WTO. Its rule-based nature was contrasted to power-based dispute settlement under the *General Agreement on Tariffs and Trade 1947* (GATT), its ambitious timelines compared to long delays in both international tribunals and domestic courts. Even when negotiations to reform WTO rules were going poorly (which happened often), WTO disputes continued to be resolved. Compliance with the recommendations and rulings of the WTO's Dispute Settlement Body (DSB) was a key measure of the effectiveness of this system, and generally compliance was good.

Today, the WTO itself and the dispute settlement system are being severely tested by developments in the international community, from the imposition of unprecedented tariffs to more frequent invocation of exceptions including public morals and national security, and perhaps most of all by the United States' blocking of appointments to the WTO Appellate Body, which continues at the time of writing. Especially at such a time, an investigation into the effectiveness of the WTO dispute settlement system is crucial to understanding both why the system has worked for so long and how it may continue to function and evolve despite more recent challenges.

Dr Sivan Shlomo Agon's book goes to the heart of these important issues, beginning and ending with the question of whether compliance with DSB rulings is the best way of determining the effectiveness of the WTO dispute settlement system. Departing from most of the existing literature on this system, Shlomo Agon contests compliance as a central measure of its effectiveness. Instead, drawing on social science literature on organizational effectiveness, she posits a goal-based framework for assessing the effectiveness of WTO dispute settlement. In establishing this framework, she identifies both the ultimate goals of the system—such as preserving the balance of rights and obligations between WTO Members and conferring legitimacy on the WTO and its underlying norms—and its intermediate goals (which include WTO-consistency, preventing unilateralism, and legitimating the dispute settlement system itself).

This goal-based framework enables a more nuanced evaluation of WTO dispute settlement than has previously been conducted. By selecting a range of significant completed cases for in-depth analysis, and by supplementing doctrinal and documentary research with extensive interviews with key actors, Shlomo Agon enhances our understanding of the goals of the WTO dispute settlement system and the reasons for its longstanding success. Bringing fresh insights to well-known disputes from *EC – Bananas* to *US – Clove Cigarettes*, she demonstrates the multiplicity of goals in WTO dispute settlement, the potential for such goals to intersect and conflict, and the reality of goal-shifting, whereby the goals of the system change over time and between different types of disputes.

While cautioning against a return to the power-based GATT system, Shlomo Agon emphasizes the importance of considering the possible unintended consequences of an overly legalistic dispute settlement system in the WTO, such as obviating the need to resolve issues in WTO negotiations, leaving them to be resolved instead through WTO disputes. Rather than viewing imperfect compliance as a flaw in the system, Shlomo Agon argues that 'flexibility in the resolution of disputes … may work to sustain [the] enduring functioning and effectiveness' of the WTO and WTO dispute settlement, 'i.e., their ability to achieve their various policy goals in the long run'. This notion of tolerating non-compliance as a means of sustaining the WTO and its dispute settlement system provides an important message to trade negotiators as they continue to navigate proposals for reform and avenues for rescuing the WTO Appellate Body and the organization as a whole.

This book offers a note of hopefulness to current debates, because if the goals of the WTO dispute settlement system do and have changed in the past, the system may be more amenable to reform and continued functioning in the future. And a resilient dispute settlement system could help secure the future of the WTO itself.

Andrew D Mitchell
Tania Voon
May 2019

Preface

The replacement of GATT with the World Trade Organization (WTO) at the end of the Uruguay Round of trade negotiations (1986–1994) marked the beginning of a new age of dispute settlement in the multilateral trading system. Following a deal struck between the US, which sought to strengthen the multilateral dispute settlement mechanism, and other trading partners that wanted to curtail US power to use unilateral trade measures, the GATT's 'power-oriented' mechanism gave way in 1995 to a reformed, more 'rule-oriented' dispute settlement system (DSS) under the WTO's auspices. The rules and procedures of the legalized WTO DSS were laid down in a special agreement, known as the Dispute Settlement Understanding (DSU). Among its various innovations, the DSU established a compulsory and binding dispute settlement procedure that eliminated the option, previously available to Members under GATT, to stall the dispute settlement process by blocking the establishment of a panel or the adoption of its report. No less important, the DSU instituted a standing Appellate Body (AB) of seven jurists charged with reviewing issues of law and legal interpretations developed by panels in accordance with customary rules of interpretation of public international law.

These two fundamental reforms paved the way, in turn, for a new chapter in the history of international adjudication and global economic governance. Since its inception in 1995, the legalized WTO DSS has considered hundreds of trade disputes between WTO Members. Developed and developing countries alike have become active players in the system, which has earned a reputation as the 'jewel in the crown' of the WTO. Under the lead of the AB, a rich and coherent body of WTO jurisprudence has emerged, covering issues ranging from classic trade measures such as subsidies and anti-dumping duties, to novel trade-restrictive policies in areas such as tobacco control and climate change mitigation. Scholars across disciplines have devoted extensive research efforts to studying the DSS's design and operation, often applauding the system's high judgment-compliance rates and its contribution to entrenching the rule of law in international trade relations. In parallel, businesses, the media, and NGOs throughout the world have attentively followed DSS proceedings, spurred by their recognition of this adjudicative system as a dominant site having the power to affect their interests and concerns.

At the same time, and almost from the start, the judicialized WTO DSS has been the subject of controversy and criticism, taking blows from actors within and outside the multilateral trade circle. Prevalent critiques have targeted, among other things, the alleged engagement of WTO panels and the AB in judicial activism, as well as their undue encroachment on state regulatory autonomy. Criticism has likewise been levelled at the institutional imbalance between the WTO's judicial and political arms, intensified by the tradition of consensus-based political decision-making at the WTO that has rendered negotiating breakthroughs difficult to achieve and made it essentially impossible for WTO Members to overturn DSS rulings.

Against this background, critical questions have arisen: Is the WTO DSS effective? How exactly is the effectiveness of this judicialized dispute settlement mechanism to be defined and measured? Is its effectiveness all about compliance, as common wisdom seems to suggest? If not, what goals, beyond compliance, is the WTO DSS expected to achieve? Has it fulfilled these objectives so far, and how can their achievement and the system's effectiveness be enhanced in a rapidly changing global environment? These questions about the effectiveness, impact, and possible improvement of the WTO DSS motivated the writing of this book.

It was a few years back, when the WTO DSS was approaching its twentieth anniversary, that I started delving into these questions. I was struck by the pivotal role this rules-based dispute settlement mechanism has grown to play in the multilateral trading system and the leading position it has gained among international courts and tribunals. Yet, these effectiveness-related questions seem to have become even more acute as I reached this book's finish line, with the WTO DSS making headlines around the world as it faces the biggest crisis in its 24 years of existence. The immediate trigger of the unprecedented crisis besetting the DSS at the time of wrapping up this book is the US backlash against the system, observed in the Trump administration's continued blocking of new appointments to the AB, a development that threatens to severely undermine the functioning of the entire WTO dispute settlement structure. At the core of the US criticism of the DSS, which predates the Trump administration, are concerns over procedural as well as substantive aspects of the system's design and operation, especially what the US considers as the AB's 'judicial overreach'. Such concerns had already led the previous Bush and Obama administrations to block the (re)appointment of some individual AB members. However, fuelled by qualms regarding multilateralism and mandatory international adjudication, as well as by heightened political and economic tensions with China, the Trump administration has raised long-lasting US concerns about the WTO judiciary to new levels. Within this context, it has moved to block the initiation of the formal process for selecting any new AB members, an action signalling the US perceived need for systemic reform of the WTO DSS, especially its appellate instance.

As things stand while writing these words, unless there is a significant shift in US policy, only one AB member will remain in office by December 2019, thus bringing the number of sitting members below the required three to hear appeals. Should that happen, the WTO DSS would be left without its formal appellate review process and panel rulings would become binding only if all the parties to the dispute agree not to invoke their right of appeal. Such events could, in turn, incapacitate the DSS in a period it may be needed most, when critical challenges are facing the multilateral trading system centred around the WTO. In this respect, I need mention only the WTO's struggle to overcome the long-standing stalemate in multilateral negotiations, the continuing surge in regional trade agreements, the urge for protectionism and unilateralism manifested in the trade policies recently adopted by some major players, and the sharp escalation of the US-China trade war by means of a dramatic increase in tariffs. In this turbulent environment, failure to resolve the AB crisis could result in the further spread of tit-for-tat retaliatory tariffs around the world, culminating in reduced security and predictability as well as lower economic growth for all the actors involved. More fundamentally, failure to solve the current DSS impasse runs the risk of weakening the bulwarks of the multilateral rules-based order and returning to a power-based trading system in which powerful states can impose their will through unilateral trade measures at the same time that the interests of small players are left out on a limb.

As I finalize the writing of this book, therefore, the story of the legalized WTO DSS has largely become a story of an international court on trial, the fate of which is currently shrouded in uncertainty. The potential consequences of the present DSS crisis are nevertheless clear to all. Hence, in an effort to prevent the paralysis of the DSS in the very near future (i.e., in December 2019), various short-term solutions have been offered with a view to ensuring that trade disputes will continue to be resolved within the multilateral WTO framework. However, as implied by several DSS reform proposals recently put forward by WTO Members in an attempt to address US concerns, preservation of the WTO's two-stage binding adjudicative system in the long term will likely require some changes, perhaps as part of a more-comprehensive WTO reform aimed at modernizing the Organization so that it can better meet the evolving demands of world trade.

And so, as in the years leading to the Uruguay Round negotiations, the multilateral trading system and its dispute settlement mechanism are (again) in crisis. It is somewhat ironic that the crisis has been instigated by the very same country that originally pushed for the creation of the WTO and its strengthened dispute settlement apparatus. Still, this state of unrest may nevertheless be leading us to another transformative stage in the evolution of the multilateral trading system, where its DSS may once more be subjected to reform.

A fundamental condition for informed and meaningful reform of the WTO DSS, however, is a better understanding of the effectiveness of this judicial system as it currently operates, as well as of the appropriate measures against which its performance is to be put on trial and judged. While the general assessment of the WTO DSS has so far been quite positive, its effectiveness cannot continue to be measured against narrow conventional benchmarks, such as the number of disputes filed or the compliance rate generated. Rather, the effectiveness of the DSS must be evaluated more broadly, against the multiple (and at times contradictory) goals entrusted to the system by its 'mandate providers', the community of WTO

Member states. To that end, this book offers a comprehensive, nuanced, and dynamic analytical framework for studying, thinking, and arguing about the effectiveness of the WTO DSS—a framework that transcends classic standards such as compliance, considers the wide corpus of institutional goals prescribed for the DSS, and takes the conflictual and shifting nature of these goals into account. The book carries out this research endeavour while crafting a revealing insider's account of the WTO DSS, drawn from dozens of interviews with WTO practitioners involved in the inner workings of the DSS. Through this insider's look and a detailed examination of landmark WTO disputes, the book uncovers the oft-hidden dynamics of WTO adjudication and provides a fresh perspective on the DSS's operation, the diverse roles it plays, the outcomes it produces, and the undercurrents affecting its effectiveness.

In these challenging times for international economic cooperation, for the WTO, and for the DSS lying at its heart, it is my hope that this book can make an important contribution towards a deeper and more complete understanding and assessment of the benefits (as well as the costs) this international adjudicative body generates. Hopefully, the book's insights will also prove valuable in sculpting any future DSS reform.

Sivan Shlomo Agon
May 2019

Acknowledgements

In writing this book, a long and challenging intellectual and personal journey, I have benefited greatly from the guidance and support of many individuals and institutions to whom I owe a debt of gratitude. First, I am deeply grateful to Yuval Shany and Tomer Broude, the supervisors of the dissertation at the foundation of this book, who have supported me enormously throughout the work on this research project. Their high academic standards, expertise, dedication, and friendship have been a major source of advice and inspiration. I cannot possibly express the extent of my gratitude to them. I also owe sincere thanks to Moshe Hirsch and Arie Reich, as well as to my dissertation's referees, Robert Howse and Jeffery Dunoff, for their precious time and valuable comments.

My thanks also go to the WTO Secretariat and its Legal Affairs Division for hosting me as an intern and visiting scholar during my research. Without these unique experiences, I would not have been able to gain direct access to the dispute settlement system standing at the centre of this book, nor to meet and learn from those who are regularly involved in its workings. I wish to thank, in particular, Valerie Hughes and Maria Pereyra for allowing me to take part in the WTO internship program, and to Gabrielle Marceau for inviting me to arrive at the WTO once again, as a visiting scholar, in order to complete the field research required for this book. This is a great opportunity for me to also thank the numerous interviewees—WTO adjudicators, staff members of the WTO Secretariat, ambassadors, trade delegates, and practicing lawyers at the ACWL and private law firms—for sharing with me their valuable knowledge, experience, and insights, without which this work would not have reached fruition. The scholarship I received from the ERC Project on the Effectiveness of International Adjudication covered expenses related to this vast qualitative research. Funding awarded by the Research Authority at Bar-Ilan University supported the subsequent writing of this book.

Special words of thanks are reserved for my style editor—Nina Reshef—for her professionalism, enthusiasm, and remarkable devotion throughout the process. At the final stages of this work, I likewise benefited from the exceptional technical assistance of Gal Ben-Haim, Daria Chill, and Eden Farber. Still, I alone am responsible for what I have written, and all errors in the pages that follow are my own. My thanks further go to the team at OUP for their great effort and professional assistance in publishing my work. Special thanks are due in this respect, to Merel Alstein, the international law commissioning editor, to Jack McNichol, the commissioning assistant in charge of this book, to Tania Voon and Andrew Mitchell, the editors of the International Economic Law series, and to Rajalakshmi Senbagaraman , the book's project manager.

Then there is my family. I do not have enough words to express my gratitude to my parents, Shlomit and Haim Shlomo, for their endless love, care, support, and reassurance, which sustained me every step of the way. These extraordinary individuals, the first to instil in me the love of learning and exploring, stood by me unconditionally in the face of every challenge I encountered. This book is dedicated to them.

Finally, this book would not have seen the light of the day had it not been for the unwavering help, support and commitment of my beloved husband, Zohar Agon. I thank you, for much more than this book.

Contents

PART II WHEN TRADE AND NONTRADE VALUES COLLIDE: LINKAGE DISPUTES FROM A GOAL-BASED PERSPECTIVE

PART III WHEN DISPUTES WON'T GO AWAY: PERENNIAL DISPUTES FROM A GOAL-BASED PERSPECTIVE

List of Abbreviations

AB	Appellate Body
ACP	Africa, the Caribbean, and the Pacific
ACWL	Advisory Center on WTO Law
AJIL	American Journal of International Law
ASEAN	Association of Southeast Asian Nations
CETA	Comprehensive Economic and Trade Agreement
CRTA	Committee on Regional Trade Agreements
DG	Director General
DISC	Domestic International Sales Cooperation
DSB	Dispute Settlement Body
DSS	Dispute Settlement System
DSU	Dispute Settlement Understanding
EC	European Communities
ECJ	European Court of Justice
EEC	European Economic Community
EJIL	European Journal of International Law
EJIR	European Journal of International Relations
EPA	European Partnership Agreement
EU	European Union
FCTC	Framework Convention on Tobacco Control
FSC	Foreign Sales Corporations
FTA	Free Trade Agreement
GATS	General Agreement on Trade in Services
GATT	General Agreement on Tariffs and Trade
HQB	High-Quality Beef
ICJ	International Court of Justice
ITO	International Trade Organization
MERCOSUR	Mercado Común del Sur
MFN	Most-Favoured Nation
MOU	Memorandum of Understanding
NAFTA	North American Free Trade Agreement
NGO	Nongovernmental Organization
PPM	Processes and Production Methods
PRS	Price Range System
RTA	Regional Trade Agreement
SEA	Single European Act
SPS	Sanitary and Phytosanitary Measures
TBT	Technical Barriers to Trade
TPP	Trans-Pacific Partnership
UK	United Kingdom

US	United States
USTR	United States Trade Representative
VCLT	Vienna Convention on the Law of Treaties
WHO	World Health Organization
WTO	World Trade Organization

Introduction

International Judicial Effectiveness and the WTO Dispute Settlement System: Framing the State of the Field

The World Trade Organization (WTO) Dispute Settlement System (DSS) opened its doors on 1 January 1995. Considered by many to be 'a fundamental pillar' of the multilateral trade system and global economic governance,[1] and a leading actor among international courts and tribunals,[2] this adjudicative institution, currently under substantial pressure, is a rather complex social construct.[3] It is expected to achieve multiple goals, and those goals often conflict with one another. It is constituted in a dynamic global environment where numerous actors, interests, and constraints face it with competing demands that constantly generate shifts in the means and efforts taken in pursuit of its manifold goals. The WTO DSS, established when the WTO took over from the General Agreement on Tariffs and Trade (GATT) as the structure overseeing the multilateral trading system, is also a composite of the old and the new, where traditional elements of GATT diplomacy are intertwined with modern ingredients of an enhanced legal nature. It is a compulsory adjudicatory system embedded in what is still a 'Member-driven organization'; yet at the same time, it forms part of a broader project of international adjudication, motivated by the will to bolster the rule of law in international relations. Because of this diversity and complexity, analysis of the effectiveness of the WTO DSS can be a difficult and challenging task.

However, in the existing literature on the WTO DSS, the system and assessment of its effectiveness often appear not that complicated. While largely projecting a favourable view of DSS performance so far, this literature, in line with most research on the effectiveness of international courts in general, tends to follow rather 'crude

[1] 'Azevêdo Urges Commonwealth to Play Full Part in Strengthening the Multilateral System' (*WTO News*, 11 September 2018) <https://www.wto.org/english/news_e/spra_e/spra233_e.htm> accessed 18 December 2018 [hereinafter *WTO News* 2018].

[2] Richard Stewart and Michelle Sanchez Badin, 'The World Trade Organization: Multiple Dimensions of Global Administrative Law' (2011) 9 Int'l J Const L 556, 562.

[3] As elaborated later in the Introduction, at the time of completing this book project (January 2019), the major source of stress facing the WTO DSS is the attack launched against it and, especially, against its Appellate Body (AB), by the United States in the form of blocking the appointment of AB Members, what may deprive this body of the personnel needed to adjudicate cases as of December 2019. See Rachel Brewster, 'The Trump Administration and the Future of the WTO' (2019) 44 Yale J Int'l L (forthcoming).

and/or intuitive definitions' of judicial effectiveness, which often 'equate' this notion with usage rates and compliance with judicial decisions.[4] Thus, in accordance with the dominant models in the field, the effectiveness of the WTO DSS has often been assessed against its usage record, namely, the number of disputes filed with the system and, most commonly, against the benchmark of WTO Members' compliance with adverse DSS rulings.[5] Yet, usage rates and judgment compliance, though targeting aspects of importance to the operation of the WTO DSS, and other international courts, constitute, at most, limited proxies for judicial effectiveness.

[4] Yuval Shany, *Assessing the Effectiveness of International Courts: A Goal-Based Approach* (OUP 2014) 4. For a discussion and critique of the tendency in the current literature on international courts to equate judicial effectiveness with judgment-compliance and usage rates see also 4–5; Emilie M Hafner-Burton, David G Victor, and Yonatan Lupu, 'Political Science Research on International Law: The State of the Field' (2012) 106 AJIL 47, 93. For illustrative works on the effectiveness of international courts focusing on compliance and usage rates, see, e.g. Laurence R Helfer and Anne-Marie Slaughter, 'Toward a Theory of Effective Supranational Adjudication' (1997) 107 Yale LJ 273; Eric A Posner and John C Yoo, 'Judicial Independence in International Tribunals' (2005) 93 Calif L Rev 1; Aloysius P Llamzon, 'Jurisdiction and Compliance in Recent Decisions of the International Court of Justice' (2009) 20 EJIL 815; Colter Paulson, 'Compliance with Final Judgments of the International Court of Justice since 1987' (2004) 98 AJIL 434; Constanze Schulte, *Compliance with Decisions of the International Court of Justice* (OUP 2004). For a discussion of the more general trend to assess the effectiveness of international law and institutions through the lens of state compliance with international legal prescriptions, see Lisa L Martin, 'Against Compliance' in Jeffrey L Dunoff and Mark A Pollack (eds), *Interdisciplinary Perspectives on International Law and International Relations: The State of the Art* (CUP 2013) 591; Robert Howse and Ruti Teitel, 'Beyond Compliance: Rethinking Why International Law Really Matters' (2010) 1 Global Pol'y 127.

[5] See Manfred Elsig, Bernard Hoekman, and Joost Pauwelyn, 'Thinking About the Performance of the World Trade Organization: A Discussion Across Disciplines' in Manfred Elsig, Bernard Hoekman, and Joost Pauwelyn (eds), *Assessing the World Trade Organization: Fit for Purpose?* (CUP 2017) 28 (noting that '[t]he predominant approach to assessing the performance of WTO dispute settlement is less than satisfactory. Most legal scholars and WTO insiders ... have focused on either usage rates, that is, how many disputes have been filed at the WTO, or compliance with adverse rulings issued by WTO panels or the Appellate Body'). For illustrative works on the WTO DSS focusing on usage-rate effectiveness measures and, in particular, judgment compliance, see, e.g. Giorgio Sacerdoti, 'The WTO Dispute Settlement System: Consolidating Success and Confronting New Challenges' in Manfred Elsig, Bernard Hoekman, and Joost Pauwelyn (eds), *Assessing the World Trade Organization: Fit for Purpose?* (CUP 2017) 148–52; Arie Reich, 'The Effectiveness of the WTO Dispute Settlement System: A Statistical Analysis' (2017) EUI Working Paper 2017/11 <https://papers.ssrn.com/sol3/papers.cfm?abstract_id=2997094> accessed 18 December 2018; William J Davey, 'The WTO and Rules-Based Dispute Settlement: Historical Evolution, Operational Success, and Future Challenges' (2014) 17 J Int'l Econ L 679, 687–90 [hereinafter Davey 2014]; Gabriele Spilker, 'Compliance with WTO Dispute Rulings' (2012) NCCR Working Paper 2011/25 <http://www.nccr-trade.org/fileadmin/user_upload/nccr-trade.ch/wp1/Compliance_Spilker_2012.pdf> accessed 18 December 2018; Valerie Hughes, 'Why Is the WTO Dispute Settlement System So Successful?' (2012) Video Lecture <https://www.wto.org/english/tratop_e/dispu_e/event_archive_e.htm> accessed 18 December 2018; Edward Lee, 'Measuring TRIPS Compliance and Defiance: The WTO Compliance Scorecard' (2011) 18 J Intell Prop L 401; William J Davey, 'Compliance Problems in WTO Dispute Settlement' (2009) 42 Cornell Int'l LJ 119; Donald McRae, 'Measuring the Effectiveness of the WTO Dispute Settlement System' (2008) 3 Asian J WTO & Int'l Health L & Pol'y 1; Gary Horlick and Judith Coleman, 'A Comment on Compliance with WTO Dispute Settlement Decisions' in Merit E Janow, Victoria Donaldson, and Alan Yanovich (eds), *WTO: Governance, Dispute Settlement and Developing Countries* (Juris Publishing 2008) 771; Bruce Wilson, 'Compliance by WTO Members with Adverse WTO Dispute Settlement Rulings: The Record to Date' (2007) 10 J Int'l Econ L 397; John H Jackson, 'The Role and Effectiveness of the WTO Dispute Settlement Mechanism (with Comments and Discussion)' in Susan M Collins and Dani Rodick (eds), *Brookings Trade Forum* (Brookings Institution Press 2000) 179.

In effect, usage rates only reveal the number of complaints lodged with an international court (in the case of the DSS this figure is 574 for the period 1 January 1995 to 30 December 2018).[6] They 'do not say anything about the total number of violations or disputes that are out there, including those that have *not* been filed'.[7] In other words, usage rates reveal little if anything about the actual impact of an international court, such as the WTO DSS, on state conduct,[8] whereas both high- and low-usage records may suggest substantial court impact on states or, alternatively, negligible influence.[9] High-usage rates may, for example, be indicative of disputants' perceptions of the court's usefulness and effectiveness as a means for resolving disputes or securing compliance with treaty provisions, but also of the courts' inability to introduce, over time, legal stability and predictability within the treaty regime in which it operates, conditions assumed to induce rule compliance and reduce the number of legal disputes.[10] In a similar vein, low-usage rates may attest to the court's perceived unattractiveness and ineffectiveness; yet they may also imply that the court's legal shadow effectively incentivizes disputing parties towards out-of-court settlements, or rule compliance, before the presentation of formal disputes,[11] a tendency suggesting that the court's normative power has meaningful sway over those subject to its jurisdiction.

It follows, then, that usage rates may provide mixed indications about DSS effectiveness. Moreover, a narrow focus on those instances where the DSS has been used, and on outputs such as the number of disputes filed or rulings issued, may fall short of capturing those effects and outcomes the system may generate *without* a formal judgment being rendered or even *without* a case being filed. Such shadow effects, exerted prior to a ruling or without at all activating the DSS, are no less vital for an analysis of its functioning and effectiveness.[12] A WTO practitioner interviewed by the author put it nicely:

[6] See 'Chronological List of Disputes Cases' (*WTO*) <https://www.wto.org/english/tratop_e/dispu_e/dispu_status_e.htm> accessed 30 December 2018 [hereinafter List of Disputes]. The number of cases filed with the WTO DSS has often been invoked as indicative of the effectiveness and success of the system, especially when compared with the more modest record of the GATT DSS, under which 300 disputes were brought during its forty-seven years of existence. See, e.g. 'WTO Disputes Reach 500 Mark' (*WTO News*, 10 November 2015) <https://www.wto.org/english/news_e/news15_e/ds500rfc_10nov15_e.htm> accessed 18 December 2018; 'Azevêdo Says Success of WTO Dispute Settlement Brings Urgent Challenges' (*WTO News*, 26 September 2014) <https://www.wto.org/english/news_e/spra_e/spra32_e.htm> accessed 18 December 2018. See also Reich (n 5) 1; Davey 2014 (n 5) 687–88.

[7] Joost Pauwelyn, 'The WTO 20 Years On: "Global Governance by Judiciary" or, Rather, Member-driven Settlement of (Some) Trade Disputes between (Some) WTO Members' (2016) 27 EJIL 1119, 1121 (emphasis original).

[8] Andrew T Guzman, 'International Tribunals: A Rational Choice Analysis' (2008) 157 U Pa L Rev 171, 188.

[9] Shany (n 4) 5; Elsig, Hoekman, and Pauwelyn (n 5) 28.

[10] Yuval Shany, 'Assessing the Effectiveness of International Courts: A Goal-Based Approach' (2012) 106 AJIL 225, 227; Shany (n 4) 5.

[11] Shany (n 10) 227.

[12] As Hudec has noted some time ago, 'no functioning legal system can wait until' such time that a ruling is out or formal proceedings are underway 'to exert its primary impact'. Robert E Hudec, *Enforcing International Trade Law: The Evolution of the Modern GATT Legal System* (Butterworth Legal Publishers 1993) 360. Busch and Reinhardt have similarly stressed that the effectiveness and success of

> To determine the success of the dispute settlement system, you have to look at the circumstances in which it is not used, probably more than the circumstances in which it is used, because just the existence of the system ensures that there is a certain amount of adherence to [WTO] rules even when the adjudicator is not called on to adjudicate the dispute.[13]

Is Judicial Effectiveness All About Compliance?

The even more prevalent tendency, particularly among jurists, to assess the effectiveness of the DSS by focusing on compliance with WTO rulings—understood as 'a causal relationship between judicial decisions and state practice, leading to a convergence of the two'[14]—is equally problematic. This focus, predicated on the assumption that compliance with WTO rulings offers a useful measure for evaluating how well the DSS fares in upholding the rule of law and in securing obedience to WTO norms,[15] is surely tempting when dealing with an international adjudicatory body like the WTO DSS. Promoting rule compliance constitutes a central goal of international courts. It likewise embodies the aspirations of lawyers operating in the anarchic international system to bolster international law's substantive legal prescriptions[16] and foster an 'international culture of compliance'.[17] The extensive interest in compliance also coincides with the general narrative of the judicialization of international law in recent decades as signifying 'a shift from a power-based to a rules-based international system'[18] and as representing the creation of a 'new world order based on the rule of international law'.[19] This same narrative holds true especially for the move observed in the multilateral trade setting from the diplomacy-oriented DSS in place under the GATT to a more legalized

the WTO DSS hangs on its ability to encourage settlement bargaining and compliance 'in the shadow of weak law', without judicial proceedings being initiated or without a judgment being delivered. See Marc L Busch and Eric Reinhardt, 'Bargaining in the Shadow of the Law: Early Settlement in GATT/WTO Disputes' (2000) 24 Fordham Int'l LJ 158, 158–60.

---

13 Interview with private attorney (Geneva, 23 April 2012).

14 Yuval Shany, 'Compliance with Decisions of International Courts as Indicative of their Effectiveness: A Goal-Based Analysis' in James Crawford and Sara Nouwen (eds), *Select Proceedings of the European Society of International Law 2010* (Hart Publishing 2012) 230.

15 ibid.

16 Jacob Katz Cogan, 'Noncompliance and the International Rule of Law' (2006) 31 Yale J Int'l L 189, 191.

17 Louis Henkin, *International Law: Politics and Values* (Kluwer Law International 1995) 45.

18 Ruti Teitel and Robert Howse, 'Cross-Judging: Tribunalization in a Fragmented but Interconnected Global Order' (2009) 41 NYU J Int'l L & Pol 959, 961. See also Bernhard Zangl, 'Is There an Emerging International Rule of Law?' (2005) 13 Euro Rev 73.

19 Antonio Cassese, 'On the Current Trends Towards Criminal Prosecution and Punishment of Breaches of International Humanitarian Law' (1998) 9 EJIL 2, 8. See also Shany (n 10) 225–26; John B Bellinger, 'International Courts and Tribunals and the Rule of Law' in Cesare PR Romano (ed), *The Sword and the Scales: The United States and International Courts and Tribunals* (CUP 2009) 2.

DSS following formation of the WTO.[20] Finally, focusing on unchanging, one-dimensional benchmarks such as judgment compliance greatly simplifies effectiveness assessment of complex institutions like the WTO DSS, by rendering such a research endeavour more manageable and measureable.[21]

Yet, despite their intellectual and practical appeal, the prevalent models gauging DSS effectiveness through the narrow lens of compliance are less than satisfying. This is not because of what they reveal about the DSS (which enjoys a relatively high judgment-compliance rate),[22] but because of the many things they do not disclose. Among other things, effectiveness models focusing on states' compliance with WTO rulings (second-order compliance) tell us little, if anything, about the overall compliance record with WTO rules (first-order compliance).[23] Since the study of compliance rates with DSS rulings explores the system's impact in those cases where such judgments were *in fact* issued, it does not reveal the broader 'shadow' effect the DSS may be exerting on the conduct of states other than the immediate disputants, nor whether the system is effective in generally entrenching the rule of law in the WTO setting. In other words, judgment-compliance rates tell us little about the role of the DSS in the larger WTO legal order and whether its existence and the rulings it delivers affect the attitude of prospective parties to

[20] On the legalization of the WTO DSS as representing 'an ambitious attempt at strengthening the "international rule of law"', see Ernst-Ulrich Petersmann, 'How to Promote the International Rule of Law? Contributions by the World Trade Organization Appellate Review System' (1998) 1 J Int'l Econ L 25, 31. See also David Evans and Gregory C Shaffer, 'Introduction' in Gregory C Shaffer and Ricardo Meléndez-Ortiz (eds), *Dispute Settlement at the WTO: The Developing Country Experience* (CUP 2010) 1.

[21] Martin (n 4) 591.

[22] Although studies on the DSS disclose rather high judgment-compliance rates, the rates reported vary. According to the WTO website, the compliance rate with dispute settlement rulings 'is very high, at around 90%'. See *WTO News* 2018 (n 1). Davey reports in his studies on an implementation rate of more than 80 per cent. See William J Davey, 'WTO Dispute Settlement: Promise Fulfilled?' in Inge Govaere, Reinhard Quick, and Marco Bronckers (eds), *Trade and Competition Law in the EU and Beyond* (Edward Elgar 2011) 197–200; William J Davey, 'The WTO Dispute Settlement System: The First Ten Years' (2005) 8 J Int'l Econ L 17, 46–48. Disaggregating the data on judgment compliance further, Horlick and Coleman (n 5) find rates of 67.1 per cent for full compliance with WTO rulings, 24.1 per cent for partial compliance, and 8.9 per cent for noncompliance. Finally, Epstein and others report about 66 per cent full compliance, 13 per cent some compliance, and 21 per cent no compliance. See David Epstein, Sharyn O'Halloran, and Amy L Widsten, 'Implementing the Agreement: Partisan Politics and WTO Dispute Settlement' in James Hartigan (ed), *Trade Disputes and the Dispute Settlement Understanding of the WTO: An Interdisciplinary Assessment* (Emerald Group Publishing Limited 2009) 124. The varying compliance rates, resulting inter alia from the different conceptualizations and coding methods applied in each study, attest to the elusiveness of the concept of compliance and the methodological difficulties associated with its operationalization when determining whether respondents have indeed brought themselves into compliance with WTO rules.

[23] Elsig, Hoekman, and Pauwelyn (n 5) 28; Manfred Elsig, 'WTO Dispute Settlement and the Study of Compliance' (2015) 14 J Int'l Trade L & Pol'y 112, 113. On the distinction between first-order and second-order compliance, see also Alasdair R Young, 'Effective Multilateralism on Trial: EU Compliance with WTO Law' in Spyros Blavoukos and Dimitris Bourantonis (eds), *The EU Presence in International Organizations* (Routledge 2011) 116–17 ('Compliance can be with respect to the international rules themselves ("first-order compliance") or authoritative decisions by an international third-party concerning failure to comply with the rules in the first place ("second-order compliance")').

litigation, discourage future violations of the underlying legal norms,[24] and generally pull Members towards compliance with WTO rules.[25]

As a matter of fact, judgment-compliance rates may indicate very little about the actual compliance pull of DSS rulings vis-à-vis the specific disputing parties addressed.[26] As Shany explains, compliance with an international court's rulings depends, among others, on the nature of the decisions issued, which may themselves impose more or less demanding legal standards on losing parties.[27] A 'low-aiming' court, for example, 'which issues timid substantive judgments or minimalist remedies may generate high levels of compliance yet yield only minor impact on the state of affairs and poorly contribute to the policy problem it was designed to address'.[28] Consequently, while high compliance rates may sometimes indicate strong judicial impacts, signifying the court's success in holding defendants accountable to agreed-upon international rules, they may also denote weak, readily met, and ineffective standards.[29]

Yet, beyond such limitations, a fundamental conceptual weakness of the common compliance-based effectiveness models—all predicated on the premise of rule compliance as the fixed primary goal to be attained by the DSS[30]—lies in these models' incomplete assumptions regarding DSS goals and, in consequence, in the crucial aspects of the system's operation they leave out of its effectiveness account. First, common approaches gauging the DSS effectiveness through the limited lens of compliance rule out consideration of the *multiple* organizational goals that WTO Members expect the DSS to achieve, of which compliance may not be the most prominent a priori. Second, existing effectiveness models disregard the complex interrelations and *conflicts* between the DSS's multiple goals, as well as the trade-offs such conflicts impose between the outcomes produced by the

[24] Guzman (n 8) 187. For these reasons, Guzman has chosen to focus on the tribunal's ability to encourage compliance with the legal obligations underlying the international regime of which the tribunal forms a part.

[25] Carlos M Vazques and John Jackson, 'Some Reflections on Compliance with WTO Dispute Settlement Decisions' (2002) 33 L & Pol'y in Int'l Bus 555, 566 (noting that 'compliance with primary obligations may well be occurring under the surface, influenced if not caused by the existence of a dispute settlement regime').

[26] Elsig, Hoekman, and Pauwelyn (n 5) 28–29.

[27] Shany (n 14) 230–32.

[28] Shany (n 4) 5.

[29] cf Kal Raustiala and Anne-Marie Slaughter, 'International Law, International Relations and Compliance' in Walter Carlsnaes and others (eds), *Handbook of International Relations* (Sage 2002) 539 (noting that 'while high levels of compliance can indicate high levels of effectiveness, they can also indicate low, readily met and ineffective standards').

[30] On the perception of compliance as the primary goal of the DSS, see, e.g. John H Jackson, 'International Law Status of WTO Dispute Settlement Reports: Obligation to Comply or Option to "Buy Out"?' (2004) 98 AJIL 109, 123 (referring to compliance as the 'critical and central goal' of the WTO DSS); Guzman (n 8) 188 (arguing that '[t]he most compelling potential purpose for a tribunal is to support some underlying legal obligation' and that '[t]he dispute resolution provisions of the WTO … are intended to increase compliance with rules contained in the WTO agreements'); Piet Eeckhout, 'Remedies and Compliance' in Daniel Bethlehem and others (eds), *The Oxford Handbook of International Trade Law* (OUP 2009) 443.

system. Third, current effectiveness models are also static in nature, based on the supposedly unchanging character of DSS goals and the persistent supremacy of compliance among its objectives. Such models thus overlook important *shifts* in emphasis amongst the various goals of the DSS, which occur over time or across different types of WTO disputes, and the resulting effects of such shifts on the DSS effectiveness analysis. Finally, the dominant effectiveness models, by focusing on compliance, risk discounting the vital role that measured amounts of noncompliance may play in maintaining the long-term viability and effectiveness of the DSS, and the WTO regime as a whole, by providing a flexibility mechanism or escape valve in the face of occasionally intense political or economic pressures.

What is missing in the current literature on the WTO DSS is, therefore, a more comprehensive, nuanced, and dynamic framework for studying, thinking, and arguing about the effectiveness of the system—a framework that transcends classic standards such as compliance, considers the broad corpus of institutional goals entrusted to the DSS, and takes the conflicting and variable nature of these goals into account. This book seeks to fill this gap. Drawing on the rich social science literature on organizational effectiveness, the book puts forward a more sophisticated, multidimensional goal-based framework for analysing the effectiveness of the WTO DSS, in which the multiple, conflicting, and shifting goals underlying the system serve as key effectiveness benchmarks. In so doing, as detailed below, the book develops an elaborate account of the aims guiding the DSS's work, the diverse roles it plays, the pressures and challenges it confronts, and the outcomes it produces, thereby opening the door for a more complex understanding of the DSS's operation and the undercurrents affecting its effectiveness.

As recent developments make clear, this research endeavour is particularly timely for both academic and practical reasons. With the WTO's negotiation function struggling to overcome its stagnation, regional trade agreements proliferating, and contestation of the normative foundations of global economic integration intensifying, 'the credibility of the WTO as a functioning international organization' depends, more than ever, as William Davey has put it, 'on ensuring the effectiveness of its dispute settlement function'.[31] At this precise moment in time, however, the WTO DSS appears to be showing 'signs of stress'[32] in the face of serious systemic challenges 'that are affecting its current operation and that threaten its future effectiveness'.[33] These 'grave trials' facing the system[34] relate, inter alia,

31 Davey 2014 (n 5) 679–80.

32 Sacerdoti (n 5) 148.

33 Terence P Stewart, 'The Broken Multilateral Dispute System' (2018) Asia Society Policy Institute Research Paper, 4 <http://www.stewartlaw.com/Content/Documents/Terence%20P.%20Stewart%20-%20The%20Broken%20Multilateral%20Trade%20Dispute%20System.pdf> accessed 18 December 2018.

34 Xu Feibiao, 'At a Crossroad: Reforming the WTO is Imperative but Consensus Will Be Necessary' *Beijing Review* (Beijing, 6 September 2018) <http://www.bjreview.com/Opinion/201808/t20180831_800139958.html> accessed 30 December 2018.

to the increasing number and complexity of cases reaching its docket,[35] and, in particular, to the growing political and economic competition between the United States and China, the world's largest economic powers, competition that escalated in 2018 through the recourse of the two countries to tit-for-tat unilateral trade measures outside the multilateral rules-based system.[36] Most pressing, however, at the time of finalizing the writing of this book, is the US backlash against the DSS—observed in the continued blocking of new appointments to the Appellate Body (AB), which the United States accuses of judicial 'overreach'[37]—a development that threatens to grind the DSS to a halt at a time when it may be needed most.[38] And so, it is the United States—the driving force behind the creation of the judicialized WTO DSS—that now seems to hold this system hostage and to risk undermining its future functioning.[39] At the same time, the United States, like the rest of the WTO membership, keeps on bringing new disputes to the system at an increasing pace.[40]

This recent chain of events raises and hones, in turn, a range of fundamental questions, among them: What should be done to secure the future effectiveness of the WTO DSS? Has this judicial system really been effective, as the general wisdom seems to suggest?[41] If so, what does the recent US offensive against the DSS say about the system's efficacy? Has the system been, perhaps, 'too' effective, or the opposite? Should WTO Members thus undo the judicalization of WTO dispute settlement or, rather, move further along the judicialization path?

[35] Sacerdoti (n 5) 148–49.

[36] Gregory Shaffer, 'A Tragedy in the Making? The Decline of Law and the Return of Power in International Trade Relations' (2019) 44 Yale J Int'l L (forthcoming).

[37] ibid.

[38] The AB is composed of seven members who decide cases in panels of three. These members hold four-year terms, which are renewable once. Their appointment (or reappointment) requires consensus of all WTO Members so that any Member can veto a candidate's selection. At the time of wrapping up this book (January 2019), the Trump Administration's policy is to formally object to all motions to nominate or renew the terms of AB members. As of 1 October 2018, only three AB members remained in office. Unless the United States stops blocking the selection process, or some other solution is found to the problem, only one AB member will remain as of December 2019. Hence, 'the crisis is here with a clearly defined time frame to keep the dispute settlement system functioning'. Terence P Stewart, 'The Future of the WTO – Will Reform Happen in a Timely Manner?' (2018) Washington International Trade Association Research Paper, 2 <http://www.stewartlaw.com/Content/Documents/11-07-18%20TPS%20-%20The%20Future%20of%20the%20WTO.PDF> accessed 18 December 2018; Shaffer (n 36).

[39] Shaffer (n 36); 'America Holds the World Trade Organization Hostage' *The Economist* (23 September 2017) <https://www.economist.com/finance-and-economics/2017/09/23/america-holds-the-world-trade-organisation-hostage> accessed 12 December 2018.

[40] During 2018, the United States initiated eight disputes before the WTO DSS. Furthermore, during that same year, thirty-nine disputes were filed with the DSS. This is the highest annual total in twenty years. See List of Disputes (n 6).

[41] See, e.g. Sacerdoti (n 5) 147–48; Davey 2014 (n 5); Robert Howse, 'The World Trade Organization 20 Years On: Global Governance by Judiciary' (2016) 27 EJIL 9, 11; Brewster (n 3); A V Ganesan, 'The Appellate Body in its Formative Years: A Personal Perspective' in Gabrielle Marceau (ed), *A History of Law and Lawyers in the GATT/WTO: The Development of the Rule of Law in the Multilateral Trading System* (CUP 2015) 545; Michelle Limenta, *WTO Retaliation: Effectiveness and Purposes* (Hart Publishing 2017) 2; Cherie O'neal Taylor, 'Beyond Retaliation' (2017) 38 Nw J Int'l L & Bus 55, 60–61.

To be able to answer these queries seriously, let alone to consider what changes are needed in the structures and processes of the DSS so as to enhance its effectiveness, we should first formulate a more coherent conception of what 'WTO DSS effectiveness' means, identify the appropriate measures against which the system's effectiveness is to be put on trial, and develop a better understanding of the theoretical and practical complexities pertaining to an effectiveness examination of this adjudicative system. This book sets out to do so. In carrying out these tasks, the book does not engage in an overall effectiveness assessment of the WTO DSS, nor does it profess to offer a decisive answer to the question of whether the DSS has been effective so far in reaching the various goals for which it was created. While the book does illuminate and address important dimensions of effectiveness and ineffectiveness in the DSS's operation, its main ambition is to lay down a broad and dynamic conceptual framework for studying judicial effectiveness at the WTO, together with the analytical tools that could inform future thinking and research in search of responses to the series of questions raised above.

Research Agenda and Objectives

While a broad methodological framework for analysing the effectiveness of the WTO DSS is missing from current debates, foundations for such a framework may be traced in the social sciences, where questions of organizational effectiveness have long been the subject of academic inquiry. Under the dominant model in the field, known as the goal-based approach, 'effectiveness' is defined as the extent to which an organization attains its goals, that is, the desired outcomes it ought to generate in the eyes of relevant constituencies.[42] In following this approach, the book conceives WTO DSS effectiveness as the level to which this body attains the goals set for it by the WTO and its Member states (the 'mandate providers'),[43] those that fund, monitor, and use this adjudicative system.[44] Under the goal-based approach as applied to the WTO DSS, therefore, the goals underlying the system constitute the key organizational effectiveness criteria. These goals are, in turn, to be juxtaposed against the actual outcomes the system generates.

Above all, the goal-based approach advanced in the book provides us with a multidimensional benchmark from which to conduct an effectiveness analysis,

[42] The goal-based model is discussed at length in Chapter 1.

[43] The reasons for selecting the 'mandate providers' as the primary group of goal setters among the other possible constituencies (e.g. individual states, WTO adjudicators, or members of the WTO Secretariat) are explained in Chapter 1.

[44] A more general move towards the application of the goal-based approach to the study of the effectiveness of international courts has been taken by Shany (n 4), as part of a five-year research project funded by the European Research Council on the Effectiveness of International Adjudication. The ideas for the present book were initially developed by the author during her time as a member and a PhD candidate participating in the mentioned research project.

that is, it takes into account the DSS's manifold purposes, going beyond compliance, when evaluating the system's performance. Yet by broadly conceptualizing effectiveness, this approach urges us to look even further, beyond the breadth of DSS goals, to uncover the real-life intricacies underlying the system's operation and effectiveness as these arise from the multiple and conflicting nature of its objectives, together with the trade-offs demanded between them. Crucially, despite its centrality to any discussion regarding the success (or failure) of the DSS, the fundamental question of the system's underlying goals and the complexities emanating from their multifarious and often contradictory nature 'has been virtually ignored by government officials, practitioners and academics alike'.[45] The goal-based approach pursued in this book promises to begin addressing this gap.

What is more, the goal-based approach provides a fertile framework from which to generate new hypotheses about the DSS's goals and their operationalization in the real world, with important descriptive and normative implications for the study of the work and effectiveness of the system. One novel hypothesis advanced here is referred to as 'goal shifting', according to which the goals of the DSS change over time and by context. Thus, contrary to existing studies on the DSS, which perceive its organizational goals as static elements, the book conceives these goals as dynamic in at least two senses. First, DSS goals, or their relative weight, shift *vertically*, along the various stages of the dispute settlement process and/or along the system's life trajectory. Second, DSS goals, or their relative salience, shift *horizontally*, across disputes, because of the distinctive features and challenges presented by the different types of cases reaching its docket. This notion of 'horizontal' goal shifting essentially suggests that while all WTO disputes share certain commonalities (e.g. they are all addressed under the same WTO procedures and involve competing trade-related interests), these disputes differ in meaningful ways that generate variations in the dominant goals pursued as the DSS turns from one dispute category to another. Hence, in contrast to the tendency in writings about the DSS and its effectiveness to treat all WTO disputes as one monolithic unit in which the key objective is compliance, this book submits that these disputes should be viewed as disparate phenomena, each in its own way.

Thus, within the DSS's caseload, one may find a growing number of cases referred to as 'linkage' (or 'trade-and') disputes, disputes that involve trade-restrictive national policies in areas such as health and environment, and which invoke the persisting friction between the WTO's trade liberalization aim and 'nontrade' societal

[45] Bryan Mercurio, 'Retaliatory Trade Measures in the WTO Dispute Settlement Understanding: Are There Really Alternatives?' in *Trade Disputes and the Dispute Settlement Understanding* (n 22) 404. See also Henrik Horn and Petros C Mavroidis, 'International Trade: Dispute Settlement' in Andrew T Guzman and Alan O Sykes (eds), *Research Handbook in International Economic Law* (Edward Elgar Publishing 2007) 190 (noting that 'there is something unsatisfactory about the fact that the empirical literature on the DS system in the ... WTO attempts, to a large extent, to evaluate performance of the system, without explicitly specifying what it is meant to achieve').

values. Other disputes filed with the DSS reflect the increasing tension between the multilateral trade system centred on the WTO and regional trade agreements (RTAs), which have dramatically expanded and grown in number over the last two decades. In addition, the DSS's long list of cases contains several high-stake, perennial conflicts between major economic powers, conflicts having systemic implications for the operation and stability of the cooperative WTO regime, among them some intense transatlantic trade feuds. Finally, the north–south divide is also being felt within the WTO dispute settlement arena, with Members asking the DSS 'to apply law and technicalities to a tremendously charged social-political relationship, as it has in the other fields of tension'.[46]

And so, despite their commonalities, these and other types of WTO disputes have different characteristics, presenting the DSS with distinct legal, political, economic, and institutional challenges. As the notion 'horizontal goal shifting' suggests, these challenges shift the relative weight assigned to the multiple goals sought by the DSS, including its compliance objective, and trigger the latent conflicts among them. In other words, the diverse challenges raised before the DSS yield varying emphases and trade-offs between its objectives when moving across the different categories of cases coming before it. Such goal-shifting tendencies, closely investigated in this book, for the first time, by means of a legal, interview-based analysis of several categories of WTO disputes, are therefore crucial for understanding the DSS's operation and for critically gauging its effectiveness and outcomes. In particular, the goal-shifting phenomenon fundamentally challenges the convention viewing compliance as the key objective to be achieved by the DSS over time and across disputes and, in consequence, as the primary measure of its effectiveness. By framing, instead, the DSS's goals as complex, nonbinary constructs that change with shifts in the modalities in which the system operates, the goal-shifting concept developed in the book significantly expands the existing discourse on the DSS and its effectiveness, showing how perceiving its goals and functioning in static terms can lead to an imprecise understanding of the system's performance and judicial outcomes.

This book thus seeks to contribute to the existing literature on the WTO DSS along three main axes: First, drawing on a theoretical model borrowed from organizational studies, the book advances a multidimensional approach for analysing the effectiveness of the WTO DSS—a goal-based approach that defines DSS effectiveness in terms of goal attainment. Second, in devising this goal-based effectiveness framework, the book ploughs new ground to develop a substantially more nuanced and comprehensive account of DSS goals, recasting those goals as multi-faceted, often conflicting constructs that force this adjudicative system to strike complex trade-offs in its goal-attainment endeavours. Third, the book introduces

[46] Tomer Broude, *International Governance in the WTO: Judicial Boundaries and Political Capitulation* (Cameron May 2004) 27–28.

the novel concept of goal shifting, pointing to the idea that DSS goals alternate in time and across disputes, an idea illuminating why we need to move from a static to a dynamic analytic perspective when studying the work of the DSS and the goals steering its operation and determining its effectiveness. As elaborated below, the book makes these theoretical contributions while pursuing a robust qualitative empirical research design, basing its analysis on dozens of in-depth interviews with the actors (lawyers, adjudicators, bureaucrats, and diplomats) participating in the WTO DSS operations. Finally, since the question of international judicial effectiveness lying at the heart of this book is not unique to the WTO DSS but is of relevance to the numerous other courts operating at the international level, the book's theoretical and empirical contributions may inform and enrich broader debates on the goals, functions, and effectiveness of international adjudication. This is so particularly at this moment in time, when the backlash against international courts appears to be on the rise.[47]

The Book's Contents

The book is divided into four major parts. Part I (Chapters 1–3) establishes the underpinnings of the WTO DSS goal-based effectiveness framework. To this end, Chapter 1 sets out the theoretical and methodological foundations of the goal-based approach as gleaned, with relevant adaptations, from the social science literature on organizational effectiveness. The chapter addresses the main elements and concepts of the goal-based effectiveness model as applied to the DSS, together with the measurement challenges it faces, thereby highlighting the model's promise, but also its limitations.

Drawing on the conceptual bases set forth in Chapter 1, the book then moves on to lay down the substantive building blocks of the WTO DSS goal-based effectiveness framework in the form of the multiple goals prescribed for this system by its mandate providers, against which its performance is to be evaluated. With a view to establishing the relevant context for identifying and analysing these goals, Chapter 2 provides a brief overview of the origins and evolution of the WTO DSS and explains its current design and procedures. Based on a multisource analysis, including in-depth interviews with WTO practitioners, Chapter 3, in turn, maps out the matrix of DSS goals while probing both their complementary and contradictory relationships. The chapter starts with an account of the system's ultimate ends (i.e. the overarching, long-term purposes of the DSS): promoting the security and predictability of the multilateral trading system, maintaining and

[47] Mikael Rask Madsen, Pola Cebulak, and Micha Wiebusch, 'Backlash Against International Courts: Explaining the Forms and Patterns of Resistance to International Courts' (2018) 14 Int'l J L in Context 197.

restoring the negotiated balance of concessions between WTO Members, sustaining the operation of the WTO and the realization of its goals, and conferring legitimacy upon the WTO edifice and rules. Chapter 3 continues with a discussion of the DSS's intermediate goals, those organizational goals that are more instrumental in nature and conducive to the attainment of the system's longer-term and open-ended objectives. These goals include inducing compliance with WTO rules, fostering the positive and prompt settlement of disputes among WTO Members, clarifying WTO law, levelling the playing field between WTO Members, preventing unilateralism, and legitimizing the operation, authority, and outputs of the DSS itself.

Having so reconstructed the WTO DSS as a system of multiple, mutually reinforcing and contradictory goals, the book proceeds in Parts II, III, and IV, with an examination of the operationalization of these goals in the real world, exploring their interplay, especially the conflicts and shifts taking place among them, while considering the implications of these phenomena for the DSS's effectiveness analysis. A core aim of these three major parts is, therefore, to probe the book's central proposition concerning the variable nature of DSS's goals, which shift in time and across different types of disputes. The three consecutive parts carry out this research endeavour through in-depth, interview-based analysis of specific cases falling under three categories of WTO disputes, while offering a fresh and original reading of some of the most important cases to have reached the DSS's docket so far.

More specifically, Part II (Chapters 4–6) focuses on 'trade-and' disputes. These include cases that transcend the WTO's core trade domain by calling for judicial oversight of those national regulations that restrict international trade in the name of 'nontrade' values such as health and environmental protection. For the reasons detailed in Chapter 4, this category of cases has long subjected the WTO and its DSS to pressing legitimacy challenges from stakeholders inside and outside the multilateral trading system. Through a close examination of two representative trade-and disputes—the early *US-Shrimp* and the more recent *US-Clove Cigarettes*—Chapters 5 and 6, respectively, show how the heightened legitimacy concerns aroused by trade-and cases have shaped the DSS's goal-attainment patterns, engaging this judicial system in an intensified quest after its two legitimization objectives. The first, the ultimate end of the DSS, as a 'regime court', to bestow legitimacy on the WTO edifice among constituencies inside and outside the multilateral trade setting; and the second, legitimation of its own authority as an international court among external audiences while sustaining the internal support of WTO Members, what can be considered a fundamental intermediate goal of the DSS. As Chapters 5 and 6 show, these two interrelated legitimacy-oriented aims have occasionally collided, events indicating the limits to the DSS's ability to attain concurrently its manifold goals and, it follows, the built-in limits set on its effectiveness.

Part III (Chapters 7–9) takes stock of the DSS's goal-attainment patterns in the category of 'perennial' disputes, the highly intense and recidivist conflicts involving major trade partners, loaded histories, politically empowered stakeholders, and national policies and interests of compelling economic, political, or symbolic importance. Chapter 7 explains why these high-stake conflicts are such hard cases, immune to compromise and resistant to compliance with adverse DSS rulings. As such, these disputes place heavy strain on the WTO and its DSS, and are often viewed as 'impossible' or 'wrong' cases for the latter to address.

Chapters 8 and 9 transmit, in turn, a picture of the DSS's complex operations and goal-attainment efforts when addressing perennial conflicts, as illustrated through the case studies of *EC-Bananas* and *EC-Hormones*, the famous transatlantic trade rows that came to a close in recent years, almost two decades into the WTO's existence. The respective chapters demonstrate how in certain disputes—and in contrast to the conventional wisdom—the DSS is not geared primarily to mechanically enforce compliance with WTO rules; instead, it plays an augmented role in the interstice between law and politics. They show that when dealing with high-stake perennial conflicts, the DSS becomes a repeat player in a broader political process aimed at the settlement of the dispute, where the system plays a prominent function in, first, containing the protracted dispute within defined legal parameters, neutralizing its political aspects, and forestalling unilateral actions, all required to sustain the cooperative WTO framework while the dispute endures. Second, during breakdowns in the political process, the mandatory DSS, through its binding procedures and rulings, further serves as a mechanism to stimulate renegotiation and to construct focal points around which the parties can collaborate on the road towards a settlement and reestablishment of their reciprocal balance of concessions.

Alongside this goal shifting, Part III also dwells on some of the more salient conflicts that became cornerstones of the DSS's goal structure. The two-decade-long trade feuds examined, which eventually ended with mutually satisfactory (albeit not fully WTO-compliant) settlements, have brought to the fore the fundamental tension between the DSS's aim to secure rule compliance and legal predictability, and its desire to preserve a previously negotiated balance of concessions through amicable settlements and flexible rebalancing acts, thought to sustain the viability of the WTO in the long run. As Chapters 8 and 9 show, in certain circumstances, political or economic exigencies may make such goal conflicts inescapable. Still, while the resulting outcomes in such instances may fall short of full legal compliance, they may nevertheless be conducive to the long-term effectiveness of the DSS and the cooperative WTO regime.

Finally, Part IV of the book extends the goal-based analytic framework applied in Parts II and III to an additional category of WTO disputes: those reflecting the growing friction between the WTO's multilateral trade system and the network of RTAs proliferating around the globe. Looking at a series of prominent RTA-related cases that came before the WTO DSS, the extensive analysis carried out in Chapter 10 shows that the dynamic reality of goal shifts and goal conflicts experienced within the DSS is not unique to trade-and and perennial disputes. Similar processes can be observed in the histories of other classes of WTO disputes, an analysis of which is likely to disclose different DSS goal-attainment patterns evidencing new goal priorities and trade-offs, and resulting in varying dimensions of judicial effectiveness and ineffectiveness, adjusted to the new operational environments.

Chapter 11 concludes. It sums up the key findings of the study while discussing the results emerging from a comparative analysis of the three categories of WTO disputes examined. The chapter then revisits the central arguments put forth in the book and articulates the lessons to be learned for the study of the goals, operation, and effectiveness of the WTO DSS, and international courts more broadly. It also discusses some of the insights to be offered with respect to possible institutional changes or reforms of the DSS with a view to ensuring its future effectiveness. The chapter closes with several observations that go beyond effectiveness, pertaining to the costs and unintended consequences attendant on more effective and empowered international adjudication.

The Research Approach: Sources and Methods

In its efforts to develop a sophisticated and multifaceted goal-based framework for analysing the effectiveness of the WTO DSS and the complex dynamics of the goals guiding the DSS's operation, the present book applies a multimethod research approach. Specifically, it weaves together legal and institutional analysis with a robust qualitative empirical research design consisting of in-depth case study analyses and intensive semistructured interviews with WTO practitioners. Here I elaborate these methodological choices and their benefits in the areas explored.

Comparative Case Study Analysis

As noted in the above overview of its contents, the book takes a case study approach to the investigation of WTO DSS performance and goal dynamics, especially the goal-shifting phenomenon, by looking at three categories of WTO cases: trade-and disputes, perennial conflicts, and RTA-related clashes. Several reasons underlie the selection of these groups of cases. First, since these dispute categories present the WTO and its DSS with different sets of problems and pressures, their investigation provides the *variation* required by the study in order to examine whether the relative weight ascribed to the various DSS goals indeed shifts across WTO disputes, contingent on their type and features.[48] Also guiding the choice of the three categories of cases is their relevance to our research objectives.[49] As indicated above and demonstrated throughout the book's chapters, each category challenges in its own way the convention perceiving compliance with WTO rules and decisions as the primary desired end of the DSS, and thus as the key outcome variable by which its effectiveness should be measured. In addition, each of the three categories touches upon central institutional, political, and legal issues of concern to the DSS and the WTO at present, a point that opens a useful window for understanding the ties between the DSS and its institutional environment, as well as the way in which the latter shapes DSS goal-attainment efforts and instigates conflicts between its multiple goals.

Within each category of cases, specific WTO disputes are analysed in a manner providing the reader with an insightful account of the causes leading to their eruption, the actors, interests, norms, and challenges at play, and the ways in which these factors affected the judicial acts and goal-attainment efforts carried out by the DSS. In the trade-and dispute category, we analyse the *US-Shrimp* and *US-Clove Cigarettes* cases, while in the perennial dispute category we examine *EC-Hormones* and *EC-Bananas*.[50] In the burgeoning group of RTA-related cases, the viewpoint taken is slightly broader, covering the most prominent cases so far falling into this category, among them: *Turkey-Textiles*, *Mexico-Soft Drinks*, *Brazil-Tyres*, and *Peru-Agricultural Products*.

There are, of course, limitations to the case method. These are grounded predominantly in the small number of cases investigated, which narrow the basis for scientific generalization.[51] While recognizing its limitations, the case study approach nonetheless seems particularly appropriate for the present research. Notably, without in-depth knowledge of different categories of WTO disputes, and without access to the details of the specific cases belonging to each category, it becomes impossible to accurately identify, or trace, the conflicts and shifts materializing between the multiplicity of DSS objectives, and to explain how the system's diverse goal-attainment patterns in each category are shaped by the unique challenges invoked. Investigation and explanation of such phenomena in depth and within their real-life settings require a detailed consideration of contextual factors, which the case study method allows.[52]

[48] Alexander L George and Andrew Bennett, *Case Studies and Theory Development in the Social Sciences* (MIT Press 2005) 83 (noting that '[c]ases should … be selected to provide the kind of … variation required by the research problem').

[49] ibid ('the primary criterion for case selection should be the relevance to the research objective of the study').

[50] The reasons underlying the choice of these specific categories and cases are elaborated in Chapters 4 and 7 of the book.

[51] George and Bennett (n 48) 17; Robert K Yin, *Case Study Research: Design and Methods* (4th edn, Sage Publications 2009) 15.

[52] George and Bennett (n 48) 19; Yin (n 51) 18.

Furthermore, the case study design implemented here—consisting of both within-case analyses and cross-case comparisons (across the selected disputes in each category, and across the three dispute categories considered)—may enhance our ability to draw inferences from the research.[53] First, within-case analysis of two trade-and disputes, for example, allows making cross-case comparisons and examining whether similar goal-attainment patterns are exhibited in both disputes. Common patterns, if observed in both cases, may produce more compelling evidence and improve our ability to make broader claims regarding the DSS goal-attainment patterns in the dispute category to which the case studies belong.[54] Second, juxtaposing the distinct dispute categories examined enables, in turn, comparisons between different types of WTO cases for the purpose of identifying variations in the DSS's goal-attainment efforts. Comparisons across distinct dispute categories that reveal varied goal-attainment patterns may allow us to draw broader inferences, beyond the categories investigated here, about how the DSS operates and how its goals shift in the movement between the different classes of cases comprising its docket.

In-depth Qualitative Interviews

As is the case with other international courts and institutions, the world of dispute settlement at the WTO and the inner workings of the DSS largely remain wrapped in a veil of confidentiality, with only a few insiders and cognoscenti privy to the processes and practices involved. The book breaks this mould by providing a revealing account of the complex, oft-hidden dynamics of WTO dispute settlement as experienced by and seen through the eyes of a rather closed circle of WTO insiders. Hence, the analysis and findings presented here are grounded in unique empirical data, culled by means of fifty-six in-depth, semistructured interviews carried out by the author with WTO practitioners. This qualitative research method, still uncommon in legal scholarship on the WTO DSS, joins the examination of primary legal materials (e.g. DSS rulings, WTO agreements, and other official WTO documents) and secondary sources (e.g. the Dispute Settlement Understanding negotiating history, news reports, and legal, economic, and political science scholarship), while informing the analysis with the testimonies and first-hand knowledge of practitioners in the field.

The interviews were conducted between March 2012 and April 2013. Five interviews took place in Brussels, two over the phone, with the vast majority held in

[53] See George and Bennett (n 48) 18 (noting that 'there is a growing consensus that the strongest means of drawing inferences from case studies is the use of a combination of within-case analysis and cross-case comparisons within a single study or research program'); John Gerring, *Case Study Research: Principles and Practices* (CUP 2007) 12–13, 22, 31.

[54] cf Yin (n 51) 38–39, 61.

Geneva during the author's five-month stay at the WTO in 2012, a position providing access to key WTO actors having first-hand knowledge of the DSS's work and the specific cases examined. Interviewees included AB members, WTO panellists, senior and midlevel staff members belonging to the WTO Secretariat, WTO ambassadors, Chairpersons of the WTO Dispute Settlement Body, legal counsels in trade delegations, and lawyers from private law firms and the Advisory Centre on WTO Law. In each of the cases investigated, an attempt was made to interview informants with different positions and opposing interests in the dispute in order to obtain multiple perspectives and develop a more holistic account of the dispute and the DSS's practices.[55] Some of the informants were involved in more than one of the cases addressed, an element reflected in the lengthier interviews conducted. In general, the interviews lasted between one and one and a half hours. All participants but two permitted recording the conversation.[56]

The interviews were designed to gain a fuller picture of the case studies by eliciting information excluded from DSS rulings and other public records (such as what occurred 'behind the scenes'), as well as to obtain participants' perceptions of the challenges facing the DSS in the dispute categories examined and the ways in which such challenges were woven into the judicial choices made and goals pursued by the DSS. Beyond their relevance to the selected cases, the interviews provided a supplementary source for identifying the various goals of the DSS, together with an opportunity to elicit the meanings informants associated with those goals, both necessary to gain a better understanding of what actors in the DSS's operative environment believe are the system's aims as opposed to what they perceive the DSS to be doing in fact.

With these ends in mind, the interviews were conducted according to a semistructured interview guide composed of open-ended questions that first addressed the specific case/s the interviewees were involved in,[57] and then the more general issue of WTO DSS goals. The semistructured nature of the interviews permitted informants to convey their own narratives of the cases investigated and to share their knowledge and experience with the DSS at length. At the same time, this format gave both the interviewees and the author the leeway needed to take the

[55] This approach made it possible to compare different perspectives and examine whether the interviewees corroborated one another. On the use of 'triangulation' as a method for controlling for bias in qualitative research, see Gregory Shaffer and Tom Ginsburg, 'The Empirical Turn in International Legal Scholarship' (2012) 106 AJIL 1, 4.

[56] For reasons of anonymity, the interviewees are cited with generic titles such as 'WTO official' or 'EU official'.

[57] The interview would generally open with a background question, inviting the interviewee to speak on how he or she became involved in the dispute at issue. Informants' responses were thereafter sought for answers to questions such as: 'What, if anything, distinguishes this dispute from other disputes filed with the WTO DSS?'; 'What were the main challenges the DSS had to face in this dispute?'; 'What impact, if any, did these challenges have on the operation of the DSS?'; 'What goals did the DSS try to achieve in this case?', etc. While these sorts of questions were repeated in all the interviews, other questions were designed for the dispute at issue or the broader class of WTO disputes to which it belonged.

conversation down unexpected paths.[58] Through the questions and the evolving conversation, an understanding emerged of how the interviewee perceived the dispute at issue; the problems and challenges it presented before the DSS; the dynamics, actions, and expectations of relevant actors; the goals the DSS sought to achieve; and the eventual outcomes brought about.

Before analysing the data, all the interviews were transcribed. Analysis then followed with detailed coding of the interviews according to multiple categories, developed and honed as the study progressed. While the findings presented in the book resulted from the continuous dialogue between the interviews, the literature and other pertinent sources, the interviews revealed information and perceptions otherwise unavailable. They provided knowledge about WTO dispute settlement in action, as it is experienced and practised in the real world. Most crucially, the interviews laid bare the gap between the existing literature on DSS effectiveness, which tends to focus on compliance, and actual practice, which more than once has led the DSS to look beyond compliance and to prioritize other institutional goals. The combination of first-hand reports, together with institutional and legal analysis, has allowed me, so I hope, to make a persuasive claim about the complexity of the aims underlying the DSS, the need for this adjudicative system to incessantly adapt the dominant goals pursued to varying operational contexts, and the consequent need for a shift to a multidimensional and dynamic framework for thinking about and studying this system's effectiveness.

[58] Michael Quinn Patton, *Qualitative Research and Evaluation Methods* (Sage Publications 2002).

PART I
THEORY, CONTEXT, GOALS

1

Reconceptualizing Judicial Effectiveness at the WTO

Towards a Goal-Based Approach

1.1 Introduction

> Our society is an organizational society. We are born in organizations, educated by organizations, and most of us spend much of our lives working for organizations.... In contrast to earlier societies, modern society has placed a high moral value on ... effectiveness and efficiency. Modern civilization depends largely on organizations as the most ... efficient form of social grouping.[1]

In a very real sense, we are living in an organizational world 'in which the major actors in local, national, and international policy events are organizations and networks of organizations'.[2] The prevalence of organizations in almost all areas of domestic and international life, and the consequent desire of governmental agencies, private firms, and the public to evaluate the performance of these organizations, have spurred extensive research efforts in the social sciences, primarily in public administration and organizations studies, so as to determine what constitutes organizational effectiveness and how best to measure it. As Quinn and Rohrbaugh have noted,[3] 'the effectiveness literature represents the central theme in organization theory'. Sowa, Selden, and Sandfort have added, furthermore, that this is particularly so in the case of public organizations, where questions of effectiveness 'have become increasingly important, as government ... , clients, and the public

[1] Amitai Etzioni, *Modern Organizations* (Prentice Hall 1964) 1.

[2] Pamela S Tolbert and Richard H Hall, *Organizations: Structures, Processes, and Outcomes* (10th edn, Prentice Hall 2009) 18.

[3] Robert E Quinn and John Rohrbaugh, 'A Spatial Model of Effectiveness Criteria: Towards a Competing Values Approach to Organizational Analysis' (1983) 29 Mgm't Sci 363, 370. See also Hal G Rainey, *Understanding and Managing Public Organizations* (5th edn, Jossey-Bass 2014) 147 ('Virtually all of management and organization theory is concerned with performance and effectiveness, at least implicitly').

exert increased pressure' on such organizations 'to demonstrate their impact on complex social problems'.[4]

The rich social science literature on organizational effectiveness provides a number of conceptual approaches and analytical tools that, taken together, may foster the development of a more comprehensive and methodical framework for studying and assessing the effectiveness of the World Trade Organization (WTO) Dispute Settlement System (DSS) that, like other courts at the national and international level, can be considered a public organization.[5] In this chapter I present the theoretical foundations of such a framework, which is borrowed with some adaptations from that vast body of social science literature. After discussing the main approaches developed in the social sciences to defining organizational effectiveness, I elaborate the reasons for my selection of the goal-based approach to serve as the basis for the study into the effectiveness of the WTO DSS. I then review the central concepts associated with this approach, while focusing on organizational goals, goal multiplicity, goal conflict, and goal shifting. Finally, I discuss several methodological determinations that should be made before applying the proposed WTO DSS goal-based effectiveness framework. These include the selection of the goal setters to inform the DSS's effectiveness analysis, the choice of performance indicators, and the determination of the time frame in which effectiveness is to be measured.

1.2 Choosing Among Multiple Criteria of Organizational Effectiveness: A Goal-Based Approach for Analysing the Effectiveness of the WTO DSS

The fundamental question that any effectiveness-related research ought to begin with is what constitutes an *effective* organization. As organization theory makes clear, no universal definition or criterion can be used to define and assess organizational effectiveness across all kinds of organizations.[6] Organizations vary, and so do the methods we employ to gauge their effectiveness.[7] Organization theory therefore offers several criteria and approaches to organizational effectiveness,[8]

[4] Jessica E Sowa, Sally C Selden, and Jodi R Sandfort, 'No Longer Unmeasurable? A Multidimensional Integrated Model of Nonprofit Organizational Effectiveness' (2004) 33 Nonprofit & Voluntary Sector Q 711, 712.

[5] See Yuval Shany, 'Assessing the Effectiveness of International Courts: A Goal-Based Approach' (2012) 106 AJIL 225, 227.

[6] Kim S Cameron and David Whetten, 'Some Conclusions about Organizational Effectiveness' in Kim S Cameron and David A Whetten (eds), *Organizational Effectiveness: A Comparison of Multiple Models* (Academic Press 1983) 262–63; Raymond F Zammuto, *Assessing Organizational Effectiveness: Systems Change, Adaptation, and Strategy* (SUNY Press 1982) 26.

[7] Sowa, Selden, and Sandfort (n 4) 713; Richard W Scott and Gerald F Davis, *Organizations and Organizing: Rational, Natural, and Open Systems Perspectives* (5th edn, Prentice Hall 2007) 202.

[8] See Scott and Davis (n 7) 326–27.

each of which may suit some types of organizations, but may be inapplicable to others.

Within the earliest and still dominant approach in the field, known as the 'rational system' or 'goal-based' approach, 'organizational effectiveness' is defined as the extent to which an organization attains its goals.[9] The premise underlying this definition is that organizations are inherently goal-attaining entities.[10] These 'social structures' are deliberately constructed for the collaborative pursuit of certain policy goals,[11] 'both formally specified and implicit'.[12] Put differently, organizations are 'purposeful' in the sense that their activities and the interactions of their participants are coordinated to achieve specific goals.[13] For this reason, their effectiveness should be gauged by examining how well they are performing with respect to these goals, namely, the 'desired outcomes' they are expected to generate.[14]

While widely accepted in the social science literature, the rational system approach provides only one effectiveness criterion. Another is offered by the 'natural system approach', also known as the 'system resource model'. In contrast to the former, the natural system approach views organizations as, first and foremost, social collectivities whose primary interest lies in ensuring survival. In other words, it views the entity's survival as the organization's overriding goal.[15] Accordingly, the natural system approach defines organizational effectiveness in terms of the organization's viability or survivability,[16] conceived as the 'ability to exploit its environment in the acquisition of scarce and valued resources to sustain its functioning'.[17] Hence, in contrast to the goal-based approach, the natural system model holds that organizational 'inputs … are more important than … outputs because an organization's ability to maintain sufficient resources for survival is the most important criterion of effectiveness'.[18]

[9] James L Price, 'The Study of Organizational Effectiveness' (1972) 13 Soc Q 3; Richard W Scott, *Organizations: Rational, Natural, and Open Systems* (5th edn, Prentice Hall 2003) 351–52; Melissa Forbes and Laurence E Lynn Jr, 'Organizational Effectiveness and Government Performance: A New Look at the Empirical Literature' (Draft of November 2006) 8; Robert D Herman and David O Renz, 'Theses on Nonprofit Organizational Effectiveness' (1999) 28 Nonprofit & Voluntary Sector Q 107, 108; Tolbert and Hall (n 2) 186–87.

[10] Scott and Davis (n 7) 35. As the authors explain: 'The term *rationality* in this context is used in the narrow sense of technical or functional rationality. … and refers to the extent to which a series of actions is organized in such a way as to lead to predetermined goals with maximum efficiency. Thus, rationality refers not to the selection of the goals but to their implementation'.

[11] Scott (n 9) 11; Etzioni (n 1) 3; Richard L Daft, *Organization Theory and Design* (10th edn, Cengage Learning 2010) 11.

[12] Sowa, Selden, and Sandfort (n 4) 71.

[13] Scott (n 9) 26.

[14] Scott and Davis (n 7) 36; Etzioni (n 1) 6.

[15] Scott (n 9) 352; Tolbert and Hall (n 2) 190.

[16] See, e.g. David McKevitt and Alan Lawton, *Public Sector Management: Theory, Critique and Practice* (Sage Publications 1994) 226.

[17] Stanley E Seashore and Ephraim Yuchtman, 'Factorial Analysis of Organizational Performance' (1967) 12 Admin Sci Q 377, 393. See also Stanley E Seashore and Ephraim Yuchtman, 'A System Resource Approach to Organizational Effectiveness' (1967) 32 Am Soc Rev 891.

[18] Sowa, Selden, and Sandfort (n 4) 713.

The third major view of organizational effectiveness is the 'open system approach'. Compared with the previous two, this approach places greater stress on the organization's interaction with its external environment. As Scott notes, the open system approach 'views organizations as being highly interdependent with their environments and engaged in system-elaborating as well as system-maintaining activities'.[19] It follows that under this approach, an effective organization is one that interacts in a well-balanced and sustainable manner with its environment, meaning that it acquires inputs and transforms them into the goods or services that satisfy stakeholders' needs, while maintaining a sustainable equilibrium between organizational inputs and outputs.[20] Emphasizing the importance of a return, the open system approach recognizes profitability—the excess of returns over expenditures—as a key effectiveness criterion. In like manner, viewing the organization's long-term well-being as dependent on its ability to detect and respond to subtle changes in its environment, this approach sets adaptability and flexibility as crucial criteria of the organization's effectiveness in acquiring vital resources and achieving growth.[21]

While one can find additional models of organizational effectiveness in the social science literature,[22] the rational, natural, and open system approaches 'account for much of the variance in measures of effectiveness'.[23] Among the three, the goal-based approach, as explained below, appears to provide the most suitable framework for conceptualizing the effectiveness of an international court such as the WTO DSS.[24] First, like other international institutions, the DSS is a social structure created by states 'to support the collaborative pursuit of specified goals',[25] such as solving coordination problems or generating certain collective goods.[26] Second, the organizational goals underlying the DSS represent core concepts for its institutional analysis.[27] These goals demarcate the domain in which the DSS may legitimately operate, affect distribution of its resources, and serve as guidelines for behaviour, providing criteria for selecting among alternative actions and

[19] Scott (n 9) 352.

[20] Wesley A Martz, 'Evaluating Organizational Effectiveness' (dissertation, Western Michigan University, 2008) 38–39.

[21] Scott (n 9) 352; Rainey (n 3) 166.

[22] See Kim S Cameron and David A Whetten, 'Organizational Effectiveness and Quality: The Second Generation' in John C Smart (ed), *Higher Education: Handbook of Theory and Research* (Agathon Press 1996) 267.

[23] Scott (n 9) 351.

[24] Yuval Shany, *Assessing the Effectiveness of International Courts* (OUP 2014) 6–8, 13–16.

[25] Scott and Davis (n 7) 11.

[26] Kenneth W Abbott and Duncan Snidal, 'Why States Act through Formal International Organizations' (1998) 42 J Conflict Resol 3; Bruce M Russett and John D Sullivan, 'Collective Goods and International Organization' (1971) 25 Int'l Org 845. See also Helmut Breitmeier, *The Legitimacy of International Regimes* (Ashgate Publishing 2008) 26–28 (discussing the perception of institutions as instruments to the achievement of goals in international politics and the advantages offered by a goal-attainment standard for a study of international regimes' effectiveness).

[27] cf Mayer N Zald, 'Comparative Analysis and Measurement of Organizational Goals: The Case of Correctional Institutions for Delinquents' (1963) 4 Sci Q 206, 207.

policies.[28] By focusing on the concept of organizational goals, the goal-based model thus goes beyond formal dictates when addressing the effectiveness of the DSS, to look at how the system actually operates. Third, the goal-based approach offers a comprehensive, institution-specific, normative benchmark for performance evaluation in the form of goal attainment, thereby enabling to assess DSS effectiveness against some preconceived idea of the socially desirable ends this adjudicative system should achieve and the manner in which it should conduct its business.[29] Finally, by broadly conceptualizing effectiveness, the goal-based approach, as elaborated below, urges us not only to examine the performance of the DSS against its idiosyncratic goals, it also encourages us to uncover the real-life complexities underlying the DSS's operation and effectiveness, as these emerge from the phenomena of goal multiplicity, goal conflict, and goal shifting characterizing this system.

In contrast, the natural and open system approaches, although highlighting important dimensions of organizational performance, seem ill-suited to serve as the dominant frameworks for measuring the effectiveness of public organizations, particularly adjudicating institutions such as the WTO DSS. First, the distinctive legal, institutional, and financial status of public organizations renders effectiveness criteria such as resource acquisition, value maximization, flexibility, and organizational survival—prevalent in the analysis of private sector and for-profit organizations—less appropriate in the public domain.[30] For example, the resource-acquisition criterion, generally useful in cases where the organization's inputs and outputs are clearly connected,[31] may arguably not apply in the case of public organizations, let alone international courts like the WTO DSS, where acquired resources are often only loosely connected to the outputs and impacts—such as norm clarification, norm compliance, and dispute settlement—these courts generate. Furthermore, in the public sector, resource acquisition, profitability, and survivability—measures inherent to the open and the natural system approaches—usually serve only as *means* for achieving some *socially desired* goals.[32] Effectiveness assessment in the public sector cannot, in consequence, stop at whether organizations, in this case international courts, have acquired sufficient resources and guaranteed their survival; rather, such assessment must also attend to the question of whether the organizational survival 'they have just guaranteed is also producing social value defined in terms of an important mission that they could achieve'.[33]

[28] Scott and Davis (n 7) 36; Richard H Hall and John P Clark, 'An Ineffective Effectiveness Study and Some Suggestions for Future Research' (1980) 21 Soc Q 119, 119–20.

[29] On the normative aspects of the goal-based approach see Shany (n 5) 230–31; Shany (n 24) 14–16.

[30] Daniel P Forbes, 'Measuring the Unmeasurable: Empirical Studies of Nonprofit Organization Effectiveness from 1977 to 1997' (1998) 27 Nonprofit & Voluntary Sector Q 183, 184; Mark H Moore, 'Managing for Value: Organizational Strategy in For-Profit, Nonprofit, and Governmental Organizations' (2000) 29 Nonprofit & Voluntary Sector Q 183, 194–95; Rainey (n 3) 150.

[31] Cameron and Whetten (n 22) 267; Martz (n 20) 40.

[32] Moore (n 30) 195–96.

[33] ibid.

Finally, within the context of the present book, the weaker normative content of the natural and the open system approaches makes them less suitable for a legal study interested in questions of organizational effectiveness in international adjudicative institutions such as the WTO DSS. To illustrate, the open system approach, by focusing on an organization's interactions with its environment, evaluates organizational impacts without juxtaposing them against a specific normative benchmark. This approach asks what organizations do, and not what organizations *should* do.[34] For a study anchored in law and interested in developing a critical perspective on international adjudication and judicial institutions like the one nested within the WTO setting, the choice of an effectiveness model that identifies judicial impacts but also examines the alignment of these impacts with the attainment of certain specific goals seems more appropriate.[35] For the same reasons, the natural system approach, which regards survivability and resource acquisition as the key parameters of organizational success, appears even less suitable in our case.

That said, following the attempts of organization theorists to combine the various effectiveness models, each highlighting different but 'significant and enduring features of organizations',[36] the WTO DSS goal-based framework developed here incorporates pertinent concepts taken from the open and the natural system approaches. Thus, unlike early versions of the goal-based model that viewed organizations as closed systems, sealed off from their environment, the goal-based effectiveness framework advanced in this book conceives the DSS as an open system that is dependent on flows of external resources and information,[37] closely linked to its overarching WTO regime, and embedded in a dynamic global environment that affects and shifts its goal-attainment efforts. Similarly, in line with the natural system model, the goal-based approach pursued here recognizes that international courts, like other organizations, while engaged in achieving specified goals, are also involved 'in other activities required to maintain themselves as a viable social unit'.[38] The approach proposed, as elaborated below, thus embraces the concept of 'maintenance' or 'support' goal, required to sustain the DSS's ability to act and survive, as suggested by the natural system model. The key effectiveness criterion followed in this book nevertheless remains that of goal attainment.

34 Shany (n 24) 15.

35 ibid.

36 On the attempts of organization theorists to combine the three perspectives into more complex models see Scott (n 9) 102–22. See also Quinn and Rohrbaugh (n 3).

37 cf Scott (n 9), who states that unlike early rational system models that featured 'the organization as a closed system, separate from its environment and encompassing a set of stable and easily identified participants' (ibid 28), 'a new generation of theories has … focused on the organization as a rational system, but with a difference: now the organization is also viewed as an open system' (ibid 111).

38 ibid 352.

1.3 Organizational Goal and Goal Categories

As the above suggests, the idea of shared goals, collaboratively pursued, is a defining feature of organizations, private and public.[39] Goals consequently 'constitute a central point of reference in the study of organizations',[40] particularly under the rational system (or goal-based) approach, which verily defines organizational effectiveness in terms of attainment of those goals underlying the organization. In developing a goal-based effectiveness framework for the WTO DSS, therefore, a precise understanding is required of what we mean by 'organizational goals' and the types of organizational goals that can serve as normative yardsticks against which to measure DSS effectiveness.

As Etzioni puts it, an organizational goal is a desired state of affairs 'which the organization as a collectivity is trying to bring about'.[41] Or, in the words of Richard Scott, organizational goals are 'conceptions of desired ends'—ends that the organization attempts to achieve through the performance of task-oriented activities.[42] These desired ends vary, in turn, along numerous dimensions and across different constituencies, as captured in the typologies developed in organization theory to explain crucial aspects of goal variation.[43] Charles Perrow, for example, distinguishes between *official* and *operative* goals.[44] Whereas official goals are 'the general purposes of the organization as put forth in the charter, annual reports, public statements by key executives and other authoritative pronouncements',[45] operative goals are 'the relatively specific immediate ends an organization seeks, reflected in its actual operations and procedures'.[46]

In analysing the goals lying at the basis of the proposed WTO DSS goal-based effectiveness framework, this book applies several typologies that hinge on Perrow's distinction, but which break that distinction down into more specific and refined

[39] Tolbert and Hall (n 2) 186–87.

[40] Scott (n 9) 22. See also Edward Gross, 'The Definition of Organizational Goals' (1969) 20 Brit J Soc 277 ("The central concept in the study of organizations is that of the organizational goal. One might even claim that the notion of a goal is coincidental with that of an organization.... It is the dominating presence of a goal which marks off an "organization" ... from all other kinds of systems').

[41] Etzioni (n 1) 6. When so defined, an organizational goal should be distinguished from 'private' or 'personal' goal, which relates to a future state that an individual or subunit within the organization desires for the organization, or for himself. See Lawrence B Mohr, 'The Concept of Organizational Goal' (1973) 67 Am Pol Sci Rev 470; Price (n 9) 5; Gross (n 40) 278. Given that the present research, like most effectiveness studies, takes the organization as a whole as the appropriate level of analysis for assessing effectiveness (Scott (n 9) 353), it goes beyond the agendas and objectives held by subunits within the organization. Organizational performance is therefore explained in terms of the 'organizational goals' that exist beyond the 'private goals' pursued by individuals.

[42] Scott (n 9) 22; Rainey (n 3) 150 ('An organizational goal is a condition that an organization seeks to attain').

[43] Tolbert and Hall (n 2) 15.

[44] Charles Perrow, 'The Analysis of Goals in Complex Organizations' (1961) 26 Am Soc Rev 854, 855–56. For similar distinctions see Hall and Clark (n 28) 120; Zald (n 27) 209.

[45] Perrow (n 44) 855.

[46] Rainey (n 3) 150; Perrow (n 44) 855.

goal categories. This it does by distinguishing DSS goals according to their source, hierarchical level, and form of articulation. These distinctions, recently woven together by Yuval Shany in the context of international courts,[47] provide important insights into the environments in which international courts such as the WTO DSS operate, the diverse constituencies they serve, and the nature of the goals they are expected to achieve. Such distinctions can assist us in identifying and then classifying DSS goals in a way that captures 'our legal sensibilities about form and authority' while facilitating a more precise and comprehensive assessment of goal attainment.[48]

And so, the first distinction to be drawn between the DSS's goals rests on the source of those goals—that is, the identity of the goal setters.[49] Here we distinguish between *external* goals, prescribed for the WTO DSS by extraneous constituencies (e.g. WTO Member states or the general public), and *internal* goals,[50] set by actors belonging to the system itself (e.g. WTO adjudicators or WTO Secretariat staff).[51] This distinction draws important attention to the diverse goals that each constituency, inside and outside the system, expects the DSS to achieve and, in consequence, the range of effectiveness criteria that may be used when gauging its effectiveness. Moreover, the internal/external distinction, beyond its taxonomical value, also has great normative significance for international courts like the WTO DSS. Thus, whereas the internal goals of international courts are generally not legally binding and may be amended by the court itself (as in the case of goals prescribed in court-formulated rules of procedure or in past rulings), international courts are obliged, as a matter of law, to follow the goals set out in their constitutive treaties, concluded by their so-called 'mandate providers'—an external community of states and international organizations.[52] As discussed later in this chapter, it is for this reason, inter alia, that the goal-based effectiveness framework developed herein embraces the goals set for the DSS by its mandate providers as the primary normative benchmarks to guide its effectiveness analysis.

The second distinction to be drawn is based on the goals' 'level of abstraction' or hierarchical level, that is, between *ultimate ends* and *intermediate goals*.[53] Ultimate

[47] Shany (n 24) 17–20.

[48] Shany (n 5) 232.

[49] Shany (n 24) 18.

[50] ibid. Similar distinctions between external and internal goals, addressing the expectations and needs of the organization's external and internal constituencies, can be found in Mohr (n 41) 475; Zald (n 27) 208.

[51] See, e.g. Andrew T Guzman, 'International Tribunals: A Rational Choice Analysis' (2008) 157 U Pa L Rev 171, 184 (discussing the possibility that an international tribunal 'will develop some other set of priorities and goals, distinct from those of any state party. These priorities and goals might involve an enlargement of the tribunal's power and jurisdiction, the advancement of a particular view of the law, or some other objective').

[52] Shany (n 24) 18.

[53] ibid 18–19. Along similar lines, Seashore and Yuchtman differentiate between three hierarchical categories of organizational goals: 'At the top of the hierarchy is the ultimate criterion', which may often be immeasurable. Below are the 'penultimate criteria', which are then followed by subsidiary variables, also referred to as 'subgoals' that serve as 'means for achieving goals' higher up in the hierarchy. Seashore and

ends represent the overarching goals that the DSS is to attain in the long run. Such goals are usually stated in rather open-ended language; they address the broad mission that the system is designed to achieve. Goals of this type may therefore be associated with a certain level of 'goal ambiguity', allowing greater interpretive leeway in deciding their exact scope and meaning in practice.[54] Intermediate goals, on the other hand, are instrumental to the achievement of the system's open-ended (or broader) longer-term objectives. In other words, these are shorter-term goals that serve as means for the realization of the system's ultimate ends. As noted by Rainey, '[g]oals always link together in chains of means and ends, in which an immediate objective can be expressed as a goal but ultimately serves as a means to a more general or longer-term goal'.[55] In the case of the DSS (see Chapter 3), an illustrative example of such an immediate objective is the peaceful settlement of disputes, considered instrumental in promoting the DSS's ultimate ends of fostering a stable multilateral trade setting and maintaining the balance of concessions between WTO Members. Yet, the DSS has various other intermediate goals, such as preserving its institutional legitimacy, a goal often referred to as a *maintenance* or *support goal*, namely, a goal that may not necessarily have intrinsic value but is essential for preserving the system's ability to operate and survive.[56]

Within the goal-based effectiveness model proposed here, the distinction between ultimate ends and intermediate goals is of significant analytical value. The distinction promises to illuminate the complex interrelations existing between the DSS's various goals, help differentiate between its short- and long-range objectives, and facilitate identification of causal chains in the system's judicial outcomes. Thus, for example, this distinction may explain how the realization of certain immediate goals by the DSS incrementally leads to the attainment of the system's more general, long-term objectives or, conversely, how suboptimal functioning with respect to some intermediate goals hinders realization of related ultimate ends.

The last distinction to be delineated between DSS goals refers to the goals' method of articulation. According to this typology, a distinction can be drawn between *explicit*, *implicit*, and *unstated* goals.[57] Whereas *explicit* goals are objectives expressly stipulated in official instruments published by the system or its

Yuchtman (n 17) 378–79. See also Mohr (n 41) 477–78 (discussing the concept of 'sub-objectives' that 'are instrumental to the achievement of other organizational purposes'); Beryl A Radin, *Challenging the Performance Movement: Accountability, Complexity, and Democratic Values* (Georgetown University Press 2006) 15 (distinguishing between an 'intermediate outcome', namely an 'outcome that is expected to lead to a desired end but is not an end in itself', and an 'end outcome', that is, 'the end result that is sought').

[54] On this type of goal ambiguity, referred to in the literature as 'mission comprehension ambiguity', see Young Han Chun and Hal G Rainey, 'Goal Ambiguity and Organizational Performance in U.S. Federal Agencies' (2005) 15 J Pub Admin Research & Theory 529, 532.

[55] Rainey (n 3) 155.

[56] Gross (n 40) 282–87; Charles Perrow, *Organizational Analysis: A Sociological View* (Tavistock Publications 1970) 134.

[57] Shany (n 24) 19.

stakeholders (e.g. the DSS's constitutive treaty, known as the Dispute Settlement Understanding (DSU)),[58] *implicit* goals are concealed in these instruments but can be inferred by way of interpretation.[59] *Unstated* goals, on the other hand, are objectives that the institution's official mandate fails to enumerate but which have been espoused by stakeholders or by the institution itself, independently of any formal text.[60] Though unstated, such goals, as shown in Chapter 3, are no less vital for the DSS's functioning and effectiveness because they often reflect constituencies' common beliefs regarding inherent goals, fundamental to the system's operation, such as conferral of legitimacy on the international cooperative regime in which the DSS is embedded.

As in other organizations, then, the goals of the DSS vary in the form of their articulation, their level of generality, their temporal nature, and the identity (external or internal) of their respective constituencies. Hence, under the goal-based approach, a fundamental decision is to be made regarding the specific group of constituencies whose goals for the DSS will serve as its normative effectiveness baseline. As implied above and further explained in Section 1.6, below, this book presents an effectiveness model that identifies as a normative baseline the goals set for the DSS by one dominant group of external constituencies—the mandate providers—that is, the international organization and Member states that fund, monitor, and use the DSS, as well as those that control its operation and reform.

1.4 Goal Multiplicity and Goal Conflict

Whereas identifying one key category of goal setters along the lines just mentioned narrows the focus of any given effectiveness assessment to a single set of baseline goals, most organizations still exhibit multiple goals as part of that set. This state of goal multiplicity results from the complex and heterogeneous nature of contemporary organizations. It also results from a reality where diverse constituencies (belonging to the same group of goal setters) bestow manifold and competing demands upon the organization, requiring the latter to respond to diverse interests and pursue a variety of goals.[61] Within such multipurpose organizations, certain

[58] Understanding on Rules and Procedures Governing the Settlement of Disputes, 15 April 1994, Marrakesh Agreement Establishing the World Trade Organization, Annex 2, 1869 UNTS 401.

[59] Jackson uses a similar distinction between explicit and implicit goals, with the latter 'not so explicitly expressed in the DSU'. John H Jackson, *Sovereignty, the WTO, and Changing Fundamentals of International Law* (CUP 2006) 146.

[60] Shany (n 24) 19. Similar ideas may be found in early organization theory literature. See James D Thompson and William J McEwen, 'Organizational Goals and Environment: Goal-Setting as an Interaction Process' (1958) 23 Am Soc Rev 23, 28–29 (noting that '[g]oals appear to grow out of interaction, both within the organization and between the organization and its environment. While every enterprise must find sufficient support for its goals, it may wield initiative in this'); Donald R Cressey, 'Achievement of an Unstated Organizational Goal: An Observation on Prisons' (1958) 1 Pac Soc Rev 43.

[61] Rainey (n 3) 163. Victoria Buenger and others, 'Competing Values in Organizations: Contextual Influences and Structural Consequences' (1996) 7 Org Sci 557, 560.

types of goal conflict are clearly unavoidable.[62] Short-term and long-term goals may be incompatible at times. Conflicts may likewise arise between competing intermediate objectives, or between explicit and unstated goals, so that maximizing one goal may inevitably take away from the other.[63]

These goal-multiplicity and goal-conflict complexities have major implications for organizational performance and effectiveness analysis. First, they highlight the often-great diversity of outcomes the organization is expected to achieve during its performance of specific tasks and, consequently, the many dimensions against which its effectiveness can (and ought to) be measured. Second, since these manifold goals are not always arranged in a clear hierarchy, ambiguity may be generated as to which goals should be given preference in the event of conflict or competition over organizational resources, a situation requiring the organization to constantly prioritize between its multiple objectives.[64] Finally, goal multiplicity and goal conflict expose the constraints placed on organizational effectiveness, as in a world of multiple and competing institutional goals, organizations are often required to trade off one goal against another.

Like other institutions, the DSS—a quasi-judicial body nested within the complex WTO edifice and subject to the demands of diverse constituencies in the multilateral trade system—has multiple organizational goals. Whereas some of these goals, as shown in Chapter 3, are interrelated and complementary, others are potentially conflictual. Thus, for example, Article 3 of the DSU asks the DSS to promote the prompt settlement of disputes, as well as clarify WTO law through well-reasoned rulings, without explicitly indicating which goal should take precedence in cases of conflict, or how a balance between the goals is to be struck. Yet, one can easily see how expeditious dispute settlement proceedings, crucial for a global economic system to remain viable, may not always coincide with the production of high-quality legal outputs. In a similar vein, the goal of fostering the amicable settlement of disputes may at times come at the expense of full compliance with WTO rulings and rules because mutually agreed solutions, reached in the shadow of the law, may lead to greater flexibility in outcomes that moves away from strict compliance with WTO rules.

Recognition of goal multiplicity and identification of the goal tensions that push and pull at the DSS are therefore invaluable for the development of a goal-based approach to assessing this adjudicative system's effectiveness. Among other things, these concepts may help explain why the DSS, like all organizations, sometimes achieves some rather than other goals in a more satisfactory manner while exhibiting different dimensions of effectiveness and ineffectiveness for each. Also,

62 David F Gillespie, 'Discovering and Describing Organizational Goal Conflict' (1978) 1 Admin Soc Work 395.

63 Rainey (n 3) 151.

64 On this problem of 'priority goal ambiguity' in public organizations, see Chun and Rainey (n 54) 535.

uncovering the DSS's multiple objectives and their underlying conflicts may bring to light the inevitable trade-offs the system faces when pursuing its manifold goals, thereby revealing the relative weight of each, compliance included. In Chapter 3, I analyse, inter alia, the tensions latent in the fabric of DSS goals, whereas in later parts of the book, I explore the manifestation of these tensions in the real world, together with their ramifications for the DSS's effectiveness assessment.

1.5 Goal Shifting

Goal shifting, another feature associated with organizational goals, ought to be considered in the development of the WTO DSS goal-based effectiveness framework. As Thompson and McEwen have noted, in many analyses of organizational goals and performance, 'the goals of the organization are often viewed as a constant'.[65] Yet goals in effect define the sought-for relationships between the organization and its environment. As a complex and evolving system of numerous parts in constant interaction with one another and the environment,[66] changes that occur in the organization, its surroundings, or both may also generate shifts in the organizational goals pursued, their scope, application, and priority.[67] Hence, as several commentators have suggested, these goals should not be viewed as static elements, but rather as dynamic constructs.[68]

Following this line of thought, and unlike effectiveness studies, including on the WTO DSS, which employ a static approach to organizational performance and regard goals as constant variables,[69] the goal-based model advanced herein views DSS goals as dynamic concepts that change along two axes, the vertical and the horizontal.

First, I argue, the goals pursued by the DSS, or their relative weight, shift vertically along the various stages of the dispute settlement process (i.e. the consultation stage, the panel proceedings, the Appellate Body (AB) process, and the

[65] Thompson and McEwen (n 60) 23.

[66] Benoit Morel and Rangaraj Ramanujam, 'Through the Looking Glass of Complexity: The Dynamics of Organizations as Adaptive and Evolving Systems' (1999) 10 Org Sci 278; Donde P Ashmos, Dennis Duchon, and Reuben R McDaniel Jr, 'Organizational Responses to Complexity: The Effect on Organizational Performance' (2000) 13 J Organizational Change Mgm't 577.

[67] Thompson and McEwen (n 60) 23; Tolbert and Hall (n 2) 189–90.

[68] Thompson and McEwen (n 60) 23; Yamen Barlas and Hakan Yasarcan, 'A Comprehensive Model of Goal Dynamics in Organizations: Setting, Evaluation and Revision' in Hassan Qudrat-Ullah, J Michael Spector, and Paal Davidsen (eds), *Complex Decision Making* (Springer 2008) 296 ('In more sophisticated and realistic goal-seeking models, the goal is not fixed; it varies up and down depending on current conditions, called a "floating goal" structure'); John D Sterman, *Business Dynamics: Systems Thinking and Modeling for a Complex World* (McGrew-Hill 2000) 532 (discussing the concept of 'floating goals' and noting that '[t]he goals float with the ebb and flow of the system itself').

[69] For a critique of organizational effectiveness research that is 'limited to the assessment of static criteria', see Robert E Quinn and Kim Cameron, 'Organizational Life Cycles and Shifting Criteria of Effectiveness: Some Preliminary Evidence' (1983) 29 Mgm't Sci 33, 41.

implementation stage) because of the distinctive structures and attributes found at each stage. This does not prevent DSS goals or their relative salience from also shifting vertically throughout the system's life, as societal changes within the system and its surroundings may affect its goals and functions.[70] Such changes, however, may occur gradually and informally, depending on shifting needs, circumstances, and stakeholders' priorities; these changes, therefore, may not always be reflected, especially in real time, in modifications to the system's formal mandate. Identification of DSS goals, a mission carried out in Chapter 3, thus requires going beyond the letter of the DSU to extrapolating those goals from multiple sources, while examining what intertemporal goal shifts, if any, have occurred since the DSS's inception.

Alongside these vertical goal-shifting trends, I submit, the goals of the DSS, or the relative weight ascribed to them, also shift horizontally, across different types of WTO disputes. Such horizontal goal shifting may result from a variety of factors, including the subject matter of the dispute, the WTO obligations involved, the social values at stake, or the systemic challenges and external pressures confronting the WTO and its DSS. Such forces, and the dynamic environment in which they come into play, create a context that influences and constrains the choices facing the DSS, events that shape the dominant goals pursued by the system in specific categories of conflicts. As a result, while in all WTO disputes the DSS is expected to achieve a broad set of goals, the diverse features and challenges associated with the different types of cases reaching its docket may shift the emphasis placed on these goals as the DSS moves from one dispute category to the other. This horizontal goal-shifting hypothesis is closely examined through a comparative analysis of three categories of WTO disputes in later parts of the book.

Taken together, vertical and horizontal goal shifting have important ramifications for the study of the WTO DSS. First, they challenge the common view of DSS goals as static constructs, suggesting instead that these goals, including the oft-cited compliance objective, are embedded in dynamic and discursive practices of changing audiences, interests, and pressures, which regularly cause the relative prominence of DSS objectives to shift. Second, these goal-shifting notions further imply that the static effectiveness studies so prevalent in the field, based on the premise of compliance as the DSS's fixed primary goal, may fall short of capturing its actual goal-attainment patterns and thus be blind to the full diversity of the outcomes the system produces. Finally, vertical and horizontal goal shifting critically suggest that an effective adjudication system is one that not only achieves its goals, but is also capable of adapting itself and its goal-attainment efforts to changes and new challenges.[71] These goal-shifting notions thus stress that even when applying

[70] Tolbert and Hall (n 2) 189–90; Shany (n 5) 235; Gross (n 40) 293.

[71] A similar line of thought may be found in Ashmos, Duchon, and McDaniel (n 66) 589, who study the effect on performance of an organization's responses and adaptation to turbulence and change in its environment, including the adaptation of the goals pursued.

a goal-based approach to assessing effectiveness, there is no room for a 'one-size-fits-all' examination.

Taken as a whole, goal shifting and the goal-based effectiveness model in which it forms a part provide the foundations for a more rigorous and dynamic conceptual framework for analysing the operation and effectiveness of the WTO DSS. We next address key methodological determinations to be made when carrying out research pursuant to this analytical framework.

1.6 Key Design Parameters in Applying the WTO DSS Goal-Based Framework

The preceding sections have laid down the theoretical underpinnings of the WTO DSS goal-based effectiveness framework, its key definitions, typologies, concepts, and complexities. Any effectiveness study seeking to apply this framework must in turn address several key research design parameters. These mainly concern the selection of the specific category of stakeholders whose goals for the DSS will serve as the normative effectiveness benchmarks, the translation of those goals into performance indicators, and the delineation of the time frame during which the system's effectiveness is to be measured.

Goals in the Eyes of Whom? Selecting a Key Constituency

As noted earlier, organizations speak to a range of external and internal constituencies,[72] each of which sets different goals for the organization to achieve.[73] The WTO DSS is no exception. Among its various constituencies one may count WTO Member states, WTO adjudicators, WTO Secretariat staff, industries and entrepreneurs, members of the legal community, adjacent international organizations, the general public, and others. These constituencies, because of their different interests, expectations, and aspirations, present diverse goals to the DSS and, consequently, diverging sets of criteria for measuring its effectiveness. A fundamental question therefore arises when gauging DSS effectiveness: which goals, belonging to which constituencies, should be used? More concretely, since the concept of effectiveness requires a referent, we need to specify from whose perspective DSS effectiveness is to be measured, that is, the choices and expectations of which goal setters should inform the measurement framework.

[72] Terry Connolly, 'Organizational Effectiveness: A Multiple-Constituency Approach' (1980) 5 Acad Mgm't Rev 211.

[73] Rainey (n 3) 155 (noting that different coalitions and stakeholders have different goals that they want the organization to achieve).

The answer to this question may vary, of course, depending on the purpose and interest of the research in question. As indicated earlier, this book embraces the set of DSS goals prescribed by one dominant group of external stakeholders—the mandate providers—as the normative baseline for analysing DSS effectiveness. When speaking of 'mandate providers', I am referring to the international organization in which the DSS is embedded, the WTO, and its Member states. The main reasons behind this methodological choice are delineated below.[74]

First, the focus on the mandate providers is predicated on the fact that these stakeholders created the DSS and drafted its mandate, in the form of the DSU. They are also the ones who fund, control, and oversee DSS operations. Acting collectively through the WTO's Dispute Settlement Body (DSB)—a political forum comprised of representatives of all WTO Members—the mandate providers are in charge of administrating the entire WTO dispute settlement process. These stakeholders are responsible for referring disputes for adjudication through the panels they establish, for conferring a binding legal status on DSS rulings by adopting panel and AB reports, for supervising implementation of DSS rulings, and for authorizing 'retaliation' when these rulings are not implemented. These same stakeholders also determine the composition of the panels[75] and select (and reappoint) AB members, with the consensus of all WTO Member states or, conversely, forestall the nomination of new AB members, as done (at the time of writing) by the United States. What is more, in fulfilling these responsibilities, WTO Members are provided with ample opportunities to formally express their support or, alternatively, their discontent with the judicial choices made by WTO adjudicative bodies,[76] a capacity that may prospectively affect DSS policy and conduct.

[74] For further discussion of the reasons for focusing on the goals set forth by the mandate providers in the area of international courts, see Shany (n 24) 31–35.

[75] The WTO Secretariat maintains an indicative list of governmental and nongovernmental individuals that may be selected as panellists and proposes nominations for the panel to the parties to the dispute. In case the parties oppose such nominations and are unable to agree on the composition of the panel, panellists are appointed by the WTO director-general.

[76] This was the case, for example, with respect to WTO Members' attempts to communicate to the AB their dissatisfaction with its position regarding the admissibility of amicus curiae submissions in WTO proceedings. See DSB, Minutes of Meeting of 6 November 1998 (14 December 1998) WT/DSB/M/50; General Council, Minutes of Meeting of 22 November 2000 (23 January 2001) WT/GC/M/60. A more recent example can be found in the pronouncements made at the DSB meeting pending the adoption of the AB report in the case of *Canada-Renewable Energy*, where some Members expressed their concerns about certain parts of the legal interpretation developed by the AB. See DSB, Minutes of Meeting of 24 May 2013 (31 July 2013) WT/DSB/M/332. Finally, notable expressions of discontent with the judicial choices and decisions rendered by the AB over the years have been voiced by the United States, particularly in those instances where the AB has overruled panel decisions in favour of the United States regarding measures taken by the latter under anti-dumping and countervailing duty laws. However, the most pointed criticism seems to be reflected in the pronouncements made by the current Trump administration—at DSB meetings, as well as outside the formal WTO setting—parallel to that administration's prolonged blockage of the process for selecting new AB members. See, e.g. 'Statements by the United States at the Meeting of the WTO Dispute Settlement Body, Geneva, December 18, 2018' (*US Mission to International Organizations in Geneva*, 18 December 2018) 9–35, 44 <https://geneva.usmission.gov/wp-content/uploads/sites/290/Dec18.DSB_.Stmt_.as-deliv.fin_.public.pdf> accessed 29 December 2018; 'The President's 2018 Trade Policy

The unique position of the mandate providers in the life of the DSS, expressed in their continuing influence on its design, procedures, and activities, assigns their goals for the system a distinctive role in its operation. Their leverage vis-à-vis the DSS suggests that the goals they have set constitute a crucial point of reference for its actual practice and for predicting and assessing its behaviour. In addition, any act perceived by the mandate providers as seriously deviating from their goals and expectations (often alluded to as 'agency slack'[77]), may invite strong political reactions, potentially threatening the legitimacy of the DSS, which largely relies on the mandate providers' continued support for its authority. Subject to such 'legitimacy pressures', DSS independence to pursue aims and policies as it sees fit is constrained,[78] a situation that ensures significant DSS attentiveness to the mandate providers' goals and preferences.

The identification of the goals set by the mandate providers as the DSS's key effectiveness benchmarks in the research resting at the heart of this book is further supported by the fact that these stakeholders constitute the system's exclusive users. Following the dispute settlement practice under the WTO's predecessor, the General Agreement on Tariffs and Trade (GATT), disputes before the DSS continue to be conducted in the classic, bilateral fashion, between complaining and responding Member states, with no other actor entitled to file a legal complaint before the WTO DSS. Hence, when carrying out research on DSS effectiveness, it makes considerable sense to focus on the goals set for the system by those principal actors who directly consume the services it offers, and shape the disputes it is called upon to adjudicate. As a senior WTO official and former WTO ambassador put it: 'The owners of the [dispute settlement] system are the Members, and the owners of a case are the parties to the case. . . . It is for them [i.e. for Member states] to make a judgment whether it's a failure or not'.[79] It should further be recalled in this respect that since the mandate providers are also the ones authorized to revise the DSS's constitutive instrument once failures or shortcomings are identified, an effectiveness scheme incorporating their perspectives and goals may ease the introduction of reforms to the DSS's mandate, structure, and procedures more so than effectiveness studies focusing on other categories of goal setters.

Agenda' (*USTR*, 2018) 22–28 <https://ustr.gov/sites/default/files/files/Press/Reports/2018/AR/2018%20Annual%20Report%20I.pdf> accessed 29 December 2018.

[77] The term 'agency slack' refers to those agency's actions considered undesirable by its principals. See Darren G Hawkins and others, 'Delegation under Anarchy: States, International Organizations, and Principal-Agent Theory' in Darren G Hawkins and others (eds), *Delegation and Agency in International Organizations* (CUP 2006) 8.

[78] Shany (n 24) 33. For a discussion of the concept of 'constrained independence', which refers to the various mechanisms that restrict the choices available to independent international judges, including possible challenges to their legitimacy, see Laurence R Helfer and Anne-Marie Slaughter, 'Why States Create International Tribunals: A Response to Professors Posner and Yoo' (2005) 93 Calif L Rev 899, 942–54.

[79] Interview with senior WTO official (Geneva, 23 March 2012).

The selection of the mandate providers as the cornerstone of the DSS's goals and effectiveness analysis can also be justified from a normative standpoint. First, as is the case with other international courts, the normative legitimacy of the DSS derives in large part from the consent of WTO Member states to its creation and jurisdiction. This source of legitimacy, rooted in the purposeful and consensual delegation of power from national governments to the DSS, represents the traditional justification for the exercise of authority by such international adjudicative institutions.[80] It is further reflected in the 'principal-agent' as well as 'trusteeship' theories of international courts, in which the latter are conceptualized as 'agents' or 'trustees' of Member-state principals who, by consenting to delegate authority to international courts for the pursuit of specified goals, confer legitimacy upon the mandate and operation of these courts.[81] While state consent alone no longer seems sufficient to sustain international courts' claim for legitimacy, it remains a central justification for these courts' increasing public authority,[82] and it reinforces the proposition that international courts such as the DSS should faithfully pursue the goals of the mandate providers who endowed them with judicial powers.

Second, as a matter of law, briefly noted earlier, the DSS is under legal obligation to follow the goals articulated in its constitutive treaty by its mandate providers. In fact, the DSU explicitly stresses this obligation by elaborating the contents and limits of this duty. Thus, in laying down the DSS's mandate, the DSU not only specifies the goals the system ought to achieve and the legal powers designated to support their attainment, it also states in Articles 3.2 and 19.2 that in executing these powers and pursuing its goals, the DSS 'cannot add to or diminish the rights and obligations' of Members provided in the WTO agreements. Failure to respect these legal prescriptions, or departure from the prescribed goals, may be viewed at some level as lacking justification,[83] what may consequently diminish the legitimacy the DSS draws from the legal mandate to which WTO Member states consented.[84]

[80] Jan Klabbers, Ann Peters, and Geir Ulfstein, *The Constitutionalization of International Law* (OUP 2009) 39; Armin von Bogdandy and Ingo Venzke, 'In Whose Name? An Investigation of International Courts' Public Authority and Its Democratic Justification' (2012) 23 EJIL 7, 8; Nienke Grossman, 'The Normative Legitimacy of International Courts' (2013) 86 Temple L Rev 61, 65–67.

[81] Karen J Alter, 'Agents or Trustees? International Courts in their Political Context' (2008) 14 EJIR 33; Manfred Elsig and Mark A Pollack, 'Agents, Trustees, and International Courts: The Politics of Judicial Appointment at the World Trade Organization' (2014) 20 EJIR 391. For a survey of relevant literature on the topic, see Emilie M Hafner-Burton, David G Victor, and Yonatan Lupu, 'Political Science Research on International Law: The State of the Field' (2012) 106 AJIL 47, 85–86 and accompanying footnotes.

[82] Klabbers, Peters, and Ulfstein (n 80) 39; Armin von Bogdandy and Ingo Venzke, *In Whose Name? A Public Law Theory of International Adjudication* (OUP 2014) 3.

[83] Grossman (n 80) 66 ('A court that evades or ignores the limitations placed upon its authority by states threatens its legitimacy').

[84] cf Daniel Bodansky, 'The Legitimacy of International Governance: A Coming Challenge for International Environmental Law?' (1999) 93 AJIL 596, 605 ('Legal legitimacy is what connects an institution's continuing authority to its original basis in state consent. The authority of the International Court of Justice, for example, derives from its Statute, to which UN member states consented').

Third, the goals set for the DSS by the mandate providers deserve preference over those of other goal setters, such as WTO adjudicators, because they represent the end results of a deliberative and, at least to some degree, transparent process, carried out by state representatives acting on behalf of nations and their citizenry. Such a process, seen for example in the context of the talks on possible improvements to WTO dispute settlement procedures (known as the DSU Review),[85] allows all participants to air their views, requires them to publicly justify their positions and, eventually, to collectively articulate the agreed-upon results. In this sense, as Shany notes, 'the goal-setting process undertaken by the mandate providers may generate more procedural and outcome legitimacy than other less-articulated and less-deliberated goal-setting processes (such as goals set by court judges or by politicians in any specific country)'.[86] Furthermore, the need of negotiating states to gain domestic constituencies' support for the mandate bestowed on an international court increases the probability that the goals they have set for the court will reflect broader conceptions of the desired ends and public goods it is expected to promote.[87]

Finally, the focus on the mandate providers' goals is also sensible from a practical, methodological point of view. The results of the goal-setting process initiated by an international court's mandate providers are usually enumerated in an official, publicly available document, often in the form of an international treaty. As noted earlier, these same goals may be articulated at varying levels of generalization, with some goals perhaps exhibiting a degree of ambiguity, a feature common to public organizations given the political environments in which they operate[88] and the need to cope with policy conflicts and competing interests.[89] Indeed, at the international level, the political difficulties encountered by negotiators may often consciously drive them towards 'constructive ambiguity' when drafting treaties.[90] In any event, the treaty establishing an international court usually constitutes the primary if not the sole written specification of its goals. Furthermore, such a treaty is often accompanied by some form of publicly available commentary that sheds light on the treaty's preparation and the rationales underlying the goals assigned to

[85] On the DSU Review negotiations, see <www.wto.org/english/tratop_e/dispu_e/dispu_negs_e.htm> accessed 30 December 2018.

[86] Shany (n 24) 34.

[87] ibid 34–35.

[88] Jung Wook Lee, Hal G Rainey, and Young Han Chun, 'Goal Ambiguity, Work Complexity, and Work Routineness in Federal Agencies' (2010) 40 Am Rev Pub Adm 284; Sanjay K Pandey and Hal G Rainey, 'Public Managers' Perceptions of Organizational Goals Ambiguity: Analyzing Alternative Models' (2006) 9 Int'l Pub Mgm't J 85.

[89] Sanjay K Pandey and Bradley E Wright, 'Connecting the Dots in Public Management: Political Environment, Organizational Goal Ambiguity, and the Public Manager's Role Ambiguity' (2006) 16 J Pub Admin Research & Theory 511, 514.

[90] Ernst-Ulrich Petersmann, 'Strategic Use of WTO Dispute Settlement Proceedings for Advancing WTO Negotiations of Agriculture' in Ernst-Ulrich Petersmann and James Harrison (eds), *Reforming the World Trading System: Legitimacy, Efficiency, and Democratic Governance* (OUP 2005) 128–29.

the court.[91] As a result, research into these goals, as set by the mandate providers, offers more concrete and identifiable benchmarks for analysing the effectiveness of the WTO DSS than do studies focused on more fragmented and obscure goal-setting processes.

For the reasons listed, this book takes mandate providers as the dominant category of goal setters to inform the WTO DSS effectiveness framework. This does not mean that other research projects cannot be envisaged under the goal-based model, such as studies directed towards the goals set by other external or internal stakeholders (e.g. WTO adjudicators, WTO Secretariat staff, or individual states, among others). In fact, even a project like the present one cannot entirely disregard the expectations shared by other constituencies. More than once, the decision to address the expectations of other DSS stakeholders—for instance, private economic actors (producers and exporters) operating in the international trade arena—may benefit the mandate providers themselves. Similarly, the WTO DSS's capacity to satisfy the goals sought by its mandate providers may occasionally be influenced by its ability to accommodate the concerns and expectations of other stakeholders—for example, environmental lobby groups, human rights activists, and other international organizations—who have shown interest in the WTO, and particularly its DSS, as the multilateral trading system has pushed further into policy areas such as public health and the environment. Thus, to the extent that the goals set for the DSS by its mandate providers allude to, hinge on, or overlap the desired ends of other stakeholders, they should be considered as integral to the inquiry into DSS goals conducted in Chapter 3.

Measuring Goal Attainment: Selecting Effectiveness Indicators

Identification of a key category of goal setters—in this case, the mandate providers—and mapping the goals they expect the DSS to achieve, represent only the first stage of a goal-based inquiry into DSS effectiveness. Once these goals are identified, an assessment of DSS effectiveness requires translation of these goals into viable performance indicators. Selection of such indicators, as Richard Scott notes, is '[a]mong the most critical decisions to be made in attempting to assess organizational effectiveness'.[92] In the social science literature, three types of indicators have been identified: structures, processes, and outcomes.[93]

[91] Thus, in the case of the WTO DSS, the relevant materials from the Uruguay Round negotiations on dispute settlement, which led to adoption of the DSU and creation of the DSS, are publicly available online. See <www.wto.org/english/docs_e/gattdocs_e.htm> accessed 30 December 2018. The Uruguay Round's negotiating history is also documented in the following four-volume set: Terence P Stewart, *The GATT Uruguay Round: A Negotiating History (1986-1992)* (Kluwer Law and Taxation Publishers 1993).

[92] Scott (n 9) 363.

[93] ibid 363–68; Cameron and Whetten (n 22) 277–78.

Structure (or *input*) indicators are used to examine whether the tangible and intangible resources or assets available to the organization (e.g. budget, employees, and legal powers) enable it to meet its objectives. *Process* indicators serve to evaluate whether the organizational processes in place facilitate achievement of the organization's aims, whereas *outcome* indicators are applied to assess whether the organization's outputs and their social effects are consistent with the organization's goals.[94] Hence, while structure indicators focus on inputs and measure the capacity of the organization to function and generate the desired outcomes, process indicators assess efforts by focusing on the quantity and quality of the activities carried out by the organization.[95] Ultimately, outcome indicators—often regarded as the optimal type of effectiveness indicators—evaluate achievements, assessing the impact and value-added generated through activation of the organization's structures and work processes.[96]

Since the goal-based approach to organizational effectiveness requires us to compare the organization's goals (or desired ends) against the outcomes (i.e. actual ends) it achieves, we can conclude that the key to assessing DSS effectiveness involves, first and foremost, the evaluation of its judicial outcomes. Thus, if one goal of the DSS is to support the operation of the WTO regime and its underlying objectives, among them, trade liberalization, an investigation of DSS effectiveness should utilize those outcome indicators reflecting the extent to which DSS rulings have induced changes in trade flows in disputed areas,[97] or generated revision of trade-restrictive practices.[98] Similarly, should a desired end be promotion of positive settlement of disputes in the shadow of WTO law, evaluation of DSS performance with respect to this goal should look into indications revealing, inter alia, the degree to which DSS operations facilitate pre-ruling, as well as post-litigation settlements.[99]

Yet, although outcome indicators represent the quintessential measures of effectiveness, many of a public organization's goals, including those of the DSS, cannot readily be transformed into objective and result-oriented indicators.[100] This observation rests on the ambiguous character of some of the goals pursued (e.g. in the

[94] Shany (n 5) 238. As Shany notes, an important distinction is to be made between *outputs* and *outcomes*. Thus, while 'outputs' refer to 'the direct products of an organization's operations (for example, decisions, speeches, and legal briefs)', 'outcomes' 'are the effects of such outputs on the external state of the world'. See Shany (n 5) 248.

[95] Forbes and Lynn (n 9) 9–10; Scott (n 9) 366–67; Scott and Davis (n 7) 327–28; Radin (n 53) 15.

[96] Scott (n 9) 363; Forbes and Lynn (n 9) 9.

[97] cf Chad P Bown, 'On the Economic Success of GATT/WTO Dispute Settlement' (2004) 86 Rev Econ & Stat 811.

[98] See Marc L Busch and Eric Reinhardt, 'Developing Countries and GATT/WTO Dispute Settlement' (2003) 37 J World Trade 719.

[99] Sivan Shlomo Agon and Yuval Shany, 'The WTO Dispute Settlement System' in Yuval Shany, *Assessing the Effectiveness of International Courts* (OUP 2014) 217.

[100] Jung Wook Lee, Hal G Rainey, and Young Han Chun, 'Of Politics and Purpose: Political Salience and Goal Ambiguity of US Federal Agencies' (2009) 87 Pub Admin 457, 460. See also Gillespie (n 62) 399 ('organizations have both highly quantified and less quantified (qualitative) goals').

case of the DSS, conferral of legitimacy on the WTO), as well as the nonquantifiable nature of some of the public goods produced (e.g. international cooperation or the international rule of law). In addition, unlike organizations operating in the private sector, public organizations like the DSS exercise less control over their inputs, and the social impacts they generate often take place in complex legal and political environments. Taken together, these factors render a cause-and-effect analysis of their organizational performance especially difficult to conduct.[101]

In such instances, therefore, when the goals of the DSS cannot be translated into objective, quantifiable outcome indicators, and causal chains between the system's operation and, for example, changes in state practice may not be easily identified, the system's performance may be measured with the use of qualitative indicators, that is, indicators based on the subjective perceptions of performance levels by relevant actors. Effectiveness assessment in such instances would also benefit from supplemental use of structure and process indicators.[102] Although the latter types of indicators do not directly assess goal achievement, they may assist in evaluating the capacity of the DSS for effective performance by highlighting how the system's structures and processes support its operation and ultimately encourage, or curtail, its effectiveness.[103] Thus, for example, the investigation of structural indicators, such as judicial independence, reputation, personnel (e.g. number of judges, size of the legal secretariat, and quality of personnel), resources (e.g. budget and facilities), or jurisdictional powers (e.g. scope of jurisdiction, binding effect of rulings, and enforcement mechanisms),[104] could assist us, by way of 'reverse engineering', in identifying how the DSS is expected to perform and whether the structures in place are likely to yield the desired outcomes.[105] Moreover, the examination of such structural attributes may explain discrepancies between the goals prescribed for the DSS and the actual outcomes it delivers, thereby directing our attention to those structural conditions more conducive to the system's goal-attainment efforts.

In a similar fashion, an investigation into the quantity and quality of the procedures followed by the DSS may also help us predict the extent to which it may achieve its purposes. For example, adherence to basic standards of transparency and due process in the conduct of panel and AB proceedings can be expected to enhance DSS legitimacy among some target audiences, an outcome that may heighten the impact of DSS rulings. Establishment of a participatory, deliberative judicial process, drawing on information from sources beyond the immediate disputants, likewise, may result in rulings offering improved normative guidance—an

[101] Forbes and Lynn (n 9) 9; Scott (n 9) 364; Shany (n 5) 239.

[102] Lee, Rainey, and Chun (n 100) 460.

[103] Patricia W Ingraham and Amy Kneedler Donahue, 'Dissecting the Black Box Revisited: Characterizing Government Management Capacity' in Caroline J Heinrich and Laurence E Lynn Jr (eds), *Governance and Performance: New Perspectives* (Georgetown University Press 2000) 292.

[104] For a survey of relevant structural indicators in the context of international courts, see Shany (n 24) 58–59.

[105] Guzman (n 51) 203 ('Tribunal design can influence outcomes').

outcome that may also generate greater compliance with WTO law. Alternatively, disproportionate recourse to WTO countermeasures by developed countries when compared with developing countries may undermine confidence in the DSS, thus weakening its ability, as a rules-based system, to redress asymmetries of power and level the playing field between WTO Members. As in the case of structural indicators, we can conclude that an examination of DSS processes may assist in predicting and understanding how well the system works, knowledge that may contribute to improving its outcomes and performance.[106]

Setting a Time Frame

One last critical issue to be addressed by any study seeking to apply the goal-based approach to assessing the effectiveness of the WTO DSS concerns the time frame within which the system's performance is to be evaluated. As Cameron and Whetten note, '[t]he adage, "Timing is everything", has a special significance for research on organizational effectiveness'.[107] The temporal unit used when evaluating organizational effectiveness can influence the outcomes of the assessment in several ways.[108] First, as various studies have shown, short-term versus long-term measures of effectiveness often produce different results.[109] Such differences may emerge from a deliberate organizational decision to sacrifice performance in one time frame in the hope of increasing it in another.[110] They may also result from variations in the temporal scope of the goals the organization pursues. Consider the DSS goals, for example. These goals, as indicated above, consist of several ultimate ends (i.e. the overarching general goals the DSS ought to attain in the long run) alongside more-circumscribed, short-term, intermediate goals that are instrumental for achieving the DSS's long-term objectives. In light of this goal structure, if a short time frame is selected for assessing DSS goal-based effectiveness, the attainment of some intermediate goals, such as promoting the positive resolution of disputes or the prevention of unilateral actions, is likely to be detected; yet the same examination may not fully capture DSS performance with respect to ultimate ends such as enhancing WTO legitimacy, which tend to be achieved incrementally, over a long period of time.[111]

[106] Sowa, Selden, and Sandfort (n 4) 715 ('To improve outcomes, organizations need to understand how their structures and processes enable or hinder those outcomes').

[107] Cameron and Whetten (n 22) 275.

[108] Tolbert and Hall (n 2) 198.

[109] Cameron and Whetten (n 22) 275 (referring to studies that found some organizations to be less effective in the short term but relatively effective in the long term, and vice versa).

[110] ibid 275–76. See also Scott (n 9) 352 (noting that organizations may focus attention on short-range indicators to the neglect of other, more-enduring measures of performance).

[111] cf Cameron and Whetten (n 6) 272 ('effects and outcomes sometimes cannot be detected if the wrong time frame is selected because they may occur incrementally over a long period of time').

Time considerations are also important because organizations, including international courts like the DSS, go through life-cycle stages, during which their performance fluctuates.[112] Hence, the time unit selected for assessing their performance can have a significant impact on the assessment's results. For example, an analysis focusing on an organization's early years may reveal concentrated efforts to finalize procedures, acquire resources, and entrench its legitimacy and authority. As the organization matures, such efforts may be expected to recede, with other goals gaining priority.[113] It thus follows that a goal-based effectiveness study of the WTO DSS that involves assessment of the system's formative years can be expected to yield different outcomes when compared with one focusing on later stages in the system's life cycle. Such variations in DSS effectiveness may be eclipsed, however, if the study's temporal framework covers the entire span of the system's operation. That is, assessment of DSS performance in a single period encompassing its entire lifespan may risk obscuring fluctuations in its performance and goal attainment.[114] An effectiveness study that allows us to compare different phases of the DSS's life cycle may therefore provide a more nuanced understanding of its performance and the factors influencing its effectiveness.

Finally, we should recall that not only organizations change and develop over time; external environments change as well, to confront organizations with varying types and levels of constraints as time goes by.[115] Constraints once acute may subside, and new challenges may arise, thereby generating shifts in the organizational goals to be pursued. Part II of the book presents one such example, found in the strong public criticism directed at the WTO and its trade liberalization ethos at the turn of the twenty-first century. The strident criticism, calling into question both the substance and procedures of WTO governance, has posed an unprecedented challenge to the authority and legitimacy of the WTO and the DSS, consequently leading the DSS to enhance its emphasis on its legitimation objectives, as compared with its predecessor under the GATT regime. The enduring impasse in the WTO's legislative arm provides another illustrative example. On the one hand, the long-lasting stalemate has reduced Members' threats to overturn DSS rulings and has heightened the normative role of the DSS in clarifying and developing WTO law. Yet, the same weakness evidenced by the WTO's negotiating branch with respect to delivering substantive outcomes in the form of new trade rules has contributed to the surge in preferential trade agreements outside the multilateral trade system. In turn, this development has placed new challenges before the DSS, forcing it to shift and adapt its goal-achievement efforts accordingly (see Part IV). Such goal-shifting events further stress the importance of the selected unit of time

[112] Scott (n 9) 352; Cameron and Whetten (n 22) 276; Tolbert and Hall (n 2) 198.
[113] cf Scott (n 9) 352–53.
[114] Shany (n 24) 23.
[115] Tolbert and Hall (n 2) 198.

when assessing DSS effectiveness and, in particular, the need to be sensitive to the possibility of goal fluctuations during the selected period.[116]

Choices on '[h]ow to incorporate the temporal dimension' in organizational effectiveness assessment, as Tolbert and Hall note, 'is essentially one of judgment'.[117] One should nonetheless exercise this judgment call against the various considerations just discussed. To be more precise, decisions must be made with regard to the time frame of reference for analysing DSS goal attainment, the nature and phasing of environmental constraints, and the historical situation of the system.[118]

1.7 Beyond Goal Attainment: Efficiency and Cost-Effectiveness

The goal-based approach advanced in this book offers a broad yet intuitive framework for studying the effectiveness of the WTO DSS in terms of goal attainment. At the core of this approach lies a rather compelling normative argument, according to which international courts such as the DSS should fulfil the objectives for which they have been delegated legal powers. Still, this approach, by focusing on 'the relations between the results … realized and the intended results',[119] does not capture any unintended or unexpected outcomes that the DSS may be generating. This approach likewise fails to account for the costs invested in achieving the intended objectives. The goal-based model, despite its reach, therefore leaves certain aspects of DSS functioning unexplored irrespective of their relevance for understanding the system's conduct and assessing its performance.

To fill in the missing parts of the picture, a comprehensive approach to organizational performance evaluation must go beyond goal attainment. Such is the case with the DSS as well, where the proposed goal-based framework should be extended along two complementary dimensions. First, a goal-based effectiveness analysis of the DSS should be accompanied by investigation of the unintended or unforeseen consequences created in the system's pursuit of its various goals. Naturally, the social impacts generated by the DSS may not be limited to realization of its predefined aims. One should therefore also consider the degree to which the system's operation may be projecting additional and unanticipated costs and benefits (or negative and positive externalities) onto its environment.[120] For example, it may be the case that by means of its legal interpretations, the DSS not only clarifies WTO law—an explicit goal assigned to the DSS in its mandate—but also sheds

[116] Shany (n 5) 235.
[117] Tolbert and Hall (n 2) 198.
[118] ibid.
[119] Bart Prakken, *Information, Organization and Information Systems Design: An Integrated Approach to Information Problems* (Kluwer Academic 2000) 45.
[120] Tolbert and Hall (n 2) 12; Shany (n 5) 237.

light on lacunas in the respective legal arrangements, thereby alerting 'decision makers in the non-dispute settlement part' of the WTO system to the presence of policy problems that may have to be addressed in future negotiations.[121] Similarly, through the resolution of bilateral trade disputes between WTO Members, the DSS may raise the profile of certain global issues (e.g. the friction between trade and the environment),[122] thereby stimulating international cooperation aimed at their resolution.

Yet, by fulfilling its mandate, the DSS may also be producing negative externalities. Thus, while the judicialized WTO DSS may be removing ambiguities in WTO legal texts and inducing compliance with WTO law, some suspect that the DSS's apparent effectiveness in promoting these goals has been realized to the detriment of the WTO's legislative arm, a situation making it more difficult for WTO Members to negotiate new trade rules in the fear that these may expose them to further compulsory judicial scrutiny by the DSS.[123] In a similar vein, through its resolution of WTO disputes implicating conflicting international norms or overlapping international jurisdictions, the DSS may be inadvertently exacerbating rather than defusing international tensions and fragmentation.[124]

As these examples suggest, the DSS may be effective (in the sense of fulfilling all of its goals) yet 'inefficient by generating considerable costs and negative externalities that may offset some or all of the benefits' embedded in the achieved objectives.[125] And vice versa: the DSS may fail to meet certain desired ends but still be efficient in producing unforeseen benefits that compensate for its relatively ineffective goal-achievement record.[126] Evaluation of DSS performance should thus complement the study of its goal attainment by examining the system's 'efficiency', that is, the costs and benefits of its performance independent of its organizational goals. This may allow us to form a more informed opinion about whether the benefits generated by the DSS outweigh the costs and negative externalities it produces.[127]

[121] Jackson (n 59) 150.

[122] Laura Yavitz, 'The WTO and the Environment: The Shrimp Case that Created a New World Order' (2002) 16 J Nat Res and Envtl L 203, 205.

[123] See, e.g. A V Ganesan, 'The Appellate Body in its Formative Years: A Personal Perspective' in Gabrielle Marceau (ed), *A History of Law and Lawyers in the GATT/WTO: The Development of the Rule of Law in the Multilateral Trading System* (CUP 2015) 545; interview with WTO ambassador (Geneva, 24 July 2012) (suggesting that the existence of a stronger, compulsory DSS has contributed to the impasse in multilateral trade negotiations as it has led negotiators to pursue clearer treaty texts (leaving adjudicators with less interpretative leeway), and thereby restraining the use of constructive ambiguity in moving negotiations forward).

[124] See Pieter Jan Kuijper, 'Conflicting Rules and Clashing Courts: The Case of Multilateral Environmental Agreements, Free Trade Agreements and the WTO' (2010) International Centre for Trade and Sustainable Development Issue Paper 10, 34–38 <www.ictsd.org/downloads/2011/12/conflicting-rules-and-clashing-courts.pdf> accessed 30 December 2018.

[125] Shany (n 24) 28.

[126] ibid.

[127] ibid 27–29.

Second, a goal-based effectiveness analysis of the DSS may also be complemented by an investigation of the system's *cost-effectiveness*, namely, the relationship between the system's inputs and outputs.[128] Organizational effectiveness as defined here explores whether an organization's goals have been achieved but without taking the allocation and amount of means used for that purpose into account.[129] Because most organizations, especially public organizations like the DSS, possess limited resources, organizational performance is generally subject to tight cost constraints.[130] An analysis of DSS cost-effectiveness may thus illuminate the relationship between the goals attained by the system and the resources invested to achieve those goals,[131] what would also broaden our understanding of the system's *relative* effectiveness.[132] A cost-effectiveness analysis may likewise allow us to consider whether the resources invested in the creation and maintenance of the DSS could have been employed to advance other, alternative projects, which may have produced better results. It follows that expanding the research framework beyond goal attainment, to encompass efficiency and cost-effectiveness, as Shany notes, 'may facilitate not only discussion of judicial performance and outcome, but also of the justifications for the existence of international courts' such as the WTO DSS.[133]

1.8 Conclusions

Employing social science methods for evaluating the effectiveness of the WTO DSS provides us with new opportunities for the study of judicial effectiveness at the WTO. The goal-based approach followed in this book appears to offer a particularly comprehensive, straightforward conceptual structure for assessing the DSS's effectiveness, while at the same time bringing the challenges that may be associated with such an assessment to the fore. Against this backdrop, the present chapter has sought to delineate the conceptual contours of the WTO DSS goal-based effectiveness framework within which the multiple, conflicting, and shifting goals assigned to the system by its mandate providers serve as key effectiveness criteria. As has been suggested, this effectiveness framework, focusing on assessment of goal attainment, may nonetheless be extended by examining the DSS's efficiency and cost-effectiveness.

[128] ibid 28–29.

[129] Prakken (n 119) 45 ('Effectiveness makes clear whether that target is reached while ignoring the means that were used').

[130] Forbes and Lynn (n 9) 10.

[131] Prakken (n 119) 45. Note that Prakken uses the term 'efficiency' (not 'cost-effectiveness') to describe 'the relation between the results we achieved and the means we used'.

[132] Shany (n 24) 28.

[133] ibid 28–29.

The richer and more nuanced understanding of DSS effectiveness promised by the goal-based approach entails, of course, a more complex analytical process. It requires the assessment of DSS performance against multiple yardsticks, some easily translated into objective, quantitative performance indicators, with others less amenable to quantification. Also not to be overlooked in such a study are the tensions latent in DSS goals and goal shifting over time and across disputes, factors having weighty implications for the system's operation and effectiveness analysis. The time has come, therefore, to identify the plethora of goals underlying the DSS and, while so doing, laying down the substantive normative benchmarks of the DSS's goal-based effectiveness framework, against which the performance of this adjudicative system is to be evaluated.

2

Goals in Context

The Evolution, Structure, and Nature of the WTO Dispute Settlement System

2.1 Introduction

Under the goal-based approach, a methodical and comprehensive investigation into the effectiveness of the World Trade Organization (WTO) Dispute Settlement System (DSS) ought to start from a rather fundamental question: What are the goals (i.e. the desired outcomes) this system is to generate? In contrast to the 'thick brush' approach associated with some current writing on the effectiveness of international courts, the goal-based model followed in this book requires us to invest substantial efforts in identifying the unique set of goals designated for the WTO DSS by those who authored the system's mandate. The present chapter takes the first step in that direction by elaborating the institutional and historical background necessary for identifying DSS goals, a mission continued in Chapter 3.

The WTO DSS was established in 1995 against the backdrop of the multilateral trading system as it had evolved during the fifty-year existence of the WTO's predecessor, the General Agreement on Tariffs and Trade (GATT 1947). The history of dispute resolution under GATT, the reforms introduced to the multilateral dispute settlement mechanism as the WTO supplanted GATT, and the desired outcomes those reforms were meant to achieve largely shaped the design, procedures, and objectives of the WTO DSS in their present form. To understand the operation of the WTO DSS and its underlying goals, as well as to grasp some of the grave trials faced by the system these days, one must therefore understand the regime from which this adjudicative system emerged and the challenges that led to its creation.

In what follows, this chapter provides a brief account of that history, together with a review of the GATT dispute settlement mechanism and the flaws that generated calls for its reform. On this basis, the chapter then turns to present the dispute settlement system put in place with the transition from the GATT to the WTO, while addressing the main improvements it introduced and describing its structure and procedures. The chapter closes with some reflections on the hybrid legal/diplomatic, bilateral/multilateral character of the WTO DSS, reflected in the system's structure and procedures as well as in its goals. This dual character, as illustrated later in the book, nurtures many of the shifts, conflicts, and subsequent trade-offs exhibited between the system's goals throughout its operations.

2.2 The Evolution of the Multilateral Dispute Settlement System

The eighth and final round of negotiations under the GATT, known as the 'Uruguay Round', marked a pivotal turning point for the multilateral trade system. Launched in Punta del Este, Uruguay, in September 1986, and concluded in Marrakesh, Morocco, in March 1994, the Round led to the formation in 1995 of a new institutional framework for regulating international trade, what became known as the WTO. The Uruguay Round also expanded the substantive scope of the multilateral trade regime by subsuming new areas (e.g. intellectual property and services) within its regulatory reach, while at the same time introducing numerous improvements to existing GATT 1947 provisions and to the rules formulated in the previous Tokyo Round of trade negotiations. By the time it was concluded, the Uruguay Round ensured, therefore, that the multilateral trade system would be subject to profound transformation, especially as the entire set of agreements negotiated during the Round constituted a 'single undertaking', meaning that all trading partners were required to accept the full roster of obligations canonized in the thick treaty text, which had taken eight years to negotiate.

Among its innovations, the Uruguay Round subjected the WTO's broader multilateral trade edifice to a new dispute settlement system, often referred to as one of the Round's main achievements.[1] The system's rules and procedures were detailed in a special agreement—the Dispute Settlement Understanding (DSU), which established a sophisticated, multistage, legalized dispute settlement mechanism comprised of compulsory and exclusive jurisdiction, binding decisions, and a permanent Appellate Body (AB). And yet, this WTO adjudicative system is not an entirely new construct. Rather, it was built upon the dispute settlement procedures developed under the GATT over five decades.

Dispute Settlement Under the GATT and the Road to the Uruguay Round

The GATT was born in 1947 as a provisional agreement, aimed at fostering peace and stability in the postwar trading system through the progressive liberalization of national markets. Its drafters' original intent was to situate the GATT within the institutional setting of the International Trade Organization (ITO). They therefore dedicated scant space to dispute settlement within the text of the GATT treaty, contrary to Chapter VIII of the ITO Charter, which laid down a rather elaborate

[1] Peter Van den Bossche and Werner Zdouc, *The Law and Policy of the World Trade Organization: Law, Text, Cases and Materials* (3rd edn, CUP 2013) 160.

procedure for the 'Settlement of Differences'.[2] These procedures were supposed to provide the GATT with the necessary dispute settlement apparatus. However, because key signatories of the ITO Charter eventually chose to abstain from its ratification, the ITO never came into being. This left the GATT with only two general paragraphs devoted to dispute settlement—Article XXII on Consultations and Article XXIII on Nullification or Impairment of Benefits.

Despite such a meagre foothold, the procedures instituted to implement these provisions over five decades of practice evolved into a relatively effective system for the resolution of disputes between the GATT Contracting Parties.[3] What was initially 'a rudimentary, power-based system for settling disputes through diplomatic negotiations' was gradually transformed into a more formal system for settling disputes through adjudication,[4] especially after the reforms introduced to the system by the conclusion of the Tokyo Round of multilateral trade negotiations in 1979.

Under the GATT DSS as it developed, bilateral consultations with a view to achieving a solution mutually agreeable to the parties were to be held at the initial stage of the dispute settlement process. If no settlement was reached, the dispute could be referred to an ad hoc 'panel' once a consensus decision was reached by the GATT Contracting Parties, acting through the GATT Council. The ad hoc panel consisted of three or five experts, most often diplomats and trade officials, serving in their individual capacity and not as representatives of any government (compared with the 'working parties', composed of state representatives subject to the respective governments' instructions, which addressed the disputes brought to the GATT in its early years).[5] Once established, the panel's function was to review the facts of the dispute together with the applicable GATT provisions, and to arrive at an objective assessment of the matter before it. The panel would then deliver its decision (referred to as a 'report') to the GATT Contracting Parties, which had to adopt the report by consensus for it to become legally binding. Should the respondent not change its behaviour in the wake of an adverse panel ruling, the Contracting Parties were empowered to authorize the complainant to suspend trade concessions or other GATT obligations vis-à-vis the respondent. Such authorization, however, was actually given in one case only.[6]

Overall, the GATT DSS was perceived to have achieved an impressive record in dispute resolution.[7] Yet it suffered from several notable deficiencies that

[2] Havana Charter for an International Trade Organization and Final Act and Related Documents: United Nations Conference on Trade and Employment, Havana Cuba, 21 November 1947 to 24 March 1948, UN Doc ICITO/1/4/1948.

[3] John H Jackson, *Sovereignty, the WTO, and Changing Fundamentals of International Law* (CUP 2006) 137.

[4] Van den Bossche and Zdouc (n 1) 159.

[5] John H Jackson, 'The Case of the World Trade Organization' (2008) 84 Int'l Aff 437, 442.

[6] Jackson (n 3) 139.

[7] Robert E Hudec, *Enforcing International Trade Law: The Evolution of the Modern GATT Legal System* (Butterworth Legal Publishers 1993) 361–62.

adversely affected its performance. Most crucial was the positive consensus rule requiring all state parties to agree on every decision, from beginning to end of the dispute settlement process. In practice, this gave any party (usually the defending party) the virtual right to block the formation of a panel, the adoption of its ruling, and the authorization of sanctions for noncompliance and, thereby, to effectively leave the dispute unresolved. This blocking power, 'deemed to be the most significant defect' in the GATT dispute settlement process,[8] became ever more acute as 'the number, visibility, and importance of cases' increased during the 1980s.[9]

The blocking (or veto) power introduced, in turn, an additional challenge in the form of unilateral retaliatory threats and actions, used as a tool to enforce GATT market access commitments upon noncomplying trade partners, especially by the United States. During the 1970s and 1980s, in response to dissatisfaction with GATT dispute settlement procedures, an increasing trade deficit, and a growing perception within the United States that it 'was giving more than it was getting in terms of its national interests in the GATT and that its trading partners were exploiting GATT rules and their lack of enforcement to their advantage', the United States enacted a series of domestic legislative reforms intended to address its trade problems.[10] The best-known of these was Section 301 of the Trade Act of 1974, by which the US Congress invested the president with the authority to take unilateral retaliatory measures against any country's foreign trade policy should the United States deem it to be GATT-illegal or unjustified, unreasonable, or discriminatory. Under this 'unilateral' approach to addressing trade disputes, when a foreign government blocked the GATT dispute settlement process, the United States often found itself threatening unilateral trade retaliation unless the respective government agreed 'to change its trade practices in accordance with Washington's demands'.[11] This American approach to the resolution of trade disputes, referred to by many as 'aggressive unilateralism',[12] was viewed unfavourably by the rest of the world.[13]

Further difficulties associated with the GATT DSS included the scanty elaboration of its goals and procedures, the delays in decision-making absent binding timelines, the sporadic participation of developing countries, and the

[8] Jackson (n 3) 141.

[9] Judith L Goldstein and Richard H Steinberg, 'Regulatory Shift: The Rise of Judicial Liberalization at the WTO' in Walter Mattli and Ngaire Woods (eds), *The Politics of Global Regulation* (Princeton University Press 2009) 224.

[10] T N Srinivasan, 'The Dispute Settlement Mechanism of the WTO: A Brief History and an Evaluation from Economic, Contractarian and Legal Perspectives' (2007) 30 World Econ 1033, 1038; Goldstein and Steinberg (n 9) 224–25.

[11] Goldstein and Steinberg (n 9) 225.

[12] See Jagdish Bhagwati and Hugh T Patrick (eds), *Aggressive Unilateralism: America's 301 Trade Policy and the World Trading System* (University of Michigan Press 1990).

[13] Goldstein and Steinberg (n 9) 225.

fragmentation of dispute settlement procedures between the GATT and the Codes concluded by the end of the Tokyo Round of trade talks.[14]

Hence, despite the pragmatic drift in the development of the GATT DSS and the improvements introduced to the system throughout its fifty years of operation, discontent with the DSS among GATT Contracting parties, aggravated during the 1980s, led many to call for its reform. This discontent, however, reflected broader dissatisfaction with the GATT system in the early 1980s, when it became clear to state parties that the GATT 1947 rules were no longer compatible with the international trading system as it was evolving, and that a new round of negotiations 'was needed to restore confidence in the GATT multilateral trading system'.[15] GATT members ultimately agreed to launch that new round in September 1986, in Punta del Este, Uruguay, where they adopted the Punta del Este Ministerial Declaration that established the framework for the eighth and final round of GATT trade talks, commonly referred to as the Uruguay Round. The Ministerial Declaration, which placed dispute settlement high on the Round's negotiating agenda, expressed the need for far-reaching reform in these words:

> In order to ensure prompt and effective resolution of disputes to the benefit of all contracting parties, negotiations shall aim to improve and strengthen the rules and procedures of the dispute settlement process, while recognizing the contribution that would be made by more effective and enforceable GATT rules and disciplines. Negotiations shall include the development of adequate arrangements for overseeing and monitoring of the procedures that would facilitate compliance with adopted recommendations.[16]

The WTO DSS, negotiated during the Uruguay Round and provided for in the DSU (a WTO agreement entirely dedicated to dispute resolution), addressed many of the above-mentioned shortcomings associated with the GATT dispute settlement procedures.

2.3 The WTO DSS: Structure and Procedures

With the formation of the WTO and adoption of the DSU, the multilateral DSS went through a major reform. The DSU constituted a unified DSS, endowed with

[14] See Jackson (n 3) 143–44; William J Davey, 'Dispute Settlement in GATT' (1987) 11 Fordham Int'l LJ 51, 81–90.

[15] Gilbert R Winham, 'The Evolution of the World Trading System: The Legal and Institutional Context' in Daniel Bethlehem and others (eds), *The Oxford Handbook of International Trade Law* (OUP 2009) 20.

[16] Ministerial Declaration on the Uruguay Round, Declaration of 20 September 1986, GATT BISD 33S/19 (1987).

exclusive jurisdiction over all disputes arising between WTO Members under the various WTO agreements, including those addressing new subject areas such as services, foreign investment, and intellectual property. The DSU further set strict time frames for every stage of the dispute settlement process. It explicitly forbade unilateral sanctions and instituted a permanent appellate instance of jurists in addition to various procedures for ensuring improved implementation of DSS rulings. Most importantly, the DSU eliminated the ability of any one Member to stall the dispute settlement process. Thus, in lieu of the GATT's problematic positive consensus requirement, the DSU applied a 'reverse consensus' rule to all stages of the dispute settlement process. In consequence, progress along the various stages—consultations, panel proceedings, appellate review, and implementation—could be halted only if all WTO Members agree to oppose it. Since chances of reaching such a consensus are generally rather low, the establishment of panels, the adoption of panel and AB rulings, and the authorization of trade sanctions for noncompliance have all become virtually automatic under the DSU, rendering the WTO DSS more compulsory and legally binding.

Under the legalized WTO DSS, the formal dispute settlement process is initiated when one or more Member states (the complainant/s) file a 'request for consultations' with another WTO Member (the respondent), declaring the legal basis for the complaint against a specific trade measure taken by the latter.[17] Once such a request is submitted, initial consultations between the complainant and respondent are mandatory. Hence, 'consultations' between the Members concerned constitute the first step of the WTO dispute settlement process. Consultations are carried out as confidential negotiations between the parties, aimed at resolving the dispute amicably through a mutually acceptable solution—the WTO's preferred mode of dispute resolution, as explicitly stated in Article 3.7 of the DSU. While many disputes do not proceed beyond this stage,[18] the DSU mandates that if the dispute is not resolved within sixty days of receipt of the request for consultations, the complainant may request the establishment of a panel to adjudicate the case.

Pursuant to the DSU's reverse consensus rule, once a panel is requested, the Dispute Settlement Body (DSB)—a formal organ comprised of all WTO Members and responsible for the administration of WTO disputes—must establish such a panel unless a consensus exists *against* its formation, thus effectively endowing the complainant with a *right* to a panel. The panel normally consists of three independent experts appointed ad hoc by the WTO Secretariat from a roster of trade administrators, practitioners, academics, lawyers and diplomats deemed qualified by virtue of their training or experience. Once formed, the panel reviews the factual record and the legal questions raised in the dispute, and issues its report.

[17] For a thorough presentation of the DSS procedure, see Van den Bossche and Zdouc (n 1) 156–311.

[18] William J Davey, 'The WTO and Rules-Based Dispute Settlement: Historical Evolution, Operational Success, and Future Challenges' (2014) 17 J Int'l Econ L 679, 688–89.

With a view to facilitating an amicable settlement, the panel first issues the report to the parties involved (the 'interim report').[19] Upon its circulation to the general WTO membership, the panel report becomes publicly available. Following its circulation, both sides may appeal the panel decision before the AB, a standing adjudicative instance comprised of seven members, each appointed by the DSB for a four-year term (which may be renewed once). The AB reviews the panel's determinations and legal interpretations; it may either uphold, modify or reverse the panel's findings and conclusions. After it is finalized, the AB report, together with the panel report (as modified by the AB), is adopted virtually automatically by the DSB, thereby acquiring binding legal force. Where the panel or the AB finds a measure to be in breach of WTO law, it recommends that the responding party bring the measure into conformity with the relevant WTO agreement/s. Under DSU Article 19.1, the panel and the AB are further authorized to suggest, in their ruling, ways in which the respondent could bring itself into compliance with WTO law. This option, however, has rarely been employed.[20]

Following adoption of the panel and AB decisions, the dispute reaches the final stage, implementation. At this point, the responding party is given a 'reasonable period of time' (usually fifteen months) to bring its measure into conformity with WTO rules. If disagreement arises as to whether the implementation steps taken by the respondent have indeed brought its measure in line with WTO law, further proceedings may be initiated under DSU Article 21.5 to evaluate compliance ('compliance review proceedings').

In cases where the respondent fails to bring its measure into conformity within the reasonable period of time, Article 22 of the DSU provides access to two temporary remedies, pending withdrawal of the measure found to be WTO-inconsistent. The first is voluntary compensation, to be granted to the complainant by the respondent, based on mutual agreement between the parties. Absent such agreement, and as a measure of last resort, the complainant has the right to seek DSB authorization to suspend concessions or other obligations under the WTO covered agreements with respect to the respondent. Retaliatory sanctions of this sort are prospective and bilateral in nature, taking the form of imposition of tariffs or other trade barriers by the complainant vis-à-vis the respondent. Pursuant to DSU Article 22.4, such retaliatory measures shall be set on a level 'equivalent to the level of the nullification or impairment' caused by the respondent's violation whereas under Article 22.6, any disagreement over the proposed level of suspension is to be resolved through arbitration. Like compensation, the suspension of concessions shall—according to Article 22.8—be temporary and 'shall only be

[19] Wolfgang Alschner, 'Amicable Settlements of WTO Disputes: Bilateral Solution in a Multilateral System' (2014) 13 World Trade Rev 65, 69–70.

[20] Joseph Pelzman and Amir Shoham, 'WTO DSU-Enforcement Issues' in James Hartigan (ed), *Trade Disputes and the Dispute Settlement Understanding of the WTO: An Interdisciplinary Assessment* (Emerald Group Publishing 2009) 376–77.

applied until such time as the measure found to be inconsistent with a covered agreement has been removed'.

This is the place to note that at any point along this multistage process, the disputing parties may engage in negotiations to resolve their dispute amicably, in keeping with the DSU's explicit preference for mutually acceptable settlements.[21] WTO disputes are therefore 'launched with a negotiation, which the parties may continue during formal WTO dispute settlement consultations, during the panel process, through the end of the panel and appellate process, and afterwards'.[22] According to DSU Article 3.5, negotiated solutions reached between the parties to matters formally raised under the WTO dispute settlement provisions shall be consistent with the WTO agreements, whereas Article 3.6 further subjects such solutions to notification to the DSB so as to avoid possible interference with the rights of other WTO Members under the same or other WTO agreements. Adherence to the latter requirement, however, 'has not been universal'; notifications made by WTO Members 'do not always include details'; furthermore, no means of verifying whether a notification has not omitted some relevant points is currently in place.[23]

Finally, it should be noted, alongside the formal dispute settlement procedures described above, the DSU provides WTO Members with the option of resorting to good offices, conciliation, and mediation (Article 5), as well as arbitration (Article 25). These routes, however, have so far rarely been utilized.[24]

2.4 The Hybrid Nature of the WTO DSS: A Tale of the Old and the New

> [N]egotiations [are constantly] going on about the role and nature of the dispute settlement [system].... Members want to be able to use it

[21] Alschner (n 19) 69–70.

[22] Amelia Porges, 'Settling WTO Disputes: What Do Litigation Models Tell Us?' (2004) 19 Ohio St J Disp Resol 141, 143. See also Jonas Tallberg and James McCall Smith, 'Dispute Settlement in World Politics: States, Supranational Prosecutors, and Compliance' (2014) 20 EJIR 118, 125–26.

[23] Porges (n 22) 163. See also Alschner (n 19) 90–92.

[24] Michelle T Grando, *Evidence, Proof, and Fact-Finding in WTO Dispute Settlement* (OUP 2009) 22. A WTO ambassador and panellist commented in this regard that although WTO Members have the possibility to resort to these alternative means for dispute resolution, Members rarely do so because of the legal complexity usually characterizing WTO disputes. Interview with WTO ambassador (Geneva, 23 July 2012). Note, however, that in response to the crisis besetting the WTO DSS at the time of finalizing this book (resulting from the US blocking of appointments to the AB), some have suggested using an ad hoc appeal arbitration procedure under DSU Article 25 as an interim solution should the AB become dysfunctional as of December 2019. See Jennifer Hillman, 'Three Approaches to Fixing the World Trade Organization's Appellate Body: The Good, the Bad and the Ugly?' (2018) Institute of International Economic Law Research Paper <https://www.allnews.ch/sites/default/files/files/20181212_Georgetown-Hillman_Good_Bad_Ugly_Fix-to_WTO_AB.pdf> accessed 30 December 2018.

> for their [own] purposes but they don't want it to get too strong, because then they might be left behind at some point, and they will have to comply even though they don't agree. And at the same time, you know, when they want to use it against others, it needs to be strong, so . . . it is a dialectic, going back and forth all the time.
>
> —Interview with a former EU official (Geneva, 9 July 2012)

As this comment implies and as recent developments in the multilateral trading system have aptly illustrated, throughout the history of the GATT, and now the WTO, there has been some ambivalence over the appropriate role, nature, and strength of the multilateral dispute settlement procedure.[25] Two competing viewpoints have occupied debates on this issue among diplomats and academics since the GATT's inception.[26] According to the first, diplomacy-oriented perspective to trade dispute resolution, 'not legal principles and lawyers, but economic policy and diplomats should be the driving forces in the dispute settlement procedure'.[27] This procedure, it has been argued, should not be 'juridical' or 'legalistic', but simply be one that would assist states 'to resolve differences through negotiation and compromise'.[28] In contrast, the second, rule-oriented approach has favoured a more disciplined, judicial, and legalistic dispute settlement process by which an impartial third-party adjudicator could make objective rulings about alleged inconsistencies with the multilateral trade rules.[29]

As many have observed, with the formation of the WTO in 1995, the multilateral DSS edged away from its diplomatic orientation under the old GATT, towards the second and more legalistic approach to the settlement of international trade disputes.[30] As implied above, disputes under the GATT were addressed through a mechanism that was, in many respects, power-oriented and political in nature.[31] Consensus was required to complete any step of the dispute settlement process. Panellists were often diplomats who saw their 'principal task' as crafting outcomes which would be acceptable to both parties and thus amenable to adoption.[32]

[25] On this issue, see also Srinivasan (n 10) 1035; Giovanni Maggi and Robert W Staiger, 'The Role of Dispute Settlement Procedures in International Trade Agreements' (2011) 126 Q J Econ 475, 476, 486–87; John H Jackson, 'Dispute Settlement in the WTO: Policy and Jurisprudential Considerations' (1998) Research Seminar in International Economics, University of Michigan, Discussion Paper 419, 2 <https://ideas.repec.org/p/mie/wpaper/419.html> accessed 30 December 2018.

[26] Alschner (n 19) 69.

[27] ibid.

[28] Jackson (n 25) 2.

[29] ibid 3; Alschner (n 19) 69.

[30] See, e.g. Judith Goldstein and Lisa L Martin, 'Legalization, Trade Liberalization, and Domestic Politics: A Cautionary Note' (2000) 54 Int'l Org 603, 603–04, 626; Srinivasan (n 10) 1035.

[31] Arie Reich, 'From Diplomacy to Law: The Juridicization of International Trade Relations' (1997) 17 Nw J Int'l L & Bus 775, 794–99.

[32] Joseph H H Weiler, 'The Rule of Lawyers and the Ethos of Diplomats: Reflections on the Internal and External Legitimacy of WTO Dispute Settlement' (2002) 13 Am Rev Int'l Arb 177, 184.

Secrecy surrounded large parts of the process, whereas disputes were treated as 'discrete eruptions between members requiring "settlement"', even if they impinged upon systemic issues of relevance beyond the particular dispute.[33] Within this framework, the GATT DSS placed considerable emphasis on negotiation and settlement, and was largely considered to be designed to reach mutually agreeable solutions rather than delivering judgments based on legal principles.[34] As noted by Weiss, under the GATT DSS, the goal to be achieved was 'not legal consistency, predictability, and certainty. . . . The dominant aspect of GATT disputes was that of "settlement", of a balanced accommodation of interests rather than a vindication of rights in a "victory versus defeat" pattern'.[35]

Hence, although the GATT DSS evolved through practice towards a more judicialized system over the course of its history, it continued to be 'governed by elements of diplomacy and consensus';[36] 'its fundamental purpose remained to facilitate the diplomatic settlement of trade disputes between contracting parties'.[37] It was thus only with the conclusion of the Uruguay Round and the creation of the WTO and its reformed DSS that the rule-oriented approach to dispute settlement in the multilateral trade system came to prevail.[38] Historically, this shift towards greater legalization resulted mainly from a deal struck between the United States, which sought to strengthen the multilateral dispute settlement system, and other trading partners, among them the EU and Japan, which favoured a less judicial DSS, but nonetheless decided to accept a more judicial-like system in exchange for the US commitment to use the new system in lieu of taking unilateral measures under the so-called Section 301 of the 1974 US Trade Act.[39] Interestingly, twenty five years later, at the time of finalizing the writing of this book, it is the United States, the driving force behind the creation of the WTO DSS, that has come to raise serious challenges to the judicialized nature of the DSS and to threaten reverting the system 'to the pre-1995 regime' of the GATT through the continuous blocking of nominations to the AB.[40] At the same time, the EU, China, and many other trading partners appear to have become the advocates of the legalized DSS as it emerged from the paradigmatic shift that took place in the turn from the GATT to the WTO.

[33] ibid 183.

[34] Matthias Oesch, *Standards of Review in WTO Dispute Resolution* (OUP 2003) 4.

[35] Friedl Weiss, 'Improving WTO Procedural Law: Problems and Lessons from the Practice of Other International Courts and Tribunals' in Friedl Weiss (ed), *Improving WTO Dispute Settlement Procedures* (Cameron May Limited 2000) 21.

[36] Claus-Dieter Ehlermann, 'Six Years on the Bench of the "World Trade Court": Some Personal Experiences as Member of the Appellate Body of the World Trade Organization' (2002) 36 J World Trade 605, 607.

[37] Richard H Steinberg, 'Judicial Lawmaking at the WTO: Discursive, Constitutional, and Political Constraints' (2004) 98 AJIL 247, 250.

[38] Oesch (n 34) 5.

[39] Davey (n 18) 686; Robert Hudec, 'The New Dispute Settlement Procedure: An Overview of the First Three Years' (1999) 8 Minn J Global Trade 1, 13.

[40] Gregory Shaffer, 'A Tragedy in the Making? The Decline of Law and the Return of Power in International Trade Relations' (2019) 44 Yale J Int'l L (forthcoming).

This being said, one should not overstate the 'legal paradigm shift' captured in the move to the WTO.[41] Not only did the GATT DSS gradually become more legalized over time,[42] but the WTO DSS itself retained some meaningful aspects of GATT diplomacy.[43] And so, despite its much-acclaimed juridification, the WTO dispute settlement mechanism, as Ehlermann notes, is essentially a 'hybrid one', combining 'traditional' features of trade diplomacy, such as mandatory consultations, confidential procedures, and a clear preference for bilateral, mutually agreed settlements of disputes, with 'new' elements of legal adjudication, such as compulsory jurisdiction, quasi-automatic adoption of rulings, standing appellate instance, law interpretation, and norm compliance.[44] Or, as another AB member put it:

> [T]he WTO [DSS has] ... two layers.... The first layer is modelled after arbitration, an old-type arbitration even. You have confidentiality, you have [bilateral] agreements of the parties.... The second layer is modelled after adjudication, not even simple, but higher adjudication. But somehow you impose, for example, confidentiality of procedures. It's completely irrelevant for a tribunal. Moreover, a tribunal which is supposed to control the interpretation of the law.... So, these are the type of things [that are brought together in the WTO DSS] ... they are not very coordinated.[45]

The hybrid character of the WTO DSS, stemming from the increasing penetration of legal structures, actors, and concepts into what was formerly an inherently diplomatic domain, has resulted, as Conti notes, in 'a multifaceted tension between law and diplomacy' in the system's design and processes.[46] In a similar vein, the DSS's dual character has resulted in an underlying tension between bilateralism and multilateralism in a system designed to enforce multilateral rules and provide systemic predictability through legal interpretation, but which is embedded in what is clearly a bilateral dispute settlement structure. One WTO legal officer described this latter tension between the bilateral (or private) and the multilateral (or public) aspect of the DSS rather succinctly:

> The WTO system is a hybrid ... a multilateral system and also a private [system], or at least a bilateral arbitration [system], when it comes to dispute settlement....

41 Weiler (n 32) 179–81.

42 For a detailed overview of this gradual process, see Gabrielle Marceau, Amelia Porges, and Daniel Ari Baker, 'Introduction and Overview' in Gabrielle Marceau (ed), *A History of Law and Lawyers in the GATT/WTO: The Development of the Rule of Law in the Multilateral Trading System* (CUP 2015) 1.

43 Weiler (n 32) 180.

44 Claus-Dieter Ehlermann, 'Policy Conclusions' in Federico Ortino and Ernst-Ulrich Petersmann (eds) *The WTO Dispute Settlement System 1995-2003* (Kluwer Law International 2004) 102.

45 Interview with former AB member (Geneva, 19 April 2012).

46 Joseph A Conti, *Between Law and Diplomacy: The Social Context of Disputing at the World Trade Organization* (Stanford University Press 2011) 1.

> The [first aspect] ... has systemic public importance, whereas private arbitration is simply a means of resolving a dispute between two [parties].... The WTO system has elements of both.... [T]here are aspects to the system that are essentially bilateral ... for example ... the objective of resolving the dispute at hand ... it's about resolving a particular dispute, in a particular point in time between two Members. But, of course, the system at the same time is not ... only a bilateral means of dispute settlement ... it also has multilateral public aspects to it. And so, whenever the panel is interpreting a provision ... [the] interpretations [developed] ... are not specific to the particular dispute. The essence of treaty interpretation in WTO dispute settlement is that interpretations developed in one case ... will have a bearing ... on future cases. There is nothing private or bilateral about interpretation. And ... there are tensions ... between ... these two objectives of seeking to ... facilitate the resolution of the dispute at hand, seeking the Members concerned to reach a mutually agreed solution ..., while at the same time, the system clearly has broader multilateral aspects to it, for instance, treaty interpretation.[47]

This dual nature of the WTO DSS and the tensions resulting therefrom, as the last quotation implies, are reflected not only in the system's structure and procedures but also in its underlying goals, examined in the following chapter. Such tensions, to which we come back later in the book, generate in turn inevitable conflicts, shifts and trade-offs between DSS goals, thereby affecting the system's operation and effectiveness in meaningful ways.

[47] Interview with WTO legal officer (Geneva, 13 March 2012).

3
The WTO Dispute Settlement System
Goals

3.1 Introduction

Our stress on organizational goals for assessing judicial effectiveness demands that we now explore the fundamental question of precisely which goals its mandate providers expect the World Trade Organization (WTO) Dispute Settlement System (DSS) to achieve. Despite the fundamental nature of this question, as several commentators have indicated, there remains a 'lack of clarity' among government officials, practitioners, and academics concerning 'the aims and objectives of the DSS',[1] accompanied by an ongoing debate 'about the role that it should serve'.[2] In this context, by tying effectiveness to goals, the goal-based approach advanced in this book urges us to delve deeper into the question of what aims underlie the DSS, the spectrum of functions it should play, and the nature of the relations between them. In what follows we take stock of these multiple aims as prescribed for the DSS by its mandate providers, thereby laying down the substantive building blocks of the WTO DSS goal-based effectiveness framework against which its performance is to be evaluated.

A convenient starting point in identifying the various goals of the DSS is found in Article 3 of the Dispute Settlement Understanding (DSU), where the authors of the DSU listed several of the objectives the system ought to pursue. I do not, however, limit my investigation to an examination of the DSU text. I go further, to analyse the DSU's negotiation history, official WTO documents (e.g. those promulgated within the framework of the DSU Review negotiations on possible improvements to WTO dispute settlement procedures), DSS rulings, interviews with WTO practitioners, and the academic literature on the DSS written by scholars in law, political science, and economics. These diverse sources reveal an intricate matrix of ultimate ends and intermediate goals, which at times complement and at times contradict one another. As explained in Chapter 1, this goal multiplicity results, inter alia, from the broad range of tasks entrusted with the DSS, the varied

[1] Bryan Mercurio, 'Retaliatory Trade Measures in WTO Dispute Settlement Understanding: Are There Really Alternatives?' in James Hartigan (ed), *Trade Disputes and the Dispute Settlement Understanding of the WTO: An Interdisciplinary Assessment* (Emerald Group Publishing 2009) 404.

[2] Giovanni Maggi and Robert W Staiger, 'The Role of Dispute Settlement Procedures in International Trade Agreements' (2011) 126 Q J Econ 475, 476, 486–87.

demands imposed by its constituencies, and the convoluted institutional and political environment in which the system is nested. In turn, this goal multiplicity contributes to the conflicts reflected in DSS goals, conflicts that are further nurtured by the hybrid nature of the system, which, alongside modern elements of legal adjudication, preserves 'traditional' elements of trade diplomacy inherited from the WTO's predecessor, the General Agreement on Tariffs and Trade (GATT).

In concert with the goal typologies introduced in Chapter 1, the present chapter analyses the WTO DSS goal structure, beginning with the system's ultimate ends—the overarching purposes the DSS is expected to fulfil in the long run, which frame the broad mission it is designed to achieve. The chapter then follows with the system's more specific, intermediate goals, those which serve as means for realizing the former, more general, often open-ended objectives.

3.2 Ultimate Ends

Providing Security and Predictability to the Multilateral Trading System

The first of the WTO DSS's ultimate ends, explicitly set down in Article 3.2 of the DSU, echoed in its negotiating history and the ongoing talks on it possible reform,[3] as well as in the views of WTO officials and practitioners,[4] is to provide 'security and predictability to the multilateral trading system'. Obviously, security and predictability are essential conditions for the efficient conduct of the governments participating in the multilateral trading system. Among other things, a predictable

[3] For discussions of this ultimate end in the framework of the Uruguay Round negotiations, see, for example, Summary and Comparative Analysis of Proposals for Negotiations, Note by the Secretariat, Negotiating Group on Dispute Settlement (3 November 1987) GATT Doc MTN.GNG/NG13/W/14 [hereinafter November 1987 GATT Secretariat Note]; Summary and Comparative Analysis of Proposals for Negotiations, Note by the Secretariat, Negotiating Group on Dispute Settlement (26 February 1988) GATT Doc MTN.GNG/NG13/W/14/Rev.1 [hereinafter February 1988 GATT Secretariat Note]. The centrality of this ultimate end of the WTO DSS has been reiterated during the DSU Review negotiations. See, e.g. Minutes of Meetings of 13–15 November 2002, Special Session of the Dispute Settlement Body (31 March 2003) TN/DS/M/6; Minutes of Meetings of 14 October 2002, Special Session of the Dispute Settlement Body (27 February 2003) TN/DS/M/5 [hereinafter Minutes of Meeting of October 2002]; Report of the Chairman, Ambassador Ronald Saborío Soto, Special Session of the Dispute Settlement Body (6 August 2015) TN/DS/27, 1 [hereinafter Report of the DSB Chairman 2015]. Finally, the salience of this objective has been recently re-emphasized by many WTO Members during the discussions of proposed amendments to the DSU raised in an attempt to solve the crisis faced by the DSS as a result of the continued US blocking of the process for selecting new AB members. See, e.g. Communication from the European Union, China, Canada, India, Norway, New Zealand, Switzerland, Australia, Republic of Korea, Singapore, and Mexico to the General Council (11 December 2018) WT/GC/W/752/Rev.2, 1.

[4] See, e.g. interview with private attorney (Brussels, July 19 2012) (noting that the goal of the WTO DSS is to maintain predictability and order in the multilateral trade system); interview with WTO ambassador (Geneva, 23 July 2012); interview with former WTO legal officer (Geneva, 30 March 2012); interview with Ecuadorian official (Geneva, 25 July 2012).

trading environment is conducive to the reduction of mutual suspicions and misunderstandings that could result in trade wars among WTO Members. Yet, while WTO agreements are negotiated and signed by governments, the multilateral trading system, as the panel in *US-Section 301* emphasized, is 'composed not only of states but also, indeed mostly, of individual economic operators' (e.g. producers, importers, and exporters), the main actors affected by a lack of security and predictability in international trade.[5] Accordingly, it was important for the WTO founders to foster, by means of the DSS, stable and certain market conditions that would support intergovernmental cooperation as well as 'individual economic activity in national and global' marketplaces.[6] Or, as a WTO ambassador put it, since WTO rules increasingly affect private economic operators in addition to Member states, the DSS is expected to provide such private actors with the necessary conditions of legal 'security and predictability.... Investors and trade actors need to know the rules of the game and well understand the rules of the game' in order to conduct their business.[7]

However, the provision of these fundamental conditions, as a former Appellate Body (AB) member forcefully asserted, does not imply legal stagnation. A core goal of the DSS, he continued, is clearly 'to stabilize the [multilateral trading] system' by 'guaranteeing uniformity of behavior' and keeping state conduct 'within the limits' of WTO law through 'control [of] the interpretation of the law' and the curbing of treaty 'auto-interpretation' by Member states ('a grave congenital illness of international law').[8] That said, '[s]tabilize doesn't mean freeze'; rather, it means that 'if there's an evolution [in the law], it's an evolution which is visible. You could see that things are moving in a certain direction', which makes them predictable. 'Without that', this AB member emphasized, the WTO system could not be sustained; otherwise, it would be 'like driving without tools of circulation'.[9] Early on in its jurisprudence, the AB acknowledged as much:

> WTO rules are reliable, comprehensible and enforceable. WTO rules are not so rigid or so inflexible as not to leave room for reasoned judgements in confronting the endless and ever-changing ebb and flow of real facts in real cases in the real world. They will serve the multilateral trading system best if they are interpreted with that in mind. In that way, we will achieve the 'security and predictability' sought for the multilateral trading system by the Members of the WTO through the establishment of the dispute settlement system.[10]

[5] *United States–Section 301–310 of the Trade Act of 1974*, Report of the Panel, 27 January 2000, WT/DS152/R, para 7.76.
[6] ibid, paras 7.71, 7.73, 7.75.
[7] Interview with WTO ambassador (Geneva, 24 July 2012).
[8] Interview with former AB member (Geneva, 19 April 2012).
[9] ibid.
[10] *Japan–Taxes on Alcoholic Beverages*, Report of the Appellate Body, 1 November 1996, WT/DS8/AB/R, WT/DS10/AB/R, WT/DS11/AB/R, 31.

In order for achievement of the rather abstract ultimate end of providing security and predictability to be feasible, it is essential for the DSS to advance other, more concrete intermediate goals. These include, inter alia, the interpretation and application of the law in a clear, coherent, and consistent manner; the inducement of compliance with WTO rules; the assurance of positive solutions to disputes; and the prevention of destabilizing, unilateral enforcement actions, the last being a lesson learned from the GATT's history.

Maintaining and Restoring the Balance of Benefits between WTO Members

As detailed in the previous chapter, the principal goal assigned to the GATT DSS was 'to provide for an orderly process for maintaining or restoring the balance of concessions between Contracting Parties'.[11] This goal fitted well the diplomacy-oriented approach to dispute settlement prevalent under the GATT, which aimed at achieving a balanced accommodation of states' reciprocal trade concessions (rather than adherence to agreed rules).[12] Although the WTO DSS's mandate providers created a more rule-based system, as Palmeter and Alexandrov note, '[m]embership in the WTO, as was the case with GATT, is not a matter simply of adhering to a set of legal rules'.[13] The WTO is also a reciprocity-based system, founded on a delicate negotiated balance of rights and obligations specified in the WTO agreements, as well as of additional trade concessions exchanged between its Members.[14] Within this framework, one of the major goals of the WTO DSS is to maintain that balance of trade benefits and restore it whenever a scofflaw member upsets it.[15]

[11] Terence P Stewart (ed), *The GATT Uruguay Round: A Negotiating History (1986-1992)*, vol 2 (Kluwer Law and Taxation Publishers 1993) 2669.

[12] Friedl Weiss, 'Improving WTO Procedural Law: Problems and Lessons from the Practice of Other International Courts and Tribunals' in Friedl Weiss (ed), *Improving WTO Dispute Settlement Procedures* (Cameron May Limited 2000) 21.

[13] David Palmeter and Stanimir A Alexandrov, 'Inducing Compliance in WTO Dispute Settlement' in Daniel L M Kennedy and James D Southwick (eds), *The Political Economy of International Trade Law: Essays in Honor of Robert Hudec* (CUP 2002) 654.

[14] Joost Pauwelyn, 'Enforcment and Countermeasures in the WTO: Rules are Rules–Toward a More Collective Approach' (2000) 94 AJIL 335, 339. See also Simon A B Schropp, *Trade Policy Flexibility and Enforcement in the World Trade Organization: A Law and Economics Analysis* (CUP 2009) 191–92.

[15] John Linarelli, 'The Role of Dispute Settlement in World Trade Law: Some Lessons from the Kodak-Fuji Dispute' (2000) 31 L & Pol'y Int'l Bus 263, 348 ('The DSB exists in the nation state system of reciprocity.... In a reciprocity based system, the DSB focuses on the balance of concessions ... to either preserve or restate the WTO bargain struck by the WTO members'). See also Rodney D Ludema, 'Optimal International Trade Agreements and Dispute Settlement Procedures' (2001) 17 Eur J Pol Econ 355, 357; Thomas A Zimmermann, *Negotiating the Review of the WTO Dispute Settlement Understanding* (Cameron May 2006) 72.

This rebalancing goal is reflected in the explicit language of Article 3.3 of the DSU, which provides that the settlement of disputes is essential for the 'maintenance of a proper balance between the rights and obligations of Members'. This objective is also present in the negotiating history of the Uruguay Round[16] and in the remedies of compensation and suspension of *equivalent* concessions stipulated in DSU Article 22.[17]

While remaining central to its mission, a potential tension exists between the rebalancing objective and other goals of the DSS, especially securing the predictability of the multilateral trade system and fostering compliance with WTO rules. This tension largely stems from the fact that under the current DSS, with its de jure and de facto preference for mutually agreed solutions,[18] the negotiated balance of benefits may not necessarily be restored through withdrawal of the WTO-inconsistent measure, but rather through bilateral recalibration of the original bargain between the disputing parties in a settlement[19] that effectively tolerates ongoing violations of WTO law.[20] In some cases, however, as Part III of this book illustrates, it is the ability of the DSS to preserve a pre-existing equilibrium through a rebalancing act that protects the long-term economic, political, and legal security of the WTO regime by introducing a contractual flexibility mechanism in times of heightened political or economic pressures.[21]

[16] See, e.g. Statement by the Spokesman of the European Community at the Meeting of 5–6 April, Negotiating Group on Dispute Settlement (5 April 1990) GATT Doc MTN.GNG/NG13/W/39, 1 [hereinafter 1990 Statement of the European Community]; Comparison of Existing Texts and Proposals for Improvements to the GATT Dispute Settlement System, Note by the Secretariat, Negotiating Group on Dispute Settlement (21 September 1988) GATT Doc MTN.GNG/NG13/W/29/Rev.1, 4–5; Summary and Comparative Analysis of Proposals for Negotiations, Note by the Secretariat, Negotiating Group on Dispute Settlement (22 June 1988) GATT Doc MTN.GNG/NG13/W/14/Rev.2, 2.

[17] See, e.g. Peter B Rosendorff, 'Stability and Rigidity: Politics and Design of the WTO's Dispute Settlement Procedure' (2005) 99 Am Pol Sci Rev 389, 391; Michelle Limenta, *WTO Retaliation: Effectiveness and Purposes* (Hart Publishing 2017) 10.

[18] See DSU art 3.7 ('A solution mutually acceptable to the parties to a dispute ... is clearly to be preferred').

[19] Interview with former WTO legal officer (Geneva, 30 March 2012) (noting that the DSS 'is out there to achieve some balance, through a settlement or through rule-compliance').

[20] Jonas Tallberg and James McCall Smith, 'Dispute Settlement in World Politics: States, Supranational Prosecutors, and Compliance' (2014) 20 EJIR 118, 126.

[21] Leslie Johns and Peter B Rosendorff, 'Dispute Settlement, Compliance and Domestic Politics' in *Trade Disputes and the Dispute Settlement Understanding* (n 1) 159; Rosendorff (n 17) 389–90. Other commentators have advanced a similar argument based on efficient breach theory. Such commentators argue that WTO law does not require compliance at all costs, and that the DSS works, de facto, as a system of 'breach and pay', that is, as a contractual flexibility device allowing Members to adjust the bargain when it proves mutually disadvantageous, thereby sustaining the WTO cooperative regime in the long run. See, e.g. Warren F Schwartz and Alan O Sykes, 'The Economic Structure of Renegotiation and Dispute Settlement in the World Trade Organization' (2002) 31 J Legal Stud S179; Joel P Trachtman, 'The WTO Cathedral' (2007) 43 Stan J Int'l L 127; Eric A Posner and Alan O Sykes, 'Efficient Breach of International Law: Optimal Remedies, "Legalized Noncompliance", and Related Issues' (2011) 110 Mich L Rev 243.

Regime Support: Sustaining WTO Operation and Realization of Its Goals

The WTO DSS is institutionally embedded in the broader framework of norms and mechanisms comprising the multilateral trading system. And, like other regime courts situated within international governance structures, it was created in part to 'enhance the success and effectiveness of the regime'.[22] Hence, as one of the constitutive elements of the WTO,[23] the DSS is expected to sustain the operation of the multilateral trading system, to keep Member states within its normative community, and to support the realization of its underlying goals,[24] among which we can list promoting global welfare and development through trade liberalization, and 'deeper objectives . . . such as establishing stability and peaceful economic relations'.[25] The DSU attests to this regime-support goal when stipulating, for instance, in Article 3.3, that the prompt settlement of disputes 'is essential to the effective functioning of the WTO'.

Upholding the WTO cooperative regime and multilateral objectives is thus realized by the DSS by facilitating the positive and timely resolution of disputes, where possible through the conclusion of mutually agreed solutions. Yet, the DSS further advances this regime-maintenance goal by containing existing conflicts within defined legal parameters, defusing their political aspects,[26] and forestalling across-the-board deterioration through unilateral actions, all with a view to sustaining the WTO's stability and allowing disputants to continue collaborating on other fronts while awaiting their conflict's resolution.[27] As one state official commented:

> [O]ne function that . . . [the dispute settlement] system plays is that . . . whatever problem we have with some other country, we can handle it here . . . and just take it out of the agenda with the other country, at least, for a while, . . . and say, 'well, we can continue to discuss whatever you want, it is true that we have a commercial dispute, but that's being dealt in the WTO [DSS]. So, let's keep it there'. That's one

[22] Benedict Kingsbury, 'International Courts: Uneven Judicialization in Global Order' in James Crawford and Martti Koskenniemi (eds), *The Cambridge Companion to International Law* (CUP 2012) 218.

[23] See Marrakesh Agreement Establishing the World Trade Organization, 15 April 1994, 1867 UNTS 154, art III:3 [hereinafter WTO Agreement].

[24] Yuval Shany, 'Assessing the Effectiveness of International Courts: A Goal-Based Approach' (2012) 106 AJIL 225, 246; interview with private attorney (Geneva, 16 July 2012) (noting that one goal of the DSS, as part of the WTO, is to 'assure that the system remains workable').

[25] Joseph H H Weiler, 'The Rule of Lawyers and the Ethos of Diplomats: Reflections on the Internal and External Legitimacy of WTO Dispute Settlement' (2002) 13 Am Rev Int'l Arb 177, 181.

[26] Interview with former WTO legal officer (Geneva, 30 March 2012). See also Donald McRae, 'Measuring the Effectiveness of the WTO Dispute Settlement System' (2008) 3 Asian J WTO & Int'l Health L & Pol'y 1, 13.

[27] Interview with WTO legal officer (Geneva, 4 April 2012) (noting that the DSS maintains the functioning and stability of the multilateral trade regime by 'removing the threat of unilateralism' and by containing 'protectionist clashes').

> of the goals ... [of] the system.... [to] isolate these disputes which, in some cases, may contaminate the entire relationship with the other country in ... the WTO.[28]

For the DSS, the ultimate end of regime support, as we will see in the following, is also promoted along other channels, including the enforcement of WTO rules that embody the multilateral trading system's objectives, as well as the clarification of the contents of WTO agreements in light of new and unforeseen circumstances. Such reinterpretation of the basic legal texts ensures the adaptability of the multilateral cooperation regime and its viability over time.[29]

Legitimizing the WTO and Its Underlying Norms

Like other global governance institutions, the WTO must possess legitimacy in order to thrive and provide the valuable goods of international cooperation.[30] 'Legitimacy' in the case of the WTO, as in other contexts, has both a normative and a sociological meaning.[31] To say that the WTO is legitimate in the normative sense is to assert that it has the 'right to rule' as a matter of moral theory[32]—meaning that the authority it exercises is normatively justified because it meets certain 'objective' notions or standards of fairness and justice (e.g. democratic accountability, legality, transparency, respect for human rights, and so forth).[33] To say that the WTO is legitimate in the sociological sense points to whether its authority, as an empirical matter, is *perceived* as justified by those whom it purports to govern,[34] that is, whether affected stakeholders such as WTO Members, private economic operators, and civil society groups accept the WTO's claim for authority.[35] Sociological legitimacy is thus a subjective quality, defined by the actual acceptance

[28] Interview with Ecuadorian official (Geneva, 17 July 2012).

[29] cf Yuval Shany, *Assessing the Effectiveness of International Courts: A Goal-Based Approach* (OUP 2014) 39 (arguing that international courts, by 'clarifying and updating international law norms', work to strengthen the 'conduct-regulating quality' of those norms, and to maintain 'the norms as a legitimate and effective articulation of the policy or value preference that the lawgivers sought to pursue').

[30] Allen Buchanan and Robert O Keohane, 'The Legitimacy of Global Governance Institutions' (2006) 20 Ethics & Int'l Aff 405.

[31] ibid 405.

[32] ibid. Christopher A Thomas, 'The Uses and Abuses of Legitimacy in International Law' (2014) 34 Oxford J Legal Stud 729, 738.

[33] Daniel Bodansky, 'Legitimacy in International Law and International Relations' in Jeffrey L Dunoff and Mark A Pollack (eds), *Interdisciplinary Perspectives on International Law and International Relations: The State of the Art* (CUP 2013) 324, 327; Shany (n 29) 139.

[34] Bodansky (n 33) 327.

[35] See, e.g. Daniel Bodansky, 'The Concept of Legitimacy in International Law' in Rüdiger Wolfrum and Volker Röben (eds), *Legitimacy in International Law* (Springer 2009) 313. See also Junne CA Gerd, 'International Organizations in a Period of Globalization: New (Problems of) Legitimacy' in Jean-Marc Coicaud and Veijo Aulis Heiskanen (eds), *The Legitimacy of International Organizations* (United Nations Publications 2001) 192 (noting that in the era of globalization, the legitimacy of international organizations 'depends not only on the perceptions and attitude of governments, but also on the views ... of many other actors in global society').

of an institution's authority by relevant constituencies and by their belief that the institution's rules and decisions ought to be obeyed.[36]

While conceptually and practically distinct, the normative and sociological dimensions of legitimacy are 'closely related' and tend to affect and inform one another.[37] Thus, an institution's satisfaction of certain normative conditions (e.g. expertise, the assurance of procedural justice, etc.) may affect perception and acceptance of its authority by relevant stakeholders. Conversely, normative legitimacy depends, to some degree, on sociological legitimacy because '[a]n institution could not be normatively legitimate if no one thought it so'.[38] As Buchanan and Keohane thus stress, '[i]t is important not only that global governance institutions [like the WTO] be legitimate' in the normative sense, 'but that they are perceived to be legitimate' as well.[39] 'The perception of legitimacy matters, because, in a democratic era, multilateral institutions will only thrive if they are viewed as legitimate' by the affected publics.[40]

The DSS can play a significant role in fortifying and sustaining both dimensions of WTO legitimacy[41] because, like all courts, it embodies a 'legitimacy-conferring capacity'—the ability to legitimize not only its own decisions but also the decisions and operations of other institutions.[42] And, like other courts at the international level, one of its generic goals is to confer legitimacy on the norms and institutions that form the regime in which it operates. As elaborated by Shany on this point, although the generic goal of legitimizing the public authority of international regimes and the norms they generate 'is hardly ever mentioned in constitutive instruments of international courts', it is the unique capacity of courts to bestow legitimacy on the institutions of the regime in question, on the norms they apply and on any decision pertaining to an ongoing dispute that leads states, at least in part, to create international courts in preference to alternative, non-judicial dispute resolution or norm-enforcing mechanisms that may address the same policy problems.[43] '[*E*]*xternal* legitimization of international governance' is therefore one of the ultimate ends of international adjudication, for the WTO DSS as well.[44]

[36] Ian Hurd, *After Anarchy: Legitimacy and Power in the United Nations Security Council* (Princeton University Press 2008) 7; Thomas (n 32) 741.

[37] Daniel Bodansky, 'The Legitimacy of International Governance: A Coming Challenge for International Environmental Law?' (1999) 93 AJIL 596, 601–02; Joseph H H Weiler, 'In the Face of Crisis: Input Legitimacy, Output Legitimacy and the Political Messianism of European Integration' (2012) 34 J Eur Integration 825, 826–27.

[38] Bodansky (n 33) 327.

[39] Buchanan and Keohane (n 30) 407.

[40] ibid.

[41] Mercurio (n 1) 398; Philip M Nichols, 'GATT Doctrine' (1996) 36 Va J Int'l L 379, 458–65.

[42] See James L Gibson and Gregory A Caldeira, 'The Legitimacy of Transnational Legal Institutions: Compliance, Support, and the European Court of Justice' (1995) 39 Am J Pol Sci 459, 466.

[43] Shany (n 29) 44–46, 137. See also Armin von Bogdandy and Ingo Venzke, 'On the Functions of International Courts: An Appraisal in Light of Their Burgeoning Public Authority' (2013) 26 Leiden J Int'l L 49, 59.

[44] Shany (n 29) 137 (emphasis original).

The DSS fulfils this external legitimization goal mainly by means of its seemingly 'non-political', legalistic, rules-based approach.[45] As a senior WTO official put it, the DSS works to sustain the legitimacy of the WTO's political and legal order 'because it is based on the rule of law. It is not based on power'.[46] Thus, by providing the WTO with a forum for the resolution of disputes by professional, independent, and impartial adjudicators, based on law and reason, the DSS projects its positive halo onto the WTO as a global governance institution that channels its exercise of power and application of norms through neutral judicial procedures. By replacing power-based decision making with the rule of law and by facilitating the 'airing of disputes regardless of a party's economic power or influence', the DSS, as a mandatory adjudicating forum, further promotes a more equitable and level playing field between WTO Members[47]—an element essential for the legitimacy of the WTO regime.[48] Finally, the DSS helps legitimize the WTO governance structure by offering procedures for clarifying WTO rules and producing coherent legal interpretations that bolster the 'compliance pull' of those rules.[49] In parallel, its adaptation of WTO norms to changing and unanticipated conditions serves to preserve these norms as legitimate expressions of the policy goals pursued by WTO Members over time.

As in the case of other international courts, legitimatization of WTO governance and norms, as a formal goal, appears nowhere in the DSS's constitutive instrument. Yet, as implied here, its invaluable capacity to legitimize seems to represent one of the basic reasons for the introduction of the DSS into the WTO regime in the first place.[50] Along these lines, Cameron and Gray have noted that: '[i]nstalling an equitable dispute settlement resolution mechanism within the trading regime entrenches the legitimacy of the regime itself and provides a better incentive to comply with international trading obligations'.[51]

We should bear in mind, however, that the ability of the DSS to confer legitimacy onto the extended WTO edifice depends to a large extent on the DSS's own legitimacy in the eyes of key constituencies.[52] Without being regarded as legitimate itself, the DSS could not fulfil its external legitimization goal, nor could it adequately

[45] See James L Gibson, 'Understandings of Justice: Institutional Legitimacy, Procedural Justice, and Political Tolerance' (1989) 23 L & Soc'y Rev 469, 471 (discussing the claim that courts 'have special powers to legitimize' since they 'are thought to be non-political in the sense that they make decisions on the basis of merit and logic, shunning the favouritism, logrolling, and pork barrel so central to decision making in other political institutions'); Nichols (n 41) 462–64; Shany (n 29) 45.

[46] Interview with senior WTO official (Geneva, 23 March 2012).

[47] James Cameron and Kevin R Gray, 'Principles of International Law in the WTO Dispute Settlement Body' (2001) 50 Int'l & Comp L Q 248, 248–49.

[48] cf Julio Lacarte-Muró and Petinal Gappah, 'Developing Countries and the WTO Legal and Dispute Settlement System: A View from the Bench' (2000) 3 J Int'l Econ L 395.

[49] See Thomas M Franck, *The Power of Legitimacy Among Nations* (OUP 1990) 49–66, 142, 147–48.

[50] Shany (n 29) 137.

[51] Cameron and Gray (n 47) 249.

[52] Tom Ginsburg, 'International Judicial Lawmaking' in Stefan Voigt, Max Albert, and Dieter Schmidtchen (eds), *International Conflict Resolution* (Mohr Siebeck 2006) 172 (describing the legitimacy of the DSS as 'bundled' together with that of the organization in which it is embedded).

attain its other ultimate ends, delineated above, and the organizational objectives further discussed below. Hence, sustaining the DSS's internal legitimacy (i.e. the justification and acceptance of its own authority) constitutes an intermediate goal of the DSS (as of other international courts), facilitating the system's realization of its various other organizational aims.[53] In what follows, we discuss this and other intermediate goals the DSS is expected to promote, while analysing their occasional conflicts and complementarities.

3.3 Intermediate Goals

Inducing Compliance with WTO Undertakings

> [T]he WTO dispute settlement system is part of the WTO rules-based multilateral trading system. . . . Members spent a lot of time negotiating rules. . . . When you negotiate rules, you expect them to be followed. . . . So, . . . one of . . . [the DSS's] main objectives is, and should be, to make sure that Members follow . . . WTO rules.
>
> —Interview with ACWL lawyer (Geneva, 27 July 2012)

As the citation above underscores, a key intermediate goal of the WTO DSS is to promote compliance with the primary norms underlying the multilateral trading system so as to render those norms effective and reliable.[54] Article 3.2 of the DSU reflects this aim by stating that the DSS 'serves to preserve the rights and obligations of Members under the covered agreements'. Article 3.7 adds that absent a mutually agreed solution, the first objective of the DSS 'is usually to secure the withdrawal of the measures concerned if these are found to be inconsistent with the provisions of any of the covered agreements'. A review of the DSU's negotiating history likewise suggests that creation of a strengthened DSS, capable of effectively securing compliance with WTO rules, was among the primary motivations for reforming the GATT DSS and making it more legalized in the first place.[55] In a similar vein, the DSS's goal of inducing norm compliance is echoed in the discussions carried out within the framework of the DSU Review negotiations.[56]

[53] Shany (n 29) 46, 137.

[54] John H Jackson, *Sovereignty, the WTO, and Changing Fundamentals of International Law* (CUP 2006) 148. See also interview with senior WTO official (Geneva, 13 August 2009) (the goal of the DSS is 'to ensure that countries respect the WTO's negotiated obligations . . . it's an enforcement mechanism . . . the goal is to give further weight to the obligations and guarantee that they will always be respected; and if not, then challenged through adjudication').

[55] See, e.g. The GATT Uruguay Round (n 11) 2723–25; Richard H Steinberg, 'Judicial Lawmaking at the WTO: Discursive, Constitutional, and Political Constraints' (2004) 98 AJIL 247, 248.

[56] See, e.g. Report of the DSB Chairman 2015 (n 3) 9–10 (addressing the discussions carried out in the framework of the DSU Review regarding the reform proposals relating to the issue of securing

The DSS, for its part, works to promote this compliance inducement objective in various ways. First of all, by declaring a violation of the WTO treaty, the DSS provides the disputing parties and other Members with a more accurate assessment of the challenged behaviour, generates the reputational consequences to accompany that violation, and makes retaliation more likely and more acceptable to the rest of the WTO membership, thereby increasing the prospects of compliance.[57] In other words, as a compulsory adjudicative mechanism, the DSS operates to induce norm compliance—and thus to alleviate the enforcement problem inherent to the WTO as an international legal system relying mainly on self-enforcement by Member states[58]—by monitoring states' conduct, identifying violations, and increasing the reputational and economic costs of deviation from the treaty's stipulations.[59] As one WTO ambassador stated: in the wake of an adverse DSS ruling, 'it is still ultimately the sovereign right of a country to act'. But 'what the Dispute Settlement Understanding ... does ... [is that] it makes it increasingly more painful ... not to comply'. The DSS's finding of a WTO violation 'is public, everybody knows that you have lost ... and therefore you've got to fix it. You've got a reasonable period [of time] to fix it, which is also agreed publicly among all the Members'. And then, 'if you don't comply within that period.... the complaining party [is allowed] to ... ask the [permission of the] Dispute Settlement Body' to impose 'retaliatory' measures against the respondent.[60] Taken together, these actions increase the pressure to comply with WTO ruling and rules.

Another avenue employed by the DSS to promote compliance with WTO norms involves reinforcing their 'compliance pull' through legal interpretations that clarify the respective norms and generate information about their content.[61] By interpreting WTO law, the DSS, like other courts, serves as a mechanism for diminishing the 'indeterminacy' inherent in legal rules, elucidating what conduct is permitted and what is out of bounds under a given rule. In making WTO norms

'effective compliance' with WTO rulings and rules through the DSS). See also, Report of the Chairman, Ambassador Ronald Saborío Soto, Special Session of the Dispute Settlement Body (21 April 2011) TN/DS/25 [hereinafter Report of the DSB Chairman 2011].

[57] Andrew T Guzman, 'International Tribunals: A Rational Choice Analysis' (2008) 157 U Pa L Rev 171, 181; Andrew T Guzman, *How International Law Works: A Rational Choice Theory* (OUP 2008) 52. See also Giovanni Maggi, 'The Role of Multilateral Institutions in International Trade Cooperation' (1999) 89 Am Econ Rev 190, 191–92 (arguing that the role of the DSS 'is to identify the violation and bring it to the attention of third countries, exposing the offending country to a loss of reputation in the trading community', and thereby help 'in improving compliance' with WTO agreements).

[58] Schropp (n 14) 198 ('Self-enforcement lies in the nature of the WTO as a treaty'); Alexander Keck and Simon Schropp, 'Indisputably Essential: The Economics of Dispute Settlement Institutions in Trade Agreements' (2008) 42 J World Trade 785, 804.

[59] See, e.g. Dan Kovenock and Marie Thursby, 'GATT, Dispute Settlement and Cooperation' (1992) 4 Econ & Pol 151; Henrik Horn and Petros C Mavroidis, 'International Trade: Dispute Settlement' in Andrew T Guzman and Alan O Sykes (eds), *Research Handbook in International Economic Law* (Edward Elgar 2007) 186–88.

[60] Interview with former WTO ambassador (Geneva, 12 August 2009).

[61] Franck (n 49) 53–64.

more determinate and transparent, the DSS bolsters their legitimacy and, in consequence, their ability to pull Member states towards compliance.[62]

Promotion of compliance does not, however, stand in isolation from other DSS goals. More specifically, increased compliance with WTO rules contributes to greater stability and predictability throughout the multilateral trade system. It also fortifies the WTO's legitimacy and advances the realization of its underlying purposes. Yet, as explained above, an inherent tension exists between securing norm compliance and the goal of rebalancing the scales. Furthermore, as a WTO legal officer noted, there is a genuine tension between the DSS's aims of 'achiev[ing] rule compliance' and 'achiev[ing] pragmatic solutions for disputes' while maintaining some measure of flexibility in the process.[63] This goal conflict, illustrated in the case studies presented in Part III of the book, is built into the very language of the DSU. Thus, while the DSU seeks to ensure compliance with WTO rules, it also manifests a preference for mutually agreed solutions at every stage of the dispute settlement process as a means for restoring the balance of concessions upset by a Member's WTO-inconsistent measure. Yet while the DSU states that such negotiated solutions shall be consistent with the WTO agreements, it does not provide for a surveillance mechanism that may systematically verify their consistency with WTO law.[64] By so opening the door to bilateral solutions within the multilateral system, the DSU effectively incentivizes Members to resolve disputes without delay, while urging them to forget 'past grievances' in a manner that may moderate 'the repercussions of violations of the agreements',[65] and come at the expense of third parties' interests or the collective interest in compliance with WTO law.[66] It therefore appears that fundamental to the DSS vision 'is an inherent conflict between the desire to maintain rule integrity and the desire to facilitate the resolution of disputes',[67] the traditional goal of international courts we now address.

Fostering Positive Dispute Settlement

> [T]he purpose of the Dispute Settlement Understanding is to assist the Members in resolving their differences over how they implement … the WTO agreements and how they interpret their obligations under those

[62] ibid.

[63] Interview with WTO legal officer (Geneva, 16 March 2012). See also interview with WTO official (Geneva, 18 April 2012) (alluding to the 'tension' between 'achieving compliance and achieving a solution to a trade issue'); interview with former WTO legal officer (Geneva, 30 March 2012); Joseph Pelzman and Amir Shoham, 'WTO DSU-Enforcement Issues' in *Trade Disputes and the Dispute Settlement Understanding* (n 1) 377.

[64] Wolfgang Alschner, 'Amicable Settlements of WTO Disputes: Bilateral Solutions in a Multilateral System' (2014) 13 World Trade Rev 65, 92.

[65] Horn and Mavroidis (n 59) 188.

[66] Alschner (n 64) 66–67; Jackson (n 54) 146.

[67] Horn and Mavroidis (n 59) 188.

> agreements.... [T]he objective of dispute settlement is to resolve amicably differences.
>
> —Interview with former WTO legal officer (Geneva, 30 March 2012)

Few would deny that a key goal of international courts, including the WTO DSS, has always been and remains facilitation of the amicable settlement of individual disputes.[68] Explicit statements of this goal are found in Article 3.4 of the DSU, which stipulates that panel and AB 'rulings shall be aimed at achieving a satisfactory settlement of the matter' pending before them, and in Article 3.7, which declares that the 'aim of the dispute settlement mechanism is to secure a positive solution to a dispute'.[69] As the DSU regards mutually agreed solutions as the preferred mode for resolving disputes,[70] the DSS's dispute settlement goal consists of a critical aspect of encouraging negotiated settlements in the 'shadow of the law'—either prior to or after litigation—alongside third-party adjudication. Alluding to this key function of the DSS as it relates to the promotion of prelitigation bargaining and settlement, a WTO official observed:

> [T]he biggest benefit [of the DSS] ... is its [very] existence and the fact that because it is there, you might not actually always have to ... [reach the stage of open disputes and litigation] ... it is a preemptive system.... the absolute last resort. You shouldn't have to go there. But the fact that you have an agreement and that countries at the end can ... [turn] to the dispute settlement [system] ... means that you settle a lot [of issues] beforehand.[71]

In this sense, therefore, the mandatory DSS, through the shadow exerted by its existence and the threat of litigation it poses, serves to facilitate communication between prospective litigating states while providing incentives for the amicable settlement of disputes erupting between them. From this perspective, then, the DSS constitutes 'a coordination mechanism' that incentivizes 'WTO member bargaining under the shadow of the law and legal institutions',[72] and thereby assists the

[68] von Bogdandy and Venzke (n 43) 53; Jackson (n 54) 147.

[69] See also *Australia–Measures Affecting Importation of Salmon*, Report of the Appellate Body, 6 November 1998, WT/DS18/AB/R, para 223 (the aim of the DSS is 'to resolve the matter at issue and "to secure a positive solution to a dispute"'); *United States–Measures Affecting Imports of Woven Wool Shirts and Blouses from India*, Report of the Appellate Body, 23 May 1997, WT/DS33/AB/R, 19 ('the basic aim of dispute settlement in the WTO is to settle disputes').

[70] This preference, articulated in Article 3.7 of the DSU, has been reiterated in the framework of the DSU Review talks. See, e.g. Report of the DSB Chairman 2015 (n 3) 11 ('Mutually agreed solutions negotiated between the parties to a dispute remain acknowledged as the preferred outcome').

[71] Interview with WTO official (Geneva, 26 March 2012). See also interview with former EU official (Geneva, 9 July 2012) (noting that 'the sheer existence' of the DSS 'drives people to the negotiation table and to find a solution').

[72] Linarelli (n 15) 335.

attainment of a mutually agreed settlement before a judicial ruling is delivered and even 'before engaging in costly litigation'.[73]

Yet the shadow cast by the DSS extends beyond prelitigation bargaining to the negotiations taking place *after* a DSS ruling on the merits has been made,[74] as the ruling rendered creates 'a new bargaining situation', having the potential to push the parties closer to mutual agreement.[75] Thus, by issuing a judgment that validates a claim of WTO violation, the DSS affects the reputational balance between the complainant and respondent and opens the door for the imposition of economic sanctions on the latter, thereby establishing a new framework for settlement renegotiation[76] while reducing the respondent's ability to leave the negotiating table.[77] And, by articulating its legal interpretations and findings in the dispute, the DSS disseminates the information needed for the disputing parties to reach a common understanding of the relevant facts or the law,[78] while constructing concrete 'focal points' around which the parties can constructively move towards an agreeable settlement and reestablishment of their bilateral balance of concessions.[79] As noted by a WTO legal officer:

> [T]he general function of the dispute settlement system.... [is to] help the parties settle their dispute because ... when ... the Members start ... negotiating [following a DSS ruling] ... they will have ... a better understanding of what are their legal rights and obligations. They will have a better understanding of ... what the status of their case is in the WTO, ... [which] will be an important element in the negotiation.[80]

[73] Michael Gilligan, Leslie Johns, and Peter B Rosendorff, 'Strengthening International Courts and the Early Settlement of Disputes' (2010) 54 J Conflict Resol 5, 22.

[74] ibid 7, 10–11; interview with staff member of the AB Secretariat (Geneva, 4 July 2012).

[75] Heinz Hauser and Alexander Roitinger, 'Renegotiation in Transatlantic Trade Disputes' in Ernst-Ulrich Petersmann and Mark A Pollack (eds), *Transatlantic Economic Disputes: The EU, the US, and the WTO* (OUP 2003) 496. See also Ruth L Okediji, 'Rules of Power in an Age of Law: Process Opportunism and TRIPS Dispute Settlement' in Choi E Kwan and James C Hartigan (eds), *Handbook of International Trade: Economics and Legal Analyses of Trade Policy and Institutions*, vol 2 (Blackwell Publishing 2004) 52 ('disputes create a secondary market for renegotiation of existing bargains.... Such renegotiation takes place during the DSU process, as parties exchange information, consider competing interpretations and, ultimately, when the panel or Appellate Body issues a definitive ruling about what the standard means and/or what constitutes a violation of the standard').

[76] Hauser and Roitinger (n 75) 496 (arguing that the DSS, by 'confirming a violation of an agreement' and by 'defining the level of lawful retaliation.... establishes the two cost components of ... non-compliance and sets the frame for a new bargaining situation between the complainant and defendant').

[77] Gilligan, Johns, and Rosendorff (n 73) 11–12.

[78] On the information dissemination role of international courts see Guzman (n 57) 180–81; Eric A Posner and John C Yoo, 'Judicial Independence in International Tribunals' (2005) 93 Calif L Rev 1.

[79] Tom Ginsburg and Richard H McAdams, 'Adjudicating in Anarchy: An Expressive Theory of International Dispute Resolution' (2004) 45 WM & Mary L Rev 1229.

[80] Interview with WTO legal officer (Geneva, 4 April 2012). Along similar lines, one interviewee observed that the DSS, 'like in any litigation', serves as a 'bargaining tool' and as mechanism for generating dialogue between the disputants. Interview with private attorney (Brussels, 19 July 2012). Correspondingly, another interviewee alluded to the DSS's goal of facilitating settlement through 'renegotiation of the contract'. Interview with former WTO legal officer (Geneva, 30 March 2012).

But beyond being a salient aim in itself, the peaceful settlement of trade disputes plays a vital role in the attainment of other systemic DSS objectives. Thus, the resolution of disputes through an orderly process is conducive to the maintenance of a stable multilateral trading regime,[81] as well as the enhancement of its legitimacy, by providing an outlet for interparty grievances and purported injustices. In the same vein, the positive settlement of disputes, as DSU Article 3.3 indicates, is 'essential to the effective functioning of the WTO' and the preservation of 'a proper balance between the rights and obligations of Members'. Still, the desire to facilitate positive solutions to disputes and, specifically, to foster mutually agreed settlements, may constrain the achievement of other DSS goals. Thus, although Article 3.5 of the DSU requires mutually agreed solutions to be WTO-consistent, the preference for negotiated settlements might lead to greater flexibility in outcomes that moves away from strict compliance with WTO rules. Furthermore, as Jackson notes, 'a settlement in some cases may be detrimental to the broader goals' of the DSS.[82] This is because 'multilateral considerations and "longer term systemic goals"', such as the predictability and stability of interpretations of the treaty text, 'may generally be absent when it comes to deals struck between two disputing states where bilateral interests and the goal of solving "the instant dispute" are paramount'.[83]

Prompt Settlement of Disputes

The WTO DSS is expected not only to secure the positive settlement of disputes, but also to do it in a timely manner. Against the history of delays under the GATT dispute settlement process, the authors of the DSU sought to streamline the adjudicative process.[84] Accordingly, they stated in DSU Article 3.3 that: '[t]he *prompt* settlement of situations in which a Member considers that any benefits accruing to it ... under the covered agreements are being impaired by measures taken by another Member is essential to the effective functioning of the WTO'.[85] WTO Members have reiterated the importance of this goal during the DSU Review negotiations.[86] In a similar vein, the AB has stressed early on in

[81] The GATT Uruguay Round (n 11) 2809 ('to the extent that ... disputes between parties cannot be resolved amicably or at all, the survivability of the trading system can be jeopardized').

[82] Jackson (n 54) 146.

[83] Alschner (n 64) 67.

[84] See, e.g. November 1987 GATT Secretariat Note (n 3) 2; February 1988 GATT Secretariat Note (n 3) 2.

[85] Emphasis added.

[86] Thus, the importance of the DSS goal of prompt settlement of disputes has been stressed repeatedly during the DSU Review negotiations, particularly in the framework of the discussions of proposals regarding the 'timeframes' of WTO dispute settlement procedures. See, e.g. Report of the DSB Chairman 2011 (n 56); Report of the DSB Chairman 2015 (n 3); Minutes of Meeting of October 2002 (n 3) 8; Further Contribution of the United States on Improving Flexibility and Member Control in WTO Dispute Settlement, Communication from the United States, Special Session of the Dispute Settlement Body (24 October 2005) TN/DS/W/82, 1.

its jurisprudence that '[t]he procedural rules of WTO dispute settlement are designed to promote ... the fair, *prompt* and effective resolution of trade disputes' between Members.[87]

As the language of DSU Article 3.3 just cited suggests, the expeditious resolution of trade disputes is conducive to the efficient functioning of the WTO regime, most notably, by removing the stumbling blocks to international economic cooperation between trading partners. At the same time, the prompt settlement of bilateral conflicts may not always coincide with the DSS aim 'to provide jurisprudence that will bolster the predictability and security' of the multilateral trade system through detailed and well-reasoned rulings.[88] One WTO legal officer articulated this goal conflict as follows: '[W]hile as a complainant you are interested in the prompt settlement of the dispute, ... from a systemic point of view ... [we find] an interest in the promulgation of well-reasoned decisions that clarify the law' for the benefit of the multiple governmental and private actors taking part in the international trading system.[89] This tension between the DSS goals, it should be noted, seems to be intensifying with the rising complexity of the cases reaching this adjudicative system's docket. As one WTO legal officer stated:

> One obvious source of tension [between DSS goals] is the idea of ... prompt settlement of disputes, which suggests that [the proceedings before the] panels and the Appellate Body shouldn't take too much time.... [O]n the other hand ... [WTO adjudicators] need to undertake an objective assessment of the matter [before them], ... [meaning] that ... [they] need to thoroughly examine all the legal and factual issues [raised].... [Yet,] in recent cases, for example, in the *Aircraft* cases, that is a big challenge because you're confronted with very complex cases ... [which intensify the] tension ... between ... [the need to provide thorough legal rulings] and the objective of prompt and efficient settlement of disputes.[90]

As the DSU does not indicate which of the two goals—prompt dispute settlement or high-quality legal outputs—should take precedence in the presence of such tension, the DSS finds itself facing a measure of ambiguity regarding its goal priorities. In this state of play, some interpretative leeway seems to be left for the DSS when balancing between the competing objectives and when deciding which one should prevail in any given instance of goal conflict.[91]

[87] *United States–Tax Treatment for 'Foreign Sales Corporations'*, Report of the Appellate Body, 20 March 2000, WT/DS108/AB/R, para 166 (emphasis added).

[88] Jackson (n 54) 146.

[89] Interview with WTO legal officer (Geneva, 19 March 2012).

[90] Interview with WTO legal officer (Geneva, 4 April 2012).

[91] cf Jackson (n 54) 150 (noting that 'balancing is often necessary' given the potential clashes between the objectives pursued by adjudicative systems).

Clarifying WTO Rules and Removing Ambiguities from the Treaty Text

> [B]y the very nature of treaties, ... they are obscure [some] or most of the time; ... if they were so clear, then perhaps they would not have been agreed to. So ... diplomats usually agree to obscure language so that everyone is happy, and then leave the interpretation to the dispute settlement system.
>
> —Interview with ACWL lawyer (Geneva, 27 July 2012)

As the above quotation implies, WTO agreements are incomplete contracts of a somewhat vague nature. This incompleteness is the product of the constructive ambiguity introduced by negotiators when formulating these international agreements, the complexity and scope of the agreements, but also the uncertainty about future developments. Conflicting interpretations of WTO rules are consequently inevitable, leaving the DSS with the task of clarifying the WTO agreements and removing their legal ambiguities with the aid of interpretation.[92] Article 3.2 of the DSU explicitly embraces this function as a goal of the DSS, which it regards as designed 'to clarify the existing provisions of those agreements in accordance with customary rules of interpretation of public international law'—a phrase construed by the AB to refer to the Vienna Convention[93] rules of treaty interpretation.[94]

While the DSU entrusts the DSS with the authority to clarify WTO law, it nevertheless precludes WTO panels and the AB from adding to or diminishing Members' rights and obligations under the WTO covered agreements (see DSU Articles 3.2 and 19.2). The DSU thus explicitly cautions the DSS against judicial activism or lawmaking, proscribing it from taking 'on the role of "legislator"'.[95] That said, the line between an illegitimate act of lawmaking and a legitimate exercise of treaty interpretation and gap filling may at times be hard to draw,[96] and while distinctions between such judicial functions are prevalent in legal theory,[97] they tend

[92] See, e.g. interview with WTO legal officer (Geneva, 16 March 2012) (noting that a 'main objective' of the panel and the AB is to clarify 'the way the agreement should be interpreted'); interview with ACWL lawyer (Geneva 19 April 2012) (noting that the role of the DSS is 'to establish the clarity of the law'); Maggi and Staiger (n 2); Jackson (n 54) 148; Joel P Trachtman, 'The Domain of WTO Dispute Resolution' (1999) 40 Harv Int'l LJ 333, 334, 339–40.

[93] Vienna Convention on the Law of Treaties, 23 May 1969, 1155 UNTS 331.

[94] See *United States–Standards for Reformulated and Conventional Gasoline*, Report of the Appellate Body, 20 May 1996, WT/DS2/AB/R, 17; *Japan–Taxes on Alcoholic Beverages*, Report of the Appellate Body, 1 November 1996, WT/DS11/AB/R, 10-12.

[95] Peter Van den Bossche and Werner Zdouc, *The Law and Policy of the World Trade Organization: Law, Text, Cases and Materials* (3rd edn, CUP 2013) 185.

[96] See, e.g. Ingo Venzke, 'The Role of International Courts as Interpreters and Developers of the Law: Working Out the Jurisgenerative Practice of Interpretation' (2012) 34 Loy LA Int'l & Comp L Rev 99, 101–02; Kati Kulovesi, *The WTO Dispute Settlement System: Challenges of the Environment, Legitimacy and Fragmentation* (Kluwer Law International 2011) 182.

[97] See generally, Duncan Kennedy, *A Critique of Adjudication (fin de siècle)* (Harvard University Press 1998); H L A Hart, *The Concept of Law* (3rd edn, OUP 2012).

to be less clear-cut in practice. Moreover, it should be admitted that in interpreting and resolving gaps and obscurities in WTO agreements, the DSS, like all judicial systems, inescapably creates new rules rather than merely applying existing ones,[98] actions inviting differences to arise between 'relatively aggressive interpretations and those that remain closer to the text of the document and existing practice'.[99] As a WTO ambassador and panellist noted in this regard: 'I am clearly on the side of not . . . creat[ing] new law through the dispute settlement system'. Yet, a certain degree of lawmaking by the DSS 'is inevitable. It is part of the system and you have to do it. . . . In the process of interpretation, you are about to create some sort of law'.[100]

The tasks of clarifying and interpreting WTO agreements are invariably instrumental to the attainment of other DSS objectives. Most notably, through its 'expressive' function, by which it clarifies WTO rules and the state of the world to which they apply, the DSS works to facilitate the positive settlement of disputes between WTO Members.[101] That is to say, by resolving ambiguities in the law and the associated facts, and by communicating in favour of a particular legal outcome, the DSS, like other structures of international adjudication, influences the behaviour of the disputing states while providing them with concrete focal points around which they can more effectively coordinate towards reaching a solution to their conflict.[102] As a WTO legal officer explained:

[98] cf Kennedy (n 97) 28; Hersch Lauterpacht, *The Development of International Law by the International Court* (CUP 1982) 155 ('the fact remains that judicial law-making is a permanent feature of administration of justice in every society'); Andrew T Guzman, 'Trade, Labor, Legitimacy' (2003) 91 Cal L Rev 885, 898 ('any judicial or arbitral body will "make law" when it interprets legal texts').

[99] Guzman (n 98) 898. In this light, one should not find it surprising that over the years the WTO DSS, and especially the AB, has been accused on several occasions by Members of judicial activism and illegitimate lawmaking or gap filling. Such accusations were already made at an early stage of the DSS's life, for example, in the wake of the AB ruling in the *US-Shrimp* case discussed in Chapter 5. Notable accusations of judicial overreach during the years have been voiced by the United States, particularly when losing cases regarding anti-dumping, countervailing, and safeguard measures. Thus, for example, following the promulgation of the AB ruling in *US–Anti-Dumping and Countervailing Duties (China)* in March 2011, the United States Trade Representative stated: 'I am deeply troubled by this report. It appears to be a clear case of overreaching by the Appellate Body. We are reviewing the findings closely in order to understand fully their implications'. See 'USTR Statement Regarding WTO Appellate Body Report in Countervailing Duty Dispute with China' (*USTR*, 11 March 2011) <https://ustr.gov/about-us/policy-offices/press-office/press-releases/2011/march/ustr-statement-regarding-wto-appellate-body-report-c> accessed 31 December 2018. It should be noted, however, that such allegations of judicial overreach on the part of the United States, suggesting that certain AB rulings have added to or diminished the rights and obligations of Members under the WTO agreements, have grown particularly strong under the Trump administration. See, for example, 'The President's 2018 Trade Policy Agenda' (*USTR*, 2018) 22–24 <https://ustr.gov/sites/default/files/files/Press/Reports/2018/AR/2018%20Annual%20Report%20I.pdf> accessed 31 December 2018. For a discussion of the claims raised by the United States regarding AB judicial activism and illegitimate gap filling, see Gregory Shaffer, 'A Tragedy in the Making? The Decline of Law and the Return of Power in International Trade Relations' (2019) 44 Yale J Int'l L (forthcoming).

[100] Interview with WTO ambassador (Geneva, 23 July 2012).

[101] cf Ginsburg and McAdams (n 79) (discussing the 'expressive' function of international courts, which, through their clarification of the relevant facts and the law, construct focal points and provide signals that facilitate the settlement of international disputes).

[102] ibid.

> The [WTO dispute settlement] system is not geared to resolving theoretical issues of interpretation. The system is aimed at … helping parties find a pragmatic solution to a dispute.… [The system] ultimately sends the ball back to the parties, but hopefully by telling the parties what the interpretations of the agreement that they themselves have signed should be, that, in turn, will help them to find a solution.… Hopefully… [by] helping clarify the facts of the case or … the appropriate interpretation of the agreement, [adjudication by the DSS] would be conducive to parties finding a mutually agreed solution.[103]

But beyond its contribution to the resolution of bilateral disputes, the goal of removing the normative ambiguities occasionally found in WTO agreements has the 'salient multilateral or systemic aspect of providing clarification to all Member states regarding the type of measures and legal issues addressed in a specific case'.[104] This systemic feature has been emphasized in WTO jurisprudence, for instance, in the *US-Boeing* ruling, where the AB 'faulted … and criticized the panel … [for] not tackling a certain legal issue' raised by the complainant that, according to the AB, the panel should have addressed 'in order to clarify' the relevant WTO law to the benefit of WTO Members.[105] Thus, in response to the panel's refusal to 'tackle the issue of law' put before it and to provide the legal clarification requested by the EU,[106] based on the (erroneous) view that such clarification would require the panel 'to offer guidance on an issue that would not affect the resolution of this dispute',[107] the AB observed:

> By refusing to undertake a more comprehensive analysis of the legal issue of how the DSB is to initiate an Annex V procedure, *the Panel deprived Members of the benefit of 'a clear enunciation of the relevant WTO law'* and failed to advance a key objective of WTO dispute settlement, namely, *the resolution of disputes 'in a manner that… clarifies existing provisions of the covered agreements* in accordance with the customary rules of interpretation of public international law'.[108]

The AB then added:

> [T]he DSU stipulates that panels and the Appellate Body are to clarify relevant provisions of the covered agreements … in such a way as to preserve the rights

[103] Interview with WTO legal officer (Geneva, 16 March 2012).

[104] Interview with WTO legal officer (Geneva, 19 March 2012). See also interview with WTO ambassador (Geneva, 24 July 2012) (stressing the importance of having 'a predictable set of rules in the sense that they are interpreted clearly… for [the benefit of] all actors' in the multilateral trading system).

[105] Interview with WTO legal officer (Geneva, 13 March 2012).

[106] *United States–Measures Affecting Trade in Large Civil Aircraft (Second Complaint)*, Report of the Appellate Body, 23 March 2012, WT/DS353/AB/R, para 499.

[107] ibid, paras 486, 499–500.

[108] ibid, para 500 (emphasis added).

> and obligations of Members and contribute to the security and predictability of the multilateral trading system, consistently with the objective of securing a positive solution to individual disputes.[109]

We can therefore conclude that from a broader, multilateral perspective, DSS generation of legal interpretations in the context of bilateral disputes advances the systemic interest of the wider WTO membership in the harmonious development of WTO law and jurisprudence, as well as in the creation of a more legally stable and predictable multilateral trade system.[110] Moreover, as previously noted, coherent and reasoned legal interpretations are invaluable for promoting the legitimacy of WTO rules and, in consequence, for strengthening their compliance pull, as well as for adjusting these rules to changing and unforeseen circumstances. These benefits do not, of course, eliminate all of the tensions existing between law interpretation and other DSS institutional goals. As indicated, providing well-reasoned judgments so as to substantially remove legal ambiguities in the treaty text may verily undermine or contradict the goal of *prompt* settlement of disputes. Also to be considered is the effect of the DSU's preference for dispute settlement through mutually agreed solutions. Since such solutions may emerge at any stage of the dispute settlement process (including the period prior to the rendering of a DSS ruling), a dispute's resolution may, at times, come at the expense of clarifying the law to the benefit of the WTO's entire membership.[111]

Levelling the Playing Field and Redressing Asymmetries of Power

> INTERVIEWER: And the last question, what are the goals of the dispute settlement system? What are the goals that Member states expect the ... system ... to achieve?
>
> INTERVIEWEE: Well, in the first place, we are, no matter the level of development, we are at the same level, the same in terms of the dispute settlement mechanism.
>
> —Interview with former Guatemalan official (Geneva, 24 July 2012)

[109] ibid, para 502.

[110] For a discussion of this point, see also *United States–Final Anti-Dumping Measures on Stainless Steel from Mexico*, Report of the Appellate Body, 20 May 2008, WT/DS344/AB/R, para 161. See also Claus-Dieter Ehlermann and Nicolas Lockhart, 'Standard of Review in WTO Law' (2004) 7 J Int'l Econ L 491, 498; interview with WTO legal officer (Geneva, 19 March 2012).

[111] Interview with WTO legal officer (Geneva, 13 March 2012).

By moving away from the previous, power-oriented and diplomacy-marked GATT DSS towards a more legalistic, rule-oriented WTO DSS, the Uruguay Round negotiators sought, among other things, 'to ensure prompt and effective resolution of disputes *to the benefit of all contracting parties*'.[112] That is, they sought to establish a system that, through its rules-based approach, would bring about greater fairness to weaker countries and help redress asymmetries of power between large, powerful states and smaller or less-developed states.[113] The latter had been underrepresented in the consensual GATT dispute settlement structure and therefore limited in their ability to make legal claims and be granted redress for alleged grievances.[114] In that spirit, a Canadian official noted that: 'the creation of the DSU was meant to legalize [the dispute settlement system so as] ... to level the playing field between developing and developed countries, to take out some of ... the power politics that gets played' in international economic relations.[115]

It follows, then, that among its various goals, the legalistic WTO DSS was designed to alleviate power disparities between WTO Members by providing weaker countries with a forum where they can air their disputes regardless of their economic clout,[116] gain binding rulings against economically stronger states, and force such states to address their concerns.[117] Without such a mandatory, rules-based DSS, 'a developing country is likely to encounter refusal to negotiate by powerful countries, arbitrary standards, limited interest from third countries in their trade problem, and lack of leverage to bargain for concessions'.[118] As a former WTO ambassador and Chair of the DSB put it, a rules-based dispute settlement mechanism 'allows for the creation of an equilibrium among Member states irrespective of their size ... after all, that is what a rule of law should do'.[119]

Although the goal of levelling the playing field is not explicitly stated in the DSU, it resonates throughout the Uruguay Round negotiation history, in the literature on the WTO DSS,[120] and is openly referred to by WTO officials and trade delegates, as

[112] See Ministerial Declaration on the Uruguay Round, Declaration of 20 September 1986, GATT BISD 33S/19 (1987) (emphasis added).

[113] Jackson (n 54) 148–49.

[114] Addressing the underrepresentation of developing countries in the previous GATT DSS, Hudec noted: 'Developing countries accounted for 44 of 229 complaints (19 percent) and 29 of 223 appearances as defendant (13 percent)'. Robert E Hudec, *Enforcing International Trade Law: The Evolution of the Modern GATT Legal System* (Butterworth Legal Publishers 1993) 295.

[115] Telephone interview with Canadian official (10 August 2009).

[116] Cameron and Gray (n 47) 248–49; Andrea K Schneider, 'Not Quite a World without Trials: Why International Dispute Resolution Is Increasingly Judicialized' (2006) J Disp Resol 119, 128.

[117] Christina L Davis, 'Do WTO Rules Create a Level Playing Field? Lessons from the Experience of Peru and Vietnam' in John S Odell (ed), *Negotiating Trade: Developing Countries in the WTO and NAFTA* (CUP 2006) 223.

[118] ibid.

[119] Interview with former WTO ambassador (Geneva, 12 August 2009).

[120] See, e.g. John H Jackson, 'International Law Status of WTO Dispute Settlement Reports: Obligation to Comply or Option to "Buy Out"?' (2004) 98 AJIL 109, 120 ('A less explicit policy objective of the DS system ... is the goal of "levelling the playing field" between large, powerful states and small or relatively weak states. For the system to be creditable, it must remedy the asymmetries of power between WTO members so as to give everyone—large, small, weak, or powerful—its "day in court" and the expectation

the above statements suggest. An Ecuadorian official elaborated his views on this objective when stressing the importance of the DSS as a 'rules-based system':

> I think many developing countries . . . attach the utmost importance . . . to this, to a rules-based system. I think all countries should know that this system is based on rules and no matter how big their countries [are] or how small your country is, all of us should play by the same rules and all of us are expected to comply with whatever ruling comes from the DSU. I think that's what all countries, especially small developing countries expect from the system, . . . [it] is one of the goals which should be served [by the DSS].[121]

Needless to say, the involvement of developing and less-powerful countries in the WTO DSS is cardinal to the success and legitimacy of this judicial organ and the WTO regime as a whole. This same involvement is also crucial for the fuller integration of developing countries in the multilateral trading system together with the protection of their share in economic growth—two hallowed goals of the WTO Agreement. As noted by Julio Lacarte-Muró and Petinal Gappah, two former AB members: 'In view of the high proportion of developing countries in the WTO membership, their participation [in the dispute settlement mechanism] is vital to the credibility and acceptability of the system, and to the proper defense of their interests as well.'[122]

Multilateral Dispute Resolution and Discouragement of Unilateralism

> [O]ne of the key objectives [of the DSS] is . . . to provide a forum for Members to resolve their disputes multilaterally . . . [that is,] to [afford them] the opportunity to . . . [turn] to multilateral third-party dispute resolution as a way to avoid unilateralism in trade policy.
>
> —Interview with WTO legal officer (Geneva, 4 April 2012)

Historically, the shift towards greater legalization of the WTO DSS by the end of the Uruguay Round was not exclusively motivated by the will to level the playing field between Member states. Rather, as explained in Chapter 2, this shift resulted in large part from a deal struck between the United States,

of receiving adequate redress for harms attributed to measures that are inconsistent with the obligations of the WTO system'). See also Joseph A Conti, *Between Law and Diplomacy: The Social Context of Disputing at the World Trade Organization* (Stanford University Press 2011) 11–12; Iida Keisuke, 'Is WTO Dispute Settlement Effective?' (2004) 10 Global Governance 207, 216–18.

---

121 Interview with Ecuadorian official (Geneva, 25 July 2012).

122 Lacarte-Muró and Gappah (n 48) 395.

which sought to strengthen the GATT DSS, and those trading partners that wanted to curtail US power to use unilateral trade measures under the so-called Section 301 of the 1974 US Trade Act.[123] Thus, while the United States was interested in fortifying the GATT dispute settlement mechanism and addressing its procedural weaknesses, especially the veto power created by the consensus rule, the EU, Japan, and other trading partners wished to restrain the use of unilateral trade actions by the United States, as well as secure greater commitment by state parties to resort to the multilateral procedures instead of turning to unilateral actions when attempting to resolve disputes.[124] A trade-off of sorts was ultimately struck among the Uruguay Round negotiators. It centred on 'making multilateralism more effective ... and ... binding' through the creation of a procedurally tighter dispute settlement system that would meet the US complaints on the one hand, and 'limiting unilateralism' by obligating redress of WTO violations solely via the DSU's multilateral procedures on the other.[125]

Considered in this light, another purpose bestowed upon the WTO DSS was 'to fend off unilateralism' in international trade relations[126] and to provide a forum for Members to settle disputes with other Members through well-ordered multilateral procedures.[127] This goal is reflected in DSU Article 23, entitled 'The Strengthening of the Multilateral System', which states the following:

> 1. When Members seek the redress of a violation of obligations ... under the covered agreements ... they shall have recourse to, and abide by, the rules and procedures of this Understanding.
> 2. In such cases, Members shall:
>   (a) Not make a determination to the effect that a violation has occurred ... except through recourse to dispute settlement in accordance with the rules and procedures of this Understanding....

Article 23 of the DSU thus entrusts the DSS with the exclusive power to make determinations of compliance and noncompliance with WTO agreements, a step

[123] Robert Hudec, 'The New Dispute Settlement Procedure: An Overview of the First Three Years' (1999) 8 Minn J Global Trade 1, 12–13.

[124] The GATT Uruguay Round (n 11) 2761–62, 2777–79, 2809–10. See also Minutes of Meeting of 22 September 1988, GATT Council (17 October 1988) GATT Doc C/M/224, 34; 1990 Statement of the European Community (n 16) 1; Dispute Settlement: Communication from Canada, Negotiating Group on Dispute Settlement (28 June 1988) GATT Doc MTN.GNG/NG13/W/41, 1; Meeting of 28 September 1989, Note by the Secretariat, Negotiating Group on Dispute Settlement (13 November 1989) GATT Doc MTN.GNG/NG13/16, 6; Meeting of 7 December 1989, Note by the Secretariat, Negotiating Group on Dispute Settlement (15 December 1989) GATT Doc MTN.GNG/NG13/17, 4.

[125] Interview with former US official (Geneva, 11 July 2012); Hudec (n 123) 13.

[126] Keisuke (n 120) 215; Horn and Mavroidis (n 59) 188.

[127] Van den Bossche and Zdouc (n 95).

necessary to avoid unilateral determinations of WTO violations, which might lead to precarious unilateral actions in the international trading system.

The DSS's goal of fending off unilateralism is closely tied, in turn, to some of its other organizational objectives, most notably, the fortification of the multilateral trade system's security and predictability.[128] Thus, by channelling conflicts through the multilateral dispute settlement process, the DSS helps inhibit 'the escalation or spread of "uncontrolled wars" which would emerge from unilateral action or arbitrary retaliation',[129] and which could risk the security of the WTO system. In addition, as a WTO official went on to elaborate, by restraining unilateralism and enabling Members to manage their disputes through the mandatory DSU-devised procedures, the DSS assists in providing some degree of order and normative stability for the cooperative WTO regime, ensuring that it remains workable, especially in times of turbulence:

> [For situations] where … one of the parties feels that the other party is not complying, you need to have some kind of set rules because otherwise … what you have is the law of the jungle … [Members] taking the matters into their own hands. And, of course, for an organization like the WTO, which is so large and with such a diverse membership, the ability … to take matters into your own hands … varies enormously depending on the countries. And if you had that kind of situation where anybody was taking their trade sanctions individually in such an intense trading environment that we have right now, you could have … an [overall] escalation of trade sanctions … in the world. So, hopefully, the [dispute settlement] system defuses a lot of the disputes, helps Members to comply, and therefore prevents this kind of breakdown of the whole system.[130]

As the last comment implies, dispute resolution through the multilateral procedures governed by the DSS along with the restraints the latter places on unilateral actions, may further contribute to creating a more level playing field between WTO Members because economically strong states, contrary to what occurred during the GATT era, are now prohibited, at least formally, from initiating unilateral measures when seeking to protect their trade interests. Finally, and not least importantly, each instance of recourse to the multilateral procedures of the DSS as a venue for resolving the trade disputes erupting between Members reaffirms the DSS's authority and thereby reinforces its legitimacy, the last organizational goal to be discussed here.

[128] *United States–Import Measures on Certain Products from the European Communities*, Report of the Panel, 10 January 2001, WT/DS165/R, para 6.14 ('An important reason why Article 23 of the DSU must be interpreted with a view to prohibiting any form of unilateral action is because such unilateral actions threaten the stability and predictability of the multilateral trade system …').

[129] Zimmermann (n 15) 37.

[130] Interview with WTO legal officer (Geneva, 16 March 2012).

Sustaining WTO DSS Legitimacy

> [T]here is this notion of legitimacy that I think is part and parcel of all tribunals.
>
> —Interview with private attorney (Geneva, 16 July 2012)

As Gibson and Caldeira note, '[f]or legal institutions, no attribute is more important than legitimacy. Legitimacy provides courts authority; it allows them the latitude necessary to make decisions contrary to the perceived immediate interests of their constituents. Since courts typically have neither the power of the "purse nor the sword"', the authors stress, this attribute 'is essential to judicial effectiveness'.[131]

Legitimacy, then, while a valuable end in itself, is also a critical tool in the achievement of court effectiveness—i.e. a court's ability to fulfil the very objectives for which it was created.[132] Because international courts such as the WTO DSS 'lack both the kind of democratic legitimation possessed by domestic institutions in liberal democracies, and the strong law-enforcement facilities available at the domestic level', their legitimacy is all the more essential to their success and the realization of the expectations attendant to their operations.[133] Thus, in order to produce authoritative clarifications of WTO law and strengthen the compliance pull of WTO rules, it is crucial that the interpretation of these rules be conducted by a court whose authority is recognized as legitimate by those to whom the rules apply.[134] In like manner, in order for the DSS to confer legitimacy on the WTO regime, the DSS must itself be considered legitimate because, arguably, 'only legitimate institutions can bestow legitimacy on other institutions'.[135]

One last (unstated but inherent) intermediate goal of the WTO DSS (as of other international courts) is, therefore, to sustain its legitimacy,[136] namely,

[131] Gibson and Caldeira (n 42) 460.

[132] Shany (n 29) 137–38. See generally Mark H Moore, 'Managing for Value: Organizational Strategy in For-Profit, Nonprofit, and Governmental Organizations' (2000) 29 Nonprofit & Voluntary Sector Q 183, 200–02 (referring to building organizational legitimacy and support in the non-profit sector as a valuable end in itself, as well as a necessary instrument in the pursuit of the organization's mission).

[133] Yuval Shany, 'Stronger Together? Legitimacy and Effectiveness of International Courts as Mutually Reinforcing or Undermining Notions' in Nienke Grossman and others (eds), *Legitimacy and International Courts* (CUP 2018) 354; Nienke Grossman, 'The Normative Legitimacy of International Courts' (2013) 86 Temple L Rev 61, 63.

[134] Franck (n 49). See also Tomer Broude, *International Governance in the WTO: Judicial Boundaries and Political Capitulation* (Cameron May 2004) 70 (arguing that 'a judiciary and its decision must themselves satisfy the requirements of legitimacy in order to command compliance').

[135] Shany (n 24) 265.

[136] Shany (n 29) 137 (noting that 'maintaining *internal* legitimacy' constitutes 'an *intermediate* goal of international courts. Such internal legitimacy is a prerequisite for conferring external legitimization on other norms and the institutions creating them and for facilitating the attainment of the court's ultimate ends'). See also Nick Huls, 'Introduction: From Legitimacy to Leadership' in Nick Huls, Maurice Adams, and Jacco Bomhoff (eds), *The Legitimacy of Highest Courts' Rulings: Judicial Deliberations and Beyond* (TMC Asser Press 2009) 13 ('Every legal system tries in its own way to create legitimacy for its courts').

to sustain a justifiable and acceptable authority to decide cases and issue judgments that are worthy of respect and obedience by those they address.[137] Here as well it is important that the DSS maintain its *normative* legitimacy by possessing some 'objective' qualities (e.g. transparency, expertise, and success in solving collective problems) that morally justify its right to exercise authority.[138] Yet, it is also essential that the DSS be *sociologically* legitimate, meaning that its authority be *perceived* as justified by those affected by it—states, private economic operators, and civil society groups, among others—and that its decisions be viewed by the latter as authoritative, even if they do not agree on the merit of any specific decision made.[139] As Weber noted a century ago, the more an institution is perceived as legitimate, the more stable and effective it is likely to be.[140] For this reason, Bodansky adds, 'writers speak not only of the legitimacy of power, but of the power of legitimacy'.[141]

3.4 Conclusions

The goals described throughout this chapter comprise the corpus of missions envisioned for the WTO DSS by its mandate providers. These goals constitute the substantive foundations of the DSS goal-based effectiveness framework advanced in this book; hence, they serve as the primary normative benchmarks against which the system's effectiveness is to be measured. When woven together, they shed light on the many dimensions of DSS operation, what stresses the need for a broad framework for analysing its effectiveness, one that goes beyond compliance and accounts for the system's various complementary and conflicting goals, as well as for the anticipated trade-offs associated with these objectives.

Based on the theoretical underpinnings outlined in Chapter 1, together with the comprehensive set of DSS goals identified in the present chapter, the book now turns to an examination of the shifting nature of these goals, their internal conflicts on the ground, and the ramifications of these phenomena for the system's effectiveness analysis. The book carries out this endeavour by means of an in-depth, interview-based investigation of three categories of WTO disputes. Doing so

[137] Nienke Grossman, 'Solomonic Judgments and the International Court of Justice' in *Legitimacy and International Courts* (n 133) 44; Harlan Grant Cohen and others, 'Legitimacy and International Courts – A Framework' in *Legitimacy and International Courts* (n 133) 4.

[138] Grossman (n 133).

[139] Sivan Shlomo Agon, 'Clearing the Smoke: The Legitimation of Judicial Power at the WTO' (2015) 49 J World Trade 539, 545–47. On international courts and the sociological dimension of legitimacy more generally, see, Nienke Grossman, 'Legitimacy and International Adjudicative Bodies' (2009) 41 Geo Wash Int'l L Rev 107; Erik Voeten, 'Public Opinion and the Legitimacy of International Courts' (2013) 14 Theoretical Inquiries L 411.

[140] Max Weber, *Economy and Society: An Outline of Interpretative Sociology*, vol 1 (Guenther Roth and Claus Wittich (eds), Bedminster Press, 1968) 31.

[141] Bodansky (n 37) 603.

allows it to show how the unique challenges confronting the DSS in each category influence DSS goal-attainment efforts, generate changes in the stress placed on its diverse goals, and render goal trade-offs inevitable, events crucially affecting the assessment of the system's effectiveness and performance throughout. The first category of cases we examine is that of 'trade-and' disputes.

PART II

WHEN TRADE AND NONTRADE VALUES COLLIDE

Linkage Disputes from a Goal-Based Perspective

4

Linkage Disputes and the Enduring Quest for Legitimacy

4.1 Linkage Disputes: Setting the Scene

The expanded reach of the multilateral trade regime in the post–Uruguay Round era and its growing influence on nontrade policy domains provoked strong public criticism against the World Trade Organization (WTO) soon after its establishment in 1995, portraying this international organization 'as a ruthless vehicle of economic globalization, oblivious ... of other values ... of the international community'.[1] Such criticism was a major source of what came to be known as the WTO legitimacy crisis by the turn of the millennium.[2] The WTO's judicial system, for its part, could not avoid this source of tension. In fact, it was not before long that the WTO Dispute Settlement System (DSS) found itself at the forefront of the thorny 'trade-and' debate, as cases involving competing trade and nontrade values were brought before it since its inception. Examples of such 'linkage' (or 'trade-and') disputes include the early *US-Gasoline*[3] and *US-Shrimp*[4] disputes, involving trade-restrictive environmental regulations; the *Korea-Beef* case, dealing with consumer protection issues;[5] the *EC-Asbestos*[6] and *EC-Biotech*[7] cases, concerning health-related concerns; and the *US-Gambling* case that implicated measures aimed at protecting public morals.[8] Alongside these cases, the WTO DSS has faced in recent years a new and intense wave of complex trade-and disputes, inviting close scrutiny of novel national regulations such as tobacco-control policies (*US-Clove*

[1] Georges Abi-Saab, 'The Normalization of International Adjudication: Convergence and Divergencies' (2010) 43 NYU J Int'l L & Pol 1, 14.

[2] Daniel C Esty, 'The World Trade Organization's Legitimacy Crisis' (2002) 1 World Trade Rev 7.

[3] *United States–Standards for Reformulated and Conventional Gasoline*, Report of the Appellate Body, 20 May 1996, WT/DS2/AB/R.

[4] *United States–Import Prohibition of Certain Shrimp and Shrimp Products*, Report of the Appellate Body, 6 November 1998, WT/DS58/AB/R.

[5] *Korea–Measures Affecting Imports of Fresh, Chilled and Frozen Beef*, Report of the Appellate Body, 10 January 2001, WT/DS161/AB/R, WT/DS169/AB/R.

[6] *European Communities–Measures Affecting Asbestos and Asbestos-Containing Products*, Report of the Appellate Body, 5 April 2001, WT/DS135/AB/R.

[7] *European Communities–Measures Affecting the Approval and Marketing of Biotech Products*, Report of the Panel, 21 November 2006, WT/DS291/R.

[8] *United States–Measures Affecting the Cross-Border Supply of Gambling and Betting Services*, Report of the Appellate Body, 20 April 2005, WT/DS285/AB/R.

Cigarettes[9] and *Australia-Plain Packaging*[10]), eco-labelling schemes (*US-Tuna II*),[11] animal welfare measures (*EC-Seal Products*[12]), and climate change mitigation policies (*Canada-Renewable Energy*[13] and *India-Solar Cells*[14]).

This growing list of trade-and disputes has sparked 'a fresh debate on the WTO's infringement of state sovereignty',[15] and reignited questions over the legitimacy of the DSS when called upon to address sensitive issues that go beyond the WTO's core 'trade' province. Thus, for example, following its announcement of the US tobacco regulation as WTO-inconsistent in *US-Clove Cigarettes*, the Appellate Body (AB) was blamed for 'placing itself in the position of the regulator'[16] and for undermining the legitimacy of its overarching WTO edifice.[17] Remarks along these lines, suggesting undue encroachment on WTO Members' regulatory autonomy and their 'rights to pursue legitimate and important public policy measures', also followed promulgation of the latest *Tuna-II* rulings.[18]

With the continued salience of critiques of economic globalization (vividly illustrated recently in Europe and the United States), the intensification of certain trade-and problems (e.g. tobacco control, illegal fishing,[19] and climate change),

[9] *United States–Measures Affecting the Production and Sale of Clove Cigarettes*, Report of the Appellate Body, 24 April 2012, WT/DS406/AB/R.

[10] *Australia–Certain Measures Concerning Trademarks, Geographical Indications and Other Plain Packaging Requirements Applicable to Tobacco Products and Packaging*, Reports of the Panels, circulated 28 June 2018, WT/DS435/R, WT/DS441/R, WT/DS458/R, WT/DS467/R. Note that the four complainants in the *Plain Packaging* case were Cuba, the Dominican Republic, Honduras, and Indonesia. On 19 July 2018, Honduras appealed its panel report. The Dominican Republic also appealed the panel ruling on 23 August 2018. At its meeting on 29 August 2018, the DSB adopted the panel reports with respect to Cuba and Indonesia, in the absence of any appeal against those two reports.

[11] *United States–Measures Concerning the Importation, Marketing and Sale of Tuna and Tuna Products*, Report of the Appellate Body, 13 June 2012, WT/DS381/AB/R.

[12] *European Communities–Measures Prohibiting the Importation and Marketing of Seal Products*, Reports of the Appellate Body, 18 June 2014, WT/DS400/AB/R, WT/DS401/AB/R.

[13] *Canada–Certain Measures Affecting the Renewable Energy Generation Sector; Canada–Measures Relating to the Feed-In Tariff Program*, Reports of the Appellate Body, 24 May 2013, WT/DS412/AB/R, WT/DS426/AB/R.

[14] *India–Certain Measures Relating to Solar Cells and Solar Modules*, Report of the Appellate Body, 14 October 2016, WT/DS456/AB/R.

[15] Prateek Bhattacharya and Jayant Raghu Ram, 'Settling Trade Disputes: Butter, not Guns' (2012) 4 Trade L & Dev 1, 7.

[16] See the US statement pending the adoption of the AB report in *US-Clove Cigarettes* at DSB, Minutes of Meeting of 24 April 2012 (27 June 2012) WT/DSB/M/315, para 75.

[17] Todd Tucker, 'Summarizing WTO Appellate Body Decision on U.S. Flavored Tobacco Ban' (*Public Citizen*, 27 April 2012) 20 <http://www.citizen.org/documents/memo-appellate-body-clove-ruling-04-12.pdf> accessed 20 December 2018.

[18] See 'Statements by the United States at the Meeting of the WTO Dispute Settlement Body, Geneva, January 11, 2019' (*US Mission to International Organizations in Geneva*, 11 January 2019) 3–16 <https://ustr.gov/about-us/policy-offices/press-office/press-releases/2019/january/statements-united-states-january-11> accessed 17 January 2019. See also 'Statements by the United States at the Meeting of the WTO Dispute Settlement Body, Geneva, December 3, 2015' (*US Mission to International Organizations in Geneva*, 3 December 2015) 1–5 <https://geneva.usmission.gov/2015/12/03/statement-by-the-united-states-at-the-december-3-2015-dsb-meeting/> accessed 20 December 2018.

[19] For a discussion of this environmental issue and recent WTO disputes related to it, see Kathleen Auld, 'Trade Measures to Prevent Illegal Fishing and the WTO: An Analysis of the Settled Faroe Island Dispute' (2018) 17 World Trade Rev 665.

and the low prospects of legislative solutions materializing in the WTO's negotiating arm, the flow of trade-and disputes is expected to persist and thereby fuel further challenges to the legitimacy of the WTO and its DSS among regulating Members, as well as stakeholders outside the multilateral trade circles (e.g. civil society actors, other international institutions, and the general public). The situation was summarized by a WTO practitioner as follows:

> [W]e are moving into a phase ... where the ... [WTO DSS] has to face nontrade concerns that impact on trade, and it's more and more the case.... [Those disputes] move to the forefront of WTO litigation, and maybe for a while, the WTO was hoping that this would go away, but I don't think it will.... [And] if as a court you start moving into this field and making decisions on issues that people feel about in terms of values, ... [which] might differ from one country to the next, then that's dangerous territory because ... once a judgment is made, you will get ... [a] reaction: 'Who are they to decide? ... How come they know? And shouldn't that be [decided] in a democracy? Shouldn't that be decided by a majority, not by a bunch of judges ... in a faraway country?'[20]

In that spirit, an AB member noted that 'the issue of legitimacy ... gets raised on a much more general level and ... much broader throughout society' in those disputes that touch upon nontrade values and interests.[21]

Due to the significant part that trade-and disputes have come to play in WTO adjudication, and the intensified legitimacy challenges they present, this class of disputes is ideal for examining how heightened external and internal legitimacy pressures shape DSS goal-attainment efforts, sharpen conflicts and trade-offs between its goals, motivate shifts in their relative weights, and consequently affect the DSS's effectiveness in realizing its multiple organizational objectives. In the framework of the present book, trade-and disputes therefore form a valuable site for exploring the goal-conflict and goal-shifting phenomena described in Chapter 1 and for assessing their ramifications for the development of a comprehensive and dynamic WTO DSS goal-based effectiveness scheme. In like manner, this dispute category, because of the systemic legitimacy concerns it raises before the DSS and its overarching WTO regime, provides an opportunity for challenging the conventional wisdom claiming rule compliance to be the unwavering primary goal pursued by the DSS and the most important outcome against which its effectiveness should be measured.

[20] Interview with WTO practitioner (Geneva, 9 July 2012). Other interviewees expressed similar views. See, e.g. interview with WTO panellist (Geneva, 23 July 2012); interview with senior WTO official (Geneva, 23 March 2012).

[21] Interview with AB member (Geneva, 27 April 2012).

With a view to achieving these various research objectives, the investigation of the DSS's operation and goal-attainment patterns in trade-and disputes is carried in this second part of the book by means of a comparative, interview-based analysis of two case studies: the early case of *US-Shrimp*, concerning the WTO consistency of an import ban on shrimp harvested with methods harmful to sea turtles (Chapter 5), and the later *US-Clove Cigarettes* dispute, addressing an anti-tobacco regulation prohibiting flavoured cigarettes, aimed at reducing youth smoking (Chapter 6). The analysis of this pair of cases against the broader body of WTO jurisprudence in trade-and disputes testifies to how the enhanced legitimacy threats awakened have prodded the DSS under the lead of the AB to heighten its quest for legitimation in this class of cases. This quest for legitimacy, the analysis shows, has taken place along two parallel and at times conflicting trajectories: the first revolves around the DSS's ultimate end as a 'regime court' to confer legitimacy on the WTO among internal and external constituencies; the second concerns the DSS's intermediate goal as an international court to legitimize its own exercise of public authority among relevant audiences outside the WTO, while sustaining its internal legitimacy among WTO Members.

As demonstrated in the following chapters, the shift in emphasis towards these DSS legitimization goals in trade-and disputes is echoed in numerous testimonies by WTO practitioners involved in *US-Shrimp* and *US-Clove Cigarettes*, as well as comparable WTO cases. Moreover, this goal shifting is reflected in the *ratio decidendi* and *obiter dicta* of trade-and rulings, taking the form of a unique collection of substantive, procedural, and rhetorical legitimacy-enhancing strategies uncommon in general WTO jurisprudence. As I will show, the choice of these distinctive judicial strategies from among the others available to the DSS represents a conscious prioritization of some organizational goals over others in an attempt to craft politically palatable rulings intended to fortify WTO and DSS legitimacy among audiences inside, as well as outside, the multilateral trade system.[22]

In setting the scene for the analysis of the DSS's quest for legitimacy in trade-and disputes, unfolded in Chapters 5 and 6, this introductory chapter proceeds as follows. Section 4.2 clarifies the notion of legitimacy as employed here, and situates the analysis of the DSS's legitimation endeavours within current debates on the legitimacy of international governance. Section 4.3 then unpacks the various dimensions of the legitimacy challenge encapsulated in trade-and disputes, while placing the story of trade-and conflicts in the broader historical and institutional context of the multilateral trade system. Section 4.4 closes by elaborating on the reasons underlying the selection of *US-Shrimp* and *US-Clove Cigarettes* as the case

[22] Note that by putting forward this argument, I do not argue that legitimacy concerns are present only in trade-and disputes, nor do I mean to imply that such concerns are the sole determinant underlying the judicial choices made by the DSS in these cases. Instead, I suggest that parallel to other possible motives (e.g. good legal policy), the intensified legitimacy concerns aroused by trade-and disputes strongly affect the choices and tactics displayed by WTO adjudicators, thereby constructing a discernible judicial discourse and distinctive goal-attainment patterns.

studies appropriate for investigating DSS performance and goal-attainment patterns within the framework of trade-and disputes.

4.2 Legitimacy and Legitimation of International Governance: Meaning, Import, and Sources

Legitimacy is an elusive, open-ended concept, which is defined in a range of different ways. In the literatures of political science and international law, however, this concept is usually understood as referring to the justification and acceptance of political authority.[23] A legitimate global governance institution 'has a right to exercise authority—it has a right to rule ... —whereas an illegitimate one does not'.[24] A common distinction is drawn in this respect between two main dimensions of legitimacy: the normative and the sociological.[25] Normative legitimacy is an objective measure informed by political theory. It concerns the question of whether an institution, as a matter of moral theory, has the right to exercise authority by focusing on the standards or qualities that normatively justify its authority (e.g. its democratic pedigree, transparency, or expertise).[26] In other words, normative legitimacy refers to whether an institution's claim to authority is well founded—whether there are good reasons in support of its claim to authority.[27] Sociological legitimacy, in contrast, concerns the empirical question of whether an institution's authority is in fact 'accepted by relevant audiences, such as states and civil society groups'; whether the institution's right to rule is perceived as justified by the subjects affected, who are willing to defer even to the unpopular decisions the institution renders.[28] Hence, sociological legitimacy is a subjective, relational quality constructed between an audience and an institution, and is defined by the audience's *perception* of the institution.[29] As such, sociological legitimacy 'always involves certain actors making legitimacy claims towards specific audiences',[30] and its degree may vary across audiences and over time.[31]

[23] Daniel Bodansky, 'Legitimacy in International Law and International Relations' in Jeffrey L Dunoff and Mark A Pollack (eds), *Interdisciplinary Perspectives on International Law and International Relations: The State of the Art* (CUP 2013) 324.
[24] ibid.
[25] Allen Buchanan, 'The Legitimacy of International Law' in John Tasioulas and Samantha Besson (eds), *The Philosophy of International Law* (OUP 2010) 79.
[26] ibid 79, 85; Bodansky (n 23) 327; Allen Buchanan and Robert O Keohane, 'The Legitimacy of Global Governance Institutions' (2006) 20 Ethics & Int'l Aff 405.
[27] Daniel Bodansky, 'The Legitimacy of International Governance: A Coming Challenge for International Environmental Law?' (1999) 93 AJIL 596, 601.
[28] Bodansky (n 23) 327.
[29] Ian Hurd, *After Anarchy: Legitimacy and Power in the United Nations Security Council* (Princeton University Press 2008) 7.
[30] Joseph A Conti, 'Producing Legitimacy at the World Trade Organization: The Role of Expertise and Legal Capacity' (2010) 8 Socio-Economic Rev 131, 136.
[31] Bodansky (n 23) 335; Harlan Grant Cohen and others, 'Legitimacy and International Courts – A Framework' in Nienke Grossman and others (eds), *Legitimacy and International Courts* (CUP 2018) 4.

While conceptually and practically distinct, the normative and sociological aspects of legitimacy are related and may affect and inform one another.[32] Thus, normative legitimacy depends, to some extent, on sociological legitimacy and on people's beliefs, as '[a]n institution could not be normatively legitimate if no one thought it so'.[33] Acceptance by relevant publics (states, individuals, etc.) therefore constitutes an important—some even say necessary—element of an institution's normative justification.[34] Conversely, sociological legitimacy depends, to quite a degree, on normative legitimacy 'since beliefs about legitimacy are usually beliefs about whether an institution, as a normative matter, has a right to rule'.[35] The acceptability of an institution's authority by the relevant constituencies thus depends, in part, on how well the institution satisfies the normative tests or standards required for exercising a justified authority (e.g. equality, participation, and accountability).[36]

As indicated above, in this part of the book we take stock of the intense process of 'legitimation' followed by the WTO DSS in trade-and disputes, namely, the process by which WTO adjudicators have tried to influence the perceptions and beliefs of audiences within and outside the multilateral trade system regarding the validity and rightness of the authority exercised by the WTO and the DSS.[37] In this sense, the analysis carried out here is mainly concerned with the sociological aspect of legitimacy, understood as the quality that leads people or states to perceive authority as normatively justified and to accept it as worthy of being obeyed.

This quality of legitimacy is, clearly, critical for any type of governance, especially for institutions operating at the international level.[38] As Steffek notes, '[g]iven the strong voluntary element in rule creation and rule following in the international system', international institutions such as the WTO and its DSS are particularly dependent 'on legitimacy beliefs on the part of the ruled-over'[39] as a means to

[32] Joseph H H Weiler, 'In the Face of Crisis: Input Legitimacy, Output Legitimacy and the Political Messianism of European Integration' (2012) 34 J Eur Integration 825, 826–27; Bodansky (n 27) 601–02.

[33] Bodansky (n 23) 327.

[34] Bodansky (n 27) 601.

[35] Bodansky (n 23) 327.

[36] Yuval Shany, 'Stronger Together? Legitimacy and Effectiveness of International Courts as Mutually Reinforcing or Undermining Notions' in *Legitimacy and International Courts* (n 31) 355–56; Richard Higgott and Eva Erman, 'Deliberative Global Governance and the Question of Legitimacy: What Can We Learn from the WTO' (2010) 36 Rev Int'l Stud 449, 461.

[37] On this concept of 'legitimation' as 'the process by which actors come to believe in the normative legitimacy of an object', see Christopher A Thomas, 'The Uses and Abuses of Legitimacy in International Law' (2014) 34 Oxford J Legal Stud 729, 742–45.

[38] Jens Steffek, 'The Legitimation of International Governance: A Discourse Approach' (2003) 9 EJIR 249, 260.

[39] ibid.

motivate compliance with their legal prescriptions[40] and, more generally, as a means to secure their stability and effectiveness in carrying out their mandate.[41]

The legitimacy capital of international institutions—as of other governance structures—may derive, in turn, from the source of their authority (source-based legitimacy), the processes of governance through which this authority is exercised (process-based legitimacy), and/or the outcomes these processes produce (substantive/outcome-based legitimacy).[42] For a long time, it was the source of the authority of international institutions, rooted in state consent (i.e. the acceptance of their authority by sovereign states), that provided the primary basis for the claim of international institutions (and international law more generally) to legitimacy.[43] States were also assumed to be the exclusive legitimating community among whom an international institution's claim to legitimacy was to be sustained.[44]

However, in today's era of global governance, this no longer seems to be the case. Thus, in the burgeoning discourse on the legitimacy of international law and institutions, it has been argued that in light of the increasing depth and breadth of current global governance regimes, their legislative and adjudicative competences, their enhanced intrusion into the workings of nation-states, and their extended impact on actors at the domestic and global levels, state consent is no longer sufficient to persuade either states or other stakeholders of the legitimacy of global governance institutions.[45] Rather, to be considered legitimate, the authority of international institutions must be based on additional, more convincing, substantive and procedural grounds,[46] and must be established amidst wider circles of affected audiences, going well beyond their Member states.[47] Such claims have been particularly vocal with respect to the WTO and its DSS, especially in the context of trade-and disputes, a class of cases that has continually challenged the legitimacy of the multilateral trade institutions.

[40] Thomas M Franck, *The Power of Legitimacy Among Nations* (OUP 1990); Ian Hurd, 'Legitimacy and Authority in International Politics' (1999) 53 Int'l Org 379.

[41] cf Bodansky (n 27) 602–03; Bodansky (n 23) 336.

[42] Rüdiger Wolfrum, 'Legitimacy of International Law from a Legal Perspective: Some Introductory Considerations' in Rüdiger Wolfrum and Volker Röben (eds), *Legitimacy in International Law* (Springer 2008) 6–7; Thomas (n 37) 749–52; Hurd (n 29) 66–73; Franck (n 40) 17–18.

[43] See, e.g. Wolfrum (n 42) 6; Bodansky (n 23) 330. On state consent as the traditional basis of the legitimacy of international courts like the DSS, see Armin von Bogdandy and Ingo Venzke, *In Whose Name? A Public Law Theory of International Adjudication* (OUP 2014) 3; Armin von Bogdandy and Ingo Venzke, 'In Whose Name? An Investigation of International Courts' Public Authority and Its Democratic Justification' (2012) 23 EJIL 7, 8, 24 [hereinafter von Bogdandy and Venzke 2012].

[44] Thomas (n 37) 748.

[45] See, e.g. Wolfrum (n 42) 10–21; Bodansky (n 23) 330; von Bogdandy and Venzke 2012 (n 43) 8.

[46] See, e.g. Higgott and Erman (n 36); Buchanan and Keohane (n 26); Daniel C Esty, 'Good Governance at the World Trade Organization: Building a Foundation of Administrative Law' (2007) 10 J Int'l Econ L 509.

[47] See, e.g. Bodansky (n 23) 334; Sungjoon Cho, 'A Quest for WTO's Legitimacy' (2005) 4 World Trade Rev 391, 392–93.

4.3 The Legitimacy Matrix of Trade-and Disputes: Context and Content

The origins of the enduring legitimacy challenge facing the WTO and the DSS in cases involving nontrade interests go back to the days of the WTO's predecessor, the General Agreement on Tariffs and Trade (GATT), and are embedded in the broader trade-and debate that has clung to the multilateral trade system since the 1990s.[48] This political debate, arising with the emergence of the environment and labour-related critiques of the international trading system, came to the surface following the contentious GATT *Tuna/Dolphin* disputes in 1991 and 1994.[49] At issue in these cases was a US import ban on tuna (and tuna products) caught by fishing methods harmful to dolphins (who are known to swim above schools of tuna). Operating within the discursive practices of the closed 'club' of trade insiders, that is, the old GATT,[50] and focusing on its trade liberalization goal, the GATT *Tuna/Dolphin* panels declared the US import ban to be inconsistent with the GATT Agreement. First, based on the infamous process and production methods (PPMs) doctrine, the panels rejected the ability of a state to prohibit imports because of the way by which the goods were produced.[51] Second, following the practice of former GATT panels to narrowly construe GATT Article XX (the 'general exceptions clause'), the *Tuna/Dolphin* panels rejected US attempts to justify its trade-restrictive regulation under the environmental exceptions stipulated in this provision.[52]

Though never adopted, to many, the *Tuna/Dolphin* rulings, 'strongly supported by the insider trade policy elite and the GATT ... institution',[53] came to denote the GATT's pro-trade bias.[54] These rulings consequently sparked a fierce public debate and criticism of the WTO's predecessor for prioritizing trade over other social

[48] For an elaborate discussion of this trade-and debate, see Andrew T F Lang, 'Reflecting on "Linkage": Cognitive and Institutional Change in the International Trading System' (2007) 70 Mod L Rev 523.

[49] ibid 530.

[50] Robert O Keohane and Joseph S Nye Jr, 'The Club Model of Multilateral Cooperation and Problems of Democratic Legitimacy' in Roger B Porter and others (eds), *Efficiency, Equity, Legitimacy: The Multilateral Trading System at the Millennium* (Brookings Institution Press 2001) 264.

[51] The so-called PPMs doctrine considers illegitimate distinctions between products that are based not on the products' intrinsic attributes but, rather, on the products' process and production methods (e.g. the environment-friendly manner in which the products are being caught or made). On the PPMs doctrine see Christiane R Conrad, *Processes and Production Methods (PPMs) in WTO Law: Interfacing Trade and Social Goals* (CUP 2011).

[52] *United States–Restrictions on Imports of Tuna*, Report of the GATT Panel, 3 September 1991, DS21/R (unadopted); *United States–Restrictions on Imports of Tuna*, Report of the GATT Panel, 16 June 1994, DS29/R (unadopted).

[53] Robert Howse, 'The World Trade Organization 20 Years On: Global Governance by Judiciary' (2016) 27 EJIL 9, 21.

[54] Robert Howse, 'The Appellate Body Rulings in the Shrimp/Turtle Case: A New Legal Baseline for the Trade and Environment Debate' (2002) 27 Colum J Envtl L 491, 494.

values and for overruling the regulatory act of a sovereign state.[55] Vocal challenges to the legitimacy of the GATT DSS and the international trade regime of which it formed a part quickly followed,[56] as described by a senior US official involved in the *Tuna/Dolphin* disputes:

> [W]e knew that the response to an adverse [panel] decision would be incredibly emotional. What we didn't realize … was [that it had become] the starting point … of the anti-GATT movement.… [W]hen the *Tuna-Dolphin* cases came out … the mood that this kind of huge coalition of environment groups and consumer groups and Public Citizen and all these groups tried to create was [that] 'this is a clear and present danger to our democratic way of life. This … GATT has now become … a tool of … huge corporate interests and … others who want to destroy our environment, destroy our society … destroy our rights as consumers …'[57]

Criticism against the multilateral trade system only exacerbated when the WTO, equipped with an expanded set of rules (including extended coverage of 'behind-the-border' regulatory measures), an elaborate institutional design, and a compulsory dispute settlement mechanism, replaced GATT in 1995.[58] Among other things, critics denounced the expansion of the multilateral trade regime beyond the traditional trade domain, as well as what they considered to be the WTO's undue encroachment on state regulatory autonomy.[59] Critics further condemned the perceived prioritization of the WTO's trade liberalization goal over other social and environmental interests.[60] Yet, in addition to challenging the WTO's substantive rules and objectives, critics also contested its undemocratic and nondeliberative decision-making and adjudicative procedures, characterized by a lack of transparency and voice together with exclusion of interested stakeholders.[61] Civil society opposition to the WTO rapidly took on visual form, as seen in the 1999 protests that swept through Seattle during the third WTO Ministerial Conference, and which repeated in several subsequent WTO

[55] Ilona Cheyne, 'Law and Ethics in the Trade and Environment Debate: Tuna, Dolphins and Turtles' (2000) 12 J Envtl L 293, 294–95; Philippe Sands, *Lawless World* (Penguin Books 2005) 108.

[56] Kati Kulovesi, *The WTO Dispute Settlement System: Challenges of the Environment, Legitimacy and Fragmentation* (Kluwer Law International 2011) 88.

[57] Interview with former senior US official (Geneva, 11 July 2012).

[58] Gabrielle Marceau and Mikella Hurley, 'Transparency and Public Participation: A Report Card on WTO Transparency Mechanisms' (2012) 4 Trade L & Dev 19, 22.

[59] Andrew Lang, *World Trade Law After Neoliberalism: Reimagining the Global Economic Order* (OUP 2011) 313–14; Sarah Joseph, *Blame it on the WTO: A Human Rights Critique* (OUP 2011) 58–59; Andrew T Guzman, 'Global Governance and the WTO' (2004) 45 Harv Int'l LJ 303, 304.

[60] Tomer Broude, *International Governance in the WTO: Judicial Boundaries and Political Capitulation* (Cameron May 2004) 58; Steffek (n 38) 269–70.

[61] Broude (n 60) 58; Steffek (n 38) 270; Marceau and Hurley (n 58) 21.

gatherings,[62] thereby placing the WTO at the focus of the anti-globalization movement's attention.

The increased friction between trade and nontrade values under the extended WTO edifice and the public criticism attendant thereto have constituted some of the root causes of what became known as the WTO's 'legitimacy crisis' by the turn of the twenty-first century.[63] The WTO's judicial arm, on its part, could not have escaped this source of tension. Rather, it has repeatedly found itself at the centre of this tension,[64] as disputes involving sensitive nontrade values have continually reached its docket, from the early days of *US-Gasoline* and *US-Shrimp*, to the present era of *US-Clove Cigarettes, EC-Seal Products*, and *Australia-Plain Packaging*.

Such trade-and disputes raise, in turn, unique legitimacy challenges before the WTO DSS in its capacity as a mandatory adjudication system nested within the multilateral trade regime, and granted a limited mandate to decide disputes based on the WTO agreements. First, trade-and disputes invite international scrutiny of national value-choices reached through political structures enjoying greater democratic legitimacy than do international tribunals,[65] especially when the latter act in policy areas (such as public health and the environment) traditionally considered 'the exclusive domain of domestic regulators'.[66] As a result, trade-and disputes invoke the sensitive issue of the vertical allocation of authority between states and global governance institutions,[67] threatening WTO and DSS legitimacy among Member states and their domestic constituencies.

Second, national preferences regarding the nontrade values involved in trade-and disputes often differ from one WTO Member to the other. These disparities consequently situate the DSS in a delicate position vis-à-vis the diverse WTO membership, rendering it almost impossible to deliver an outcome that will be acceptable to all.

Third, trade-and disputes, which effectively ask the DSS to balance between trade liberalization and other social values, raise doubts as to the very competence of the DSS to decide issues going beyond the sphere of trade, and to its capacity to determine trade-offs between competing social interests.[68] Furthermore, the balancing act inherent to such linkage disputes removes them from the purely legal realm, inviting value judgments into the judicial process, contrary to the ideal perception of the latter as an objective, apolitical process, centring on questions of

[62] Manfred Elsig, 'The World Trade Organization's Legitimacy Crisis: What Does the Beast Look Like?' (2007) 41 J World Trade 75.

[63] Lang (n 59) 313–17; Andrew T Guzman, 'Trade, Labor, Legitimacy' (2003) 91 Cal L Rev 885, 896.

[64] Broude (n 60) 27.

[65] Lang (n 59) 314; Jeffrey L Dunoff, 'The Death of the Trade Regime' (1999) 10 EJIL 733, 758.

[66] Thomas (n 37) 749.

[67] Thomas Kleinlein, 'Judicial Lawmaking by Judicial Restraint? The Potential of Balancing in International Economic Law' (2011) 12 German LJ 1141, 1170; Joel P Trachtman, 'Institutional Linkage: Transcending "Trade and ..."' (2002) 96 AJIL 77.

[68] Guzman (n 63) 887; Esty (n 2) 13.

meaning and fact.[69] This 'delegalization' or 'politicization', intrinsic to trade-and disputes, further threatens to delegitimize the WTO adjudicative process and its outcomes among audiences in and outside the multilateral trade arena.[70]

Fourth, trade-and disputes invoke sensitive questions regarding the horizontal allocation of authority at the global level because the linkage problems they address are often situated at the fringes of the WTO and other international legal regimes (e.g. international environmental law).[71]

Finally, exogenous constraints on the DSS's judicial powers, such as limitations on the legal norms it may apply, embedded in its mandate, add another layer of complexity to the already convoluted legitimacy matrix of the multilateral trade institutions in trade-and cases. As Kulovesi notes, examination of non-WTO norms of international law as part of the DSS's decision-making process 'would sometimes be necessary to reach a satisfactory substantive outcome, especially in linkage disputes'.[72] Yet, the issue of the formal competence of WTO adjudicators to engage in such a judicial exercise is highly controversial.[73] While some argue that WTO panels and the AB can apply non-WTO law in disputes coming before them,[74] others are of the view that the Dispute Settlement Understanding (DSU) essentially cautions against doing so.[75] This interpretation follows from Articles 3.2 and 19.2 of the DSU, which stipulate that in their rulings, WTO adjudicators cannot add to or diminish Members' rights and obligations under the WTO covered agreements. This state of affairs confronts the WTO DSS in turn with an intricate legitimacy dilemma when called upon to address trade-and disputes. On the one hand, WTO Members may perceive attempts to stretch the boundaries of the WTO's legal framework as actions exceeding the DSS's mandate and as lacking in source legitimacy, conditions that may jeopardize the DSS's 'internal' support among at least a portion of the WTO membership.[76] On the other hand, the limits

[69] Duncan Kennedy, *A Critique of Adjudication (fin de siècle)* (Harvard University Press 1997) 27.

[70] Dunoff (n 65) 755.

[71] Kleinlein (n 67) 1170; Trachtman (n 67).

[72] Kulovesi (n 56) 136.

[73] For relevant literature, see, e.g. Kulovesi (n 56) 135–42; Erich Vranes, *Trade and the Environment: Fundamental Issues in International Law, WTO Law and Legal Theory* (OUP 2009) 69–92; Petros C Mavroidis, 'No Outsourcing of Law? WTO Law as Practiced by WTO Courts' (2008) 102 AJIL 421; Anja Lindroos and Michael Mehling, 'Dispelling the Chimera of "Self-Contained Regimes": International Law and the WTO' (2006) 16 EJIL 857; Joost Pauwelyn, *Conflict of Norms in Public International Law: How WTO Law Relates to Other Rules of International Law* (CUP 2003); Lorand Bartels, 'Applicable Law in WTO Dispute Settlement Proceedings' (2001) 35 J World Trade 499; Gabrielle Marceau, 'WTO Dispute Settlement and Human Rights' (2002) 13 EJIL 753; Joel P Trachtman, 'The Domain of WTO Dispute Resolution' (1999) 40 Harv Int'l LJ 333.

[74] See, e.g. Pauwelyn (n 73); Joost Pauwleyn, 'The Role of Public International Law in WTO: How Far Can We Go?' (2001) 95 AJIL 535.

[75] See, e.g. Trachtman (n 73) 342–43; Wolfgang Weiss, 'Security and Predictability under WTO Law' (2003) 2 World Trade Rev 183, 192–201; Gabrielle Marceau, 'Conflicts of Norms and Conflicts of Jurisdictions: The Relationship between the WTO Agreement and MEAs and other Treaties' (2001) 35 J World Trade 1081, 1102–05.

[76] Yuval Shany, *Assessing the Effectiveness of International Courts* (OUP 2014) 151; Kulovesi (n 56) 136.

imposed on the application of non-WTO law by the DSS's mandate may lead to legal outcomes regarded by audiences 'external' to the multilateral trade regime as partial, unjust, and consequently illegitimate.[77]

In light of the various complexities that inhere in trade-and disputes and the enhanced risks of delegitimation they pose to the DSS and its overarching regime, Dunoff has suggested, shortly after the establishment of the DSS, that WTO adjudicators adopt means of avoiding determinations on the merits in trade-and issues coming before them.[78] As more than two decades of WTO jurisprudence indicate, this suggestion has not been embraced by WTO adjudicators, who seem to entertain the view that abstaining from deciding such disputes would, by itself, undermine WTO and DSS credibility and legitimacy. As Claus-Dieter Ehlermann, a former AB member has noted, WTO adjudicators are not entitled to refuse to rule on a claim based on their desire to avoid politically delicate decisions because such a refusal goes counter to the DSS's mandate and the tasks it is expected to perform under the DSU.[79] His view was supported by another AB member, who stressed that 'the Appellate Body ... cannot ... not rule. And that is something that sometimes people don't keep very much in mind. It has to rule whatever happens; it doesn't matter what happens, it has to rule'.[80]

At the same time, a WTO practitioner has observed that as opposed to 'trade remedy cases' (e.g. cases addressing anti-dumping or safeguard measures), where 'there aren't enormous issues of policy lurking behind', in trade-and disputes, 'where there are issues of policy hiding behind the case ... it's natural to assume that the court is going to be politically more sensitive and craft a decision that is designed to gain some degree of public acceptance'.[81] The *US-Shrimp* and *US-Clove Cigarettes* cases examined in the following chapters indeed reveal the conscious efforts made by the DSS, under the guidance of the AB, to secure acceptance of WTO governance and judicial outcomes amidst multiple audiences, going well beyond WTO Member states, efforts that have resulted in a notable shift in emphasis in trade-and cases towards the DSS's legitimation objectives.

After briefly explaining the reasons underlying the selection of *US-Shrimp* and *US-Clove Cigarettes* as case studies well suited for the investigation of the DSS's operation and goal-attainment patterns within the context of linkage disputes, this second part of the book proceeds in Chapter 5 with a comprehensive goal-based investigation of *US-Shrimp*. Chapter 6 follows with an examination of *US-Clove*

77 Shany (n 76) 151; Kulovesi (n 56) 136.

78 Dunoff (n 65) 757–61.

79 Claus-Dieter Ehlermann, 'Six Years on the Bench of the "World Trade Court": Some Personal Experiences as Member of the Appellate Body of the World Trade Organization' (2002) 36 J World Trade 605, 633.

80 Telephone interview with former AB member (13 September 2012). See also interview with AB member (Geneva, 27 April 2012) (arguing that not ruling is 'not an option', and that, as a matter of fact, 'not ruling would also be a ruling because it would be a ruling in favor of the respondent').

81 Interview with WTO practitioner (Geneva, 16 July 2012).

Cigarettes. This part closes with a comparative assessment of the two cases, while considering the implications of the emerging findings for the evaluation of DSS performance and the development of its goal-based effectiveness framework.

4.4 Case Selection

Several considerations guided the selection of *US-Shrimp* and *US-Clove Cigarettes* as case studies appropriate for exploring the DSS's goal-attainment patterns in trade-and disputes, together with the goal shifting and goal conflicts associated with this category of cases. First, the two cases involve different WTO agreements: *US-Shrimp* addresses claims under the GATT Agreement, whereas *US-Clove Cigarettes* concerns the Technical Barriers to Trade Agreement. Second, the cases represent different periods in the life of the DSS and the WTO. *US-Shrimp* was brought before the DSS in 1996, soon after the WTO's establishment; the case ended in 2001. What became a landmark trade-and dispute was one of the first cases to raise the intricate linkage problem before the DSS, just when the WTO's legitimacy crisis was emerging. *US-Clove Cigarettes* was placed before the DSS in 2010; by then, the DSS had become a well-oiled adjudicative machine though nested within an organization trapped in prolonged political stalemate. This dispute, concluded in 2014, thus represents another stage in the life cycle of the WTO and its DSS, characterized by old but also new challenges to their legitimacy. Finally, the two cases deal with separate nontrade values: *US-Shrimp* addresses environmental protection and *US-Clove Cigarettes* concerns public health. Hence, while the cases share important characteristics, particularly the friction between trade and nontrade interests, the differences between them allow investigation of DSS judicial choices and goal-attainment efforts in trade-and disputes over time and across agreements and subject matters.

5
Escaping the Illegitimacy Net
Between Turtles and Shrimps on the High Seas

5.1 *US-Shrimp*: A Watershed in the WTO DSS's Quest for Legitimacy

As noted by the former Appellate Body (AB) member Georges Abi-Saab, the positioning of the WTO Dispute Settlement System (DSS) in 'an Organization whose pervasive atmosphere, lingering from the GATT era, is encapsulated in the mantra' of being 'a member-driven Organization', where 'members themselves take all the final decisions', has led the AB 'to stick closely to the specificities of the matter put before it, and to follow a judicial policy of "strict constructionism" in interpretation, with marked reluctance to indulge in interpretation on the basis of ... the object and purpose of the agreements'.[1] And yet, Abi-Saab added that 'this initial judicial policy', designed to allow the DSS to fulfil its mandate while satisfying the expectations and maintaining the support of its immediate institutional environment, 'has been slowly evolving towards more openness in the face of scathing criticisms of the WTO ... and its Dispute Settlement System in particular, as a ruthless vehicle of economic globalization, oblivious (and to the detriment) of other values or concerns of the international community'.[2]

The seeds of this evolving judicial process, aimed at building legitimacy for the DSS and the broader WTO edifice among audiences outside the trade circles while sustaining these institutions' support within the inner circles of WTO Members, were planted in the early trade-and dispute of *US-Gasoline* concerning a US trade-restrictive regulation aimed at reducing air pollution. Drawing on Article 3.2 of the Dispute Settlement Understanding (DSU), which requires WTO adjudicators to clarify the WTO agreements 'in accordance with customary rules of interpretation of public international law', the AB declared that those agreements are 'not to be read in clinical isolation from public international law'.[3] Hence, in contrast to the inward-looking and trade-focused approach of the old General Agreement on Tariffs and Trade (GATT) system (see Chapter 4), the AB seized the opportunity

[1] Georges Abi-Saab, 'The Normalization of International Adjudication: Convergence and Divergencies' (2010) 43 NYU J Int'l L & Pol 1, 13–14.
[2] ibid 14.
[3] *United States–Standards for Reformulated and Conventional Gasoline*, Report of the Appellate Body, 20 May 1996, WT/DS2/AB/R, 17.

International Adjudication on Trial First Edition Sivan Shlomo Agon.
Published 2019 by Oxford University Press.

in its very first case to assert that the WTO regime is firmly embedded in general international law and to confirm the 'openness' of that regime towards those parts of the international legal system representing social values other than trade.[4]

However, it was in the subsequent case of *US-Shrimp*,[5] a case that came to be seen as a watershed in the WTO DSS's quest for legitimacy,[6] that the AB assigned detailed substance to these general pronouncements. This case stands at the centre of the present chapter. In what follows, this section discusses the measure at issue in *US-Shrimp* and the infamous panel ruling rendered in the case, together with the heightened legitimacy challenges it ignited against the backdrop of the mounting criticism levelled at the multilateral trade system in the late 1990s. On these foundations, the chapter turns (Sections 5.2–5.4) to a comprehensive goal-based reading of the judicial endeavour carried out by the AB in *US-Shrimp* along the procedural, substantive, and rhetorical dimensions, tracing the goal shifts and trade-offs struck in the face of the enhanced legitimacy pressures faced by the WTO and the DSS in this case. Section 5.5 concludes the discussion while tying the goal-achievement patterns identified to the broader goal-based effectiveness framework developed in the book.

The Panel's Ruling in *US-Shrimp* and Its Aftermath

At issue in *US-Shrimp* was US legislation prohibiting imports of shrimp harvested with technologies that may adversely affect endangered species of sea turtles, unless the harvesting state had been certified by US authorities as having adopted a conservation programme comparable to that applied by the United States throughout its territory (requiring all US shrimp trawlers to use approved turtle excluder devices). India, Malaysia, Pakistan, and Thailand, adversely affected by the US import ban, filed a dispute against the United States with the WTO DSS, arguing that the US trade-restrictive environmental measure was inconsistent with the latter's obligations under WTO law.

The sensitive dispute raised in turn several challenges before the first-instance WTO panel called upon to rule on the legality of the US regulatory measure. According to one WTO official involved in the panel proceedings:

> [W]e were still in the early days of trade and environment issues, so the first ... [challenge raised before the panel] was, is the WTO a trade agreement

[4] Bruno Simma and Dirk Pulkowski, 'Of Planets and the Universe: Self-contained Regimes in International Law' (2006) 17 EJIL 483, 492, 510.

[5] *United States–Import Prohibition of Certain Shrimp and Shrimp Products*, Report of the Appellate Body, 6 November 1998, WT/DS58/AB/R [*US-Shrimp* AB Report].

[6] Robert Howse, 'The World Trade Organization 20 Years On: Global Governance by Judiciary' (2016) 27 EJIL 9, 36–39.

> only? ... [I]s its prime objective ... to promote trade? Or is it an agreement where trade is there, but ... subject to other ... more important requirements such as the ones listed in ... [GATT] Article XX, [the general exceptions clause].... [T]he second [challenge] ... was ... how should the [WTO] system interact ... with environmental agreements.... and how much of those agreements can you take [into account] ... in the interpretation and ... implementation [of the WTO agreements].[7]

The same interviewee further commented that 'at that time, the panel's opinion was, "No, we can only look at the [WTO] covered agreements".... The panel took a very commercial approach. They said, "This is a trade agreement, it's not an agreement that is dealing with the environment and trade"'.[8] Echoing the GATT *Tuna-Dolphin* rulings (discussed in the previous chapter), the panel thus found the US import ban to be in breach of GATT Article XI, which prohibits quantitative restrictions, and unjustifiable under GATT Article XX (the general exceptions clause) on the grounds that unilateral environmental measures like the disputed US measure posed a 'threat' to the multilateral trading system.[9] According to the panel, then, WTO Members were only allowed 'to derogate from GATT provisions so long as, in doing so, they do not undermine the multilateral trading system'.[10]

As a lawyer involved in *US-Shrimp* observed, once the panel's report was out in May 1998, it was clear to everyone, including the complainants, that the 'report was a bit one-sided and was going to be problematic'.[11] As expected, the panel's 'pro-trade' ruling, leaving little space for the pursuit of nontrade policies by national regulators, attracted strong public reactions.[12] It likewise stimulated further challenges to the already precarious legitimacy of the WTO regime at the end of the 1990s (see Chapter 4), while questioning 'the institutional integrity of the WTO dispute settlement system and its ability to take a balanced approach to linkage disputes'.[13] When the appeal was filed, the AB therefore 'had to choose between affirming the orthodox free trader view that prevailed within the trade policy community or acknowledging in some way and attempting to mitigate the harm to the external legitimacy of the system'.[14] At this juncture, a WTO legal officer noted:

[7] Interview with WTO official (Geneva, 22 March 2012).
[8] ibid.
[9] *United States–Import Prohibition of Certain Shrimp and Shrimp Products*, Report of the Panel, 6 November 1998, WT/DS58/R, para 7.61 [*US-Shrimp* Panel Report].
[10] ibid, para 7.44.
[11] Interview with WTO practitioner (Geneva, 16 July 2012).
[12] Kati Kulovesi, *The WTO Dispute Settlement System: Challenges of the Environment, Legitimacy and Fragmentation* (Kluwer Law International 2011) 88.
[13] ibid.
[14] Howse (n 6) 37.

> [T]he thinking of the Appellate Body was, 'Look, we're gonna sink with the ship if we don't manage to do something that will … make the system look less removed from the people, and if we don't give some hope to the Members that they … can indeed have [nontrade] policies'.[15]

Along similar lines, a practitioner involved in *US-Shrimp* observed that in the aftermath of the panel ruling, it became obvious that:

> [There was a need] to develop a solution to how the WTO could handle environmental cases, which showed some environmental sensitivity, and it was quite clear that this is going to happen at the Appellate Body proceedings. It[s] [decision] marked a complete change from what [had] happened in the GATT *Tuna-Dolphin* cases. It was … a continuation of the sensitivity [introduced] … in *Reformulated Gasoline*.[16]

And so, the intense legitimacy pressures invoked in *US-Shrimp* led the AB to adjust its goal-attainment efforts and judicial arsenal accordingly. Various procedural, substantive, and rhetorical legitimacy-enhancing strategies, discussed in detail below, were therefore incorporated into its ruling in this case in an attempt to respond to the heightened external and internal challenges posed to the authority of the WTO and the DSS.

5.2 The First Step Along the Legitimation Path: Opening the Door to *Amici Curiae*

The first step taken by the AB along the path towards strengthening WTO and DSS legitimacy in *US-Shrimp* was procedural in nature. Following GATT practice, where panels refused to address information provided by nongovernmental sources,[17] the panel in *US-Shrimp* rejected *amicus curiae* briefs submitted by environmental nongovernmental organizations (NGOs) in support of the US import ban. The panel explained its rejection by noting that 'accepting non-requested information from non-governmental sources, would be … incompatible with the provisions of the DSU', particularly Article 13, which addresses the panel's 'right to *seek* information'. It reasoned that pursuant to these provisions, information would be admissible only when it had been submitted to the panel by the parties, or sought under the panel's own initiative.[18]

[15] Interview with WTO official (Geneva, 22 March 2012).

[16] Interview with WTO practitioner (Geneva, 16 July 2012).

[17] Gabrielle Marceau and Matthew Stilwell, 'Practical Suggestions for Amicus Curiae Briefs Before WTO Adjudicating Bodies' (2001) 4 J Int'l Econ L 155, 157–58.

[18] *US-Shrimp* Panel Report (n 9) para 7.8.

The AB disagreed.[19] Criticizing the panel's interpretation as 'too literal' and 'unnecessarily technical and formal', the AB stated that under Article 13 of the DSU, the panel's 'comprehensive' authority to 'seek' information from 'any relevant source' allows it to 'either accept and consider or to reject information … submitted to it', including information from nongovernmental sources, irrespective of whether that information was requested by the panel.[20] The AB further observed that the power of panels to accept unsolicited *amicus curiae* briefs is found in the 'ample and extensive authority' the DSU grants a panel 'to undertake and to control the process by which it informs itself both of the relevant facts of the dispute and of the legal norms and principles applicable to such facts'.[21] In the wake of this interpretative exercise, described by some as 'a rather "acrobatic" interpretation' of the DSU,[22] the AB reversed the panel's finding and allowed NGOs to participate in WTO proceedings through *amicus* briefs, a decision departing from the strict government-to-government dispute settlement practice inherited from the old GATT.[23]

Above all, as von Bogdandy and Venzke note, *amici curiae* and 'NGO participation may open up legitimatory potentials' for global governance institutions such as the WTO and the DSS.[24] By expanding opportunities for public participation and promoting deliberative dialogue among wider circles of (potentially) affected stakeholders, *amicus curiae* submissions may enhance the legitimacy of the *decision-making processes* employed by international institutions.[25] In like fashion, such briefs may enhance the legitimacy of the *outcomes* these institutions generate.[26] Thus, by offering access to expertise and information from sources other than Member governments, *amicus curiae* briefs may broaden the views held by those having the power to make decisions within international institutions, helping them to better evaluate the ramifications of their decisions and, in

[19] *US-Shrimp* AB Report (n 5) paras 104–10.

[20] ibid, paras 104, 107–08.

[21] ibid, para 106.

[22] Petros C Mavroidis, 'Amicus Curiae Briefs Before the WTO: Much Ado About Nothing' in Armin von Bogdandy, Petros C Mavroidis, and Yves Mény (eds), *European Integration and International Co-ordination: Studies in Transnational Economic Law in Honour of Claus-Dieter Ehlermann* (Kluwer Law International 2002) 319.

[23] In later jurisprudence, the AB affirmed its own authority to accept amicus submission. See *United States–Imposition of Countervailing Duties on Certain Hot-Rolled Lead and Bismuth Carbon Steel Products Originating in the United Kingdom*, Report of the Appellate Body, 7 June 2000, WT/DS138/AB/R, para 39.

[24] Armin von Bogdandy and Ingo Venzke, 'In Whose Name? An Investigation of International Courts' Public Authority and Its Democratic Justification' (2012) 23 EJIL 7, 29. See also Theresa Squatrito, 'Amicus Curiae Briefs in the WTO DSM: Good or Bad News for Non-State Actor Involvement?' (2018) 17 World Trade Rev 65, 68 (alluding to the various ways in which *amicus curiae* submissions can help to alleviate aspects of the WTO DSS's 'legitimacy deficit').

[25] Steve Charnovitz, 'Nongovernmental Organizations and International Law' (2006) 100 AJIL 348, 366–67; Daniel C Esty, 'Good Governance at the World Trade Organization: Building a Foundation of Administrative Law' (2007) 10 J Int'l Econ L 509, 524–26.

[26] Charnovitz (n 25) 367.

consequence, to deliver more informed and accountable outcomes.[27] Furthermore, by providing opportunities for voice and promoting deliberative dialogue, participation through *amicus* briefs may give stakeholders a greater sense of ownership regarding the outcomes produced by those same international institutions, a step that may render such outcomes more acceptable even among those on the losing side of the debate.[28]

Being aware of these legitimatory potentials in addition to the mounting public criticism about accountability, transparency, and participation in WTO decision-making procedures, the AB's embrace of *amicus* briefs in *US-Shrimp* reflects its attempt to restructure the WTO judicial process so as to bridge the gap between the WTO and civil society[29] and make the Organization's adjudicative system more 'publicly accepted'.[30] As a former senior WTO official observed: the AB's decision on *amicus* briefs was, in effect, a 'response ... to the concerns from the environmental community' about WTO dispute settlement, which this community saw as disregarding whatever 'comes from the environmental side'.[31] In a similar spirit, an AB member sitting on the bench in *US-Shrimp* alluded to the legitimating rationale underlying the procedural decision to allow NGO participation in these words: 'In the modern world there is a great deal of attention being paid to all kinds of ... civil organizations.... [T]he reality is that ... there are groups in society that have contributions to make and they should be listened to'.[32]

The *amicus curiae* ruling therefore reveals the AB's understanding of the need to expand the (procedural) bases of WTO legitimacy while simultaneously exposing the adjudicators' shifting conceptions of the WTO's legitimating community. This change in approach suggests that this community is no longer comprised of a closed group of Member governments and trade policy insiders, the situation prevailing in the multilateral trading system since the GATT's birth in 1947.[33] Although the latter stakeholders remain 'the ones with the most privileged positions when shaping the exercise of WTO power', the AB's attempt to open up and stretch the bounds of the judicial process it orchestrates discloses its recognition of the burgeoning need to communicate with additional communities of legitimation—environmental

[27] ibid; von Bogdandy and Venzke (n 24) 29; Squatrito (n 24) 68.

[28] cf Daniel Esty, 'Good Governance at the Supranational Scale: Globalizing Administrative Law' (2006) 115 Yale LJ 1490, 1520.

[29] Daniel Bodansky, 'Legitimacy in International Law and International Relations' in Jeffrey L Dunoff and Mark A Pollack (eds), *Interdisciplinary Perspectives on International Law and International Relations: The State of the Art* (CUP 2013) 335; Jeffrey L Dunoff, 'The WTO's Legitimacy: Reflections on the Law and Politics of WTO Dispute Resolution' (2002) 13 Am Rev Int'l Arb 197, 200.

[30] Interview with WTO official (Geneva, 22 March 2012).

[31] Interview with former senior WTO official (Geneva, 17 July 2012).

[32] Telephone interview with former AB member (13 September 2012).

[33] Christopher A Thomas, 'The Uses and Abuses of Legitimacy in International Law' (2014) 34 Oxford J Legal Stud 729, 749.

groups, human rights activists, and anti-globalization protestors, among others—communities upholding 'different ideas of legitimacy' that the WTO and its DSS can no more afford to ignore.[34]

As von Bogdandy and Venzke note, international courts like the AB 'rule over procedures',[35] a feature providing them with an important source of independence in shaping their judicial process.[36] Like these commentators, we understand attempts, as seen in the *US-Shrimp* decision, to draw on this source of independence in order to foster 'more transparency and opportunities of participation', as an expression of the changing conceptions of the grounds on which the legitimacy of such decisions should be predicated, and as part of the judiciary's attempts to strengthen the 'capacity of legitimation that is nested in the judicial process itself'.[37]

5.3 The Legitimating Moves Under GATT Article XX: Setting a New Legal Framework for Trade-and Disputes

The AB's legitimation endeavour in *US-Shrimp* extended beyond the procedural domain. It further penetrated the substantive legal analysis of GATT Article XX,[38] as the United States sought to justify its otherwise GATT-inconsistent import ban pursuant to the environmental exception in Article XX(g), which allows countries to adopt trade-restrictive measures 'relating to the conservation of exhaustible natural resources if such measures are made effective in conjunction with restrictions on domestic production or consumption' of the finite resources. Here the AB was faced with the old treaty text of GATT 1947, yet with the needs to address the growing trade-environment debate and to secure a policy space for states interested in pursuing environmental regulations. As an AB member sitting on the bench in *US-Shrimp* elaborated:

[34] ibid.

[35] von Bogdandy and Venzke (n 24) 25.

[36] ibid.

[37] ibid.

[38] The text of GATT Article XX reads, in relevant parts, as follows: 'Subject to the requirement that such measures are not applied in a manner which would constitute a means of arbitrary or unjustifiable discrimination between countries where the same conditions prevail, or a disguised restriction on international trade, nothing in this Agreement shall be construed to prevent the adoption or enforcement by any contracting party of measures:

(a) necessary to protect public morals;
(b) necessary to protect human, animal or plant life or health;

...

(g) relating to the conservation of exhaustible natural resources if such measures are made effective in conjunction with restrictions on domestic production or consumption;

...'

> On the one side ... problems as the one that arose in *Shrimp-Turtle*, which concerns the environment and endangered species, is something that was not very much foreseen in the drafting of the WTO agreements. And you can see that because there is very little in the [GATT] text.... Now ... the Appellate Body.... has to rule whatever happens.... And it has to rule in terms of the provisions as they exist. It is one thing the provisions as they exist, it is another thing what you would like them to be.... [W]e all have different views of what should be the text of the WTO Agreement, but what really counts, and the only thing that counts, is the ... text as it was approved by over one hundred governments.... So that's the first thing that arose in *Shrimp*.... [S]econdly, that was ... a difficult issue, and I remember very well that the three members of the division ... had a long long debate on all aspects of the matter. And there you have ... a clash between commercial interests and environmental interests.... So there is a sharp legal contest between them, which you have to take into account. At the same time, you have to rule with equity ... as you cannot go outside the WTO agreements.[39]

As seen below, acting with these considerations in mind, the AB moved to draw on the 'standard-like' nature of GATT Article XX, which affords the adjudicators some interpretative leeway,[40] so as to introduce a new legal framework to trade-and disputes that would do 'justice to the delicate interrelationship of values and interests in such cases, some internal and some external to the trading "system"'.[41] This judicial exercise, by which the AB harnessed its law clarification goal to its WTO legitimation endeavour, has been described by some as the AB's enfranchisement of the WTO's '"external" constituencies', those who had thus far been 'marginalized as "critics"' of the system and as the '"trade and ..." people'.[42]

Redefining and Broadening the Scope of the Environmental Exception in GATT Article XX(g)

The AB commenced its legitimation effort under GATT Article XX by redefining and broadening the scope of the environmental exception concerning 'the conservation of exhaustible natural resources' enshrined in paragraph (g). Departing from the textual interpretation generally associated with WTO jurisprudence, the AB chose on this occasion to pursue a teleological, 'evolutionary' approach to the

39 Telephone interview with former AB member (13 September 2012).

40 On the standard-like nature of GATT Article XX see Joel P Trachtman, *The Economic Structure of International Law* (Harvard University Press 2008) 217–18. More generally on the distinction between 'rules' and 'standards' see ibid 212–16.

41 Robert Howse, 'From Politics to Technocracy–and Back Again: The Fate of the Multilateral Trading Regime' (2002) 96 AJIL 94, 109.

42 ibid 116.

construction of the treaty. It thus noted: "The words of Article XX(g), "exhaustible natural resources", were ... crafted more than 50 years ago'. These words, therefore, 'must be read by a treaty interpreter in the light of contemporary concerns of the community of nations about the protection and conservation of the environment'.[43] Such concerns, the AB added, are reflected in the preamble of the WTO Agreement itself, which informs the interpretation of all WTO provisions, and which 'explicitly acknowledges "the objective of sustainable development"'.[44] From the perspective embodied in the preamble, the AB inferred that the 'generic term "natural resources" in Article XX(g) is not "static" in its content' but, rather, 'evolutionary'; it then went on to address several 'modern international conventions and declarations' with a view to learning the term's exact meaning. In line with this dynamic, contextual, and teleological interpretation, the AB ultimately read the term 'exhaustible natural resources' as covering not only finite resources (e.g. gas and minerals), as suggested by the complainants based on the original intent and drafting history of GATT, but also living natural resources, such as sea turtles, which the US regulation sought to protect.[45] A WTO practitioner involved in *US-Shrimp* described the AB's interpretative course in these terms:

> [The complainants] argued that the original meaning back in the days of [the] Havana Charter should have been given effect in [Article] XX(g)—'exhaustible natural resources' meant coal and oil and things that are going to be depleted. The Appellate Body rejected that argument. They developed ... [the] notion of 'evolutionary interpretation' that the ICJ had used to redefine the meaning of 'exhaustible natural resource', and as a result they looked at the context—the preamble of the WTO Agreement—and put sustainable development firmly within Article XX. And that was profoundly important ... because environment is a concern of everyone and it should be a concern of the trade community.[46]

Shedding light on the rationale underlying this jurisprudential move, a member of the AB Secretariat's staff noted that when the AB was presented with the language of Article XX(g) it faced two interpretative alternatives. Since the generic phrase 'exhaustible natural resources' lends itself to more than one interpretation, the AB in *US-Shrimp* could have adopted either a narrow or an expansive reading of the treaty text.[47] Facing these options, the AB chose to broadly construe Article XX(g) as covering both living and nonliving entities so as to leave more regulatory space for governments to pursue environmental goals,[48] a step that would enhance,

43 *US-Shrimp* AB Report (n 5) para 129.
44 ibid.
45 ibid, paras 130–31.
46 Interview with WTO practitioner (Geneva, 16 July 2012).
47 Interview with staff member of the AB Secretariat (Geneva, 4 July 2012).
48 ibid.

they believed, the DSS's internal legitimacy among (at least some) WTO Members. At the same time, the AB's interpretative approach also gave a nod to 'constituencies and values traditionally understood as being external to the WTO and its purpose'.[49] Thus, as opposed to the 'retrospective, originalist interpretation' that would have privileged 'the supposed intentions and expectations of a fairly narrow "interpretive community" ... of ... treaty negotiators', the flexible, teleological, and contextual interpretation employed by the AB, based on evolving international law, allowed it to consider the expectations of wider constituencies in the international community as they have developed since the drafting of GATT 1947.[50]

This interpretative choice, I argue, represents in effect the AB's conscious choice between competing DSS goals and the prioritization of some organizational objectives over others. Whereas the novel evolutionary approach to treaty interpretation seems conducive to promoting the DSS's legitimization objectives, the AB's application of such a dynamic approach—implying the possibility of altering previous WTO interpretations—is less conducive to securing a legally predictable multilateral trade system and to maintaining the balance of rights and obligations originally negotiated by WTO Members.[51] For these reasons, the dynamic interpretative approach pursued by the AB as part of its legitimation effort in *US-Shrimp* was indeed criticized by some WTO Members.[52]

In any event, recourse to evolutionary and teleological interpretation was not the sole legitimating strategy used by the AB in its judicial exercise under GATT Article XX(g). Another distinctive legitimacy-enhancing tool, used in conjunction with the dynamic and teleological reading of the treaty, was the examination of non-WTO norms of international law. As briefly mentioned above, when addressing the question of whether living species (such as sea turtles) could be considered 'exhaustible natural resources', the AB referred to judgments of the International Court of Justice (ICJ) as well as to several international environmental conventions.[53] These non-WTO legal sources seem to have played an important role in *US-Shrimp*, as suggested by an AB member sitting on the bench:

> Other public international law outside the WTO treaty became a major factor in judging the appeal. Highly relevant to assessing the availability of ... [Article XX(g)] defence in that dispute was an international agreement called the Convention on International Trade in Endangered Species of Wild Fauna and

[49] Howse (n 6) 38.

[50] Robert Howse, 'Adjudicative Legitimacy and Treaty Interpretation in International Trade Law: The Early Years of WTO Jurisprudence' in Joseph H H Weiler (ed), *The EU, the WTO and the NAFTA: Towards a Common Law of International Trade?* (OUP 2000) 57–58.

[51] Arthur E Appleton, 'Shrimp/Turtle: Untangling the Nets' (1999) 2 J Int'l Econ L 477, 481–82.

[52] See, for example, the comments made by Thailand and Pakistan at the DSB meeting pending the adoption of the *US-Shrimp* decision: DSB, Minutes of Meeting of 6 November 1998 (14 December 1998) WT/DSB/M/50, 3, 5.

[53] *US-Shrimp* AB Report (n 5) paras 130–31 and accompanying footnotes.

Flora (CITES). Relevant, too, to our examination … were certain aspects of several other international conventions not among the 'covered agreements' of the WTO treaty: the 1982 UN Convention on the Law of the Sea, the Convention on Biological Diversity and the Convention on the Conservation of Migratory species of Wild Animals.

The members of the Appellate Body believed all this to be relevant. …[54]

Hence, unlike the panel that had envisaged no role for non-WTO legal sources in its ruling in *US-Shrimp*, the AB elevated these external legal benchmarks to 'crucial hermeneutic tools'.[55] When later responding to criticism of this judicial methodology by the 'insider trade policy community', Howse notes, 'Members of the Appellate Body might have suggested that they were only bringing in non-WTO international law where it was indispensable for solving interpretative controversy about the WTO agreements'.[56] Yet, he continues:

A more plausible, but not inconsistent, reading is that the Appellate Body purposely treated the issue of exhaustible natural resources in this way in order to bolster its external legitimacy at a time in which economic globalization was under persistent attack by outsider constituencies, including and especially environmental ones.[57]

Howse's reading, being compatible with the other legitimacy-enhancing strategies discussed here, is reinforced by the views of WTO practitioners who depicted the references to 'multilateral environmental conventions and instruments' in *US-Shrimp* as part of the AB's effort to show its 'awareness' of 'current environmental problems' and to express the WTO's 'greater sensitivity' to environmental concerns than that observed in past 'GATT panel reports'.[58] Yet, from a legitimacy-oriented perspective, a judicial move like the one taken by the AB, considering non-WTO legal instruments as part of its interpretative exercise, may serve additional functions. Most notably, as several commentators have observed, such an interpretation of WTO agreements, which is embedded within the broader international legal discourse and reflects the evolving law in other international legal regimes, may result in more coherent and holistic legal reasoning and thus more legitimate judicial decision-making.[59]

[54] James Bacchus, 'Not in Clinical Isolation' in Gabrielle Marceau (ed), *A History of Law and Lawyers in the GATT/WTO: The Development of the Rule of Law in the Multilateral Trading System* (CUP 2015) 513–14.

[55] Howse (n 6) 39.

[56] ibid.

[57] ibid.

[58] Interview with WTO legal officer (Geneva, 13 March 2012).

[59] Howse (n 50) 58; Andreas von Staden, 'Democratic Legitimacy of Judicial Review Beyond the State: Normative Subsidiarity and Judicial Standards of Review' (2012) 10 Int'l J Const L 1023, 1032.

That said, the suggested discomfort of WTO adjudicators with an expanded approach to using other rules of international law in their interpretations reflects the fragile standing, in terms of legitimacy, of a specialized international court like the AB when deciding cases involving competing values, some internal and some external to the regime in which it is embedded.[60] On the one hand, we have the AB's desire in such linkage cases to enhance the legitimacy of the DSS and the broader WTO edifice among external constituencies, a goal that may benefit from references to non-WTO legal sources. On the other, there is the AB's need to carry out such legitimation efforts without overly compromising the internal legitimacy of its judicial office within the trade community, particularly among WTO Members who may view the recourse to non-WTO law as judicial overreach (as later witnessed in some of the negative reactions to the AB's recourse to nontrade law in *US-Shrimp*).[61] With these DSS legitimation goals pulling in different directions, trade-offs between the competing objectives seem inevitable.

GATT Article XX Chapeau: The Emergence of the 'Balancing' Discourse and the 'Procedural Turn'

After learning that living species such as sea turtles could be considered 'exhaustible natural resources',[62] and that the US ban on the importation of shrimp was aimed at the conservation of such natural resources, as well as applied in conjunction with restrictions on domestic harvesting of shrimp,[63] the AB concluded that the US trade-restrictive measure was 'provisionally' justified under Article XX(g).[64] This conclusion, implicitly deviating from the traditional process and production methods (PPMs) doctrine (see Chapter 4),[65] stands in sharp contrast to dispute settlement practice under GATT, which made it 'almost impossible to

[60] Thomas Kleinlein, 'Judicial Lawmaking by Judicial Restraint? The Potential of Balancing in International Economic Law' (2011) 12 German LJ 1142, 1164.

[61] See, e.g. DSB, Minutes of Meeting of 6 November 1998 (14 December 1998) WT/DSB/M/50, 14.

[62] *US-Shrimp* AB Report (n 5) para 134.

[63] ibid, paras 142, 145.

[64] ibid, para 147. Paragraph (g) of GATT Article XX sets out a three-tier test requiring that a measure: (1) relate to the 'conservation of exhaustible natural resources'; (2) 'relate to' the conservation of exhaustible natural resources; and (3) be 'made effective in conjunction with' restrictions on domestic production or consumption. As just noted, in *US-Shrimp*, the AB found that the US trade-restrictive measure satisfied all three requirements.

[65] See Appleton (n 51) 491–92 (noting that in finding the US measure to satisfy the requirements of Article XX(g), the AB 'appears to have ruled, without explicitly stating', that measures distinguishing between products based on their process and production methods (rather than the products' intrinsic qualities) could be justified under GATT Article XX). See also, John H Jackson, *Sovereignty, the WTO, and Changing Fundamentals of International Law* (CUP 2006) 191 ('The Appellate Body, in the *Shrimp-Turtle* case, basically endorsed the possibility of a PPM, without ever mentioning the PPM problem or mentioning that it was shifting in emphasis, at least for that particular case, away from the more traditional attitudes towards PPMs in GATT'); Howse (n 6) 37.

justify public policies' under the exceptions specified in paragraphs (a) to (j) of Article XX.[66]

Based on the finding that the US measure fell within the terms of Article XX(g), the AB then turned to an examination of the measure under the introductory clause—the 'chapeau'—of GATT Article XX. This second part of the two-tier analysis required under Article XX, the AB elucidated, is aimed at preventing the abuse or misuse of the policy exceptions provided in this provision,[67] by ensuring that trade-restrictive measures are not *applied* in a manner constituting a means of 'arbitrary or unjustifiable discrimination between countries where the same conditions prevail' or a 'disguised restriction on international trade'.[68] Under the chapeau, the AB's quest for legitimacy in *US-Shrimp* continued.

Thus, following the seeds planted in *EC-Hormones*—where it had been stated that 'merely characterizing a treaty provision as an "exception" does not by itself justify a "stricter" or "narrower" interpretation of that provision'[69]—in its analysis of the chapeau, the AB reframed the relationship between the WTO's trade rules and the nontrade policy exceptions of Article XX in terms of 'balance'. Resorting once again to contextual-teleological interpretation, the AB determined that the chapeau of Article XX 'embodies the recognition on the part of WTO Members of the need to maintain a balance ... between the right of a Member to invoke the exceptions of Article XX ... and the substantive rights of other Members under the GATT [Agreement]'.[70] According to the AB, then, the task of interpreting and applying the chapeau is essentially 'a search for an appropriate *line of equilibrium* between, on the one hand, the right of Members to adopt ... trade-restrictive ... measures that pursue certain legitimate societal values or interests and, on the other hand, the right of other Members to trade'.[71]

And so, '[a]lthough the GATT has no specific language authorizing a balancing test',[72] and despite the 'accepted principle of interpretation that exceptions are to be interpreted narrowly', the AB advocated achieving a balance between the GATT's general rules and exceptions, and thus between trade liberalization and other social interests.[73] Seen through a legitimacy-oriented lens, the significance of the balancing act introduced to the chapeau is patent. By the end of the 1990s, this balancing analysis appears to have become a vital tool for the WTO and its DSS in

[66] Howse (n 6) 48.

[67] *US-Shrimp* AB Report (n 5) para 151.

[68] ibid, paras 150, 160.

[69] *European Communities–Measures Concerning Meat and Meat Products (Hormones)*, Report of the Appellate Body, 13 February 1998, WT/DS26/AB/R, WT/DS48/AB/R, para 104.

[70] *US-Shrimp* AB Report (n 5) para 156.

[71] Peter Van den Bossche and Werner Zdouc, *The Law and Policy of the World Trade Organization: Law, Text, Cases and Materials* (3rd edn, CUP 2013) 574 (emphasis original).

[72] WTO, *World Trade Report: Exploring the Links between Trade, Standards and the WTO* (2005) 135–41 <https://www.wto.org/english/res_e/booksp_e/anrep_e/world_trade_report05_e.pdf> accessed 30 December 2018.

[73] Van den Bossche and Zdouc (n 71) 547. See also Jackson (n 65) 190.

their attempts to regain legitimacy and public acceptance when considered against the emerging trade-and debate and the intensifying criticism of the multilateral trading system.[74] As Esty has noted, 'beyond strengthening its legitimacy through a commitment to more transparent procedures', the WTO needed 'rules ... that better balance the (sometimes) competing goals of ... trade ... and economic efficiency on the one hand, with environmental protection, human rights ... and other virtues on the other'.[75] The balancing approach read into the chapeau in *US-Shrimp* represented an attempt to respond to such calls, signalling to WTO Members but also to civil society actors and adjacent international regimes the AB's recognition of the broader context of the policy choices made at the WTO, as well as its ability to perform cross-issue balancing where noneconomic values are at play. As a senior WTO official noted, *US-Shrimp*, which gave 'a little more latitude to governments in terms of this whole issue of connecting ... trade concerns with ... nontrade [concerns]', was a 'reaction' to the criticism launched at the multilateral trade regime and 'a sort of ... rebalancing' of what had been seen in the *GATT Tuna* cases:

> [The *GATT Tuna* cases] led to a realization in everybody's heart that we have to be careful of not sort of interpreting our own ... GATT regime in such a way as to ... make it kind of trade über alles ... that we are seen as trade is pulling all over these [nontrade] concerns.[76]

As several commentators have stressed, the alternative of focusing on a narrow set of trade values and sticking to a strict textual reading of the WTO treaty, rather than balancing between trade and nontrade values, could have not only further damaged the credibility of the WTO and its DSS amidst regulating Members and external constituencies; it could have ultimately resulted in the inability of the WTO 'to maintain a degree of legitimacy that would enable it to carry out' its own economic objectives 'relating to trade liberalization'.[77]

Yet, alongside the appropriateness of the balancing analysis for cases involving conflicting trade and nontrade interests, together with the avenues of legitimation this type of analysis opened up for the multilateral trade institutions, this weighing of factors, when performed by a judiciary is, by nature, case specific because no clear rules are in place to guide comparison of the competing interests at stake. Indeed, the AB noted as much in *US-Shrimp* when it ruled that 'the location of the line of equilibrium, as expressed in the chapeau [of Article XX], is not fixed and unchanging; the line moves as the kind and the shape of the measures at stake vary

74 Daniel C Esty, 'The World Trade Organization's Legitimacy Crisis' (2002) 1 World Trade Rev 7, 18–19. For a discussion of balancing as a legitimacy-enhancing tool for an international adjudicative body like the DSS in the fragmented international legal system, see Kleinlein (n 60) 1143, 1162–70.

75 Esty (n 74) 19.

76 Interview with senior WTO official (Geneva, 11 July 2012).

77 Jackson (n 65) 190; Esty (n 74) 18.

and as the facts making up specific cases differ'.[78] In consequence, balancing may endow considerable strategic space to WTO adjudicators,[79] thereby increasing the risk of undue judicial intrusion on the regulatory autonomy of sovereign states, that is, the danger that the regulatory priorities and value choices reached through political processes at the national level would ultimately be replaced with those of international adjudicators.

Mindful of this risk and in order to avoid serious legitimacy challenges to WTO judicial intervention, the AB, in marking out the line of equilibrium under the chapeau in *US-Shrimp*, chose not to engage itself in substantive review of the US measure in the sense of determining the relative importance of the competing trade and environmental interests at issue and whether the right balance had been struck between them by the national regulator.[80] The specific measure was understood 'as an expression of the US population's own environmental priorities and values—its own way of balancing the relative importance of trade and environmental protection'—with the AB not seeing its task as second-guessing the substantive policy call made at the national level.[81] Instead, the AB limited its judicial review under the chapeau of Article XX to 'the procedural side of the balancing test'.[82] It therefore assessed whether the US measure, as applied, was disproportionate, discriminatory, or unreasonable,[83] while focusing on the regulatory design and procedures through which the United States pursued its environmental policy objectives.[84]

Following this new 'proceduralist' approach, the AB articulated three main reasons that eventually led to the US measure being found to be applied in a manner constituting 'arbitrary and unjustifiable discrimination', contrary to the chapeau's requirements. First, it determined that the US measure imposed a uniform, rigid requirement (adoption of essentially the same regulatory programme employed by the United States) on all other WTO Members wishing to export shrimp to the United States without inquiring into the programme's appropriateness for the conditions prevailing in those exporting countries.[85] Second, the United States failed to engage the complainants in 'serious, across-the-board negotiations' with the objective of concluding an international agreement for the protection of sea turtles—as it had with other WTO Members—before enforcing its import ban against them.[86] Third, the procedures followed by the US authorities

[78] *US-Shrimp* AB Report (n 5) para 159.

[79] Kleinlein (n 60) 1162, 1167; Niels Petersen, 'How Rational is International Law?' (2009) 20 EJIL 1247, 1257.

[80] Andrew Lang, *World Trade Law After Neoliberalism: Reimagining the Global Economic Order* (OUP 2011) 324.

[81] ibid.

[82] Mads Andenas and Stefan Zlepting, 'Proportionality: WTO Law–in Comparative Perspective' (2007) 42 Tex Int'l L J 371, 411–12.

[83] ibid.

[84] Lang (n 80) 323–24; Howse (n 6) 51–53.

[85] *US-Shrimp* AB Report (n 5) paras 162–64, 177.

[86] ibid, paras 166–72.

when deciding whether to grant certification to exporting countries were not transparent, did not afford affected states an opportunity to be heard, and provided no formal reasoned decision or procedure for appeal, thus resulting in a denial of 'basic fairness and due process' to the respective states.[87]

Significantly, then, the finding of the US measure as failing to meet the requirements of the chapeau of Article XX turned not on its substantive content but on various deficiencies in the procedures and operational features defining the context in which the regulatory measure was applied. This 'procedural turn', as several commentators have observed, constituted another jurisprudential strategy developed by the AB in response to the internal and external legitimacy challenges faced by the WTO and the DSS, which cases such as *US-Shrimp* had intensified.[88] As Lang has noted, '[p]rocedural review seems ... to be a necessary response to the legitimacy deficit of the WTO'.[89] Such a judicial review limits WTO intrusiveness and exhibits greater deference to regulating Members and the collective preferences of their societies, affording them the space to pursue their preferred substantive regulatory objectives. Moreover, in many instances, as in *US-Shrimp*, such procedural review results in Members being asked to fine-tune their WTO-inconsistent regulatory schemes through relatively technical, administrative adjustments without forcing them to make major, substantive changes in their chosen policy instruments.[90]

That said, while this kind of procedural review sends national regulators and domestic constituencies positive signals regarding their regulatory space, it simultaneously provides for strict judicial scrutiny of the design and decision-making processes underlying the domestic regulation, needed to prevent abuse of this policy space and of WTO exceptions for protectionist or discriminatory ends.[91] In so doing, the proceduralist review embraced by the AB reserves an appropriate role for the WTO and its DSS in orienting domestic regulation and serves to sustain the integrity of WTO rules and institutions.[92]

5.4 The Concluding 'Explanatory Paragraphs'

When seeking to trace the goal-attainment efforts of the WTO DSS in the *US-Shrimp* trade-and dispute, it is instructive to not only look at the *ratio decidendi* of the case (analysed above), but to also take a careful look at the paragraphs chosen by the AB to close its ruling in this case. As should be clear by now, although the

87 ibid, paras 178–84.
88 Lang (n 80) 326. See also Howse (n 6) 45, 51–53, 66–67.
89 Lang (n 80) 327.
90 Howse (n 6) 47, 52.
91 ibid 51–53; Andenas and Zlepting (n 82) 412.
92 Howse (n 6) 51–53; Lang (n 80) 327.

AB had considered the US trade-restrictive measure to be provisionally justified under Article XX(g), it nonetheless found that some aspects of the measure failed to meet the requirements of the Article XX chapeau. Therefore, the US defence under Article XX failed, meaning that its import ban, which violated GATT Article XI (the prohibition on quantitative restrictions), was ultimately not entitled the protection afforded by Article XX as a whole. Cognisant of the fact that this final legal outcome could be interpreted as yet another 'victory' of trade over the environment and might possibly generate negative legitimacy consequences for the WTO and its DSS, the AB chose to end its ruling in *US-Shrimp* with the two 'explanatory paragraphs' cited below. Using 'straightforward language' similar to that first seen in the trade-and dispute of *US-Gasoline*,[93] in these paragraphs, the AB went out of its way to emphasize 'the policy space for Members to enact environmental legislation and the limited nature of its ruling' in the case.[94] This language is worth quoting at length:

> In reaching these conclusions, we wish to underscore what we have *not* decided in this appeal. We have *not* decided that the protection and preservation of the environment is of no significance to the Members of the WTO. Clearly, it is. We have *not* decided that the sovereign nations that are Members of the WTO cannot adopt effective measures to protect endangered species, such as sea turtles. Clearly, they can and should. And we have not decided that sovereign states should *not* act together bilaterally, plurilaterally or multilaterally, either within the WTO or in other international fora, to protect endangered species or to otherwise protect the environment. Clearly, they should and do.
>
> What we *have* decided in this appeal is simply this: although the measure of the United States in dispute in this appeal serves an environmental objective that is recognized as legitimate under paragraph (g) of Article XX of the GATT 1994, this measure has been applied by the United States in a manner which constitutes arbitrary and unjustifiable discrimination between Members of the WTO, contrary to the requirements of the chapeau of Article XX. For all of the specific reasons outlined in this Report, this measure does not qualify for the exemption that Article XX of the GATT 1994 affords to measures which serve certain recognized, legitimate environmental purposes but which, at the same time, are not applied in a manner that constitutes a means of arbitrary or unjustifiable discrimination between countries where the same conditions prevail or a disguised restriction on international trade. As we emphasized in *United States–Gasoline*, WTO Members are free to adopt their own policies aimed at protecting the environment as long as, in so doing, they fulfill their obligations and respect the rights of other Members under the *WTO Agreement*.[95]

[93] *US-Gasoline* (n 3) 29–30.
[94] Van den Bossche and Zdouc (n 71) 582.
[95] *US-Shrimp* AB Report (n 5) paras 185–86 (emphasis original).

These 'explanatory paragraphs' illustrate the unique justificatory language chosen by the AB to close its ruling in *US-Shrimp*, language rarely resorted to in WTO jurisprudence and mainly seen in other trade-and disputes.[96] From a legal perspective, as several WTO practitioners stressed, these paragraphs constituted *obiter dicta* having no bearing on the legal conclusions already reached in the case.[97] That raises the question of what purpose were these paragraphs designed to serve. Responding to this question, WTO practitioners interviewed by the author unfolded the multifaceted legitimating objectives encapsulated in these 'political *obiter dicta*',[98] and the multiple audiences to which they were communicated.

Expression of Vertical and Horizontal Institutional Sensitivity

As discussed in the previous chapter, linkage disputes such as *US-Shrimp* often revolve around sensitive issues regarding the allocation of authority in multilevel governance.[99] Such issues, as significant factors in the complex legitimacy matrix facing the DSS in trade-and disputes, were especially prominent in *US-Shrimp*. This case called for the DSS to pass judgment on a national regulation located at the border between the WTO and international environmental law, thereby raising issues touching upon the vertical allocation of authority between states and international organizations, and the horizontal allocation of authority between adjacent international regimes. In such instances, it has been argued, in order to sustain confidence in the authority of the WTO and the DSS, WTO adjudicators must display 'institutional sensitivity' towards the regulating states whose measures are being reviewed as well as the international regimes having expertise and interest in the nontrade policy problems under discussion.[100]

This sort of institutional sensitivity may take, in turn, different stylistic and substantive forms, including: deference in treaty interpretation to other international norms and legal regimes relevant to or proficient in the disputed matter; expression

[96] See, e.g. *US-Gasoline* (n 3) 29–30; *China–Measures Affecting Trading Rights and Distribution Services for Certain Publications and Audiovisual Entertainment Products*, Report of the Appellate Body, 19 January 2010, WT/DS363/AB/R, para 335; *United States–Measures Affecting the Production and Sale of Clove Cigarettes*, Report of the Appellate Body, 24 April 2012, WT/DS406/AB/R, paras 235–36.

[97] Interview with WTO practitioner (Geneva, 16 July 2012) (noting that these explanatory paragraphs are 'for public consumption', whereas 'the legal decision is really made by that point'); interview with WTO legal officer (Geneva, 13 March 2012); telephone interview with former AB member (13 September 2012).

[98] 'Political obiter dicta' is the term used by Tulio Treves to describe 'legitimizing statements' used by international courts as tools to strengthen the legitimacy of their judgments and to make them 'more acceptable to the losing party and to public opinion'. Tullio Treves, 'Aspects of Legitimacy of Decisions of International Courts and Tribunals' in Rüdiger Wolfrum and Volker Röben (eds), *Legitimacy in International Law* (Springer 2008) 178.

[99] Kleinlein (n 60) 1170.

[100] ibid 1170–73; Robert Howse and Kalypso Nicolaidis, 'Enhancing WTO Legitimacy: Constitutionalization or Global Subsidiarity?' (2003) 16 Governance 73, 75; Howse (n 50) 62.

of respect for other global governance structures and for the regulatory autonomy of national governments; and adoption of less-intrusive standards of review or application of certain margins of appreciation in the examination of the regulatory decisions of national authorities.[101] Substantive elements of institutional sensitivity along these lines, as we have seen above, were featured in a number of the legitimacy-enhancing strategies utilized by the AB throughout the exercise of its interpretative powers in *US-Shrimp*. In the concluding explanatory paragraphs, however, this institutional sensitivity appears to have taken a more stylistic, rhetorical form. Thus, at the closing of its ruling, the AB articulated rather clearly its recognition of the regulatory right of 'sovereign nations that are Members of the WTO', the importance of 'protection and preservation of the environment' as policy objectives, and the desirability of interstate cooperation when promoting these objectives in 'other international fora', all the while stressing that its ruling against the United States is not to be read as negating any of the above.

When commenting on these statements, WTO practitioners exposed the underlying legitimatory rationale behind these expressions of vertical and horizontal institutional sensitivity and their salient 'political' aspect. Thus, an AB member serving during *US-Shrimp* conceptualized the 'kind of political language' introduced in the explanatory paragraphs as 'a sort of political caveat'. These paragraphs, he continued, were aimed at environmental organizations and, most particularly, 'for the US senate and the US House of Representatives' so as to show the WTO's 'political sensitivity' to the national regulator and to signal WTO adjudicators' reticence regarding 'stepping on the legislator's power'.[102] Another AB member sitting on the bench in *US-Shrimp* stated that these paragraphs were addressed, first and foremost, to Member governments as a means of declaring recognition of their regulatory rights, while adding that the need to introduce such unusual language into the judgment followed from the specific 'characteristics and … nature of the case'.[103] Finally, a WTO practitioner also involved in the proceedings similarly pointed to the associated 'political … and legitimacy concerns' that had led the AB to resort to such deferential language. He further stressed the horizontal dimension of institutional sensitivity embedded in these explanatory paragraphs, noting that although the AB 'never made grand pronouncements about the relationship between WTO law and international environmental law', it did show 'some degree of sensitivity concerning environmental issues' by using, inter alia, the sort of appeasing language found at the end of the *US-Shrimp* ruling.[104] This overt manifestation of institutional sensitivity on the part of the AB, it should be noted, marked a notable departure from previous practice of GATT/WTO panels, which had failed

[101] For a discussion of these various forms of institutional sensitivity, see, e.g. Howse and Nicolaidis (n 100) 87–88; Kleinlein (n 60) 1170–72; von Staden (n 59).

[102] Interview with former AB member (Geneva, 19 July 2012).

[103] Telephone interview with former AB member (13 September 2012).

[104] Interview with WTO practitioner (Geneva, 16 July 2012).

to perform such acts of political legitimation, rationalized by the idea that they were enforcing observance of a single value: free trade.[105]

An 'Explaining and Defending' Act of Legitimation

> [In] any case ... that comes before the WTO, [where] ... issues of health, environment ... are dealt with ... what the panel and the Appellate Body would have ... on their minds is also how their ... findings will be viewed by the broader epistemic community, the invisible colleagues out there. You don't write the panel report and the Appellate Body report only for the Members, certainly not in those cases. So that's why if you take some of the environmental cases like ... *Shrimps-Turtles*, you read the Appellate Body report and then at the very end of the report the Appellate Body says, 'Oh we want to emphasize that we have not decided that, we have not determined that a Member may not do [that]....' So there are messages, there are messages and for whom are these messages? These messages are not necessarily only for the Members. The messages are also for the ... NGO community out there that follows these proceedings very closely.[106]

The explanatory paragraphs in *US-Shrimp*, as this excerpt suggests, were not addressed solely to WTO Members or other international regimes as another means of expressing institutional sensitivity. They were, in fact, delivered to a broader audience—NGOs, anti-globalization activists, colleagues, and the general public—written as an 'explaining and defending' act of legitimation, needed to counter possible critiques of the DSS ruling and more general criticisms being levelled at the multilateral trade institutions at that time.[107] Such criticisms, it appears, forced the AB to engage in a direct justificatory discourse with extended circles of stakeholders, aimed at persuading them of the validity of its decision, the rules it interprets and applies, and the governance structure of which it is a part. The explanatory paragraphs in *US-Shrimp*, as the following testimony of a practitioner involved in the case suggests, should thus be viewed in a broader historical, political, and institutional context:

> [These paragraphs] are out there so that people see that they have considered these [environmental] issues and thought of these issues.... [I]t's for public

[105] Howse (n 50) 62.

[106] Interview with WTO legal officer (Geneva, 4 April 2012).

[107] cf Jens Steffek, 'The Legitimation of International Governance: A Discourse Approach' (2003) 9 EJIR 249, 250, 258, 269–70 (discussing legitimation by global governance institutions through 'explaining and defending' acts and engagement in a justificatory discourse with actors in civil society).

consumption.... They ... try to maintain their legitimacy. They show it in these politically sensitive issues. And don't forget, after the [*GATT*]-*Tuna* cases, people were in Geneva dressing up in Godzilla costumes ... showing the WTO to be a monstrous ... organization. And this created a great deal of hostility towards the GATT and the early WTO.[108]

A senior WTO official commented along similar lines: these paragraphs were addressed to 'the outside world'. They were inserted into the ruling for reasons related to the 'legitimacy of the WTO, to avoid having people say "Well, the Appellate Body.... they think trade is everything"'. These paragraphs are there '[t]o remind people, the nontrade people, that nontrade issues exist out there' and that we 'respect it'.[109]

Against this backdrop, the following statement, made by a senior WTO staff member officiating during the *Shrimp* case, aptly weaves together the various legitimatory dimensions and audiences targeted by the 'political *obiter dicta*' inserted at the end of the AB ruling:

Those are statements that I hate, as a lawyer, but I can see why they do it.... [I]n *Shrimp*, it was a very sort of explosive stuff, and at any moment you had people who were over-interpreting what the Appellate Body was doing, from the environmental community, so to say. So what's the intention when you see something like this: 'We are not saying this. We're only saying that'.... [T]he idea [is] to show how limited the reach of your decision is and that's extremely important. Again, in order to show [that] there is policy space, [and that] 'we are not anti-environmental'.... Courts are doing that all the time. The European Court [of Justice] also does that.... [In] all courts which are ... subject to ... very strong scrutiny from Member states, from society at large.... then you get this sort of defensive reasoning, 'We've only decided this, not that'.[110]

5.5 Conclusions

When describing the institutional goals underlying the AB's 'politically crafted' decision in *US-Shrimp*, a WTO practitioner involved in the case commented that:

All courts need to maintain legitimacy. They need to maintain some degree of public acceptance and approval ... and the *Shrimp* case ... fit[s] into the category of cases where the Appellate Body needed to craft a decision that was sensitive

[108] Interview with WTO practitioner (Geneva, 16 July 2012).
[109] Interview with WTO official (Geneva, 5 July 2012).
[110] Interview with former senior WTO official (Geneva, 17 July 2012).

to certain realities, and ... this goal was important to them, to maintain public approval and legitimacy, and stay within the boundaries of the law at the same time.[111]

The analysis presented in this chapter shows, indeed, how the heightened challenges to WTO and DSS legitimacy in this linkage dispute resulted in a unique assemblage of procedural, interpretive, and rhetorical judicial strategies by means of which the AB sought to deliver a decision that would sustain its two legitimization goals—legitimation of the contested authority of the WTO regime in tandem with legitimation of the DSS's own authority as an international court vis-à-vis audiences inside and outside the multilateral trade system. The specific judicial strategies employed, which are closely related to the internal and external legitimacy challenges evoked, and which mark a stark departure from previous GATT/WTO traditions, represent the AB's conscious choice to prioritize some judicial policies over others, the recourse to which may have better promoted other DSS goals.

It should be noted at this point that following the AB ruling in *US-Shrimp*, the United States introduced several changes to its regulatory programme along the lines laid out in the ruling. Dissatisfied with the implementation steps taken by the United States, Malaysia, one of the original complainants, initiated compliance review proceedings under Article 21.5 of the DSU.[112] As Howse has noted, in the face of the loud criticism of the AB ruling within the insider trade community, some believed that the AB 'would back off on this second round and find a way to close the door once again to environmentally based trade restrictions'.[113] Instead, the AB, this time joined by the panel,[114] found that the United States had appropriately addressed its concerns under the Article XX chapeau and thereby declared the revised US environmental regulation WTO-compliant, a step that brought the dispute to an end.

We are now in a better position to conclude that this outcome of compliance nonetheless tells us very little about the complex goal-attainment patterns and judicial mechanisms employed by the DSS in *US-Shrimp*, or how the systemic legitimacy challenges it confronted generated shifts towards some organizational goals rather than others along with trade-offs between the multiple objectives. This outcome tells even less about how the shifts in emphasis towards the DSS's legitimization goals, and the various jurisprudential techniques harnessed to the AB's quest for legitimacy (e.g. the use of teleological interpretations or less-intrusive proceduralist review) worked to facilitate achievement of the DSS's compliance

[111] Interview with WTO practitioner (Geneva, 16 July 2012).

[112] *United States–Import Prohibition of Certain Shrimp and Shrimp Products–Recourse to Article 21.5 of the DSU by Malaysia*, Report of the Appellate Body, 21 November 2001, WT/DS58/AB/RW.

[113] Howse (n 6) 42.

[114] *United States–Import Prohibition of Certain Shrimp and Shrimp Products–Recourse to Article 21.5 of the DSU by Malaysia*, Report of the Panel, 21 November 2001, WT/DS58/RW.

objective in this case. Clearly, an understanding of these goal-shifting trends, as well as of the mutually complementing and contradicting relationships marking DSS goals, is vital for assessing the system's operation and effectiveness in such a case. This is all the more so since, as the following chapter shows, the goal-attainment patterns observed in *US-Shrimp* were not a one-time event; similar patterns were followed in later trade-and disputes.

6

Legitimating Behind the Smoke Screen in the Battle Over Clove Cigarettes

As noted in Chapter 4, recent years have confronted the World Trade Organization (WTO) Dispute Settlement System (DSS) with an intense wave of complex linkage disputes, calling WTO adjudicators to scrutinize novel domestic policies in areas such as animal welfare, tobacco control, and climate change. Included in these cases is the famous *US-Clove Cigarettes* dispute, where the WTO-consistency of a US anti-tobacco regulation was legally challenged. This dispute, serving as the second case study in our investigation into the DSS's goal-attainment endeavours in the category of trade-and disputes, forms the subject of the analysis carried out in the present chapter. Before embarking on this analysis, however, we first review several prominent sites in the DSS's jurisprudence in trade-and disputes leading from the early *US-Shrimp* case, examined in Chapter 5, to the more recent *US-Clove Cigarettes* dispute, examined here. In so doing, we portray the continuum of which this latter dispute forms a part, a continuum that represents a long and enduring quest of the WTO DSS for legitimacy.

6.1 From *US-Shrimp* to *US-Clove Cigarettes*, and in Between

And so, the landmark *US-Shrimp* case constituted only the starting point in the search of the WTO DSS for legitimacy in trade-and disputes. As described below, this quest continued and evolved further in later jurisprudence, often exhibiting similar goal-attainment patterns to those identified in *US-Shrimp*, characterized by a notable shift in emphasis towards the DSS's legitimation objectives and a range of distinctive judicial strategies aimed at facilitating achievement of these objectives. Thus, following the path marked in *US-Shrimp*, WTO adjudicators pursued a similar expansive approach to the interpretation of WTO exceptions in subsequent jurisprudence, allowing a broad range of national regulatory measures to fall within their scope, an approach that secured greater policy space for Members and domestic constituencies in the protection of nontrade values.[1] For example, in line with the expansive interpretation of the environmental exception in *US-Shrimp*,

[1] Henrik Andersen, 'Protection of Non-Trade Values in WTO Appellate Body Jurisprudence: Exceptions, Economic Arguments, and Eluding Questions' (2015) 18 J Int'l Econ L 383, 399.

the Appellate Body (AB), in cases such as *US-Gambling*[2] and *China-Publications*,[3] endorsed a broad reading of the term 'the protection of public morals', one that would ensure the respect for national collective preferences under the public morals exception enshrined in Article XX(a) of the General Agreement on Tariffs and Trade (GATT) and Article XIV(a) of the General Agreement on Trade in Services (GATS).[4] This 'broad reading', as Howse has observed, 'appears to cross-cut all substantive fields of regulation, focusing on whether the measure in question is deemed by a given society to be derived from the fundamental beliefs or values of that society'.[5]

A comparable, rather expansive interpretive approach was also followed in cases such as *Korea-Beef*, *EC-Asbestos*, and *Brazil-Tyres*, where the AB moved to tone down the 'necessity' test included in several exceptions in GATT Article XX and its GATS counterpart. Thus, instead of the strict 'least trade-restrictive means' requirement of the old GATT, under which a trade-restrictive measure had to be indispensable to be considered 'necessary', the AB introduced a 'weighing-and-balancing' test[6] of 'the trade restrictiveness of the measure against the importance of the non-trade values at stake and the measure's effectiveness in pursuing those values'.[7] It has been argued that the introduction of this 'weighing-and-balancing' test embodied another step in the legitimation endeavour launched in *US-Shrimp*, by which the AB tried to relax the requirements of the general exceptions clause and incorporate into WTO law 'jurisprudential techniques to respond to the WTO's internal and external legitimacy crisis',[8] techniques that would show 'that the system is capable of handling problems of intersection'.[9] As a WTO official noted:

> *[US-]Shrimp* was one part of the process of the Appellate Body to rewrite the GATT jurisprudence on Article XX.... [W]hen you look at the jurisprudence on Article XX, in the whole exercise from *Gasoline* to ... *Korea-Beef* and all the like... the idea was, it will be easier to pass the tests under [the] sub-paragraphs of

[2] *United States–Measures Affecting the Cross-Border Supply of Gambling and Betting Services*, Report of the Appellate Body, 20 April 2005, WT/DS285/AB/R.

[3] *China–Measures Affecting Trading Rights and Distribution Services for Certain Publications and Audiovisual Entertainment Products*, Report of the Appellate Body, 19 January 2010, WT/DS363/AB/R.

[4] Robert Howse, 'The World Trade Organization 20 Years On: Global Governance by Judiciary' (2016) 27 EJIL 9, 62.

[5] ibid.

[6] See, e.g. *Korea–Measures Affecting Imports of Fresh, Chilled and Frozen Beef*, Report of the Appellate Body, 10 January 2001, WT/DS161/AB/R, WT/DS169/AB/R, paras 164, 166; *European Communities–Measures Affecting Asbestos and Asbestos-Containing Products*, Report of the Appellate Body, 5 April 2001, WT/DS135/AB/R, para 172; *China-Publications* (n 3) paras 239–42; *US-Gambling* (n 2) paras 304–08; *Brazil–Measures Affecting Imports of Retreaded Tyres*, Report of the Appellate Body, 17 December 2007, WT/DS332/AB/R, paras 178, 182, 210.

[7] Andrew Lang, *World Trade Law After Neoliberalism: Reimagining the Global Economic Order* (OUP 2011) 320–21.

[8] ibid 321–23.

[9] Interview with WTO practitioner (Geneva, 16 July 2012).

> [Article] XX.... So basically, the Appellate Body ... played a political role.... [I]t had to send a message to the countries that were in favour of environmental protection that 'yes, Article XX is operational', because the way it was interpreted in the GATT [era], basically, you could never meet the requirements of Article XX.[10]

In further elaborating on the legitimacy-related objective underlying the judicial exercise of broadening the scope of Article XX exceptions, the same WTO official stressed that this 'whole process of ... weakening the requirements to meet the first step of Article XX' was aimed 'to make the system acceptable'.[11] Along similar lines, other interviewees observed that the 'less strict perception of the rules' exhibited by the DSS in trade-and cases was triggered by a desire 'to put the WTO [in] a better position in ... global governance as a responsible organization that not only promotes a rule-based system for trade, but recognizes that there are other areas ... that are important for the international community and that deserve respect as well'.[12]

This is the place to note that while GATT Article XX has become a central site in the DSS's quest for legitimacy in trade-and disputes, this quest has transcended the bounds of the general exceptions clause, extending its reach to other GATT provisions[13] and WTO agreements, such as the Agreement on Sanitary and Phytosanitary Measures (SPS). Illustrative in this regard are the SPS disputes of *EC-Hormones* and *US-Continued Suspensions*, concerning the EU import ban on hormone-fed beef. In these consecutive cases, the AB opted for a range of judicial choices aimed at devising a more deferential framework for the discussion of competing trade and nontrade values, an approach that afforded a wider regulatory space for domestic decision-makers when instituting health-related SPS measures.[14] In the early *EC-Hormones*, for example, the AB relaxed the standard of review applied in proceedings under the SPS Agreement,[15] noting that this standard 'must reflect the balance established in that agreement between the jurisdictional competences conceded by the Members to the WTO and the jurisdictional competences retained by the Members for themselves'.[16] The AB also loosened the panel's interpretation of the risk assessment requirement of SPS Article 5.1 by allowing regulating states, inter alia, to base their trade-restrictive SPS measures on nonmainstream scientific opinion.[17] Highlighting the

[10] Interview with WTO official (Geneva, 22 March 2012).

[11] ibid.

[12] Interview with WTO ambassador and panellist (Geneva, 24 July 2012).

[13] See, e.g. Lang (n 7) 316–20 (discussing the legal developments in trade-and disputes with respect to GATT Articles I and III, which resulted in 'a less intrusive form of a regulatory oversight, and a greater degree of deference to domestic regulatory choices').

[14] Markus Wagner, 'Regulatory Space in International Trade Law and International Investment Law' (2014) 36 U Pa J Int'l L 1, 56–61.

[15] Lang (n 7) 339.

[16] *European Communities–Measures Concerning Meat and Meat Products (Hormones)*, Report of the Appellate Body, 13 February 1998, WT/DS26/AB/R, WT/DS48/AB/R, para 115.

[17] ibid, para 194.

legitimating element captured in these judicial choices, a former WTO official involved in *EC-Hormones* noted:

> [T]hey were young, they wanted to control their legitimacy, they didn't want to be seen as the trade-only-body that strikes down a major health measure. At the same time, they did strike down [the EU import ban], but on narrow grounds, and in a way that was perhaps more acceptable to the EU.[18]

Yet, in the second round of *EC-Hormones* (known as *US-Continued Suspension)*, the AB 'took it a step further ... [toward] giving more leeway to regulating countries'.[19] On this occasion, the AB seized the opportunity to further refine the deferential standard of review applicable to SPS trade-and disputes,[20] as well as to introduce a rather deferential threshold for Members interested in adopting provisional trade-restrictive SPS measures.[21] An EU official involved in the *Hormones* saga interestingly conceptualized 'the willingness of the Appellate Body as manifested in *Continued Suspension* to address nontrade concerns' as 'a signal to the outside world ... [that] "we are not a ... body that only cares about trade. We ... have a holistic view ... we know that this is important and we will give it ... as much room as possible under the system".... [I]t was ... a signal ... which is important for such a case'.[22]

In addition, on the procedural front, the AB (and the panel) in *US-Continued Suspension* decided to allow public observation of WTO judicial hearings for the first time.[23] Hence, despite the resistance of many third parties and the lack of consensus on this matter in the Dispute Settlement Understanding (DSU) review process, the AB found a basis in this high-profile dispute for opening up WTO hearings to the public upon the parties' request, thereby bringing to an end 'the consistent practice of sixty years of GATT/WTO dispute settlement conducted behind closed doors'.[24] While Article 17.10 of the DSU states that the appellate proceedings 'shall be confidential', the AB circumvented this confidentiality requirement by observing that this requirement is 'relative' and 'has its limits' and

[18] Interview with former WTO official (Geneva, 30 March 2012).

[19] Interview with WTO practitioner (Geneva, 30 March 2012).

[20] *United States–Continued Suspension of Obligations in the EC–Hormones Dispute*, Report of the Appellate Body, 14 November 2008, WT/DS320/AB/R, paras 587–617. This point was stressed by several interviewees: interview with WTO official (Geneva, 18 April 2012); interview with WTO official (Geneva, 28 March 2012); interview with EU Official (Brussels, 18 July 2012).

[21] *US-Continued Suspension* (n 20) paras 683–726. For a discussion of this issue, see Sungjoon Cho, 'United States–Continued Suspension of Obligations in the EC-Hormones Dispute' (2009) 103 AJIL 299, 303.

[22] Interview with former EU official (Geneva, 9 July 2012).

[23] *US-Continued Suspension* (n 20) Annex IV, para 11.

[24] Lothar Ehring, 'Public Access to Dispute Settlement Hearings in the World Trade Organization' (2008) 11 J Int'l Econ L 1021, 1021–22.

that it is within the AB's authority (*compétence de la compétence*) to lift confidentiality at the request of the participants.[25]

Against the background of criticism levelled at the WTO's nontransparent decision-making processes by civil society actors, opening WTO hearings to the public formed another step forward in strengthening WTO and DSS 'legitimacy and credibility' in the eyes of external constituencies.[26] Like the procedural development concerning *amicus curiae* briefs (see Chapter 5), opening WTO judicial proceedings to public observation carried the promise of making 'the proceedings appear to be more transparent and legalistic and thus (potentially) less objectionable'.[27] Moreover, by allowing public hearings the DSS enabled relevant stakeholders from outside the WTO (e.g. civil society representatives, journalists and individual citizens) to gain access to WTO proceedings, broaden their knowledge of these proceedings, and follow WTO disputes more closely than they otherwise could.[28] In these respects, the open hearings procedure thus offered a way to connect WTO judicial decision-making to affected actors beyond WTO Members, actors whose trust and confidence in the WTO and the DSS have become vital in order for the latter institutions to sustain their claim to legitimacy.

Finally, much like in *US-Shrimp*, the shift in emphasis towards the DSS's legitimization goals in the trade-and cases that followed was reflected in the embrace by WTO adjudicators of a distinctive rhetorical style. This rhetoric was aimed at conveying institutional sensitivity to Member governments and respect for the nontrade values pursued, often by reiterating the 'mantra'[29] regarding the right 'of a WTO Member to set the public health or environmental objectives it seeks to achieve, as well as the level of protection that it wants to obtain, through the measure or the policy it chooses to adopt'.[30] As several interviewees explained, when using this type of deferential language, WTO adjudicators are essentially 'choosing words in the interpretive exercise that communicate to the [WTO] membership' their recognition of the policy space left for Members under the WTO agreements,[31] and that 'the interpreter of the law' understands the importance of the nontrade goals at stake.[32] In further elucidating the rationale underlying these distinctive statements, a WTO practitioner noted:

> [A]s a matter of governance ... they are critical.... To be legitimate ... the dispute settlement system ... has to be able to communicate to Members that ... your

[25] *US-Continued Suspension* (n 20) Annex IV, paras 5–7.

[26] Ehring (n 24) 1023–24.

[27] Gregory Shaffer, Manfred Elsig, and Sergio Puig, 'The Extensive (but Fragile) Authority of the WTO Appellate Body' (2016) 79 L & Contemp Probs 237, 255.

[28] ibid.

[29] Joseph H H Weiler, 'Comment: Brazil–Measures Affecting Imports of Retreaded Tyres (DS332): Prepared for the ALI Project on the Case Law of the WTO' (2009) 8 World Trade Rev 137, 139.

[30] *Brazil-Tyres* (n 6) para 140. See also *US-Gambling* (n 2) paras 304–11; *Korea-Beef* (n 6) para 176; *EC-Hormones* (n 16) paras 104, 171–72.

[31] Interview with private attorney (Geneva, 23 April 2012).

[32] Interview with WTO legal officer (Geneva, 13 March 2012).

> nontrade aspirations can be set at a very high level and you can pursue nontrade related objectives ... that is for governance ... incredibly important.... [T]hat ... is ... important for credibility and legitimacy purposes.... But ... legally, could you come to the same conclusion without communicating to responding Members that they have a bit more flexibility? Sure, of course, you could....[33]

Yet, while many of the jurisprudential and rhetorical legitimacy-enhancing strategies enumerated here have been repeated in various trade-and disputes since *US-Shrimp*, reactions to selected strategies in some quarters of the WTO membership have led the AB to recraft some of its techniques so as to not compromise the DSS's internal legitimacy within the multilateral trade regime. This was the case, for example, in the attempt to shape a more participatory and externally accountable WTO judicial process through the precedential decision on *amicus* briefs in *US-Shrimp*, for which the AB was accused of exceeding its authority and disregarding 'the jurisdictional limits agreed [upon] by Members' in the DSU.[34] The outcry generated by this 'illegitimate' act of judicial activism among some Members reached its apex in *EC-Asbestos*,[35] which enmeshed the DSS in a legitimacy quandary involving internal and external pressures that were pulling in opposite directions. From *within* the WTO, many Member governments insisted on preserving the diplomatic and interstate nature of the DSS 'so as to enhance their "control" over it'. From *outside* the multilateral trade setting, nongovernmental organizations (NGOs) and civil society actors urged the system to become more open and transparent.[36]

Following these events, the AB has since been rather cautious in its approach to *amicus curiae* submissions.[37] On the one hand, the AB has never repudiated its power to accept *amicus* briefs, and its continuing acceptance of such briefs attests to its support of this practice.[38] Also, while the AB has never formally referenced *amicus* briefs in its rulings, commentators indicate that 'the AB reads them and thus is subject to the persuasive force they might have'.[39] On the other hand, given the opacity that characterizes the AB's treatment of *amicus* submissions and the frequent statements claiming that it did not find it 'necessary' to rely on them when rendering its rulings, it is hard to get a clear view as to how *amicus* briefs

[33] Interview with private attorney (Geneva, 23 April 2012).

[34] DSB, Minutes of Meeting of 6 November 1998 (14 December 1998) WT/DSB/M/50, 5, 10 [hereinafter DSB Minutes 1998].

[35] See General Council, Minutes of Meeting of 22 November 2000 (23 January 2001) WT/GC/M/60.

[36] Debra P Steger, 'The Struggle for Legitimacy in the WTO' in John M Curtis and Dan Ciuriak (eds), *Trade Policy Research* (Department of Foreign Affairs and International Trade 2003) 122–23.

[37] Maria Perez-Esteve, 'WTO Rules and Practices for Transparency and Engagement with Civil Society Organizations' (2012) WTO Staff Working Paper ERSD-2012-14, 23 <https://www.wto.org/english/res_e/reser_e/ersd201214_e.htm> accessed 30 December 2018.

[38] Shaffer, Elsig, and Puig (n 27) 254.

[39] ibid.

actually influence the outcomes of WTO disputes.[40] This resulting duality in the AB's approach to *amicus curiae* briefs reflects its fragility as an international court when trying to attain multiple competing organizational goals, in this instance, the goals of conferring legitimacy on the DSS and the WTO amidst external constituencies, while simultaneously sustaining the DSS's internal legitimacy among its mandate providers, WTO Members. It appears that the attempt to promote the former objectives has come at the price of hindering attainment of the latter, thus requiring the AB to reassess and recalibrate the trade-offs between its conflicting institutional goals.

Recourse to non–WTO international law sources of the kind observed in *US-Shrimp*—where the AB addressed several international environmental instruments under its analysis of GATT Article XX—also aroused opposition among some WTO Members. Through such references, as seen in Chapter 5, the AB sought to convey to Members and external audiences its awareness of current environmental issues and its sensitivity to the social values those instruments were meant to protect. Yet, these same references were viewed by some WTO Members as going beyond the AB's mandate, which they saw as confined to WTO law.[41] Such reactions from within the 'institution' have consequently led the AB to fine-tune its approach to non–WTO law sources. As Lang has noted: 'aware of their fragile legitimacy—and of the need to maintain the support of WTO Members', WTO adjudicators have taken a more cautious stance towards non–WTO sources in later trade-and cases that have reached their docket,[42] such as the *US-Clove Cigarettes* case, discussed below.

And so, two decades into their existence, as we shall see, the continuous flow of trade-and disputes keeps posing complex legitimacy quandaries and challenges before the WTO and its DSS. While the heated winds of Seattle and the mass protests against the WTO have subsided, legitimacy concerns have not.[43] Infused by the enduring gridlock in the WTO's legislative arm, the continuing contestation over neoliberal economic globalization (demonstrated in recent political developments in Europe and the United States), and the emergence of new trade-and issues, the DSS's prolonged quest for legitimacy in trade-and disputes has ventured in turn into new, unexplored terrains. Such was the case in *US-Clove-Cigarettes*, to which the remainder of this chapter is devoted.

[40] Gabrielle Marceau and Mikella Hurley, 'Transparency and Public Participation: A Report Card on WTO Transparency Mechanisms' (2012) 4 Trade L & Dev 19, 33–34. For a recent study addressing the question of the acceptance and consideration of *amicus* submissions by WTO panels and the AB, see Theresa Squatrito, 'Amicus Curiae Briefs in the WTO DSM: Good or Bad News for Non-State Actor Involvement?' (2018) 17 World Trade Rev 65.

[41] See, e.g. DSB Minutes 1998 (n 34) 14.

[42] Lang (n 7) 150–53.

[43] William J Davey, 'The WTO and Rules-Based Dispute Settlement: Historical Evolution, Operational Success, and Future Challenges' (2014) 17 J Int'l Econ L 679, 690.

The chapter proceeds as follows. Section 6.2 lays down the basic facts of *US-Clove Cigarettes* and recounts the intricate legitimacy setting in which the dispute unfolded. Against this backdrop, Sections 6.3–6.5 turn to an in-depth, goal-oriented analysis of the judicial effort carried out by the WTO DSS in this case. They show how the intensified legitimacy concerns aroused shaped the organizational goals pursued by the DSS and uncover the ways in which these concerns were woven into the interpretative and rhetorical choices made by WTO adjudicators in their strategic judicial space. Section 6.6 concludes while linking the goal-attainment efforts identified to the broader DSS goal-based effectiveness framework advanced in the book.

6.2 *US-Clove Cigarettes*: Facts, Context, and Legitimacy-Related Misgivings

The Facts

At issue in *US-Clove Cigarettes* was a novel US anti-tobacco regulation prohibiting flavoured cigarettes, other than tobacco or menthol.[44] Underlying this regulation—with similar measures recently adopted by other WTO Members—was the goal of protecting human health and reducing youth smoking as flavoured cigarettes make it easier for new smokers to acquire the habit by masking tobacco's unpleasant flavour. Yet, while clove cigarettes, mainly imported from Indonesia, fell under the ban, menthol cigarettes, mostly manufactured in the United States, were excluded. Prior to the US regulation's entry into force in September 2009, clove cigarettes accounted for 0.1 per cent of the US market, while menthol cigarettes were used by a quarter of the US smoking population.

In 2010, Indonesia filed a complaint against the United States before the WTO DSS, challenging the consistency of its tobacco-control regulation with both Article 2.1 and Article 2.2 of the Technical Barriers to Trade (TBT) Agreement.[45] In a finding that was not appealed before the AB, the *US-Clove Cigarettes* panel rejected Indonesia's claim under TBT Article 2.2, concluding that the US regulation was not more trade-restrictive than necessary to achieve its health objective. Yet both the panel and the AB found the US regulation to infringe the national treatment rule enshrined in TBT Article 2.1 by according less favourable treatment to imported clove cigarettes than to like menthol cigarettes of US origin. For the purposes of this book, however, no less important than this finding of a TBT violation is the way in which it was reached. Below I explore the route taken in detail,

[44] *United States–Measures Affecting the Production and Sale of Clove Cigarettes*, Report of the Appellate Body, 24 April 2012, WT/DS406/AB/R [*US-Clove Cigarettes* AB Report].

[45] Agreement on Technical Barriers to Trade Agreement, 15 April 1994, 1868 UNTS 120.

beginning with a portrait of the complex setting in which *US-Clove Cigarettes* unfolded, and which largely shaped the DSS's operation, judicial choices, and goal-attainment efforts in this case.

The Intricate Legitimacy Setting

US-Clove Cigarettes was one of three simultaneous cases brought against the United States under the TBT Agreement (the other two being *US-Tuna II*[46] and *US-COOL*[47]). Although it was presented in 2010 before a well-oiled adjudicating system with a substantive body of jurisprudence, including on trade-and issues, this case confronted the DSS with several systemic challenges. These challenges included but went beyond the need for coherence in adjudication along the concurrent TBT conflicts,[48] or the need to address legal issues of first impression with respect to core substantive provisions of the TBT Agreement.[49] Above all, as seen below, these challenges were ingrained in the 'nontrade' elements underlying the conflict and the legitimacy concerns attendant thereto.[50]

In the years that have passed since *US-Shrimp, Korea-Beef, EC-Asbestos, Brazil-Tyres*, and the like, the 'balancing' lexicon established in *US-Shrimp* seems to have become pervasive among WTO officials and state delegates alike, all of whom conceptualized the primary challenge featuring *US-Clove Cigarettes* as that of striking a balance between the trade interests and health policy at stake.[51] Thus, an AB member depicted the main challenge in *US-Clove Cigarettes* as:

> [C]learly to strike the correct balance between, on the one hand, the right of Members to have ... legislation pursuing certain nontrade related policy objectives, and on the other hand, the right of other Members ... to be protected from ... having to face trade restrictions.... [I]n that particular kind of case, the difficult task of the panel and the Appellate Body is to strike the right balance.[52]

[46] *United States–Measures Concerning the Importation, Marketing and Sale of Tuna and Tuna Products*, Report of the Appellate Body, 13 June 2012, WT/DS381/AB/R.
[47] *United States–Certain Country of Origin Labeling (COOL) Requirements*, Report of the Appellate Body, 23 July 2012, WT/DS384/AB/R, WT/DS386/AB/R.
[48] Interview with WTO legal officer (Geneva, 13 March 2012); interview with WTO panellist (Geneva, 24 July 2012).
[49] Gabrielle Marceau, 'The New TBT Jurisprudence in US-Clove Cigarettes, WTO US-Tuna II and US-COOL' (2013) 8 Asian J WTO & Int'l Health L & Pol'y 1, 6.
[50] See, e.g. interview with WTO panellist (Geneva, 24 July 2012); interview with US official (Geneva, 17 July 2012).
[51] See, e.g. interview with staff member of the AB Secretariat (Geneva, 4 July 2012); interview with WTO official (Geneva, 26 March 2012); interview with EU official (Brussels, 19 July 2012).
[52] Interview with AB member (Geneva, 27 April 2012).

The same AB member went on to emphasize:

> That balance is not our invention, that balance is in the agreements ... that balance is, by necessity, formulated in a very abstract and general way, and that has to be given meaning in a particular factual context. And these [trade-and cases] are very ... important because often they are very controversial, very political, sensitive cases.[53]

In acknowledging the complexity of this balancing act, the quoted AB member further observed that the balancing inherent to trade-and disputes 'is not a mathematical exercise. There is a judgment call that comes in, [which is] not arbitrary at all, but there is ... a judgment call that comes in ....'[54] It is exactly this 'judgment call', discussed previously in Chapter 4, that shifts cases such as *US-Clove Cigarettes* from the purely legal domain and invites challenges to WTO DSS legitimacy.

In our interviews, several other WTO practitioners echoed this same point. Thus, a state official involved in *US-Clove Cigarettes* noted that the mission entrusted to the DSS in cases of this type essentially asks the adjudicators to weigh interests that are not comparable, thereby transforming the balancing process into a rather subjective exercise in which one can never fully eliminate political judgments.[55] As a result:

> [T]he poor old judge is put before a political question and most judges, who are good judges, don't like that. They don't want to be there because to them ... [there] is the science and the art of judging, but they prefer the science.... And yet, the legislator, the horrible legislator, has sent them that problem, because ... the problem is in the treaty.... And the horrible legislator has sent to the judge what is a political problem ... [yet] nobody elected the judge and the judge is sitting there thinking, 'Well, what am I gonna do with this?'[56]

In this state of affairs, noted the same official, the DSS in *US-Clove Cigarettes*, as in other trade-and cases, faced the challenge of finding a reasonable solution to the trade-and puzzle before it without politicizing the judicial office[57]—an obviously daunting task.

In addition to the need to strike a balance between trade liberalization and Members' right to regulate, and the risk of judicial politicization associated therewith, a related legitimacy challenge raised in *US-Clove Cigarettes* concerned the *diversity* of WTO Members among which this judicial balancing exercise had to

[53] ibid. See also interview with AB Secretariat staff member (Geneva, 4 July 2012).
[54] Interview with AB member (Geneva, 27 April 2012).
[55] Interview with EU official (Brussels, 19 July 2012).
[56] ibid.
[57] ibid.

take place. WTO Members, as several interviewees stressed, do not share a unified view of how authority should be allocated between the international and national levels, and how much regulatory space ought to be left for Member governments.[58] While some WTO Members appear to expect 'a very ... narrow reading' of the notion of regulatory autonomy, fearing the 'nontrade influence' over their own economic interests,[59] others seem to expect WTO adjudicators to be rather deferential to regulating Members in cases involving nontrade policies such as *US-Clove Cigarettes*; they tend to stress that it is not the job of the adjudicators 'to intervene and tell the defending Member that it has got its politics wrong'.[60] In a similar spirit, an AB member stated that there is no consensus among WTO Members as to where exactly the balance should be struck with respect to trade-and problems. This state of play, the same AB member explained, leaves WTO adjudicators 'in the uncomfortable position of ... having to strike the balance' while staying 'within the limits' of interpretation of the treaty text, yet, at the same time, allowing 'that balance [to] shift' over time.[61] In the interstices between these contradictory expectations, we therefore find the heightened internal legitimacy challenges vis-à-vis Member governments encountered by the DSS in *US-Clove Cigarettes*.

However, parallel to these internal challenges, external legitimacy threats to the WTO and its DSS, posed by stakeholders outside the trading regime, at both the domestic and global levels, were no less prominent in this case. As it happened, timing was a crucial ingredient in *US-Clove Cigarettes*. This sensitive dispute had arisen in the midst of an intensifying worldwide anti-tobacco movement that, in the face of the global expansion of tobacco products (facilitated by trade agreements mandating the removal of import taxes and other commercial restrictions), had led to various initiatives for tobacco product regulation by national legislatures, as well as to the internationalization of tobacco-control efforts.[62] Chief among these efforts is the World Health Organization (WHO) Framework Convention on Tobacco Control (FCTC),[63] which aims 'to reduce continually and substantially the prevalence of tobacco use and exposure to tobacco smoke'. The Convention came into force in 2005; by the time *US-Clove Cigarettes* was adjudicated, the Convention had 172 Parties.[64] In addition, guidelines adopted under the

[58] Interview with senior WTO official and former state official (Geneva, 25 April 2012); interview with EU official (Brussels, 19 July 2012); interview with private attorney and former EU official (Geneva, 9 July 2012).

[59] Interview with senior WTO official and former state official (Geneva, 25 April 2012).

[60] Interview with EU official (Brussels, 19 July 2012). Other interviewees also emphasized the enhanced expectations of Members for respect towards their regulatory discretion in trade-and disputes: interview with US official (Geneva, 17 July 2012); interview with WTO ambassador (Geneva, 24 July 2012); interview with senior WTO official and former state official (Geneva, 25 April 2012).

[61] Interview with AB member (Geneva, 27 April 2012).

[62] Sergio Puig, 'Tobacco Litigation in International Courts' (2016) 57 Harv Int'l LJ 383, 388–91.

[63] WHO Framework Convention on Tobacco Control, adopted 21 May 2003, 2302 UNTS 166.

[64] *United States–Measures Affecting the Production and Sale of Clove Cigarettes*, Report of the Panel, 24 April 2012, WT/DS406/R, para 2.29 [*US-Clove Cigarettes* Panel Report].

WHO FCTC in 2010 specifically called for its Parties to introduce national regulation limiting the use of ingredients such as flavouring agents, which make tobacco products more attractive.[65] Crucially, because the WHO FCTC and its accompanying guidelines provide rules for regulating the production, sale, distribution, advertisement, and taxation of tobacco, they have the potential for intersecting with WTO agreements.[66]

The embeddedness of *US-Clove Cigarettes* in this broader network of international and national tobacco-control activities inevitably implicated the interests of yet another international organization, the WHO, as well as those of NGOs and domestic constituencies around the world (in the United States and other states having similar regulatory measures in place). When alluding to trade-and cases such as *US-Clove Cigarettes* against this background, one AB member noted that: 'There is no doubt about the fact that the legitimacy [of the WTO system] ... can possibly be questioned on a society-wide basis ... in the type of cases that concern all the [nontrade] societal values and interests', and that in such cases 'that risk is much bigger than in cases which relate to trade remedies', for example.[67]

Heightened legitimacy concerns, arising within and outside the WTO, therefore constituted the point of departure for the DSS's judicial act in *US-Clove Cigarettes*. As shown below, they led the AB (and the panel as well) to adapt its goal-attainment efforts accordingly by shifting emphasis towards the DSS's legitimation objectives and, to these ends, recalibrating the interpretative strategies applied, the choice of rhetoric used, and the final output delivered.

6.3 The Legitimating Interpretative Endeavours Under the TBT Agreement

As far as the basic functions carried out by the WTO DSS are concerned, *US-Clove Cigarettes* was like any other WTO case in which the panel and the AB were involved in the judicial exercise of interpreting the respective WTO agreements and applying the law to the facts at hand in order to promote the DSS's multiple organizational goals, among them dispute resolution and rule compliance.[68] As a

[65] Partial Guidelines for Implementation of Articles 9 and 10 of the WHO Framework Convention on Tobacco Control <http://www.who.int/fctc/protocol/guidelines/adopted/article_9and10/en/index.html> accessed 30 December 2018.

[66] Benn McGrady and Alexandra Jones, 'Tobacco Control and Beyond: The Broader Implications of United States-Clove Cigarettes for Non-Communicable Diseases' (2013) 39 Am JL & Med 265.

[67] Interview with AB member (Geneva, 27 April 2012). See also interview with staff member of the AB Secretariat (Geneva, 4 July 2012); interview with WTO panellist (Geneva, 24 July 2012).

[68] Interview with WTO legal officer (Geneva, 13 March 2012); interview with staff member of the AB Secretariat (Geneva, 4 July 2012); interview with WTO panellist (Geneva, 24 July 2012).

panellist sitting on the bench in this case noted: '[A]t the very end, our decision was a legal decision.... [P]anellists should not depart from that. We are examining [the] rights and ... obligations of the parties' under the WTO agreements. At the same time, he stressed that in the specific case:

> [W]e were *cautious with regards to the reasoning and the explanations* and put *extra care* in[to] how ... [the decision] was explained, because we knew very well that behind the [US] policy there was a very important public ... objective, and ... a lot has been said and has been written about [the] WTO and its approach to certain areas of administration such as ... public health [and the] environment.... So, it is very delicate.[69]

Substantiating this comment is another, made by an AB member, who argued that the way to handle the intensified 'risk' to the legitimacy of the DSS and the WTO in a case like *US-Clove Cigarettes*, is 'to be very aware of ... the danger, and to interpret ... very carefully'. Yet, he went on, the legal interpretations available to WTO adjudicators are constrained by the text of the WTO agreements and by the DSS's mandate, stressing that 'if ... we would go in our interpretation of the obligations ... beyond what you can reasonably read into the provisions' then another 'legitimacy problem' would emerge (i.e. vis-à-vis WTO Member states, the mandate providers).[70]

Finally, the following testimony sheds further light on the quandaries of the judicial exercise in which the AB was involved in *US-Clove Cigarettes*. In this as in all other cases, a staff member of the AB Secretariat stated, the AB was engaged in the judicial task of treaty interpretation.[71] Despite the AB's awareness of the potential policy impacts of its decision in trade-and disputes such as *US-Clove Cigarettes*, 'the AB does not make policy', 'this is what the negotiators do'; the AB 'interprets the law' and 'would never overlook the treaty provisions'.[72] At the same time, the same staff member added, 'the broader the interpretative leeway available to the adjudicators in the treaty text in this type of case, the more such policy considerations come into play'.[73] It is exactly at this junction within the strategic judicial space, I maintain, that one can identify the choices made in *US-Clove Cigarettes* between the DSS's multiple organizational goals and the way in which the adjudicators' interpretative powers were harnessed to tackling the systemic legitimacy challenges just portrayed.

[69] Interview with WTO panellist (Geneva, 24 July 2012) (emphasis added).
[70] Interview with AB member (Geneva, 27 April 2012).
[71] Interview with staff member of the AB Secretariat (Geneva, 4 July 2012).
[72] ibid.
[73] ibid.

Introducing the Balancing Approach to the TBT Agreement

Any inquiry into the enhanced judicial efforts aimed at conferring legitimacy upon the multilateral trade rules and institutions made in *US-Clove Cigarettes* ought to start from the broader legal discourse in which the AB's analysis was later on embedded. In setting the stage for its examination of the US tobacco regulation under TBT Article 2.1, the AB first framed the legal discussion under the TBT Agreement in terms of *balance*, thereby incorporating the balancing approach originally developed within the framework of GATT Article XX into the TBT Agreement. Thus, after declaring its willingness 'to make some observations of general import' on the preamble of the TBT Agreement,[74] the AB commenced its analysis with a reference to the preamble's fifth recital, which states the 'desire' of WTO Members 'to ensure that technical regulations and standards . . . do not create unnecessary obstacles to international trade'. This recital, the AB observed, 'reflects the trade-liberalization objective of the *TBT Agreement*'.[75] Yet, the AB added, this trade liberalization goal 'is qualified in the sixth recital', which explicitly acknowledges 'Members' right to regulate in order to pursue certain legitimate objectives'.[76] This recital, the AB elaborated, *counterbalances* 'the trade-liberalization objective expressed in the fifth recital'; it ' "recognizes" Members' right to regulate versus the "desire" to avoid creating unnecessary obstacles to international trade . . .'.[77]

The choice of the AB—known for its strict textual approach to treaty interpretation—to begin the legal analysis in *US-Clove Cigarettes* with a teleological account of the TBT Agreement was not accidental. By articulating the Agreement's underlying goals, the AB effectively declared the normative preferences it attributed to the rules enshrined in this Agreement, and contextualized its later reasoning within the broader value system of the legal order in which it operated.[78] It thereby set the stage for a substantive discussion of TBT Article 2.1, described below. Importantly, as Maduro has generally noted with respect to the kind of teleological reasoning displayed by the AB:

> While teleological reasoning favors a debate among alternative normative preferences in the interpretation of a rule, a simple appeal to text would hide those alternatives and preclude a debate. Teleological reasoning fosters the conditions

[74] *US-Clove Cigarettes* AB Report (n 44) paras 88–89.
[75] ibid, para 92 (emphasis original).
[76] ibid, para 94.
[77] ibid, para 95.
[78] cf Miguel P Maduro, 'Courts and Pluralism: Essay on a Theory of Judicial Adjudication in the Context of Legal and Constitutional Pluralism' in Jeffrey L Dunoff and Joel P Trachtman (eds), *Ruling the World?: Constitutionalism, International Law, and Global Governance* (CUP 2009) 368–69 (noting that teleological interpretation forces 'courts to articulate the normative preferences they attribute to the particular rules and to relate them to the normative preferences of the overall legal order'. Maduro further argues that 'by articulating the normative goals of rules and their connection to the overall value system of their legal order, courts set the stage for a substantive discussion').

necessary for such a debate in which the plurality of actors of the community of judicial discourse can participate.[79]

Hence, by articulating the diverse normative preferences embedded in the TBT Agreement—i.e. by juxtaposing the goal of 'trade liberalization' with 'Members' right to regulate'—the AB located the fundamental trade liberalization objective of the WTO regime in the broader context of competing social values and set the conditions necessary for a more-inclusive legal discourse and deliberation.

Furthermore, by framing the interplay between the above-mentioned goals of 'trade liberalization' and 'state regulatory autonomy' in terms of 'balance'—a notion absent from the TBT preamble—the AB chose to follow the legitimation path marked in earlier trade-and disputes such as *US-Shrimp, Korea-Beef*, and *US-Gambling*. Notably, although a balance between competing interests lies at the foundation of all WTO agreements, the balancing discourse, just extended to the TBT Agreement, appears to be used by WTO adjudicators primarily in trade-and disputes.[80] This tendency, as explained in Chapter 5, rests, in part, on the legitimizing attributes associated with the balancing concept and the importance of a balancing approach for the acceptability and legitimacy of processes involving adjudication between competing social values.

Against this background, the formulation of 'the object and purpose of the TBT Agreement' as 'to strike a balance between ... the objective of trade liberalization and ... Members' right to regulate'[81] constituted the first step in the AB's endeavours aimed at legitimizing the authority and outcome of the WTO and the DSS once it entered the *US-Clove Cigarettes* proceedings. With the balancing concept in mind, the AB proceeded to examine the consistency of the US regulation with the TBT's national treatment obligation. We return to the significance of balancing and its role in the context of *US-Clove Cigarettes* later below.

Bridging the Gap Created by the Missing General Exceptions Clause: Introduction of 'Legitimate Regulatory Distinctions' to TBT Article 2.1

Article 2.1 of the TBT Agreement anchors the TBT 'version' of the basic WTO 'national treatment' rule. This article—the language of which closely mirrors that of

[79] ibid 369.

[80] See interview with staff member of the AB Secretariat (Geneva, 4 July 2012) (noting that balance is part of all WTO agreements, even the Anti-dumping Agreement; yet, the issue is more prominent in agreements that implicate nontrade values); interview with US official (Geneva, 17 July 2012) (alluding to the prevalence of the balancing concept in trade-and cases, while noting that the introduction of this concept is partly a response to 'a broader discussion outside the dispute settlement system ... about the need to balance' trade with other societal objectives); interview with EU official (Brussels, 19 July 2012).

[81] *US-Clove Cigarettes* AB Report (n 44) para 174.

GATT Article III:4 national treatment provision—requires Members to ensure that their technical regulations accord 'products imported from the territory of any Member ... treatment no less favourable than that accorded to like products of national origin'. Yet, unlike the GATT trade rules, which are subject to possible derogations under Article XX, the TBT Agreement lacks a comparable exceptions clause that may justify TBT violations in the pursuit of legitimate nontrade policy objectives.[82] Clearly, such legal rigidity may severely restrict the regulatory space left for Members under the TBT Agreement and thereby undermine the legitimacy of WTO norms and the body designed to enforce them. As Franck has noted, a rule without exculpatory exception, even if clear, may appear illegitimate by producing results that are viewed as unjust, cavalier, unfair or absurd.[83] The potential implications of this legal arrangement for the internal and external legitimacy of the DSS and its overarching regime were clear to WTO adjudicators in *US-Clove Cigarettes*, as would suggest their interpretative efforts under TBT Article 2.1, described below.

For a violation of the national treatment obligation to be established, two elements must be satisfied: (i) the imported and domestic products at issue must be *like products*; and (ii) the treatment accorded to the imported product must be *less favourable* than that accorded to its domestic counterpart. Addressing the first requirement, the AB declared in *US-Clove Cigarettes* that as in the context of GATT Article III:4, the determination of *likeness* in TBT Article 2.1 is about the *competitive relationship* between and among the products at issue, as reflected in the four traditional likeness criteria: the product's physical properties, end-uses, consumers' tastes and habits, and tariff classification.[84] Based on the evidence on record, the AB found menthol and clove cigarettes to be 'like products', indicating, inter alia, that they shared the same end-uses (both were *capable* of 'satisfying an addiction to nicotine' and 'creating a pleasurable experience associated with the taste of the cigarette'),[85] and were sufficiently competitive and substitutable from the point of view of relevant consumers (among them, young smokers and potential young smokers).[86]

While arriving at the same conclusion, the first-instance panel had taken a different approach to the determination of likeness. According to the panel, the context of the TBT Agreement, as provided by the preamble's reference to

[82] Note that the question of whether GATT Article XX applies to the TBT Agreement (or other WTO instruments) was not directly addressed in *US-Clove Cigarettes*. This question was addressed in a previous case, known as *China-Raw Materials*, where the AB clarified that GATT Article XX was available for justifying violations only of GATT or other WTO provisions that expressly refer to GATT. In line with this ruling, Marceau notes, the AB did not consider that GATT Article XX could justify TBT violations in *US-Clove Cigarettes*. See Marceau (n 49) 10.

[83] Thomas M Franck, *The Power of Legitimacy Among Nations* (OUP 1990) 73–74.

[84] *US-Clove Cigarettes* AB Report (n 44) paras 104–20.

[85] ibid, paras 131–32.

[86] ibid, paras 133–45.

'measures necessary ... for the protection of human ... life or health', suggests that product likeness under TBT Article 2.1 should not be construed primarily from a competition-oriented perspective (as is the case under GATT Article III:4). Rather, a purpose-based (or 'aim-and-effect') approach should be followed, under which the legitimate regulatory *objective* of the trade-restrictive regulation must inform the likeness analysis.[87] In this modified goal-based definition of 'like products',[88] the panel had apparently sought to introduce GATT Article XX-like flexibilities into the TBT Agreement so as to enable what it considered justified violations of Article 2.1.[89]

The AB, it should be clear from the above, rejected this purpose-based approach to the determination of 'likeness', reasoning that given the multiplicity of objectives usually underlying states' trade-restrictive measures, it would be too difficult to determine the likeness of products on the basis of a measure's regulatory objectives; it therefore applied the competition-based perspective developed in the context of the GATT Agreement.[90] Still, the regulatory aim underlying a technical regulation played a salient and rather novel role in the second part of the AB's analysis of the national treatment obligation, which concerns the 'less favourable treatment' test, where the AB went to great lengths to introduce an important qualification to TBT Article 2.1 while infusing substantive content to the balance discourse discussed earlier.

And so, departing from the well-established jurisprudence on GATT Article III:4, the AB observed that the context of TBT Article 2.1, as well as the object and purpose of the TBT Agreement (namely, to strike a balance between trade liberalization and state regulatory autonomy), call for a particular reading of the 'less favourable treatment' requirement under TBT Article 2.1.[91] These contextual and purposeful elements, the AB elaborated:

> [W]eigh in favour of reading the 'treatment no less favourable' requirement of Article 2.1 as prohibiting both *de jure* and *de facto* discrimination against imported products, *while at the same time permitting detrimental impact on competitive opportunities for imports that stems exclusively from legitimate regulatory distinctions.*[92]

87 *US-Clove Cigarettes* Panel Report (n 64) paras 7.111–7.119.

88 Note that a purpose-based or an 'aim-and-effect' test to the determination of 'likeness' had been rejected in past jurisprudence on GATT Article III:4 national treatment rule. See Weihuan Zhou, 'US-Clove Cigarettes and US-Tuna II (Mexico): Implications for the Role of Regulatory Purpose under Article III:4 of the GATT' (2012) 15 J Int'l Econ L 1075, 1083–92.

89 Marceau (n 49) 10.

90 *US-Clove Cigarettes* AB Report (n 44) paras 112–13.

91 ibid, paras 169–74.

92 ibid, para 175 (emphasis added).

By stating so, the AB essentially determined that the 'less favourable treatment' requirement in TBT Article 2.1 should involve two (rather than one) analytical steps. Similar to the GATT context, there is first a need to examine whether the disputed regulation has detrimental impact on the competitive opportunities of imported products. Yet, the existence of such an impact is insufficient to meet the 'less favourable treatment' requirement under the TBT Agreement; rather, a second analytical step should be taken to establish a national treatment violation under TBT Article 2.1, that is, to ascertain 'whether the detrimental impact on imports *stems exclusively from a legitimate regulatory distinction* rather than reflecting discrimination against the group of imported products'.[93]

Notably, by adding this second step into the analysis, the AB made it clear that when reviewing domestic regulations designed to achieve noncommercial objectives under TBT Article 2.1, the measure's trade effects *as well as* its noncommercial aims (rather than the *effects* on the competitive market conditions alone) should be considered.[94] This implies that under the twofold analysis presented by the AB, a Member's technical regulation that is found to accord less favourable treatment to like imported products could nevertheless be found not to violate Article 2.1, if that detrimental impact stems exclusively from legitimate regulatory distinctions.[95] In other words, '[m]easures, including tobacco control regulations, that serve some legitimate objectives, even if they are discriminatory, can still pass the requirements of the TBT Agreement'.[96] Hence, by pursuing this interpretative route, introducing the new concept of 'legitimate regulatory distinctions'—which has no hint in the wording of Article 2.1 itself[97]—the AB effectively limited the operational scope of Members' obligations under this provision and offset the TBT Agreement's original rigidity, leaving domestic regulations that genuinely serve nonprotectionist policy objectives outside the bounds of Article 2.1.

This is the point, therefore, at which the AB's preliminary remarks about the balance enshrined in the TBT Agreement's preamble come into play. It is here as well that the interpretative exercise carried out by the AB discloses the value judgment made in its strategic judicial space. Arguably, the AB could have adhered to the narrower construction of the 'less favourable treatment' element developed in the context of GATT Article III:4, which focuses on the regulatory measure's detrimental impact on the competitive opportunities of imports, and which does not treat that measure's policy objectives as a means to exculpate such detrimental impacts. Nevertheless, the AB deliberately chose to articulate in the context of the

93 ibid, paras 180–82 (emphasis added).

94 Zhou (n 88) 1111; interview with EU official (Brussels, 19 July 2012).

95 *US-Clove Cigarettes* AB Report (n 44) para 175. For a discussion of this determination, see also Howse (n 4) 55.

96 Lukasz Gruszczynski, 'The TBT Agreement and Tobacco Control Regulations' (2013) 8 Asian J WTO & Int'l Health L & Pol'y 115, 130.

97 Marceau (n 49) 11 ('The term "legitimate regulatory distinction" is a new concept coined by the AB in *US-Clove Cigarettes* . . . without further definition or explanation. . . .').

TBT Agreement 'a new standard',[98] one that provides in effect a somewhat 'softer' version of the national treatment rule and thus allows more room for Member governments and their constituencies to pursue nontrade policy goals. Indeed, according to a staff member of the AB Secretariat, the AB in *US-Clove Cigarettes* went much beyond the earlier GATT Article III:4 jurisprudence,[99] by essentially stating that 'if a Member can show that the different treatment accorded to imported and like domestic products stems from a legitimate objective', that Member 'can discriminate'.[100] He concluded that: 'This is a huge step'.[101]

Although the AB did not state its position so explicitly, it seems that by undertaking this interpretative move—namely, by incorporating the 'legitimate regulatory distinctions' qualification into TBT Article 2.1 and by developing a distinct analytical framework separate from that traditionally applied to GATT Article III:4, the AB sought to bridge the regulatory gap created by the absence of a general exceptions clause in the TBT Agreement, one analogous to GATT Article XX.[102] Indications in this direction can be found in the ruling itself, where the AB states, almost at the outset, that the balance established in the TBT preamble between 'the desire to avoid . . . unnecessary obstacles to international trade . . . and . . . Members' right to regulate, is not, in principle, different from the balance set out in the GATT 1994' between Article III and the exceptions clause of Article XX.[103] The AB further reasoned that since 'the TBT Agreement does not contain among its provisions a general exceptions clause' comparable to GATT Article XX, the balance between trade liberalization and Members' right to regulate in the TBT context is 'found in Article 2.1 itself, read in the light of its context and of its object and purpose'.[104] As Howse has noted, these statements are remarkable; they suggest 'that the WTO's judiciary must not read provisions of the TBT Agreement that are different from, and additional to, those in the GATT in such a way as to create a "balance" that is more [trade-]liberalizing or more restrictive of domestic regulatory autonomy than the GATT itself'.[105]

[98] Interview with US official (Geneva, 17 July 2012) (noting that the AB 'articulated a new standard' with respect to the 'less favourable treatment' element in TBT Article 2.1).

[99] For an overview of previous attempts of the AB—from *EC-Asbestos* onwards—to accommodate trade and nontrade interests in its interpretation of GATT Article III:4, see Zhou (n 88) 1083–92.

[100] Interview with staff member of the AB Secretariat (Geneva, 4 July 2012).

[101] ibid. Note that the same interpretative move was followed by the AB in the subsequent TBT cases of *US-Tuna II* and *US-COOL*. See *US-Tuna II* (n 46) paras 215, 225; *US-COOL* (n 47) para 271.

[102] Interview with US official (Geneva, 17 July 2012); Gruszczynski (n 96) 130; Marceau (n 49) 10. Note that in the later case of *Canada-Renewable Energy*, a similar interpretative move was taken by the AB under the Agreement on Subsidies and Countervailing Measures, which like the TBT Agreement does not provide for a general exceptions clause. For a discussion of this move, see Sivan Shlomo Agon and Eyal Benvenisti, 'The Law of Strangers: The Form and Substance of Other-Regarding International Adjudication' (2018) 68 UTJL 598, 639–40; Andersen (n 1) 402–04.

[103] *US-Clove Cigarettes* AB Report (n 44) para 96.

[104] ibid, paras 101, 109.

[105] Howse (n 4) 54.

While some may view the AB's judicial effort to read GATT Article XX-type flexibilities into TBT Article 2.1 as an act of illegitimate gap filling, others may see it as a mindful attempt to introduce a legitimation mechanism into the text of the TBT Agreement, designed to create more regulatory space for Members and their domestic publics in the pursuit of nontrade policy objectives. As several commentators have observed in a similar context, a judicial move of the sort displayed in *US-Clove Cigarettes*—going from strictly textual interpretation (that generally dominates AB jurisprudence) towards contextual and teleological construction methods that allow for a less-intrusive interpretation of the national treatment rule—is a means to gain institutional legitimacy in response to public pressures directed at WTO adjudicators.[106] This interpretative move, which factors the policy objective of a disputed measure into the national treatment analysis, contributes to reducing the pressures on the DSS so that the WTO can ensure 'a basic level of legitimacy'.[107] Arguably, had the AB been unconcerned with such pressures, no qualification of this sort to TBT Article 2.1 would have been needed.[108]

When eventually applying its new two-prong test of 'less favourable treatment' to the present case, the AB first found that the design and application of the US tobacco regulation reflected discrimination against imports because the products banned under the regulation consisted primarily of imported clove cigarettes, whereas like domestic products (i.e. menthol cigarettes) were permitted under the same regulation.[109] In the second step of the analysis, in turn, the AB found that the disparate impact on imported clove cigarettes did not stem 'exclusively' from the US measure's legitimate regulatory objective. Thus, although the AB accepted the US claim that the objective of the disputed tobacco regulation was to reduce youth smoking, it found that while clove and menthol cigarettes both contain a characterizing flavour that increases their appeal to young people, only the first were banned. Hence, the disparate treatment accorded to imported clove cigarettes could not be justified on the basis of the regulatory objective of reducing youth smoking.[110] Finally, the AB further considered whether the reasons put forward by the United States for distinguishing between clove and menthol cigarettes—the potential negative impact on the US healthcare system and the possible development of an illicit market for menthol cigarettes—were indeed legitimate grounds for the disparate treatment. The AB was nevertheless unconvinced by these reasons,

[106] Nicholas DiMascio and Joost Pauwelyn, 'Nondiscrimination in Trade and Investment Treaties: Worlds Apart or Two Sides of the Same Coin?' (2008) 102 AJIL 48, 65.

[107] Zhou (n 88) 1082–83.

[108] Note, however, that while the AB's interpretation of Article 2.1 promises greater policy space for Members, the burden of proof is on the respondent, who must demonstrate that the detrimental impact on imports 'stems exclusively' from a legitimate regulatory distinction. See *US-Tuna II* (n 46) para 216. Moreover, the latter requirement for 'exclusivity' seems to present the respondent with a rather high legal threshold. See Gruszczynski (n 96) 132–33; interview with US official (Geneva, 17 July 2012).

[109] *US-Clove Cigarettes* AB Report (n 44) para 224.

[110] ibid, para 225.

noting that it was unclear whether these risks would materialize if menthol cigarettes were to be banned in so far that regular cigarettes would continue being marketed.[111] Nonetheless, it has been argued that the AB's dismissal of these grounds did not reflect any principled stance but, rather, the quality of the evidence submitted by the United States, which 'was of speculative nature, with weak support in empirical studies'.[112]

It thus appears that similar to *US-Shrimp* and other trade-and disputes, the final finding of the US tobacco regulation as failing to meet the requirements of TBT Article 2.1 did not rest on the substantive value choices embodied in the domestic regulatory measure but on flaws in how the measure was designed and applied. While the AB exhibited deference to the collective preferences and values reflected in the US regulation, reaffirming the ability of the United States to restrict the sale of flavoured cigarettes for reasons of public health, upon close scrutiny of how the regulation was applied it found discrimination and under-inclusiveness, leading it to see no justification for exempting menthol cigarettes from the regulation's scope.[113]

In concluding this discussion of the AB's judicial undertaking under TBT Article 2.1 in *US-Clove Cigarettes*, we cite Tania Voon, who noted that '[f]rom the perspective of WTO law', the AB's final decision 'is relatively unsurprising'. The AB 'upheld the Panel's finding that a ban affecting (almost) exclusively imported products but exempting (almost) exclusively domestically produced like products is inconsistent with the obligation of national treatment'.[114] However, as Voon also noted, the AB 'was keenly aware ... of the politically sensitive nature of its decision with respect to tobacco control regulations'.[115] Hence, within the margins of its judicial discretion and while pursuing its various institutional goals, the AB opted for legitimacy-enhancing strategies that might generate a politically palatable decision and alleviate the heightened internal and external legitimacy challenges that arose in this case. Among these strategies: resorting to contextual-teleological interpretations while introducing new concepts absent from the TBT text; incorporating the balancing approach into the TBT framework; and departing from previous GATT/WTO jurisprudence so as to infuse substantive content when balancing between trade liberalization and national regulatory autonomy. The conscious shift in emphasis towards the DSS's legitimation goals, as we show below, was not reflected only in the substantive legal analysis developed and interpretative methods used

[111] ibid.

[112] Gruszczynski (n 96) 131.

[113] Andrew Lang, 'The Judicial Sensibility of the WTO Appellate Body' (2016) 27 EJIL 1095, 1098; Howse (n 4) 52.

[114] Tania Voon, 'Appellate Body Report, United States-Measures Affecting the Production and Sale of Clove Cigarettes' (2012) 106 AJIL 824, 828.

[115] ibid.

in *US-Clove Cigarettes*; it was likewise echoed in the other legitimacy-enhancing strategies employed throughout the judicial act in this case, until its closure.

6.4 The Recourse to Institutional Sensitivity

Like other trade-and disputes, *US-Clove Cigarettes* involved sensitive problems regarding the allocation of authority under conditions of multilevel governance. This dispute called for the WTO DSS to scrutinize national regulation of a sovereign state in a policy domain (public health) that is located at the interface between two international organizations (the WTO and the WHO). This case thereby revealed problems touching upon the vertical allocation of authority between states and international organizations in addition to the horizontal allocation of authority among distinct international regimes. Following the steps taken in earlier trade-and disputes, the AB as well as the panel in *US-Clove Cigarettes* seem to have attempted to mitigate the threats to WTO and DSS legitimacy associated with such authority-allocation problems through the application of a range of horizontal and vertical institutional sensitivity tactics.[116]

Horizontal Institutional Sensitivity

The adjudication of *US-Clove Cigarettes* in a reality where aspects related to the production, sale, and distribution of tobacco are regulated in treaties concluded under the auspices of separate international frameworks—the WTO and the WHO—brought into play the *substantive norm fragmentation* predicament afflicting current international law, as well as the closely related *institutional authority fragmentation* problem.[117] It is not surprising, therefore, that in a letter sent to the AB, the WHO's Director-General expressed her interest in the case and offered technical assistance in areas covered by the WHO's mandate. While refusing the offer, the AB's decision reveals a deliberate attempt to express institutional sensitivity towards the WHO as an ingredient in its external legitimation enterprise in *US-Clove Cigarettes*.

First, when rejecting the WHO's offer, the AB found it necessary to engage in a justificatory discourse with this international organization, seeking to explain

[116] On institutional sensitivity as a legitimacy-enhancing technique in linkage disputes, see the discussion in Chapter 5, Section 5.4.

[117] Tomer Broude, 'Fragmentation(s) of International Law: On Normative Integration as Authority Allocation' in Tomer Broude and Yuval Shany (eds), *The Shifting Allocation of Authority in International Law: Considering Sovereignty, Supremacy and Subsidiarity* (Hart Publishing 2008) 104 (discussing the problems of substantive norm fragmentation and authority fragmentation in international law while presenting each as one side of the same coin).

the reasons behind the rejection. The AB explained that 'the parties had placed a considerable amount of materials regarding WHO legal instruments and the WHO's work in the area of tobacco control on the Panel record'.[118] Furthermore, the AB predicated its rejection of the WHO's offer of technical assistance (that was likely to be of a factual nature) on its mandate, accorded to the AB in DSU Article 17.6.[119] As this mandate is limited to issues of law, direct treatment of factual aspects by the AB could have given rise to allegations of judicial overreach amidst WTO Members. The approach taken by the AB, whereby it sought to communicate the reasons for declining the WHO's proposal while not straying outside its legal bounds, seems to represent therefore a middle ground between its parallel and often competing legitimacy-related needs in trade-and disputes—that is, the need to sustain the legitimacy of the WTO and the DSS among affected audiences external to the multilateral trading system, while at the same time maintaining the DSS's internal support among WTO Members (in this instance, by avoiding an uproar similar to the one that followed the DSS's decisions on *amicus curiae* briefs in *US-Shrimp* and *EC-Asbestos*).

Second, despite its decline of the WHO's offer, regard for WHO tobacco-control activity was not absent from the AB's decision in the present case. Thus, the AB found it necessary to express its recognition of 'the *importance* of Member's efforts in the World Health Organization on tobacco control' in the concluding paragraphs of its report (see Section 6.5 below), all the while stressing that its decision was not to be interpreted as preventing WTO Members from adopting tobacco-control policies.[120]

Elements of horizontal institutional sensitivity also featured in the panel's decision. This attitude was manifested already in the opening of the panel's substantive discussion in *US-Clove Cigarettes*, where it explicitly addressed the WHO by indicating, inter alia, its recognition 'of the important international efforts to curb smoking within the context of the WHO FCTC and its WHO *Partial Guidelines*'.[121] This conversation did not end there. The panel made numerous references to the WHO FCTC and its accompanying guidelines throughout its decision, particularly within its analysis of TBT Article 2.2,[122] even though none of the disputants in *US-Clove Cigarettes* were party to the FCTC.[123] As Mitchel and Voon have noted,

[118] *US-Clove Cigarettes* AB Report (n 44) para 11.

[119] ibid.

[120] ibid, para 235 (emphasis added).

[121] *US-Clove Cigarettes* Panel Report (n 64) para 7.5 (emphasis original). See also para 7.1.

[122] See, e.g. ibid paras 7.5, 7.229–7.231, 7.413–7.415, 7.427.

[123] ibid, para 2.29. Note that a similar approach towards the FCTC and its implementing guidelines, taking account of these WHO instruments, was recently displayed by the panel in the *Australia-Plain Packaging* rulings. See *Australia–Certain Measures Concerning Trademarks, Geographical Indications and Other Plain Packaging Requirements Applicable to Tobacco Products and Packaging*, Reports of the Panels, circulated 28 June 2018, WT/DS435/R, WT/DS441/R, WT/DS458/R, WT/DS467/R. Note that the four complainants in the *Plain Packaging* case were Cuba, the Dominican Republic, Honduras, and Indonesia. On 19 July 2018, Honduras appealed its panel report. The Dominican Republic also appealed the panel ruling on 23 August 2018. At its meeting on 29 August 2018, the DSB adopted the panel

while '[t]he use of non–WTO international law in WTO disputes is highly contentious', in disputes against a measure regulating tobacco flavours, 'the FCTC could arguably be used, not as law applicable in the dispute' but 'as a "factual reference" in assessing the importance of the interest at stake' or 'the relationship between the measure and the health objective'.[124] This does appear to be the way in which the panel addressed the FCTC and its accompanying guidelines in *US-Clove Cigarettes*. Thus, for example, the panel referred to these WHO legal instruments as showing 'a growing consensus within the international community to strengthen tobacco-control policies through the regulations of the content of tobacco products',[125] and as forming part of the 'extensive scientific evidence supporting the conclusion that banning clove and other flavoured cigarettes could contribute to reducing youth smoking'.[126] That being said, right at the outset, the panel situated the FCTC and its implementing guidelines under the 'Factual Aspects' heading of its decision, thereby hinting at the legal status it ascribed to these non–WTO law sources[127] so as to deflect possible accusations from WTO Members that it was going beyond the boundaries of the applicable law within the WTO dispute settlement process. The panel further noted in its ruling that the parties themselves had referred to the FCTC during the proceedings.[128] This uneasiness on the part of the panel towards the application of norms originating from other legal regimes within its own legal subsystem illustrates once more the fragile standing of such specialized international tribunals in terms of legitimacy when they are called upon to adjudicate linkage disputes in the fragmented international legal system currently in place.[129]

That said, the various references made by the panel to WHO instruments played more than a factual role in *US-Clove Cigarettes*. They also performed an important legitimizing function by embedding the panel decision in the broader international legal discourse,[130] as well as by displaying institutional sensitivity to the WHO's competency and interest in the issues at stake. As a WTO practitioner involved in the panel proceedings commented during an interview: '[W]hat was interesting, if you read through [the *Clove Cigarettes*] report... [is that] there are very many references' to the WHO FCTC; these references reflect the general mind-set

reports with respect to Cuba and Indonesia, in the absence of any appeal against those two reports. References to the FCTC and its implementing guidelines can be found, inter alia, in paragraphs 7.2604 and 7.2596 of the panel's reports.

[124] Andrew Mitchell and Tania Voon, 'Regulating Tobacco Flavors: Implications of WTO Law' (2011) 29 BU Int'l LJ 383, 412. See also Tania Voon, 'Third Strike: The WTO Panel Reports Upholding Australia's Tobacco Plain Packaging Scheme' (2019) J World Investment & Trade (forthcoming).

[125] *US-Clove Cigarettes* Panel Report (n 64) para 7.414.

[126] ibid, para 7.415.

[127] ibid, paras 2.29–2.32.

[128] ibid, para 2.29.

[129] Thomas Kleinlein, 'Judicial Lawmaking by Judicial Restraint? The Potential of Balancing in International Economic Law' (2011) 12 German LJ 1141, 1164.

[130] Andreas von Staden, 'Democratic Legitimacy of Judicial Review Beyond the State: Normative Subsidiarity and Judicial Standards of Review' (2012) 10 Int'l J Const L 1023, 1032.

of the panel, which 'was very sensitive to the fact that there is another multilateral community in the … area of health' that regulates issues related to the dispute at hand.[131]

Another interview, with a WTO panellist participating in the case, sheds further light on the rationale partially underlying the panel's references to WHO instruments, that being the problematic image that has clung to how the WTO addresses nontrade values. This interviewee cited the extensive examination 'of information of the World Health Organization' as intrinsic to the 'extra' careful approach taken by the panel when crafting and explaining its decision in *US-Clove Cigarettes*. The respective mentions, he stated, were thought to signal WTO-insiders' views of their organization as sharing the noncommercial concerns held by the wider international community.[132]

Notably, this manifestation of institutional sensitivity by the panel contrasts with the practices of early GATT/WTO panels, which had failed to display such acts of legitimation.[133] It also attests to the gradual change that has taken place among (some) WTO panellists towards trade-and issues since the controversial panel rulings in cases such as *GATT-Tuna* and *US-Shrimp*. The following statement, made by one of the panellists sitting on the bench in *US-Clove Cigarettes*, illustrates this development and the panellists' internalization of the importance of horizontal institutional sensitivity in legitimizing the authority of the WTO and its DSS within the framework of linkage disputes:

> [The] WTO is only one part of … global governance, and … it should show respect for the other pieces of the world governance [so] as to be recognized as a legitimate actor in that field. And I think that that is being done better now than before. There was a sort of arrogance in the past … and [the] WTO received a lot of heat, and it was reminded of the importance of considering objectives in other areas … [but] I think that the lesson was learned.[134]

A former AB member made a similar observation when explaining the gradual but marked change in the attitude of WTO panels towards trade-and problems:

> [Things have] changed a little bit, … as far as the WTO is concerned, since Seattle … that was a watershed in my opinion. … [WTO] legitimacy in the eyes of the international community has been severely put into question. … And they had to somehow … show that they are not a self-contained regime, completely cut

[131] Interview with WTO practitioner (Geneva, 26 March 2012).
[132] Interview with WTO panellist (Geneva, 24 July 2012).
[133] Robert Howse, 'Adjudicative Legitimacy and Treaty Interpretation in International Trade Law: The Early Years of WTO Jurisprudence' in Joseph H H Weiler (ed), *The EU, the WTO and the NAFTA: Towards a Common Law of International Trade?* (OUP 2000) 62.
[134] Interview with WTO panellist (Geneva, 24 July 2012).

> off, etc., but that they are open to the concerns of the international community in other fields as well.... [T]his explains what happened slowly.[135]

Vertical Institutional Sensitivity

The changes in attitudes of WTO adjudicators as part of their heightened quest for legitimacy have also been observed in the extensive recourse to vertical institutional sensitivity in *US-Clove Cigarettes*, a legitimacy-conferring tactic employed in several other trade-and cases. Thus, an examination of the panel and AB decisions in this case reveals conscious efforts to express deference and esteem towards WTO Member states and their regulatory autonomy not only in the legal interpretations developed (as witnessed earlier) but also in the style and terminology used. The following examples clearly illustrate these rhetorical efforts.

For example, the panel, before commencing its legal analysis in *US-Clove Cigarettes*, found it necessary to clarify that 'the WTO Agreements fully recognize and respect *the sovereign right of Members to regulate* in response to legitimate public health concerns',[136] while later stressing that 'WTO Members have *a large measure of autonomy to determine their own policies* to protect human health'.[137] Illuminating the legitimizing motivation behind these general clarifications is a comment made by a participating panellist in which he refers to previous practice in this area:

> [WTO] Member states wanted to reserve [for themselves] ... [a] space.... to implement certain policies and achieve certain objectives that are different from trade ... and there are rules [in the WTO agreements] that recognize that. And [yet], in the past ... very often it was not said [by WTO adjudicators] ... and perhaps that allowed ... these interpretations ... according to which there was a sort of ... hierarchy with regard to different kinds of [nontrade] policies, and trade policy was always more important than others in the eyes of ... WTO ... adjudicators. I believe that ... saying that in that way, making [such clarifications,] ... gives out a different kind of message: [That] [w]e have to respect the provisions [that guarantee Members a policy space] ... and that there is a recognition that Members can [pursue nontrade policies], and if they wouldn't have done this wrong, it would have been okay.[138]

[135] Interview with former AB member (Geneva, 19 April 2012).
[136] *US-Clove Cigarettes* Panel Report (n 64) para 7.2 (emphasis added).
[137] ibid, para 7.3 (emphasis added).
[138] Interview with WTO panellist (Geneva, 24 July 2012).

The general pronouncements of the panel regarding Members' regulatory autonomy join the rather deferential legal standard towards national governments it adopted in its analysis under TBT Article 2.2, which resulted in the ruling that the US tobacco-control regulation was not more trade-restrictive than necessary to fulfil its legitimate health objective.[139]

As for the AB, as discussed at length above, it introduced a relatively deferential legal standard in the context of TBT Article 2.1. Notable deferential statements concerning Member's right to regulate were also woven into the AB report. In fact, such statements were present in the preliminary remarks on the preamble of the TBT Agreement with which the AB opened its Article 2.1 analysis (addressed earlier), as well as in the paragraphs closing this analysis, which I now address.

6.5 The Reappearance of the 'Explanatory Paragraphs'

Alongside the various manifestations of horizontal and vertical institutional sensitivity in *US-Clove Cigarettes*, two paragraphs stand out in the AB's discussion under TBT Article 2.1, coming after its conclusion that the US regulation violated this provision. Using language like that first seen in the trade-and disputes of *US-Gasoline* and *US-Shrimp*,[140] the AB stated:

> In reaching this conclusion, we wish to clarify the implications of our decision. We do not consider that the TBT Agreement or any of the covered agreements is to be interpreted as preventing Members from devising and implementing public health policies generally, and tobacco-control policies in particular.... Moreover, we recognize the importance of Members' efforts in the World Health Organization on tobacco control.
>
> While we have upheld the Panel's finding that the specific measure at issue ... is inconsistent with Article 2.1 of the TBT Agreement, we are not saying that a Member cannot adopt measures to pursue legitimate health objectives such as curbing and preventing youth smoking. In particular, we are not saying that the United States cannot ban clove cigarettes: however, if it chooses to do so, this has to be done consistently with the TBT Agreement. Although Section 907(a)(1)(A) pursues the legitimate objective of reducing youth smoking by banning cigarettes containing flavours and ingredients that increase the attractiveness of tobacco to youth, it does so in a manner that is inconsistent with the national treatment

[139] On the deferential legal standard applied by the panel, see Gruszczynski (n 96) 135.
[140] See the discussion in Chapter 5, Section 5.4.

obligation in Article 2.1 of the TBT Agreement as a result of the exemption of menthol cigarettes ... from the ban on flavoured cigarettes.[141]

As noted by a member of the AB Secretariat staff, these paragraphs did not form part of the operative decision of the AB, that is, they constituted *obiter dicta* and thus had no bearing on the legal findings already reached. It should also be noted, he added, that the AB rarely resorts to this type of justificatory language in its judgments.[142] For these reasons, these 'explanatory paragraphs', which closely resemble the closing passages in *US-Shrimp*, merit special attention.

Several rationales can be suggested to explain the insertion of these paragraphs into the AB report. Among them, is the AB's desire to lay the foundations for later TBT cases (e.g. *Australia-Plain Packaging*), which were already nearing WTO adjudication at the time when the *US-Clove Cigarettes* decision was rendered.[143] Yet, the main rationale underlying the incorporation of these rare explanatory paragraphs seems to have been 'political',[144] related to the AB's willingness to address the intensified legitimacy concerns invoked in the case and to clear the smoke potentially clinging to its ruling. Interviews with WTO practitioners involved in *US-Clove Cigarettes* shed light on the multi-dimensional legitimating account encapsulated in these paragraphs, as well as the multiple audiences to which they speak.

First, as their language makes clear, these explanatory passages were addressed to WTO Members, and to the US government in particular,[145] as further expressions of institutional sensitivity towards state regulatory autonomy, what one state official involved in the case described as 'a message to the WTO Members'.[146] This same official elaborated: 'here we are listening to ... the Appellate Body saying publicly [that] it understands the importance of regulatory autonomy'. These statements represent 'an important recognition of the fact that ... regulatory autonomy is ... as much a pillar of the system of the WTO as the various provisions that speak to trade interests, because otherwise the system is not sustainable'.[147]

But these paragraphs constituted more than a means for communicating vertical institutional sensitivity towards WTO Members. Similar to *US-Shrimp*, they also served as an 'explaining and defending' act of self-legitimation by the AB[148] in the face of impending criticism against its final finding of WTO-inconsistency,

[141] *US-Clove Cigarettes* AB Report (n 44) paras 235–36.

[142] Interview with staff member of the AB Secretariat (Geneva, 4 July 2012). See also interview with WTO panellist (Geneva, 24 July 2012) (noting that these paragraphs were unnecessary 'from the legal point of view').

[143] For the panel's ruling recently rendered in the *Plain Packaging* case, see (n 123).

[144] Interview with US official (Geneva, 17 July 2012).

[145] Interview with WTO practitioner (Geneva, 16 July 2012); interview with US official (Geneva, 17 July 2012).

[146] Interview with EU official (Brussels, 19 July 2012).

[147] ibid. See also interview with senior WTO official (Geneva, 25 April 2012).

[148] On such acts of self-legitimation by international governance institutions, see Jens Steffek, 'The Legitimation of International Governance: A Discourse Approach' (2003) 9 EJIR 249, 250, 258.

anticipated from Members as well as external stakeholders. As a state official stressed in this regard, the WTO DSS, but especially the AB, is a court operating in a specific diplomatic context. Within this 'diplomatic sphere', the ability and willingness of actors to comprehend some of the issues and technicalities of litigation is at times limited; in consequence, 'the Appellate Body has to struggle because it is embedded in an immediate political context which often creates conventional wisdoms that are actually untrue, and this is part of what stresses the system'.[149] Situations thus arise where, in the face of imminent criticism against an AB ruling, the use of these explanatory paragraphs is 'the only line of defence' available for this body.[150] Along these lines, an AB member explained the rationale behind the explanatory paragraphs in *US-Clove Cigarettes* in these words:

> [I]n a way it is a pre-emptive strike ... and this technique actually goes back already a long time, but we learned from the very early cases that one got crucified in the press and in DSB statements in a way that was ... political in nature, that ... has a certain appeal because of its simplicity. And at that time, we, of course, cannot react anymore ... so, you should see this paragraph as a sort of pre-emptive strike. We put ourselves ... on the record, preparing or responding to a reaction that has not come yet, but that will come.[151]

An AB Secretariat staff member noted in the same spirit that '[b]y inserting these paragraphs, the AB wanted to make it very clear to ... people in the outside world what the AB has done'. 'The AB does not normally do that' but there are difficult situations, like the present case, in which a health-related regulation was declared WTO-inconsistent, where the AB finds it necessary to add these types of paragraphs so as to 'prevent unjustified criticism of the judgment' and 'comments' that distort its ruling, even if it is clear that such pre-emptive measures are not always successful.[152]

Interestingly, while aware of the limited force of such 'pre-emptive strikes', the AB continues to perceive such paragraphs as an essential explanatory tool in instances of heightened internal and external legitimacy concerns. In the words of an AB member:

> [P]ress releases still ignore these paragraphs and say, 'No, they ... don't allow us to protect youth from smoking'. I mean, we read this. We say, 'What can you do?' .... [W]e can't even defend ourselves publicly against [what] ... is being published....

[149] Interview with EU official (Brussels, 19 July 2012).
[150] Interview with AB member (Geneva, 27 April 2012). Other interviewees shared similar views. See, e.g. interview with senior WTO official (Geneva, 25 April 2012).
[151] Interview with AB member (Geneva, 27 April 2012).
[152] Interview with staff member of the AB Secretariat (Geneva, 4 July 2012).

> [T]he only line of defense that we have against that ... is ... including these sorts of paragraphs.[153]

Finally, when alluding to the audiences at whom those paragraphs were directed, the same AB member noted:

> So, who is the audience of such paragraphs? ... [I]t's the wide audience that doesn't really appreciate the technicalities of the reasoning.... And ... the audience is broader than that. It's also directed at government lawyers, ... the ministries involved ... just to hammer down [the expected criticism of the AB ruling].[154]

As these and other testimonies suggest, the introduction of the explanatory paragraphs into the *US-Clove Cigarettes* report represents therefore the AB's attempt to engage in a justificatory discourse with multiple legitimating audiences, wider than those usually addressed by the WTO DSS.[155] Thus, as a WTO legal officer involved in the case commented:

> [I]n these types of 'trade-and' cases ... there is a wider audience, and an audience who does not read dumping cases or other technical trade cases. And ... from the point of view of legitimacy, there are multiple considerations that panels and the Appellate Body would consider, ranging from transparency and proper reasoning, to include also the audience.[156]

In *US-Clove Cigarettes*, the wide audience the DSS strove to address in its legitimating discourse seems to have included, among others, the WHO, domestic interest groups, NGOs, the media, trade lawyers, colleagues, and the public at large.[157] Hence, although being an exemplary interstate adjudicating system, residing within a so-called member-driven organization, the explanatory paragraphs inserted in *US-Clove Cigarettes*, like those in *US-Shrimp*, aptly illustrate the distinctive multilayered discourse in which WTO adjudicators engage for the sake of tackling the persistent legitimacy challenges featuring such trade-and cases.

Yet, one last, legitimating aspect is latent in these concluding paragraphs. This aspect revolves around the issue of compliance with the ruling rendered in

[153] Interview with AB member (Geneva, 27 April 2012); interview with staff member of the AB Secretariat (Geneva, 4 July 2012).

[154] Interview with AB member (Geneva, 27 April 2012).

[155] Interview with staff member of the AB Secretariat (Geneva, 4 July 2012); interview with senior WTO official (Geneva, 25 April 2012).

[156] Interview with WTO legal officer (Geneva, 13 March 2012).

[157] Interview with WTO practitioner (Geneva, 16 July 2012); interview with US official (Geneva, 17 July 2012); interview with AB member (Geneva, 27 April 2012); interview with WTO panellist (Geneva, 24 July 2012); interview with senior WTO official (Geneva, 25 April 2012).

US-Clove Cigarettes, and relates to the stress placed in these explanatory paragraphs on the fact that by finding the US regulation to be inconsistent with TBT Article 2.1's national treatment obligation, the AB was 'not saying that the United States cannot ban clove cigarettes'. As a state official explained:

> [T]hese [paragraphs] are also compliance-related.... [T]hose extra paragraphs make [it] very clear ... that ... the US does not need to allow clove cigarettes back in the market in order to comply [with the WTO ruling]. Now ... if you are a trade person, you know that already because there are always ways to comply with [the] national treatment [rule]. But they make that very explicit, so that if you are not in the trade community, you can read this and say, 'Oh, they are not saying that the US has to let clove cigarettes back in the market'. So, in that sense ... they are trying to indicate that their decision is not ... anti-health.[158]

Note that following the AB ruling in *US-Clove Cigarettes*, and based on the novel interpretation developed therein to TBT Article 2.1, it was indeed argued that options are available for the United States to implement the ruling without allowing clove cigarettes back in the market (and without banning menthol cigarettes as well). This could be done, for instance, by citing stronger evidence showing that the different regulatory approaches taken with respect to clove and menthol cigarettes in fact stem from legitimate regulatory distinctions.[159]

In accordance with this line of argument, an AB member also alluded to the implementation-related aspect encapsulated in the explanatory paragraphs being discussed, while explaining that these paragraphs served in part to denote the limited scope of the post-litigation consequences actually emerging for the respondent from the AB ruling. In the words of this AB member:

> [I]t is useful, after having come to our conclusion, [to] ... point out what the *actual* political implications are ... or [more precisely] the *limits* of the political implications [arising for the respondent] ... because if I [just] say 'what the political implications are', then I may be suggesting that we give direction in terms of implementation, which I think we usually want to avoid, but what the limits of the political ... [implications] are, of what is actually ruled [by the AB].[160]

This approach, whereby the AB, after having arrived at its conclusion of WTO-inconsistency, underlines the actual political ramifications of its decision and

[158] Interview with US state official (Geneva, 17 July 2012).

[159] See, e.g. Robert Howse, 'Implementing the Clove Cigarettes Ruling: Comments' (*International Economic Law and Policy Blog*, 17 April 2012) <http://worldtradelaw.typepad.com/ielpblog/2012/04/implementing-clove-cigarettes.html#comments> accessed 30 December 2018.

[160] Interview with AB member (Geneva, 27 April 2012) (emphasis added).

implies that the case may be solved without the respective trade-restrictive measure being revoked, has been applied in several other trade-and disputes.[161] This was the case, for example, in the *US-Shrimp* case discussed in Chapter 5, where the AB found the US import ban to violate WTO law but simultaneously insinuated that the US trade-restrictive policy could be applied in a way that the AB would ultimately find consistent with WTO rules.[162]

This rather infrequent AB technique of going out of its way to elucidate the 'limits of the political implications' of its ruling and to signal that compliance may take place without the respondent sacrificing important national interests[163] provides, in effect, another tool within the legitimating strategy utilized by the AB in trade-and disputes. This tool is aimed not only at manifesting a sympathetic stance towards the nontrade value at stake, but also at conciliating the respondent and appeasing the compliance-related concerns of its constituencies.[164] Indeed, it has been noted, the AB's conciliating attitude in disputes involving nontrade values, often to ease the burden of compliance on losing states, 'represents a tacit acknowledgment by the Appellate Body' of the political constraints placed on its 'authority and perceived legitimacy' in such cases.[165] Putting it differently, this attitude represents the AB's tacit acknowledgement of the need, at times, for some 'give' on compliance with WTO trade commitments in order to promote other organizational goals, most notably, sustaining the overall legitimacy of the DSS and the WTO.

Before closing this section, we should note that following the AB ruling in *US-Clove Cigarettes*, the United States took several steps in order to bring itself into compliance with the ruling.[166] As part of the implementation steps taken, the United States neither banned menthol cigarettes nor allowed clove cigarettes back into its market. Instead, it laid the groundwork for a potential menthol ban by publishing an 'Advanced Notice of Proposed Rule Making concerning menthol cigarettes', which solicited public comment on potential regulatory options in relation to these products (although the United States did not commit to taking any action

[161] Interview with US official (Geneva, 17 July 2012) (noting that this 'is a pattern that we have seen repeatedly . . . they try to give a way . . . they are saying, "Well, this can be resolved in a way that respects the . . . [nontrade] value, but also takes on the trade interest". The same thing in the *Shrimp-Turtles* cases, that the compliance process didn't actually then require the US to remove the restrictions; it just required them to do some additional things to remove the . . . trade concern').

[162] For a discussion of this conciliating attitude of the AB in *US-Shrimp* and other trade-and disputes, see Geoffrey Garrett and James M Smith, 'The Politics of WTO Dispute Settlement' (2002) UCLA International Institute Occasional Paper Series, 2, 20–26 <http://escholarship.org/uc/item/4t4952d7#page-3> accessed 30 December 2018.

[163] On this tactic of international courts, see Yuval Shany, 'Compliance with Decisions of International Courts as Indicative of Their Effectiveness: A Goal-Based Analysis' in James Crawford and Sarah Nouen (eds), *Select Proceedings of the European Society of International Law* 2010 (2012) 231.

[164] Garrett and Smith (n 162) 20–26.

[165] ibid 33.

[166] The US implementation steps were notified to the DSB on its meeting of 23 July 2013. See DSB, Minutes of Meeting of 23 July 2013 (2 October 2013) WT/DSB/M/334, paras 1.44–1.45 [hereinafter DSB Minutes of 23 July 2013].

against menthol cigarettes).[167] The United States also took a series of educational measures designed to discourage young people from smoking menthol cigarettes and released a study concluding that the presence of menthol makes it harder for smokers to quit.[168] According to US statements, these actions brought it into compliance with the AB decision.[169] While disagreement arose as to whether this was truly the case, with Indonesia requesting DSB authorization of trade sanctions against the United States, no additional ruling on the matter was made: a settlement reached between the parties in October 2014 effectively brought the dispute to an end. Under this settlement, which extended certain concessions to Indonesia, the US ban on clove cigarettes remained intact.[170]

6.6 Conclusions

In the face of intensifying struggles over global tobacco control, Harold Koh has recently argued:

> [T]he battle over global tobacco control seems destined to provide a litmus test for the very legitimacy of the WTO dispute settlement process. The question will be whether responsible national governments have a right and duty to regulate to protect their residents' public health without being subjected to aggressive, meritless arbitration under economic treaties adopted for other purposes. To the contrary, those regulations are part and parcel of a global movement legally mandating government protection of public health through tobacco regulation.[171]

While views may differ as to how effective the WTO DSS was in meeting this pivotal legitimacy objective in *US-Clove Cigarettes*, the evidence presented throughout the chapter suggests that both the panel and the AB were attentive and responsive to the heightened legitimacy challenges raised in this case. This they manifested by shifting their goal-attainment efforts and judicial tools to alleviating the respective challenges through a variety of interpretive and rhetorical means they believed would yield a more politically palatable ruling, one that could be

[167] Jamie Strawbridge, 'U.S. Implementation of Adverse WTO Rulings: A Closer Look at the Tuna-Dolphin, COOL, and Clove Cigarettes Cases', 17 (*ASIL Insights*, 30 October 2013) <http://www.asil.org/insights/volume/17/issue/23/us-implementation-adverse-wto-rulings-closer-look-tuna-dolphin-cool-and> accessed 30 December 2018.

[168] ibid.

[169] DSB Minutes of 23 July 2013 (n 166) para 1.45.

[170] 'Indonesia Announces Deal with US on Clove Cigarettes Trade Dispute' (*ICTSD*, 9 October 2014) <http://www.ictsd.org/bridges-news/bridges/news/indonesia-announces-deal-with-us-on-clove-cigarettes-trade-dispute> accessed 30 December 2018.

[171] Harold Hongju Koh, 'Global Tobacco Control as a Health and Human Rights Imperative' (2016) 57 Harv Int'l LJ 433, 452.

taken by internal as well as external stakeholders to represent an acceptable balance between the competing trade and public health interests at hand. As a US official involved in the case noted:

> I think that the panel, and probably to a greater extent, the Appellate Body, tries to be aware of balancing and tries to sort of find a way... that the trade requirements in ... [WTO] rules can be adhered to, but in a way that does not ... disrespect those other [nontrade] interests ... I do think that there is a very ... conscious effort to do that.

Still, this official observed:

> I think the difficulty is that ... those other issues, be they environmental, health [or other nontrade policies] ... are ... [reached] in ... [a domestic] environment that is ... political ... it is a democratic environment and it involves a lot of different factors, and ... it is difficult ... for the Appellate Body or [the] panels to really appreciate how these things are done [at the domestic level], or what the consequences would be ... because ... they are not in a ... good position to understand how these various things are actually going to mix.... I think ... that the WTO does try to ... [take those other social values into account], but because of the nature of the organization that's very difficult for them to do that in a way that would meet the expectations on the other side. So ... that's an area [where] we've had problems in the past ... and I would expect ... [these problems] would continue and perhaps grow in the future.[172]

Like *US-Shrimp*, then, *US-Clove Cigarettes* represents another juncture in the DSS's long and ongoing quest for legitimacy in trade-and disputes, a quest aimed at securing acceptance and support for the authority of the DSS and the broader WTO regime among constituencies in and outside the multilateral trade setting. In what follows, I close this part of the book by taking a comparative look at the DSS's goal-attainment patterns as revealed in these case studies and, in the broader context of this book, address their significance in terms of WTO DSS effectiveness.

[172] Interview with US official (Geneva, 17 July 2012).

Conclusions to Part II

An Analytical Overview of Linkage Disputes

When asked what, if anything, distinguishes *US-Clove Cigarettes* from other disputes filed with the World Trade Organization (WTO) Dispute Settlement System (DSS), an Appellate Body (AB) Secretariat staff member replied: 'A number of things and nothing at the same time'.[1] This answer aptly captures the story of trade-and disputes and the DSS's goal-attainment patterns in such cases, as revealed in this second part of the book. On the one hand, as in all WTO disputes, the DSS appears to be engaged in this class of cases in the routine legal exercise of law application and interpretation while pursuing its multiple goals, including rule-compliance and dispute resolution. On the other hand, as a WTO practitioner remarked when discussing the 'interpretative exercise' carried out by the DSS in trade-and disputes:

> [U]ltimately ... [in the process of treaty interpretation] you face choices ... even within the structure of the Vienna Convention analysis you have choices of which words you choose to put meat on ... the treaty [text]. And [in trade-and disputes] ... that's when the adjudicators are most aware of their need ... to build up [the] legitimacy and credibility of the system....[2]

A qualitative empirical-legal account of *US-Shrimp* and *US-Clove Cigarettes*, coupled with insights from other trade-and disputes, indeed shows how the intensified internal and external legitimacy concerns aroused have affected the substantive, procedural, and rhetorical choices taken by the DSS in its discretionary judicial space, as well as the identity of the audiences with which it has tried to converse. Notably, the specific judicial choices made in these cases form part of the larger arsenal of judicial means and alternatives available to the DSS, recourse to which may have better promoted other institutional objectives. Yet, choices have been made that accord greater weight to selected DSS goals: those related to the

[1] Interview with AB Secretariat staff member (Geneva, 4 July 2012).

[2] Interview with private attorney (Geneva, 23 April 2012). See also interview with WTO panellist (Geneva, 24 July 2012).

legitimation of the WTO regime and the DSS itself, that is, those goals concerned with maintaining the social acceptance of the authority exerted by these global governance institutions, and with ensuring that relevant audiences—states, civil society actors, other international organizations, and the general public, among others—perceive this authority as normatively justified and as worthy of being obeyed.

A WTO practitioner aptly conveyed this idea when alluding to the prominence of the legitimacy-oriented DSS goals in trade-and disputes, and the attempts of WTO adjudicators in cases such as *US-Shrimp* and *US-Clove Cigarettes* to craft 'a decision that is designed to gain some degree of public acceptance':

> All of these decisions could have been decided the other way.... In ... *Shrimp* they could easily have reverted to the old jurisprudence from the [GATT] *Tuna/Dolphin* dispute, and likewise in the *Tuna [II]* case ... but they did not. And I think they tried to develop a line of reasoning that is going to be appreciated from the environmental perspective in *Tuna [II]* and in *Shrimp.* And in ... *Clove Cigarettes* ... they wanted to develop a line that is going to be appreciated from the public health perspective, and they did so.... [A]ll these cases could have been decided the other way ... [yet, those are] the decisions that have been written.[3]

As to the specific judicial choices taken in *US-Shrimp* and *US-Clove Cigarettes* that disclose the shift in emphasis towards the DSS's legitimation objectives, these include the following distinctive legitimacy-enhancing strategies: the move to flexible, teleological, and contextual construction methods by an adjudicatory body known for its strict textual interpretations so as to endow WTO adjudicators with greater interpretative leeway and allow them to embed the interest of free trade in the broader context of societal values; the reading of WTO provisions as reflections of a fundamental balance between trade liberalization and Members' right to regulate for nontrade values even when no general exceptions clause attesting to such a balance has been included in the applicable WTO agreement; the deliberate attempt of the DSS to manifest—in both substantive and expressive forms—vertical institutional sensitivity towards Member states and national regulatory autonomy, together with horizontal institutional sensitivity towards adjacent international regimes; the development of procedures promising more inclusive, transparent and participatory WTO decision-making; and finally, the engagement of WTO adjudicators in a rare justificatory discourse, at times through designated 'explanatory paragraphs' at the end of the ruling, aimed at clarifying to audiences inside and outside the WTO the limited political implications arising from the DSS ruling for the respondent, and signalling that the trade-and dispute at hand may be solved

[3] Interview with WTO practitioner (Geneva, 16 July 2012).

without eliminating the trade-restrictive policy found to be WTO-inconsistent. This last judicial technique perhaps most clearly reflects WTO adjudicators' acknowledgement of the political constraints encroaching on the authority and perceived legitimacy of the WTO and the DSS in trade-and cases, as well as their recognition of the resulting need for some 'give' on compliance with WTO commitments and the all-out enforcement of the multilateral trade rules so as to promote other organizational goals, among them, bolstering the very legitimacy of the WTO and its DSS.

In a similar spirit, Lang has recently observed that the distinctive line of jurisprudence gradually developed by the AB in cases involving nontrade issues encapsulates 'a vision that starts from the position that there is *a trade-off* to be made between, on the one hand, the genuine and significant economic benefits of global integration and, on the other, its political costs in the form of reduced domestic regulatory autonomy' and grave challenges to the legitimacy of the multilateral trade institutions.[4] The normative vision advanced by the AB in its trade-and jurisprudence, Lang has added, represents a 'compromise between these conflicting demands, one that captures many of the benefits of economic integration, but that avoids the legitimacy problems that have proved to come with a full throated pursuit' of GATT/WTO trade disciplines.[5] Seen through a goal-oriented lens, the vision embraced by the AB represents a compromise between the parallel but competing aims entrusted with the DSS—those geared to securing compliance with WTO rules and advancing the economic objectives embodied in WTO agreements, and those others that aim at guaranteeing the WTO and the DSS the fundamental legitimacy capital needed to secure their ability to exercise their authority and carry out their mandate. As Lang and others have further observed in this regard: 'the emergence of this new vision' in DSS jurisprudence against the legitimacy threats posed to the WTO regime from within and outside the multilateral trade circles 'has been part of the conditions providing some degree of normative stability for the regime during turbulent times'.[6]

Yet, the trade-off struck between legitimation of the WTO edifice on the one hand, and rigorous enforcement of WTO rules and their inherent liberalizing mission on the other, is not the sole trade-off envisaged between DSS goals in trade-and disputes. At times, conflicts and trade-offs arose between the DSS's two parallel legitimation objectives themselves. This was the case, for example, in *US-Shrimp* (and *EC-Asbestos*), where the AB's decisions on *amicus curiae* briefs, aimed at bolstering the external legitimacy of the DSS and the WTO regime among civil society,

[4] Andrew Lang, 'The Judicial Sensibility of the WTO Appellate Body' (2016) 27 EJIL 1095, 1103 (emphasis added).

[5] ibid.

[6] ibid. See also Robert Howse, 'The World Trade Organization 20 Years On: Global Governance by Judiciary' (2016) 27 EJIL 9, 76.

incited challenges to the DSS's internal legitimacy among WTO Members and ultimately led the DSS to fine-tune its approach to such submissions in later cases.

Hence, it is through twists and turns that the DSS, under the AB's guidance, has managed its trade-and disputes, pushing hard to attain its legitimacy-related objectives while pursuing its various other organizational goals. In turn, it is with a long yardstick that the DSS's effectiveness in such cases is to be measured, going beyond compliance and accounting for the shifts and conflicts generated between the system's multiple objectives. The taking of such a broad view is crucial because trade-and disputes and the legitimacy challenges they bring to the fore are not going to fade away; these challenges might even be exacerbated in the future given the current contestation of global economic integration in the United States and Europe, the systemic pressures facing the WTO's negotiating and adjudicative arms, and the persistent emergence of new trade-and issues.[7] In that spirit, William Davey, a former head of the WTO legal affairs division, has stated that while the AB's decisions in trade-and disputes over the years 'have lessened' the opposition to the WTO and its DSS, the 'concerns' associated with such cases 'have not disappeared'.[8] This state of affairs, Davey notes, is largely due to the fact that 'an inexhaustible supply of potentially controversial cases' involving nontrade issues can be expected to confront the DSS with legitimacy-sensitive questions in the years to come.[9]

'And where does that leave the WTO dispute settlement system'? An AB member asked as he looked towards the future:

> Well, this leaves ... [the system] in the uncomfortable position of then having to strike the balance [between the competing trade and nontrade interests], and ... have that balance within the limits of interpreting the treaty text, but have that balance shift [over time].... [T]he best example of that is, of course, Article XX(g) ... [and the] 'evolutionary interpretation' [in *US-Shrimp*].... [Yet] we will run into more and more of these problems because ... the list [of exceptions] in Article XX is a limited list.... And what has happened in recent years is [that] one ... [has consequently tried] to interpret what is in the list in a broader way ... and I'm sure that in the future we will see some very creative interpretation of the concept of 'public morals' [in GATT Article XX(a)] ... which is ... a box of Pandora [sic] that the Members kept closed ... until a few years [ago].[10]

[7] See, e.g. interview with WTO Ambassador (Geneva, 23 July 2012) (alluding to the 'fear' that given the impasse in WTO negotiations and the global need for 'solutions' of trade-and issues, more and more trade-and disputes 'are going to be brought into the system ... to have a compulsory verdict').

[8] William J Davey, 'The WTO and Rules-Based Dispute Settlement: Historical Evolution, Operational Success, and Future Challenges' (2014) 17 J Int'l Econ L 679, 690.

[9] ibid.

[10] Interview with AB member (Geneva, 27 April 2012).

Indeed, not long after *US-Clove Cigarettes*, the AB and the panel went on to push the bounds of the public morals exception enshrined in GATT Article XX(a) in the high-profile case of *EC-Seal Products*. There they found that an EU ban on seal products was necessary for the protection of public morals, understood in terms of animal welfare or inhibiting cruelty to animals.[11] A no less instructive move was recently observed in the *Brazil-Taxation* dispute, where the panel found that Brazilian society's concerns 'with respect to the need to bridge the digital divide and promote social inclusion' fell 'within the scope of "public morals" as defined and applied by Brazil'.[12]

Other cases, fuelling further challenges to the legitimacy of the WTO and the DSS, are expected to follow.

[11] *European Communities–Measures Prohibiting the Importation and Marketing of Seal Products*, Reports of the Appellate Body, 18 June 2014, WT/DS400/AB/R, WT/DS401/AB/R; *European Communities–Measures Prohibiting the Importation and Marketing of Seal Products*, Reports of the Panel, 18 June 2014, WT/DS400/R, WT/DS401/R.

[12] *Brazil-Certain Measures Concerning Taxation and Charges*, Reports of the Panel, 11 January 2019, WT/DS472/R, WT/DS497/R, para 7.568. Note, however, that since the Brazilian measure at issue failed to meet the necessity test contained in Article XX(a) of the GATT, the panel concluded that the disputed measure could not be provisionally justified under this provision. ibid, paras, 7.622, 7.625.

PART III

WHEN DISPUTES WON'T GO AWAY

Perennial Disputes from a Goal-Based Perspective

7

Trade Wars, Trade-Offs, and the International Rule of Law

7.1 Perennial Disputes: Setting the Scene

Alongside the category of trade-and disputes just examined, the World Trade Organization (WTO) Dispute Settlement System (DSS) roster of cases includes, among others, several complex, lengthy, contentious, and recurring disputes, some of which go back to the erstwhile General Agreement on Tariffs and Trade (GATT).[1] These disputes often encompass large trade volumes and/or national policies of considerable political or symbolic importance,[2] thus requiring respondents to introduce complicated legislative changes implicating multiple veto players[3] but also to initiate major shifts in ideology or resources.[4] Perhaps more crucially, these disputes often embroil politically empowered stakeholders on both sides, those who forcibly push for WTO litigation or, alternatively, against resolution of the case.[5] And, as might be expected, perennial disputes usually involve powerful states, capable of sustaining the pressure to implement adverse DSS rulings.[6] We therefore find that many of the disputes falling under this category so far are transatlantic in nature, engaging the two major economies and thus far main users of the DSS: the United States and the EU. Finally, by the time they reach the DSS, perennial disputes often exhibit a charged history and failed attempts to settle the conflict in other forums.[7] Because of these factors, politically salient cases of this type make hard cases for compromise[8] and remarkably 'hard cases for compliance'.[9] As

[1] Taylor, for example, refers to this category of complex and lengthy disputes as 'impossible' cases, and analyses the various complicating factors associated therewith. See Cherie O'Neal Taylor, 'Impossible Cases: Lessons from the First Decade of WTO Dispute Settlement' (2007) 28 U Pa J Int'l L 309, 328–38.

[2] ibid 335–37.

[3] Alasdair R Young, 'Effective Multilateralism on Trial: EU Compliance with WTO Law' in Spyros Blavoukos and Dimitris Bourantonis (eds), *The EU Presence in International Organizations* (Routledge 2011) 120.

[4] Taylor (n 1) 327, 335.

[5] ibid 336; Christina L Davis, *Why Adjudicate: Enforcing Trade Rules in the* WTO (Princeton University Press 2012) 245.

[6] Taylor (n 1) 334–35.

[7] ibid 337–38.

[8] Andrew Guzman and Beth A Simmons, 'To Settle or Empanel? An Empirical Analysis of Litigation and Settlement at the World Trade Organization' (2002) 31 J Legal Stud S205, S221; Young (n 3) 120.

[9] Young (n 3) 120; Taylor (n 1).

a matter of fact, such cases, which usually result in prolonged and obstinate noncompliance, frequently appear already at the outset to be more susceptible to nonimplementation of an adverse DSS ruling.

Perennial disputes, in turn, place serious pressures on the WTO DSS and its credibility.[10] These pressures may be long-lasting due to the likelihood of the conflicts to remain unsettled for years and to return to the DSS in different forms. Because of the key players involved and the importance of the disputed measures, these trade feuds also hold weighty implications for the parties' trading relationship and, more broadly, for the systemic stability of the WTO regime. For these reasons, perennial disputes, which 'begin, proceed, and/or end by being overly contentious, difficult, or complex', and carry heightened risks of noncompliance, have been labelled 'impossible'[11] or 'wrong' cases[12] that should never have been brought before the WTO's adjudicative system.[13] While under the old GATT DSS, such 'wrong' cases could indeed be blocked, the 'reverse consensus' rule under the legalized WTO DSS has made such blocking practically unfeasible. Perennial disputes have consequently been with the WTO DSS since its inception, from the early *EC-Bananas* and *EC-Hormones*, to *US-FSC*, *US-Zeroing*, and *US-Upland Cotton*, and today continue with cases such as *EC-Airbus* and *US-Boeing*. Unavoidably, such high-stake, perennial conflicts will continue to form part of the DSS's docket in the future; and, with the changes besetting the global economic order and the emergence of new economic powers such as China, Brazil, and India, they are expected to couple long-standing international trade rivalries with new, not less challenging and intricate ones, as the present reality suggests.

Given their complex features and the systemic challenges they present before the DSS and the WTO regime, perennial disputes are another instructive site for examining whether and how these features and challenges shape stakeholders' expectations from the DSS, shift the emphasis placed on its various goals, and stimulate conflicts and trade-offs between them. Furthermore, because of the susceptibility of perennial disputes to result in sustained noncompliance, a close analysis of the goal-attainment patterns manifested by the DSS in these cases provides a valuable opportunity for challenging the tendency in the literature to consider compliance as the fixed, primary goal to be achieved by the juridified DSS, and as the main outcome measure against which its effectiveness should be evaluated.

[10] Taylor (n 1) 341–43.

[11] ibid 316–17.

[12] Robert E Hudec, 'GATT Dispute Settlement After the Tokyo Round: An Unfinished Business' (1980) 3 Cornell Int'l LJ 145, 159–66.

[13] Taylor (n 1) 316. The rationale underlying this perception resonates with the nonjusticiability doctrine presented (and rejected) long ago by Lauterpacht, according to which disputes involving issues of 'high political importance' (including issues of great economic interests for the states concerned), should be excluded from the domain of international judicial settlement. See Hersch Lauterpacht, *The Function of Law in the International Community* (OUP 1933) 139–65; Hersch Lauterpacht, 'The Doctrine of Non-Justiciable Disputes in International Law' (1928) 24 Economica 277.

Finally, an investigation of the DSS's working patterns and the goals it serves within the context of high-stake, perennial disputes appears particularly apt at this troubling point in time, especially in light of the US–China 'trade war' that seems to be looming inside and outside the WTO DSS, with the latter facing serious challenges, posed predominantly by the United States, the historically leading force behind its creation and empowerment.

In setting the scene for the investigation into the DSS's operation and goal-attainment patterns in perennial disputes, the dispute category standing at the centre of Part III of the book, this introductory chapter proceeds as follows. Section 7.2 places the discussion of perennial disputes in the broader historical and institutional context of the multilateral trading system. It discusses the concerns over 'wrong' cases as they surfaced during the late 1970s, and then again during the 1980s, in response to increased pressure from those wishing to see the GATT DSS taking a more-legalistic, less-diplomatic form; it also examines those concerns' realization following establishment of the mandatory WTO DSS. Section 7.3 questions the common appellation of high-stake, perennial WTO disputes as 'wrong' or 'impossible' cases, owing to the problems they pose for attainment of the DSS's compliance objective. Instead, it points to the subtle shift away from compliance that seems to be taking place in such conflicts and the enhanced role the DSS comes to play at the interstice between law and politics characterizing these cases, with a view to achieving other DSS goals. Section 7.4 closes with the reasons for selecting *EC-Bananas* and *EC-Hormones* as case studies appropriate for exploring the DSS's patterns of operation, goal shifting, and goal conflict within the framework of perennial disputes.

7.2 GATT's Concerns Over 'Wrong' Cases and Their Materialization Upon Creation of the WTO

Following the conclusion of the Tokyo Round of trade negotiations in 1979, Robert Hudec published an article in which he described the concerns raised by GATT Contracting Parties during the negotiations over the creation of a stronger enforcement mechanism, believed necessary to address the then newly emerging modes of protectionism and to increase the GATT's clout vis-à-vis 'strong protectionist forces within national governments'.[14] Hudec noted that: 'A strong current of antilegalist sentiment re-emerged' at that time that argued 'against strengthening' the GATT's panel procedures.[15] In this antilegalist camp's view, adoption of more legally binding dispute settlement procedures, where panel proceedings and rulings would become readily available, would not only poison the atmosphere

[14] Hudec (n 12) 154.
[15] ibid 159.

within the GATT system (by leading parties to quicken abandonment of negotiated solutions in favour of adjudication), it could also lead to the breakdown of the GATT system by opening the door to troublesome cases that would produce judgments the losers would not implement.[16] Thus, according to negotiators contending against legalization of the GATT DSS:

> [I]f panel rulings declaring violations became routinely available, regardless of the nature of the violation, there would be a large number of instances in which governments would not comply with panel rulings. These instances of non-compliance would become conspicuous failures for the GATT, diminishing both its own prestige and that of its rules.[17]

These instances of noncompliance, which aroused concern among many Tokyo Round negotiators, Hudec labelled 'wrong' cases. In his writing, he went on to identify several categories of those so-called 'wrong' cases—disputes that might be expected to become legal failures for the GATT DSS and damage the credibility of the GATT regime.[18] The first category ('ordinary' noncompliance) consisted of cases where noncompliance was unavoidable because of the high political costs facing the respondent. Given the political realities in most GATT countries, Hudec explained, 'even the most respected legal rules will sometimes be overcome' by domestic pressures coming from an influential industry, or some peculiar economic or political situation that the government cannot afford to ignore.[19] Other classes of 'wrong' cases included disputes initiated with respect to issues over which the GATT community had either not yet reached a consensus or issues over which a past consensus had broken down.[20] Since cases falling into the latter two categories were highly likely to produce results that the losing state, and perhaps other states, would not regard as legitimate, they were likewise thought to have the potential of putting heavy strains on the GATT system.[21]

Anxious to avoid the kind of stress on the system that these and the other types of 'wrong' cases might produce, negotiators in the Tokyo Round sought to prevent such cases from reaching the GATT DSS, or at least from going through the panel process on their way to judgment.[22] To this end, the negotiators 'attempted to discourage the filing of potentially troublesome complaints, and limited access

16 William J Davey, 'Dispute Settlement in GATT' (1987) 11 Fordham Int'l LJ 51, 69–70.

17 Hudec (n 12) 159.

18 ibid 159–66.

19 ibid 159.

20 ibid 160–66. Hudec distinguished in his writing between those disputes that seek to enforce rules no longer representing consensus (cases involving 'inoperative rules') and those cases that overtax the GATT DSS by asking it to rule on cases where no consensus exists (cases capable of 'overtaxing the GATT procedure'). In each category, the problem is a lack of a generally supported rule.

21 Taylor (n 1) 324; Davey (n 16) 74.

22 Kenneth W Abbott, 'The Uruguay Round and Dispute Resolution: Building a Private-Interests System of Justice' (1992) Colum Bus L Rev 111, 119–20.

to the dispute resolution process by continuing to require a consensus decision' of all GATT Contracting Parties to establish a panel.[23] Similarly, '[f]or situations in which potentially troublesome cases did manage to enter the process', the negotiators again upheld the consensus requirement for adoption of a panel ruling, a requirement that served as 'a safety valve, a last opportunity to avoid a potentially damaging confrontation' in instances where it appeared that the ruling would not be implemented without serious conflict.[24] Against this backdrop, Frieder Roessler, a former director of the GATT Legal Affairs Division, noted that:

> [The GATT's] requirement to have a consensus ... ensured that overly difficult issues would not come to the GATT. The GATT was then very successful in solving the cases that were brought to it, but the cases that were brought to it were cases that could be resolved by it.[25]

The idea of 'wrong' cases was revisited by commentators during the Uruguay Round negotiations, in the lead-up to the adoption of the Dispute Settlement Understanding (DSU).[26] In the early days of the Uruguay Round talks, which placed dispute settlement high on the Round's negotiating agenda, William Davey, for example, alluded to the fears raised by those opposing legalization of the GATT DSS, who argued that taking a more legalistic direction in the area of dispute settlement would result in '"wrong" cases being brought into the system'—cases the resolution of which would undermine the GATT trading regime and could lead to its collapse.[27] A few years later, before the conclusion of the Uruguay Round negotiations, Kenneth Abbott echoed similar concerns. He argued that the negotiated draft of the DSU, which permitted virtually any claim to enter the dispute settlement process and provided for virtually automatic adoption of DSS rulings, would facilitate presentation of such 'wrong' cases before the GATT system. These cases in turn would generate rulings that the losing states will not observe because 'the domestic political costs are too high, because they see the rulings as incorrect, because they (and perhaps others) no longer accept the norms on which the rulings were based', or because of any number of other reasons.[28] Abbott further claimed that while compliance under the negotiated draft of the DSU would be supported by new implementation procedures and quasi-automatic authorization of retaliatory measures, '[t]here could still be cases in which a powerful contracting party would refuse to comply with a decision, even after exhausting all the available

[23] ibid 120.
[24] ibid 120, 140.
[25] Interview recorded in Geneva at the side-lines of the Legal Affairs Division thirtieth anniversary event (*WTO*, 28 June 2012) <http://www.wto.org/english/tratop_e/dispu_e/lad30bday_e.htm> accessed 20 December 2018.
[26] Taylor (n 1) 316.
[27] Davey (n 16) 70, 73–76.
[28] Abbot (n 22) 119–20, 140–41.

procedures'.[29] Legal failures of this sort, Abbot concluded, might seriously weaken the GATT as an institution.[30]

Despite these warnings, a far more legalistic dispute settlement mechanism was established by the end of the Uruguay Round, with the formation of the WTO that replaced GATT as the structure overseeing the multilateral trading system. In the wake of this development, the stated concerns over 'wrong' or 'impossible' cases seem to have materialized. The WTO's more judicialized DSS has produced over the years a series of long-lasting, charged, and very knotty trade disputes that resulted in recurring rounds of litigation and obdurate noncompliance.[31] As Davis has noted, the WTO DSS, since its establishment in 1995, has confronted 'many of the most difficult trade disputes' in areas where economic and political stakes are high and compliance is unlikely, such as '[g]overnment subsidies for aircraft development and agriculture production, regulation on food safety, and safeguards to limit textile and steel imports'.[32]

To be more specific, among the 'wrong' or 'impossible' perennial cases that have made their way to the DSS's docket we can cite: *EC-Bananas*—the two-decade-long dispute against the discriminatory EU regime for banana importation brought to the WTO by the United States and several Latin American countries after the previous GATT DSS had failed to resolve the conflict;[33] *EC-Hormones*—the protracted dispute launched by the United States and Canada against the EU import ban on beef treated with growth-hormones, the origins of which also date back to the GATT era;[34] *US-Softwood Lumber*—the long-running series of cases between Canada and the United States concerning the US import duties on allegedly subsidized Canadian lumber, which reached the WTO DSS in 2001, after being litigated before other international and national fora throughout the 1980s and 1990s;[35] and the *US-Zeroing* saga, in which the US Department of Commerce's methodology for calculating dumping margins was repeatedly challenged by WTO Members, including China, Japan, and the EU.[36] Other perennial disputes include, among others, the *US-FSC* case,[37] an extension of the famous GATT DISC

[29] ibid 142.
[30] ibid 141.
[31] Taylor (n 1) 444–45.
[32] Davis (n 5) 245.
[33] *European Communities–Regime for the Importation, Sale and Distribution of Bananas*, Report of the Appellate Body, 25 September 1997, WT/DS27/AB/R.
[34] *European Communities–Measures Concerning Meat and Meat Products (Hormones)*, Report of the Appellate Body, 13 February 1998, WT/DS26/AB/R, WT/DS48/AB/R.
[35] See, e.g. *United States–Final Countervailing Duty Determination with Respect to Certain Softwood Lumber from Canada*, Report of the Appellate Body, 17 February 2004, WT/DS257/AB/R.
[36] See, e.g. *United States–Certain Methodologies and Their Application to Anti-Dumping Proceedings Involving China*, Report of the Appellate Body, 22 May 2017, WT/DS471/AB/R; *United States–Measures Relating to Zeroing and Sunset Reviews*, Report of the Appellate Body, 23 January 2007, WT/DS322/AB/R; *United States–Laws, Regulations and Methodology for Calculating Dumping Margins (Zeroing)*, Report of the Appellate Body, 9 May 2006, WT/DS294/AB/R.
[37] *United States–Tax Treatment for 'Foreign Sales Corporations'*, Report of the Appellate Body, 20 March 2000, WT/DS108/AB/R.

case; the clashes over aircraft subsidies fought between Canada and Brazil (*Brazil-Aircraft, Canada-Aircraft*)[38] that seem to have been reawakened in 2017;[39] the lengthy conflict between Brazil and the United States over upland cotton subsidies (*US-Upland Cotton*);[40] the enduring *US-Byrd Amendment* dispute brought against the US Continued Dumping and Subsidy Offset Act of 2000 by several WTO complainants, among them the EU, Japan, Canada, and India;[41] and the gigantic, still-contended disputes between the United States and the EU over aircraft subsidies (*EC-Airbus* and *US-Boeing*).[42]

Whereas under the old GATT DSS these 'wrong' cases, all characterized by sustained noncompliance, could have largely been blocked from referral to a panel,[43] under the reformed WTO DSS, with its 'reverse consensus rule', the blocking of such cases has become effectively impossible.[44] In expressing the negative sentiments associated with this state of affairs, Karen Alter has noted: 'The cases where compliance has been the most problematic in the WTO system ... —the disputes over bananas, beef hormones and US export subsidies—were all blocked in the old system; and perhaps they should have been.'[45]

7.3 Are Those Cases Really 'Wrong'? 'Trade Wars', Trade-Offs, and the Shift Away from Compliance

As the last quotation implies, perennial WTO disputes such as those mentioned above, where noncompliance with WTO legal prescriptions was an enduring pattern, even in the face of DSS-authorized sanctions and, at times, even after the dispute was finally settled, have often been depicted by commentators as 'legal failures' and instances of WTO DSS ineffectiveness.[46] This perception is by no

[38] See, e.g. *Brazil–Export Financing Programme for Aircraft*, Report of the Appellate Body, 20 August 1999, WT/DS46/AB/R; *Canada–Measures Affecting the Export of Civilian Aircraft*, Report of the Appellate Body, 20 August 1999, WT/DS70/AB/R.

[39] *Canada–Measures Concerning Trade in Commercial Aircraft*, Request for Consultations by Brazil, 15 February 2017, WT/DS522/1, G/SCM/D114/1, G/L/1176.

[40] *United States–Subsidies on Upland Cotton*, Report of the Appellate Body, 21 March 2005, WT/DS267/AB/R.

[41] See, e.g. *United States–Continued Dumping and Subsidy Offset Act of 2000*, Report of the Appellate Body, 27 January 2003, WT/DS217/AB/R, WT/DS234/AB/R.

[42] See, e.g. *European Communities–Measures Affecting Trade in Large Civil Aircraft*, Report of the Appellate Body, 1 June 2011, WT/DS316/AB/R; *United States–Measures Affecting Trade in Large Civil Aircraft–(Second Complaint)*, Report of the Appellate Body, 23 March 2012, WT/DS353/AB/R.

[43] Karen J Alter, 'Resolving or Exacerbating Disputes? The WTO's New Dispute Resolution System' (2003) 79 Int'l Aff 783, 788.

[44] For a recent overview of the various perennial cases mentioned above, as well as others falling under this category, see Cherie O'Neal Taylor, 'Beyond Retaliation' (2017) 38 Nw J Int'l L & Bus 55.

[45] Alter (n 43) 788.

[46] See, e.g. Taylor (n 44); Gary Horlick and Judith Coleman, 'A Comment on Compliance with WTO Dispute Settlement Decisions' in Merit E Janow, Victoria Donaldson, and Alan Yanovich (eds), *WTO: Governance, Dispute Settlement and Developing Countries* (Juris Publishing Inc 2008) 771; William J Davey, 'The WTO Dispute Settlement System: The First Ten Years' (2005) 8 J Int'l Econ L 17;

means surprising. After all, the judicialization undergone by the DSS in the turn from GATT to the WTO in the mid-1990s was largely motivated by the will to strengthen the 'international rule of law' in the multilateral trading system[47] and the desire to provide 'a singularly effective mechanism by which Members can seek the full implementation of previously negotiated trade concessions'.[48] As 'a system designed to provide for the rule of law ... in international trade relations',[49] it is rather tempting to view the failure of the DSS in perennial disputes to hold states (let alone major trading powers) accountable to their original WTO treaty commitments as evidence of judicial ineffectiveness.

This perception, however, like the very designation of cases falling under the category of perennial conflicts as 'wrong cases' because of their heightened prospects of noncompliance, seems to rest on the premise of compliance as the key objective to be attained by the legalized WTO DSS across disputes, regardless of their type or nature and, in consequence, as the main yardstick of its effectiveness. The question nonetheless arises as to whether highly charged perennial disputes—some would say potential 'trade wars'—between major protagonists are indeed all about compliance; that is, whether ensuring enforcement of WTO rules, and thereby upholding the WTO rule of law, is the unwavering primary goal envisaged for the DSS in such cases. Or, perhaps, the unique challenges inherent in perennial conflicts, and their implications for Members' economic relations and the long-term viability of the cooperative WTO regime, may trigger shifts among the goals its adjudicative system is expected to promote, bringing to the fore DSS goals other than (and, at times, at the expense of) compliance, thereby exhibiting intricate trade-offs between 'trade wars' and the international rule of law.

An in-depth qualitative analysis of two such recurring perennial conflicts—the famous *EC-Bananas* and *EC-Hormones*—indeed discloses a more complex picture of the DSS's operation and goal-attainment efforts in this class of cases. This

Chad P Bown, *Self-Enforcing Trade: Developing Countries and WTO Dispute Settlement* (Brookings Institution Press 2009) 58; Marc L Busch and Eric Reinhardt, 'Transatlantic Trade Conflicts and GATT/WTO Dispute Settlement' in Ernst-Ulrich Petersmann and Mark A Pollack (eds), *Transatlantic Economic Disputes: The EU, the US, and the WTO* (OUP 2003) 483; Benjamin L Brimeyer, 'Banana, Beef, and Compliance in the World Trade Organization: The Inability of the WTO Dispute Settlement Process to Achieve Compliance from Superpower Nations' (2001) 10 Minn J Global Trade 133; Iida Keisuke, 'Is WTO Dispute Settlement Effective?' (2004) 10 Global Governance 207, 214; Alter (n 43) 788–89; Taylor (n 1) 321–27.

[47] Ernst-Ulrich Petersmann, 'How to Promote the International Rule of Law? Contributions by the World Trade Organization Appellate Review System' (1998) 1 J Int'l Econ L 25, 31. See also, Mireille Cossy, 'From Theory to Practice: Drafting and Applying the Dispute Settlement Understanding' in Gabrielle Marceau (ed), *A History of Law and Lawyers in the GATT/WTO: The Development of the Rule of Law in the Multilateral Trading System* (CUP 2015) 301–02.

[48] David Evans and Gregory C Shaffer, 'Introduction' in Gregory C Shaffer and Ricardo Meléndez-Ortiz (eds), *Dispute Settlement at the WTO: The Developing Country Experience* (CUP 2010) 1.

[49] ibid. For further discussion of this perception of the WTO DSS, and international courts more generally, see Sivan Shlomo Agon, 'Non-Compliance, Renegotiation and Justice in International Adjudication: A WTO Perspective' (2016) 5 Global Constitutionalism 238.

analysis, carried out in the two following chapters, recounts the story of a mandatory international adjudicating system that in certain disputes—and contrary to the conventional wisdom—is not geared primarily to mechanical enforcement of WTO rules but, rather, plays an enhanced role in the fissure between law and politics, where the prominent function of the DSS travels along two main paths. First, through its successive rulings and legal interpretations, the DSS serves to facilitate the amicable settlement of the dispute and the re-establishment of the bilateral balance of concessions between the parties by continually (re)framing renegotiating environments and constructing focal points around which the parties can coordinate. Second, so long as the perennial dispute endures, the DSS further plays a pivotal function in sustaining the operation of the WTO regime by managing and containing the dispute within defined legal parameters, defusing its charged political elements, preventing across-the-board deterioration through unilateral actions, and forestalling escalation of the conflict into an uncontrolled trade war.

And so, we argue, these two parallel tracks reveal a subtle-but-critical shift in perennial disputes away from compliance and towards the dispute settlement, rebalancing, and regime-maintenance goals of the DSS. Along these paths, the DSS is being recast as primarily a forum for dispute containment and repeated interaction that assists the parties to preserve their cooperative relationships while they seek readjustment of the original terms of their bargain. In other words, in high-stake, protracted conflicts of this kind, disputing before the DSS, rather than simply enforcing compliance with WTO law, serves as a mechanism by which disputants can harness the law and the judicial process to transform noncompliance into renegotiation and, eventually, into a settlement that reinstitutes their bilateral balance of benefits. Crucially, if this is indeed the case and such goal shifting occurs, one may question the initial designation of perennial disputes as 'wrong' cases (i.e. cases preferably excluded from DSS deliberation because of the likelihood of their entangling the system in sustained noncompliance). On the contrary, one may suggest that the DSS is needed in large part precisely for those intense trade rows that risk spoiling Members' broader economic and political relations; otherwise, the entire cooperative WTO enterprise may come to a halt.

As demonstrated in the following chapters, the argued shift in emphasis in perennial disputes towards the DSS's goals of settlement facilitation, rebalancing the scales, and regime maintenance emerges from the views and experience of practitioners with first-hand knowledge of *EC-Bananas* and *EC-Hormones*, as well as of comparable WTO cases. This goal shifting is further reflected in the distinctive judicial choices, interpretations, and techniques used by WTO adjudicators in these same cases, which expose a conscious prioritization of some DSS goals over others in the face of the intricacies and challenges presented to the system.

After briefly explaining the reasons underlying the selection of *EC-Bananas* and *EC-Hormones* as case studies well suited for the exploration of DSS performance and goal-attainment patterns within the context of perennial disputes, this third part of the book proceeds in Chapter 8 with a comprehensive goal-based investigation of *EC-Bananas*. Chapter 9 follows with an examination of *EC-Hormones*. This part closes with a comparative analysis of the two cases, while assessing the implications of the emerging findings for measuring DSS performance and for developing its goal-based effectiveness framework.

7.4 Case Selection

> [T]here's some category of [WTO] disputes that is different from the others. . . . [And] I . . . think [in this regard] *Bananas* and *Hormones* are the ones that are most frequently cited.
>
> –Interview with private attorney
> (Geneva, 23 April 2012)

The *EC-Bananas* and *EC-Hormones* disputes, often depicted as 'wrong' cases that enmeshed the DSS in long and abashing noncompliance,[50] constitute probably the most paradigmatic perennial disputes to reach the WTO DSS. They are therefore likely to be fruitful sources for tracing the DSS's goal-attainment patterns and the diverse roles it plays, beyond that of inducing compliance, in this class of cases.[51]

Furthermore, the two trade feuds dating back to the GATT were both concluded in recent years, almost two decades into the WTO's existence, with mutually agreed—albeit not fully WTO-compliant—settlements, after recurring rounds of WTO litigation, including recourse to WTO countermeasures. *EC-Bananas* and *EC-Hormones* thus aptly illustrate not only the shifting emphases but also the trade-offs imposed between the multiple goals and outcomes of the DSS, in particular, between compliance and settlement. In a similar vein, as opposed to ongoing perennial conflicts (e.g. *Airbus/Boeing*), the settled *Bananas* and *Hormones* disputes—the negotiated outcomes of which have been phased in until recently—offer us the opportunity to not only explore the DSS unique goal-attainment efforts as played out in perennial disputes; these cases also allow us to juxtapose the goals sought by the DSS with the actual outcomes delivered by the system, an important

[50] See, e.g. Taylor (n 1); Mark A Pollack, 'Managing System Friction: Regulatory Conflicts in Transatlantic Relations and the WTO' in *Transatlantic Economic Disputes* (n 46) 596; Brimeyer (n 46) 133–34; Bown (n 46) 59; Busch and Reinhardt (n 46) 476–78.

[51] Among the various factors making *EC-Hormones* a 'perennial' dispute (e.g. its charged prehistory, the opposing philosophies of the parties, and the complex politics of the agricultural sector) was the tension between the trade and health issues invoked. Thus, *EC-Hormones* fits the category of perennial but also that of trade-and disputes, and, as seen in Chapter 6 (Section 6.1), it exhibits many of the legitimacy-enhancing techniques apparent in other trade-and disputes such as *US-Shrimp* and *US-Clove Cigarettes*. This duality is not surprising given the multiple characteristics of any dispute, which may allow it to belong simultaneously to diverse categories of cases. Here, *EC-Hormones* is analysed from the perspective of the case as a perennial dispute—one complicating element of which is the tension between trade and health encapsulated therein.

element for a research project aimed at developing a comprehensive goal-based framework for analysing the effectiveness of the WTO DSS.

In addition, because the origins of the chosen conflicts trace back to the GATT—where the establishment of a panel to decide the case or the adoption of the panel report was blocked by the respondent—the focus on *EC-Bananas* and *EC-Hormones* (as opposed to perennial WTO conflicts that have no prior GATT history) may allow us to juxtapose the fates of the disputes under the GATT DSS and the legalized WTO DSS, and compare their performance throughout. Such an analytical exercise, in turn, may fit neatly into current debates on the nature and strength of the WTO DSS, and offer pertinent insights into the ramifications of undoing the system's judicialization or, alternatively, moving further along the judicialization path.

Finally, *EC-Bananas* and *EC-Hormones* also represent appropriate case studies for the current research because of the differences between them, including the distinct WTO agreements invoked, the different trade measures challenged, and the diverse parties involved (the United States and the EU in both disputes, Canada in *EC-Hormones*, and two competing groups of developing countries in *EC-Bananas*). These differences allow examination and comparison of the judicial attitudes and goal-attainment efforts manifested by the DSS in perennial disputes across different WTO agreements, subject matters, and political contexts.

8
The Multilateral Trade System Goes Bananas

On 8 November 2012, notification of a mutually agreed solution to the transatlantic dispute over trade in bananas, known as *EC-Bananas*, was submitted to the World Trade Organization (WTO) Dispute Settlement Body (DSB).[1] This moment signalled the end of one of the longest-running disputes in the history of the multilateral trading system. The convoluted conflict—in which third-party adjudication and negotiation were entwined and noncompliance was persistent—provides an interesting vantage point for studying the goal-attainment efforts exhibited by the WTO Dispute Settlement System (DSS) in perennial disputes, together with the goal-shifting and goal-conflict patterns characterizing these types of cases. This conflict thus stands at the centre of this chapter.

In what follows, Section 8.1 provides a brief background on the origins of the *Bananas* case. It then recounts the dispute's major turning points in the multilateral trading system—under the General Agreement on Tariffs and Trade (GATT) regime and the WTO—events crucial for understanding the protracted nature of the conflict but also the goals pursued and functions served by the WTO DSS throughout its duration. Section 8.2 identifies the main factors that made *EC-Bananas* so prolonged and resistant to resolution. On these foundations, Section 8.3 delves into a comprehensive goal-based reading of the *Bananas* saga, tracing the DSS's goal-attainment efforts and the shifts in emphasis taken towards some of its organizational objectives in the face of the challenges this case posed to the DSS and the WTO regime. Section 8.4 follows with an examination of the resulting conflicts between DSS goals and the mixed, noncompliant outcomes ultimately produced in *EC-Bananas*, while assessing their ramifications for an analysis of the system's effectiveness. Section 8.5 concludes.

[1] Notification of a Mutually Agreed Solution, *European Communities–Regime for the Importation, Sale and Distribution of Bananas* (12 November 2012) WT/DS27/98, G/L/63/Add.1, G/LIC/D/2/Add.1, S/L/17/Add.1, G/AG/W/18/Add.1, G/TRIMS/4/Add [hereinafter Notification of a Mutually Agreed Solution].

8.1 The Basic Pieces of the Puzzle

Origins of the Dispute

The origins of *EC-Bananas* trace back to the 1993 creation of a common EU regime for trade in bananas that established new terms of access to the European market—the world's largest banana market, with imports valued at roughly $2.5 billion annually.[2] Until 1993, the EU banana market was rather segmented, with each Member state applying its own trade policy.[3] At one end of the spectrum, Germany operated the largest and most liberal market, with bananas entering duty-free, primarily from low-cost suppliers in Latin America. In the middle, Belgium, Denmark, the Netherlands, and other Members applied a 20 per cent tariff on banana imports, also arriving mainly from Latin America. At the other extreme were France, the UK, and Spain, whose markets were effectively closed to banana imports from all but selected sources. Spain relied on domestic banana production from the Canary Islands, whereas France and the UK largely imported bananas on preferential terms from their former colonies in Africa, the Caribbean, and the Pacific (the ACP regions), in accordance with the special trade arrangements accorded by the EU to countries in those regions (the ACP countries), pursuant to the Lomé Convention.[4]

It took four years of hard-fought negotiations for the EU to replace this patchwork of national policies with a single European regime for the import of bananas as part of the implementation of the 1987 Single European Act.[5] This unified, highly complex and interventionist regime was announced in December 1992 and scheduled to be implemented on 1 July 1993. It consisted of a multilayered system of tariffs, quotas, and licence requirements that would benefit the ACP countries

[2] Chad P Bown, *Self-Enforcing Trade: Developing Countries and WTO Dispute Settlement* (Brookings Institution Press 2009) 49.

[3] For details see, Jaime de Melo, 'Bananas, the GATT, the WTO and US and EU Domestic Politics' (2015) 42 J Econ Stud 377, 378–80; Oliver Cadot and Douglas Webber, 'Banana Splits: Policy Process, Particularistic Interests, Political Capture, and Money in Transatlantic Trade Politics' (2002) 4 Bus & Pol 5, 8–11.

[4] Signed in 1975 (and renewed in 1979, 1984, and 1989), the Lomé Convention established an aid and trade agreement between the then European Economic Community (EEC) and developing ACP countries, many of which were ex-European colonies. The special relationship constructed in the agreement was characterized by nonreciprocal trade benefits for the ACP countries, including unlimited entry to the EU market for 99 per cent of industrial goods and many other products. Among other things, the Lomé Convention included free access of bananas from ACP countries to the EU market, enshrined in a specific banana Protocol annexed to the Convention. At least eight ACP signatories to the Lomé Convention were significant banana suppliers. The fourth edition of the Lomé Convention lapsed in February 2000. It was replaced by a new ACP-EU partnership agreement, known as the Cotonou Agreement, signed on 23 June 2000.

[5] The Single European Act (SEA) was signed in February 1986 by the Members of the then European Economic Community (EEC; precursor to the European Community and, later, the European Union) and came into force in July 1987. The SEA called, inter alia, for the establishment of a single market by 31 December 1992. It thus required the development of unified European trade regimes or rules for a variety of goods, including bananas, that until 1992 had been handled by the individual Member states.

and firms that traditionally traded in EU and ACP bananas (mainly European firms), while imposing heavy costs on the so-called dollar bananas originating in Latin American countries, where banana production was largely dominated by US-based multinational companies such as Chiquita Brands and Dole.[6] The new EU regime also inflicted substantial costs on consumers in some of the EU Member states having loose colonial ties (e.g. Germany) by requiring replacement of their previous liberal market, which allowed for the import of low-cost Latin American bananas, with a new arrangement that favoured the more expensive EU and ACP bananas. Despite the protests of these EU Members, the common EU banana policy, known as Regulation 404/93, took effect in July 1993.[7]

The GATT *Banana* Disputes

The contentious European banana regime fell afoul of various GATT/WTO rules. Particularly problematic were the trade preferences accorded by the EU to one group of banana exporters (ACP producers) but not to others (Latin American producers), an act that constituted a violation of the basic most-favoured nation (MFN) principle underlying the multilateral trading system, which requires Member states to treat all their trading partners equally. Latin American banana-producing countries thus initiated legal challenges against the EU's commercial arrangements in the area of trade in bananas already under the WTO's predecessor, the GATT.

The first legal challenge was launched while negotiations on the common EU banana regime were still underway. In 1992, a group of five Latin American countries (Colombia, Costa Rica, Guatemala, Nicaragua, and Venezuela) tried to put pressure on European negotiators by filing a dispute with the GATT DSS, challenging the GATT-consistency of the various European national banana regimes (*Bananas I*). In June 1993, the GATT panel ruled in favour of the complainants, finding the contested national schemes to violate the MFN obligation enshrined in GATT Article I and the prohibition against quantitative restrictions stipulated in Article XI.[8] The adoption of the panel report was blocked, however, by the EU and the ACP countries, using their veto power under the GATT's consensus rule.

The same Latin American countries requested the establishment of another GATT panel once the common EU banana regime took effect in July 1993

[6] Hélène Ruiz-Fabri, 'The Relationship Between Negotiations and Third-Party Dispute Settlement at the WTO, with an Emphasis on the *EC-Bananas* Dispute' in Laurence Boisson de Chazournes, Marcelo G Kohen, and Jorge E Viñuales (eds), *Diplomatic and Judicial Means of Dispute Settlement* (Martinus Nijhoff Publishers 2013) 87, 89.

[7] Karen J Alter and Sophie Meunier, 'Nested and Overlapping Regimes in the Transatlantic Banana Trade Dispute' (2006) 13 J Eur Pub Pol'y 362, 366–67.

[8] *EEC-Members States' Import Regime for Bananas*, Report of the GATT Panel, 3 June 1993, DS32/R (unadopted).

(*Bananas II*). The panel's ruling, delivered in February 1994, likewise sided with the complainants, finding the unified EU banana policy to be inconsistent with GATT rules because, inter alia, it violated the MFN requirement and discriminated against bananas grown in Latin America.[9] Yet, once again, the panel report was blocked by the EU and never adopted.

Reluctant to accept any GATT ruling regarding its banana regime, the EU nevertheless responded by requesting the GATT Council for a waiver that would allow continuation of its GATT-inconsistent trade preferences for ACP countries under the Lomé Convention. A six-year waiver from its obligations under Article I of the GATT (MFN) was granted to the EU in December 1994 (the Lomé waiver).[10] Furthermore, in anticipation of future legal challenges to its banana regime under the WTO DSS, which was scheduled to become operative on 1 January 1995 and which was expected to make it virtually impossible to block adverse legal rulings, the EU negotiated a deal with the Latin American complainants in the GATT disputes. This deal offered the five complainants a higher quota for their banana exports to Europe, a lower tariff, and a revised system of licences in exchange for a hold on further legal actions against the EU's policy.[11] In March 1994, just one month after the *Bananas II* ruling, four of the five Latin American complainants—Colombia, Costa Rica, Nicaragua, and Venezuela—agreed to the deal, known as the Framework Agreement on Banana Imports. This they did despite protests by the United States, Germany, and some other Latin American countries, which saw their access to the European market further reduced in face of the agreement.[12]

EC-Bananas at the WTO

Soon after the transition to the WTO in 1995 and the accession of Ecuador (the world's largest banana grower) to the Organization in January 1996, litigation against the EU banana regime was renewed (*Bananas III*). This time, the United States joined in the complaint filed by Ecuador, Guatemala, Honduras, and Mexico, following massive pressures from US-based firms (particularly Chiquita Brands) having large investments in the Latin American banana sector. In their rulings of May 1997 and September 1997, respectively, the panel[13] and the Appellate Body

[9] *EEC–Import Regime for Bananas*, Report of the GATT Panel, 11 February 1994, DS38/R (unadopted).

[10] The Fourth ACP-EEC Convention of Lomé - GATT Waiver (9 December 1994) GATT Doc L/7604.

[11] Cherie O'Neal Taylor, 'Impossible Cases: Lessons from the First Decade of WTO Dispute Settlement' (2007) 28 U Pa J Int'l L 309, 347.

[12] Alter and Meunier (n 7) 369.

[13] *European Communities–Regime for the Importation, Sale and Distribution of Bananas*, Report of the Panel, 25 September 1997, WT/DS27/R/USA [*EC-Bananas* Panel Report].

(AB)[14] concluded that the EU banana regime was inconsistent with WTO law. Although the EU's preferential tariffs for ACP countries were not found to be discriminatory per se because of the Lomé waiver, the EU's import quotas and import licences were found to unduly discriminate against Latin American banana exporters and American marketing companies. While the main thrust of the panel's and the AB's rulings complied with the original GATT rulings, under the WTO's reverse consensus rule, the EU could not block the adoption of the rulings and thereby prevent them from gaining legally binding status. Moreover, the same rule abolished the respondent's ability to block the move along the entire route of WTO dispute settlement, thus securing the complainants' capacity to pursue further compliance-review proceedings, or seek authorized retaliation against the EU in case the latter failed to comply with the DSS rulings against it.

Following its defeat before the panel and the AB, the EU was granted a 'reasonable period' of fifteen months to implement the DSS rulings. During this period, negotiations between the parties were conducted, parallel to the EU's working towards a revised banana policy. This work resulted in the promulgation of a new banana proposal four months into the implementation period. Despite the complainants' strong objection to the proposal, which put forward an expanded quota for banana imports from Latin America and replaced the previous import licensing system with one purportedly WTO-compatible, the proposed banana policy became effective in January 1999. However, it was not long before the first compliance panel initiated by Ecuador under Article 21.5 of the Dispute Settlement Understanding (DSU) confirmed in April 1999 that the amended EU banana policy still illegally discriminated against Latin American suppliers and US traders.[15] In a rather exceptional move, the compliance panel not only recommended that the EU bring its banana regime into conformity with WTO rules but, further to Ecuador's request, it made specific suggestions as to how the respondent could do so. Fundamental among those suggestions was the proposition that the EU shift to a 'tariff-only' banana regime, coupled with a tariff or tariff-quota preference for ACP bananas that would be covered by a suitable WTO waiver or a free trade agreement consistent with GATT Article XXIV.[16] The compliance panel's suggestions, as I detail below, 'had a significant impact on the subsequent negotiations about the resolution to the problem'.[17]

[14] *European Communities–Regime for the Importation, Sale and Distribution of Bananas*, Report of the Appellate Body, 25 September 1999, WT/DS27/AB/R [*EC-Bananas* AB Report].

[15] *European Communities–Regime for the Importation, Sale and Distribution of Bananas, Recourse to Article 21.5 of the DSU by Ecuador*, Report of the Panel, 6 May 1999, WT/DS27/RW/ECU [First Compliance Panel Report (Ecuador)]. Note that a separate request for a compliance panel was filed by the EU. The report delivered by the EU's compliance panel, however, was never adopted. *European Communities–Regime for the Importation, Sale and Distribution of Bananas, Recourse to Article 21.5 of the DSU by the European Communities*, Report of the Panel, 12 April 1999, WT/DS27/RW/EEC.

[16] First Compliance Panel Report (Ecuador) (n 15) paras 6.154–6.159.

[17] Tim Josling, 'Bananas and the WTO: Testing the New Dispute Settlement Process' in Tim E Josling and Tim G Taylor (eds), *Banana Wars: The Anatomy of a Trade Dispute* (CABI Publishing 2003) 190.

While compliance proceedings under DSU Article 21.5 were still underway, the United States, on its part, began seeking DSB authorization to suspend concessions to the EU in the amount of $520 million annually. DSU Article 22.6 arbitration ultimately set the level of authorized retaliation at $191.4 million annually,[18] which the United States started implementing on 19 April 1999 through imposition of a 100 per cent tariff on selected EU products imported into the United States. The nonagricultural products selected were designed to put pressure on EU Member states that supported the banana regime, among them, the UK and France.[19] In like manner, Ecuador, in November 1999, requested DSB authorization for 'cross-retaliation' against the EU in the spheres of services and intellectual property (rather than in consumer goods). Such authorization, the first for the WTO, was granted in March 2000, when Article 22.6 arbitration determined that Ecuador could cross retaliate against the EU in the amount of $201.6 million annually.[20]

In the end, Ecuador did not activate its retaliation rights. Yet, European concerns over the threat of cross-retaliation in the intellectual property sector,[21] alongside the sanctions employed by the United States, led the EU to engage in serious negotiations with the United States, Ecuador, and the other Latin American complainants.[22] The intense negotiations resulted in the signing in April 2001 of two nearly identical agreements, known as the 'Understandings on Bananas'. Under these agreements, concluded by the EU with the United States and Ecuador, the latter two pledged to suspend, and later terminate, their retaliatory rights. The EU, in return, committed to instituting a tariff-only regime for banana imports no later than January 2006, after a transition period during which the produce would be imported into the EU according to tariff quotas and licences distributed on the basis of past trade. Significantly, under WTO rules (Article XXVIII of the GATT), the move to a tariff-only regime effectively required the EU to reach an agreement with the Latin American MFN banana suppliers on the level of the tariff to apply under the future tariff-only system. As we shall later learn, the need to reach such an agreement remained the main stumbling block to final resolution of the *Bananas* dispute.

[18] *European Communities–Regime for the Importation, Sale and Distribution of Bananas, Recourse to Arbitration by the European Communities under Article 22.6 of the DSU*, Decision by the Arbitrators, 9 April 1999, WT/DS27/ARB [Article 22.6 Arbitration (US)].

[19] Scott D Andersen and Justine Blanchet, 'The United States' Experience and Practice in Suspending WTO Obligations' in Chad P Bown and Joost Pauwelyn (eds), *The Law, Economics and Politics of Retaliation in WTO Dispute Settlement* (CUP 2010) 238.

[20] *European Communities–Regime for the Importation, Sale and Distribution of Bananas, Recourse to Arbitration by the European Communities*, Decision by the Arbitrators, 24 March 2000, WT/DS27/ARB/ECU [Article 22.6 Arbitration (Ecuador)].

[21] James McCall Smith, 'Compliance Bargaining in the WTO: Ecuador and the Bananas Dispute' in John S Odell (ed), *Negotiating Trade: Developing Countries in the WTO and NAFTA* (CUP 2006) 271.

[22] Eckart Guth, 'The End of the Bananas Saga' (2012) 46 J World Trade 1, 6. See also Simon A B Schropp and David Palmeter, 'Commentary on the Appellate Body Report in EC-Bananas III (Article 21.5): Waiver-Thin, or Lock, Stock, and Metric Ton?' (2010) 9 World Trade Rev 7, 9.

Following conclusion of the 2001 Understandings on Bananas, the EU submitted a communication to the DSB, entitled 'Notification of Mutually Agreed Solution', wherein it argued that the Understandings reached constituted 'a mutually satisfactory solution' to the *Bananas* dispute 'within the meaning of Article 3.6 of the DSU'.[23] The United States and Ecuador, in separate communications, denied this qualification, arguing that the Understandings identified means by which the perennial dispute could be solved, but that it would be premature to take the item off the DSB agenda.[24] Yet, no less important for the EU at this stage was the need to secure WTO waivers for the trade preferences to be accorded to the ACP countries during the transition to the tariff-only regime. In November 2001, after heated negotiations, two waivers, one for its tariff preferences and the other for its special quota for ACP bananas, were granted to the EU at the WTO Ministerial Conference in Doha.[25] It then became clear, however, that if the EU wished to maintain a zero-tariff preference for ACP bananas once the tariff-only regime took effect, the WTO-consistent way to achieve that objective was to negotiate 'Free Trade Agreements' (FTAs) with the ACP countries in accordance with GATT Article XXIV.[26] Two years later, in 2003, the EU launched the so-called European Partnership Agreements (EPAs) negotiations with several groups of ACP countries.[27] 'Although EPAs remained the only way to grant the ACPs a zero-tariff treatment for bananas, many of the ACPs remained reluctant' to substitute the unilateral preferences obtained from the EU with reciprocal trade commitments under the EPAs.[28] At the time of writing, these protracted negotiations have yet to be fully completed, and the agreements reached (not necessarily as originally envisaged) have yet to be fully implemented.[29]

In addition to the waivers, it should be noted here, the Doha Ministerial Conference also laid down special procedures for two-stage arbitration in the

[23] Notification of a Mutually Agreed Solution, *European Communities–Regime for the Importation, Sale and Distribution of Bananas* (2 July 2001) WT/DS27/58.

[24] Communication from the United States, *European Communities–Regime for the Importation, Sale and Distribution of Bananas* (2 July 2001) WT/DS27/59, G/C/W/270; Communication from Ecuador, *European Communities–Regime for the Importation, Sale and Distribution of Bananas* (9 July 2001) WT/DS27/60, G/C/W/274.

[25] See European Communities–The ACP-EC Partnership Agreement, Decision of 14 November 2001, WT/MIN(01)/15; European Communities–Transitional Regime for the EC Autonomous Tariff Rate Quotas on Imports of Bananas, Decision of 14 November 2001, WT/MIN(01)/16.

[26] Guth (n 22) 8.

[27] ibid.

[28] ibid.

[29] The differing views of the participants in the EPA negotiations and the considerable number of countries involved contributed to a protracted negotiating process, which has so far resulted in several agreements. See Niels Keijzer and Lorand Bartels, 'Assessing the Legal and Political Implications of the Post-Cotonou Negotiations for the Economic Partnership Agreements' (2017) German Development Institute Discussion Paper 4/2017, 2, 6 <https://www.die-gdi.de/uploads/media/DP_4.2017.pdf> accessed 20 December 2018. For an overview of the state of play of the different EPAs, see European Commission, 'Overview of Economic Partnership Agreements' (November 2018) <http://trade.ec.europa.eu/doclib/docs/2009/september/tradoc_144912.pdf> accessed 20 December 2018.

event that the EU was unable to reach an agreement with the banana-supplying countries on the MFN tariff to apply under the tariff-only regime. Negotiations between the parties about the 'right' tariff level proved to be technically complex and politically delicate.[30] Two consecutive arbitrations, in August and October 2005, rejected, in turn, the EU's proposed MFN tariff rate (€230/ton and €187/ton, respectively), noting that the suggested rate would not maintain, at the minimum, the total market access to the EU currently enjoyed by the MFN banana suppliers.[31] In the wake of these arbitral proceedings, negotiations continued for another eighteen months. The negotiations achieved some progress towards settlement of the *Bananas* conflict, yet gaps remained, particularly on the issue of the MFN tariff rate.

On 1 January 2006, instead of establishing a tariff-only system (as agreed upon in the 2001 Understandings on Bananas), the EU put a new banana policy in place that provided a reduced MFN tariff rate of €176/ton while maintaining a special zero-tariff quota for bananas of ACP origin.[32] As the EU had failed to comply with its commitment, and as negotiations between the parties had not progressed sufficiently, actions on the WTO's legal front were renewed.[33] Colombia and Panama subsequently filed new, separate complaints against the EU banana regime in 2007. Ecuador, soon followed by the United States, launched another round of DSU Article 21.5 compliance proceedings. The compliance panels' reports were published in the spring of 2008, finding that the zero-tariff quota for ACP bananas and the MFN tariff of €176/ton violated several provisions of the GATT Agreement.[34] At the same time, while compliance proceedings were underway, the EU announced yet another amendment to its policy that eliminated the quota for ACP bananas for the first time, thus finally establishing a truly tariff-only regime. In light of this development, once the compliance panels' reports were out, the parties requested the DSB to extend the thirty-day period provided in the DSU for adoption or appeal in order to enable the parties to explore the possibility of reaching a negotiated solution. However, on 28 August 2008, the EU, followed by Ecuador, notified the DSB of their decision to appeal the compliance panels' rulings before the AB. And so, more than a decade after its first decision in the dispute, the AB

[30] Guth (n 22) 8.

[31] *European Communities–The ACP-EC Partnership Agreement–Recourse to Arbitration Pursuant to the Decision of 14 November 2001*, Award of the Arbitrator, 1 August 2005, WT/L/616; *European Communities–The ACP-EC Partnership Agreement–Second Recourse to Arbitration Pursuant to the Decision of 14 November 2001*, Award of the Arbitrator, 27 October 2005, WT/L/625.

[32] Schropp and Palmeter (n 22) 10.

[33] Guth (n 22) 9.

[34] *European Communities–Regime for the Importation, Sale and Distribution of Bananas, Second Recourse to Article 21.5 of the DSU by Ecuador*, Report of the Panel, 11 December 2008, WT/DS27/RW2/ECU [Second Compliance Panel Report (Ecuador)]; *European Communities–Regime for the Importation, Sale and Distribution of Bananas, Recourse to Article 21.5 of the DSU by the United States*, Report of the Panel, 22 December 2008, WT/DS27/RW/USA [Compliance Panel Report (US)].

found that the WTO-inconsistencies of the EU banana regime had not been fully eliminated.[35]

With the adoption in December 2008 of the reports delivered by the panels and the AB in the second series of compliance proceedings, the formal litigation in the *Bananas* saga came to an end. From this moment on, the remaining differences between the parties were sorted out through negotiations, including those conducted within the framework of the Good Offices provided by the WTO Director General.[36] A year later, in December 2009, two Agreements on Trade in Bananas were ultimately reached in Geneva (the Geneva Agreements), establishing the conditions for the final settlement of the dispute. Under the agreements reached—the Geneva Agreement on Trade in Bananas, concluded between the EU and ten Latin American countries,[37] and the Agreement on Trade in Bananas, concluded between the EU and the United States[38]—the EU committed to maintaining a tariff-only regime for banana imports. It further pledged to lower substantially but gradually its MFN banana tariffs from an initial bound tariff of €148/ton in 2009 to a final bound rate of €114/ton by 2017. The complainants, in return, agreed to terminate and settle all their pending disputes with respect to the EU banana regime. Finally, the parties to the Geneva Agreements agreed that the certification of the new EU tariff commitments on bananas in its WTO tariff schedules would mark the date of settlement of all their disputes. The two agreements, initialled in Geneva on 15 December 2009, were signed on 31 May and 8 June 2010, and formally entered into force about two years later following completion of the ratification procedures. In November 2012, following the WTO's certification of the revised EU tariff commitments on bananas, the parties jointly notified the DSB that they had reached mutually agreed solutions to the disputes on the terms set out in the Geneva Agreements, thereby officially bringing the *Bananas* saga to an end.[39] This moment, as the then Director General, Pascal Lamy, said, was 'a truly historic moment.... After so many twists and turns, these complicated and politically contentious disputes can finally be put to bed'.[40] We should note, however, that even at this

[35] *European Communities–Regime for the Importation, Sale and Distribution of Bananas, Second Recourse to Article 21.5 of the DSU by Ecuador/Recourse to Article 21.5 of the DSU by the United States*, Reports of the Appellate Body, 11 and 22 December 2008, WT/DS27/AB/RW2/ECU, WT/DS27/AB/RW/USA [AB Compliance Reports].

[36] Guth (n 22) 11–12.

[37] Geneva Agreement on Trade in Bananas (signed 31 May 2010, entered into force 1 May 2012). The text of the agreement is available at <http://ec.europa.eu/world/agreements/prepareCreateTreatiesWorkspace/treatiesGeneralData.do?step=0&redirect=true&treatyId=8501&back=8502> accessed 20 December 2018.

[38] Agreement on Trade in Bananas between the European Union and the United States of America (signed 8 June 2010, entered into force 24 January 2013). The text of the agreement is available at <http://ec.europa.eu/world/agreements/prepareCreateTreatiesWorkspace/treatiesGeneralData.do?step=0&redirect=true&treatyId=8502> accessed 20 December 2018.

[39] Notification of a Mutually Agreed Solution (n 1).

[40] 'Historic Signing Ends 20 Years of EU-Latin American Banana Disputes' (*WTO News*, 8 November 2012) <http://www.wto.org/english/news_e/news12_e/disp_08nov12_e.htm> accessed 20 December 2018.

'historic moment', EU noncompliance with WTO law continued: upon entry of the Geneva Agreements into force, the EU kept on granting tariff preferences to ACP bananas without having in place any suitable WTO waiver or exception (such as the exception for FTAs enshrined in GATT Article XXIV) for vindicating the ongoing infringement of the basic MFN rule.[41]

8.2 *EC-Bananas*: Conflict-Prolonging Factors

The *Bananas* dispute rambled through the multilateral trade system for almost two decades. At certain moments, the dispute 'had grown to such an extent that commentators feared for the very survival of the WTO' and its DSS.[42] What factors rendered the dispute so convoluted, obdurate, and, ultimately, so long-lived? Understanding the factors that prolonged the *Bananas* conflict is crucial because these factors largely shaped the challenges faced by the WTO and its judicial arm, the expectations of stakeholders from the DSS, and the main goals served by the latter in the course of the lengthy dispute.

Perhaps the most basic complicating element of *EC-Bananas* was the unusually large number of parties involved in the row.[43] Those parties included the EU's Members (the number of which increased from fifteen in 1995 to twenty-seven with the EU's enlargements in 2004 and 2007), the United States, the Latin American banana suppliers, and the ACP countries (many of which assumed a third-party status in the dispute). It is not surprising, therefore, that the first panel sitting on the bench in *EC-Bananas* opened its operative decision by stating that '[t]his case is an exceedingly complex one', involving 'almost one-third of [the WTO's] Members'.[44] Yet, more than the sheer number of parties, as detailed below, it was the specific assemblage of states, their 'group dynamics', as well as the cleavages within the different groups, that exacerbated and thus protracted the conflict. A former WTO ambassador portrayed these tangled interactions between the numerous actors involved in these words: 'all of us were against all of us'.[45]

41 For a detailed discussion of this issue, see Section 8.4 below.

42 Kevin Buterbaugh and Richard Fulton, *The WTO Primer: Tracing Trade's Visible Hand through Case Studies* (Palgrave Macmillan 2007) 87. See also interview with William Davey recorded in Geneva at the side-lines of the Legal Affairs Division 30th anniversary event (*WTO*, 28 June 2012) <http://www.wto.org/english/tratop_e/dispu_e/lad30bday_e.htm> accessed 20 December 2018 ('The most difficult case was probably *Bananas*. There was a period of time in 1999 where it looked like the system might collapse').

43 Interview with WTO legal officer (Geneva, 10 July 2012); interview with ACWL lawyer (Geneva, 27 July 2012); interview with former EU official (Geneva, 17 July 2012); Friedl Weiss, 'Manifestly Illegal Import Restrictions and Non-compliance with WTO Dispute Settlement Rulings: Lessons from the Banana Dispute' in Ernst-Ulrich Petersmann and Mark A Pollack (eds), *Transatlantic Economic Disputes: The EU, the US, and the WTO* (OUP 2003) 136–37.

44 *EC-Bananas* Panel Report (n 13) para 7.1.

45 Interview with former WTO ambassador (Geneva, 23 July 2012).

Within this constellation, the transatlantic facet of the *Bananas* conflict constituted a prominent confounding factor. As Josling has noted, '[t]he fact that the two main adversaries were the US and the EU, and that the conflict was over an agricultural product, guaranteed a level of ... defensiveness that was unlikely to be easily contained'.[46] While neither the United States nor the EU was a major banana grower,[47] the institutional configuration of agricultural trade policy making on either side of the Atlantic, as Cadot and Webber explain, facilitated the 'capture' of banana trade policy 'by highly organized, but narrow and particularistic producer[s] and above all *trading* interests'; such capture bolstered the capacity of those groups to block a settlement on what they considered unfavourable terms[48] and thereby prolong the conflict.[49] Thus, east of the Atlantic, dominant European trading firms (e.g. the British Geest and the Irish Fyffes) joined forces with ACP and EU banana growers. Together, these stakeholders were able to exert considerable influence on the design of the common EU banana regime and to conduct a well-executed, coordinated campaign lobbying for a protected market.[50] Once accorded protection in the form of Regulation 404/93—the unified EU banana policy that took effect in 1993—these actors exerted great pressure against any change to this policy.[51] West of the Atlantic, US trading firms, particularly Chiquita Brands, 'that had a strong incentive to try to defeat' the EU's banana regulation, were similarly able 'to mobilize the support of the US administration and commit it to a hard-line position in the conflict', thus further complicating efforts towards its resolution.[52]

But politically empowered domestic groups and transatlantic rivalries constituted only parts of the problem. The conflict and its intricacies cannot be understood without reference to the way in which the transatlantic struggle over trade in bananas was accompanied by new and old alliances, as the United States and the EU fought each other, 'with different groups of developing countries supporting them'.[53] Whereas the United States teamed up with the Latin American complainants, the EU lined up with the ACP countries. Coordination between the four groups of actors was highly challenging, especially when splits emerged inside the different groups, splits that were particularly conspicuous within the EU.

As previously implied, bananas had been a polemic and divisive issue within the EU for decades. Disagreements over this commodity verily threatened to impede the adoption of the Treaty of Rome (which brought about the creation of the

[46] Josling (n 17) 172.

[47] Cadot and Webber (n 3) 6.

[48] ibid 8, 15 (emphasis original).

[49] cf Christina L Davis, *Why Adjudicate: Enforcing Trade Rules in the* WTO (Princeton University Press 2012) 245 (arguing that the presence of strong interest groups on both sides of a trade dispute 'dictates against easy settlement of the dispute').

[50] Cadot and Webber (n 3) 15, 19; Buterbaugh and Fulton (n 42) 88.

[51] Buterbaugh and Fulton (n 42) 96; interview with WTO official (Geneva, 5 July 2012).

[52] Cadot and Webber (n 3) 19–24.

[53] Interview with WTO legal officer (Geneva, 10 July 2012). See also interview with former EU official (Geneva, 17 July 2012).

European Economic Community) in 1957.[54] Formation of a common EU banana regime in the early 1990s proved equally difficult. The various European Member states had different preferences concerning the importation of bananas, as reflected in the fragmented pre-1993 European banana market. Adoption of Regulation 404/93 by the EU could therefore be completed only after several years of intense negotiations and within the framework of a broader agricultural policy package. Since internal controversies among EU Members 'made it so difficult for them to come up' with a unified regime 'in the first place', a US official observed, it became clear early on that reaching an EU consensus on a revised regime that would also meet the demands of the complainants in the WTO dispute would be an extremely tricky task.[55] As a WTO legal officer noted when describing this task: 'not only [did] the EU ... [have] to negotiate with ... diverse ... [WTO] Members ... like [the] ACP [and the Latin American countries], but it also had to shepherd its own Members',[56] which remained deeply divided on the issue. Capturing the flavour of the events is this comment made by a lawyer involved in the dispute:

> [I]n the case of the European Union ... at that time it was 15 states.... [each] having different interests and ... approaches to international trade and international policy in general ... [so] how do you reconcile everybody's interests? ... [Y]ou had the Nordic countries which were pretty much ... in favour of free trade. The Germans as well.... On the other hand, you had some other countries which were more protective or more [prone to] thinking ... 'Let's help the Africans and let's help the Caribbeans ... we cannot just ... let our allies down ...'. [T]his type of internal coordination really ... requires a lot of political energy [and] ... a lot of time as well.[57]

Within this configuration, what made internal EU coordination towards resolution of the *Bananas* problem remarkably complex, beyond the divergent preferences of EU Members, was the disparate intensity of those preferences, which for many years enabled the architects of Regulation 404/93 (mainly France, Spain, Portugal, Greece, Ireland, and the UK) to maintain an uncompromising bloc against any reform that would significantly weaken the original banana regulation and bring it into conformity with WTO law.[58] Making the EU's banana regime fully WTO-compatible, Poletti and De Bièvre explain, required *unanimity* in the Council of Ministers *and* majority consent in the European Parliament because 'it entailed an overhaul of the EU's policy' towards ACP countries and a breach of 'its promise' to grant these countries preferential access to the European market under

54 Cadot and Webber (n 3) 24.
55 Interview with US official (Geneva, 17 July 2012).
56 Interview with WTO legal officer (Geneva, 10 July 2012).
57 Interview with ACWL lawyer (Geneva, 19 April 2012).
58 Cadot and Webber (n 3) 14–15, 30–31.

the Lomé Convention.[59] Given the high number of 'veto players' whose consent was needed for substantive policy reform, together with the hard-line stance taken by the advocates of Regulation 404/93, the EU, despite its repeated attempts, was able to introduce only incremental, not fully WTO-consistent modifications into its banana regime for almost two decades.[60] As one lawyer representing some of the Latin American complainants put it: *EC-Bananas* 'had to take ... such a long time because the political structure within the EU was established in such a fashion that you had to make ... mind changes in the legislatures and the relevant authorities in order to modify the whole system'.[61]

Yet, as should be clear by now, the difficulties marking *EC-Bananas* were rooted in the past—in the close historical and economic ties between the EU and the former European colonies in the ACP regions—as much as in present internal EU politics and divisions.[62] The common EU banana regime as constituted in 1993 was largely shaped by the desire of certain EU Members—especially France and the UK—to maintain the preferential trade arrangements accorded to the ACP countries under the 1975 Lomé Convention. These influential EU Members feared that absent these arrangements, small-scale banana growers in the ACP states would be eliminated from the EU market by the highly competitive Latin American banana producers backed by American corporations, an event that might lead to the destruction of the ACP countries' economies and, possibly, their political systems.[63] Moreover, while the *Bananas* case involved only one product (bananas), it called into question the EU's historical commitment to and preference for ACP countries more generally, given that the complaints targeted explicitly the discriminatory nature of the EU banana regime.[64] Against this background, a former EU official explained the enduring EU noncompliance in *EC-Bananas* and the 'impossibility to solve' the dispute for nearly two decades in these words:

> [The problem was rooted in] conflicting trade commitments.... The EU's problem was ... [its] commitment to the ACP countries, which is founded on historical

[59] Arlo Poletti and Dirk De Bièvre, 'Political Mobilization, Veto Players, and WTO Litigation: Explaining European Union Responses in Trade Disputes' (2014) 21 J Euro Pub Pol'y 1181, 1192–93.

[60] ibid 1193–94. As Poletti and De Bièvre explain, '[a]ccording to veto players theory, the potential for policy change in a given political system depends on the number of veto players, namely individual or collective actors whose consent is necessary to change the status quo. The more veto players, the smaller the set of alternative policies that can beat the status quo, and the less likely that policy change will take place'. ibid 1186.

[61] Interview with ACWL lawyer (Geneva, 19 April 2012).

[62] Interview with WTO official (Geneva, 5 July 2012); interview with former EU official (Geneva, 9 July 2012); interview with ACWL lawyer (Geneva, 19 April 2012); interview with Ecuadorian official (Geneva, 17 July 2012); interview with former WTO ambassador (Geneva, 23 July 2012).

[63] Buterbaugh and Fulton (n 42) 93–94, 102; Hunter R Clark, 'The WTO Banana Dispute Settlement and Its Implications for Trade Relations between the United States and the European Union' (2002) 35 Cornell Int'l LJ 291, 294–95, 301.

[64] Poletti and De Bièvre (n 59) 1194.

relations, which is of a very special nature, and which is not such that you can just dump it, basically.... It was not that the European market itself was being protectionist.... It was really about the ACP countries. So, it was basically the EU defending the interests of the ACP countries against other developing countries for equally legitimate concerns. And how do you want to solve that? I mean, the WTO in a sense decided each time but it was just impossible to implement it like that.[65]

A lawyer representing one of the Latin American complainants similarly stressed that this dispute 'wasn't just about changing EU protectionism'. 'The real clients of protectionism were ... the banana exporters from all the former colonies who had these preferential arrangements'. This rendered the *Bananas* case 'extremely complicated because ... the EU was arguing that ... it couldn't just abandon ... all these programs for the benefit of these poor countries'.[66]

For the EU, then, the will to complete a single European market, as envisaged in the 1987 Single European Act, while at the same time assuming responsibility for former European colonies in the ACP regions and maintaining the Lomé Convention's commitments towards these developing countries, proved highly difficult to reconcile with its WTO obligations,[67] a fact that made the political costs of WTO compliance simply too high.[68] This difficulty was further aggravated by the pressures exerted on the EU by the ACP countries to retain their postcolonial trade preferences once legal actions were initiated against the European banana regime within the multilateral trade framework.[69]

From the point of view of the Latin American complainants, however, the EU's preferential treatment of the ACP countries, understood as a means to remedy past colonial wrongs,[70] was considered legally problematic but also manifestly 'unfair', as the statement of a former Latin American official makes clear:

[O]ur understanding is that ... [the EU] wanted to protect the ACPs' market ... because they have historic relation[s] with ACP countries, some of them are

[65] Interview with former EU official (Geneva, 9 July 2012). See also interview with Ecuadorian official (Geneva, 17 July 2012) ('[I]t was very difficult to find a solution because of the linkages between the ACPs, as ... former colonies, and the European Union, and all the preferences that were being granted to them, so it was a very sensitive issue in that regard, and I think that made things even more complicated than what they were already').

[66] Interview with WTO practitioner (Geneva, 11 July 2012).

[67] Alter and Meunier (n 7) 366.

[68] Alasdair R Young, 'Effective Multilateralism on Trial: EU Compliance with WTO Law' in Spyros Blavoukos and Dimitris Bourantonis (eds), *The EU Presence in International Organizations* (Routledge 2011) 120.

[69] Alter and Meunier (n 7) 374; Buterbaugh and Fulton (n 42) 102.

[70] Interview with ACWL lawyer (Geneva, 19 April 2012) (noting that 'the main reason why the European authorities decided to maintain' the discriminatory banana import system was their belief that in this way they were 'paying back' to the former colonies the things that they 'took away from them' as colonizers); interview with WTO official (Geneva, 5 July 2012).

> ex-colonies and they have this political commitment for the development of these Members, which we found unfair to the Latin American countries because we were also ex-colonies of ... some of the Members of the European Union.... [T]his is something that [is] difficult ... to understand but you will find that the preference of the EU will be always ... ACPs ... instead of Latin American countries.[71]

Admittedly, at the same time that the EU's trade preferences were granted to ex-European colonies in the ACP regions, leading to the dependence of some of these economies on the continued sale of bananas at preferential prices in the European market,[72] trade in bananas also involved the 'livelihood of ... many ... constituents' in the Latin American countries,[73] for some of which this was 'their only or major export ... opportunity'.[74] *EC-Bananas*, therefore, was not only a north-north conflict between the major trade partners from across the Atlantic, it was also a south–south quarrel in which 'developing countries with conflicting interests' were found 'beating themselves on different sides of the table'.[75] Along with the '[d]ivisions inside the EU', an EU official stressed, 'divisions among the [two groups of] developing countries' made the *Bananas* conflict 'hellishly difficult to reconcile'.[76]

Finally, similar to the EU, ranks were not always closed around a common interest even within each group of developing countries.[77] Thus, when describing the tense interactions among the Latin American countries themselves, particularly between those relying on nationally controlled production of bananas and those where production was dominated by US-based multinationals, a former WTO ambassador candidly noted: '[W]e were all Latinos, but ... we didn't have the same position. And, different positions at that moment meant enemies. [If] [y]ou are not with me, you are against me'. The same interviewee concluded by stating that at times, 'our ... internal disputes were stronger, really stronger than the dispute with' the EU.[78]

And so, despite the ostensible legal simplicity of *EC-Bananas*, revolving mainly around straightforward issues of trade discrimination, at the core of this perennial dispute we find transatlantic rivalries, charged histories, narrow and

71 Interview with former official of Guatemala (Geneva, 24 July 2012).

72 Buterbaugh and Fulton (n 42) 93–94; Tim Josling and Tim Taylor, 'Introduction' in *Banana Wars* (n 17) 2.

73 Interview with ACWL lawyer (Geneva, 27 July 2012).

74 Interview with WTO legal officer (Geneva, 10 July 2012) (noting that for some 'Latin American countries this is really their only or major export possibility.... [Similarly,] for ... ACP countries, ... [it is vital that they] maintain this link to the EU, not politically only but also economically').

75 Interview with WTO legal officer (Geneva, 10 July 2012).

76 Interview with former EU official (Geneva, 17 July 2012).

77 Interview with WTO legal officer (Geneva, 10 July 2012); interview with private attorney (Brussels, 19 July 2012).

78 Interview with former WTO ambassador (Geneva, 23 July 2012). See also interview with former official of Guatemala (Geneva, 24 July 2012) ('[S]ome Latin American countries had different interests at different points in time. Some of these interests were moved by [the] multinational [companies].... That ... changed very much the perspective and the views with respect to dispute settlement').

well-organized economic interests, tensions emanating from supranational EU politics and postcolonialism, and splits between and within competing groups of developing countries. The manifold 'political sensitivities behind the trade of bananas', coupled with the major policy change required of the respondent, destined this old-fashioned trade dispute to be 'one of the longest disputes in the history of the GATT and WTO',[79] entangling the EU in long-lasting noncompliance with WTO rulings and rules.

8.3 *EC-Bananas*: A Goal-Based Reading

EC-Bananas—the subject of recurrent WTO litigation and enduring EU noncompliance (not fully alleviated by the settlement concluding the dispute)—has long been invoked as a failure of the legalized WTO DSS, an event that risked undermining the system's effectiveness.[80] This commonly accepted, oft-repeated version of the dispute exemplifies the conventional wisdom in the field, that of compliance being the constant prime objective expected to be achieved by the DSS and the principle measure for evaluating its effectiveness. An in-depth qualitative analysis of *EC-Bananas* nonetheless tells a more complex story of stakeholder expectations of the DSS in this protracted dispute, of the goals the DSS sought to promote, and of the outcomes it ultimately generated. The respective narrative thus calls into question the conventional wisdom.

And so, for most of those involved in *EC-Bananas*, it seems to have been rather clear from the outset that the prospects for (timely) compliance with an adverse WTO ruling, and thus for a prompt resolution of the intricate conflict, were rather low. As a lawyer representing some of the Latin American complainants stated, in 'these highly political cases ... compliance is not something that you can really achieve overnight.... When cases are ... of that political magnitude you will always find problems in compliance'.[81] A former EU official involved in the case appears to have agreed: 'I don't think that ... anybody expected that the problem would go away with just one ruling of the Appellate Body'. Although the 'EU is a big believer in the multilateral institution and wants to play by the rules, ... in *Bananas*

[79] Interview with former official of Guatemala (Geneva, 24 July 2012).

[80] See, e.g. Cherie O'Neal Taylor, 'Beyond Retaliation' (2017) 38 Nw J Int'l L & Bus 55; William J Davey, 'Compliance Problems in WTO Dispute Settlement' (2009) 42 Cornell Int'l LJ 119, 120; Bown (n 2) 59; Benjamin L Brimeyer, 'Banana, Beef, and Compliance in the World Trade Organization: The Inability of the WTO Dispute Settlement Process to Achieve Compliance from Superpower Nations' (2001) 10 Minn J Global Trade 133, 134; Karen J Alter, 'Resolving or Exacerbating Disputes? The WTO's New Dispute Resolution System' (2003) 79 Int'l Aff 783; Mark L Busch and Eric Reinhardt, 'Transatlantic Trade Conflicts and GATT/WTO Dispute Settlement' in *Transatlantic Economic Disputes* (n 43) 475–78; Petros C Mavroidis, 'The Trade Disputes Concerning Health Policy Between the EC and the US' in *Transatlantic Economic Disputes* (n 43) 244–45.

[81] Interview with ACWL lawyer (Geneva, 19 April 2012).

it was ... impossible' for the EU to implement the ruling as it was.[82] Reiterating this political impossibility, a former Latin American ambassador declared: 'I'm not defending the Europeans', but knowing the considerations and forces at play, it was clear 'that for them it was impossible to give the Latinos the same treatment as the ... ACP producers. Never ever in their life ... could [it] be possible'.[83] An Ecuadorian official went on to state that '[a]ll along we knew that ... [it] wasn't feasible' to expect the EU to give us the same treatment granted to the ACP countries, 'but we expected to have something different' in the future. Moreover, this same Ecuadorian delegate added that by the time the *Bananas* dispute was brought to the WTO, '[w]e knew that.... whatever solution we were going to find in this problem, it was going to be a political solution, not a legal solution'.[84]

Ecuador and the other complainants nonetheless chose to bring the charged *Bananas* dispute to the WTO DSS, irrespective of their apparent awareness of the high prospects of EU noncompliance and the political nature of any future resolution of the conflict. What, then, was envisaged as the DSS's role in this case? What goals, beyond compliance, was the DSS expected to attain? And what shifts and trade-offs between its multiple objectives were struck in the face of the conflict's intricacies?

As the analysis will show, rather than serving as a mechanism geared to eliciting strict compliance with WTO rulings and rules, in the perennial *Bananas* dispute, the DSS enhanced its role at the interstice between law and politics. This role was played out along two parallel tracks. First, throughout the conflict and until its final resolution, the mandatory DSS served a systemic function in containing the charged dispute within defined legal parameters and providing an outlet for the claimed interstate injustices, thereby allowing the parties to continue cooperating on other fronts, preventing unilateral actions, and deflecting destabilizing effects on the WTO regime. Second, through its successive rulings in the various litigation rounds—providing information on the relevant facts and the law, validating claims of violations, and assigning reputational and economic costs to noncompliance—the DSS further served a pivotal role in stimulating renegotiations and identifying the focal points around which the parties could progress towards a settlement and re-establishment of their reciprocal balance of concessions.[85]

[82] Interview with former EU official (Geneva, 9 July 2012); interview with former WTO ambassador (Geneva, 23 July 2012) (noting that after winning the legal case before the AB, the prospects for compliance on the part of the EU were 'zero', as the EU just 'couldn't' comply).

[83] Interview with former WTO ambassador (Geneva, 23 July 2012).

[84] Interview with Ecuadorian official (Geneva, 17 July 2012).

[85] An elaborate discussion of the role of the DSS in facilitating dispute settlement through information dissemination, identification of focal points, and stimulation of renegotiation is found in Chapter 3 of the book. For selected literature on the subject, see, e.g. Andrew T Guzman, 'International Tribunals: A Rational Choice Analysis' (2008) 157 U Pa L Rev 171, 180–83; Michael Gilligan, Leslie Johns, and Peter Rosendorff, 'Strengthening International Courts and the Early Settlement of Disputes' (2010) 54 J Conflict Resol 5, 10–11; Tom Ginsburg and Richard H McAdams, 'Adjudicating in Anarchy: An Expressive Theory of International Dispute Resolution' (2004) 45 William & Mary L Rev 1229; John Linarelli, 'The Role of Dispute Settlement in World Trade Law: Some Lessons from

As demonstrated below, this shift away from the legalistic, rule-enforcement objective of the DSS towards its goals of settlement facilitation, re-establishment of a previously negotiated equilibrium of rights and obligations, and maintenance of the cooperative WTO regime, can be derived from the ample evidence provided by insiders with first-hand knowledge of the *Bananas* dispute, as well as from the conflict's sequence of events. This goal shift, as will be shown later, can also be learned from the distinctive interpretations and judicial choices of WTO adjudicators throughout the dispute.

Evidence from the Field

Facilitating Settlement and Rebalancing the Scales Through Renegotiation

As one Ecuadorian official noted, we tend to see the WTO DSS 'as a purely legalistic system', but 'that's not the case. There's a lot of politics behind ... and in the case of ... *Bananas* the politics was present all along'.[86] In such politically intense cases, a former EU official involved in *EC-Bananas* added, the WTO DSS does not serve the 'classic straightforward' role of 'finding the truth, declaring the truth and then having everybody complying with the truth'; instead, '[i]t is being used as a leverage', 'as a tool to find the solution elsewhere', outside the formal judicial process.[87]

When elaborating this point, a staff member of the AB Secretariat involved in *EC-Bananas* noted that in convoluted cases of this sort, the DSS plays two main roles. On the one hand, 'it provides a non-negotiated solution', that is, legal answers to the disputed issues. On the other, the DSS extends its role to the post-litigation bargaining, during which the parties renegotiate on the basis of the legal findings and interpretations provided in its rulings.[88] Those roles, as played by the DSS in the *Bananas* dispute, the same official stressed, have been reiterated in other high-stake, perennial disputes, such as the ongoing transatlantic *Aircraft* conflicts.[89]

Continuing along this path, another WTO legal officer stated that in protracted and repetitive conflicts, among which we can list *EC-Bananas, US-Zeroing, US-Softwood Lumbers*, and the ongoing *US-Boeing* and *EC-Airbus* disputes, the

the Kodak-Fuji Dispute' (2000) 31 L Pol'y Int'l Bus 263, 335. For similar ideas regarding courts more generally, see Joanne Scott and Susan Sturm, 'Courts as Catalysts: Rethinking the Judicial Role in New Governance' (2007) 13 Colum J Euro L 565.

[86] Interview with Ecuadorian official (Geneva, 17 July 2012).

[87] Interview with former EU official (Geneva, 9 July 2012).

[88] Interview with member of the AB Secretariat (Geneva, 4 July 2012).

[89] ibid. Note that the same role seems to have been played by the DSS in other perennial disputes such as the twin *Aircraft* cases between Brazil and Canada, and the transatlantic dispute over GMOs. See, respectively, Nils Meier-Kaienburg, 'The WTO's "Toughest" Case: An Examination of the Effectiveness of the WTO Dispute Resolution Procedure in the Airbus-Boeing Dispute over Aircraft Subsidies' (2006) 71 J Air L & Com 191, 237; Mark A Pollack and Gregory C Shaffer, *When Cooperation Fails: The International Law and Politics of Genetically Modified Foods* (OUP 2009) 224–25, 232–33.

respective cases are not of the type where 'at the end of ... [WTO litigation] the parties are going to simply implement the rulings. They ... [will do so] but as part of ... some kind of negotiations, because the issues are simply too big and too sensitive'.[90] '[I]n these cases in particular', he stressed, 'you have to think of the dispute settlement process as part of a broader [political] process'. It is when a 'breakdown of that political process' transpires that the parties resort to the DSS as a means to move negotiations forward and facilitate a politically feasible solution, one that provides for a balanced accommodation of their concerns.[91] In such instances, the DSS, through its legal rulings, 'help[s] the parties settle their dispute because ... when they negotiate ... they ... have a better understanding of what are the legal rights and obligations.... what the status of their case is in the WTO, and that [is] ... an important element in the negotiation'.[92]

In accordance with this interpretation of the DSS's role in *EC-Bananas*, a private lawyer representing some of the ACP countries asserted that in this dispute, 'the court [was used] as a bargaining tool, and in this case, it was adequately used.... [I]n political cases like this one ... [the court] contributes to shap[ing] ... trade diplomacy'.[93] Elaborating further on this contribution, the same attorney stated: 'A legal system at the international level cannot go faster than the preparation of the mindset.... It's not equipped.... But the rulings themselves can shape and can contribute to exercising pressure on progressively amending the ... economic order'.[94]

A close look at the sequence of events in *EC-Bananas*, where judicial proceedings were braided into all the negotiations between the parties, in and 'outside Geneva, in Brussels, and in Latin American ... and ACP capitals',[95] elucidates how these DSS roles—facilitating settlement bargaining with a view to achieving a satisfactory solution that re-establishes the reciprocal balance of concessions between the parties—actually were played out.

As for the EU, the series of DSS rulings rendered in favour of the United States and the Latin American complainants, combined with the US-imposed sanctions and Ecuador's threat of cross-retaliation, assigned reputational and economic costs to its violations of WTO law and its continued state of noncompliance.[96] Such costs made the alternatives previously available to the EU, those of simply refusing to

[90] Interview with WTO legal officer (Geneva, 4 April 2012).

[91] ibid.

[92] ibid.

[93] Interview with private attorney (Brussels, 19 July 2012).

[94] ibid. See also interview with a staff member of the AB Secretariat (Geneva, 4 July 2012) (noting that *EC-Bananas* was embedded in a broader political process of negotiations between the parties, whereas the DSS played a key role in moving forward the negotiations through the series of rulings rendered over the years).

[95] Interview with WTO legal officer (Geneva, 10 July 2012).

[96] On these sorts of reputational and economic costs see Guzman (n 85) 181–83; Joost Pauwelyn, *Optimal Protection of International Law: Navigating between European Absolutism and American Voluntarism* (CUP 2008) 163–69; Giovanni Maggi, 'The Role of Multilateral Institutions in International Trade Cooperation' (1999) 89 Am Econ Rev 190, 191.

act or to engage in serious negotiations with the complainants, much more expensive,[97] thereby triggering a growing European demand for renegotiation[98] and a gradual shift in the domestic political balance towards cooperation.

And so, we can see that at an early stage of the dispute, after dissemination of the original panel and AB rulings in 1997, the EU exhibited some reluctance to seriously consult with the complaining parties; instead, as indicated in Section 8.1 above, the EU opted to devise a new banana proposal as it saw fit.[99] In like manner, despite the complaining parties' repeated claims that its proposal for reform of the banana regime would be equally WTO-inconsistent and would not meet their demands, the EU insisted that no substantive changes could be made to its suggested policy,[100] which eventually became effective in January 1999.

A significant change in Europe's noncooperative attitude appeared, however, following the compliance proceedings and Article 22.6 arbitrations conducted in 1999–2000 and the consequent authorization, granted to the United States and Ecuador by the DSB, to suspend trade concessions to the EU. As an EU ambassador involved in the case observed, the authorized retaliatory duties applied by the United States against selected EU exports since 1999 increased the EU's demand for renegotiation and helped stimulate serious discussions on the transition from the tariff-quota-licence regime to a tariff-only regime.[101] Furthermore, although Ecuador ultimately did not exercise its retaliatory rights, its threat of cross-retaliation against European intellectual property under the TRIPS Agreement heightened the pressure on the EU and elevated Ecuador's bargaining position in the negotiations leading up to the Understandings on Bananas of 2001.[102] As Smith noted:

[97] Note that absent retrospective remedies in the WTO DSS, respondents can violate WTO rules without fear of sanctions for the duration of the dispute settlement process and until retaliation is at hand. This situation allows recalcitrant Members to use the dispute settlement process to 'buy time' and prolong the application of their WTO-inconsistent policies. See Mark Wu, 'Rethinking the Temporary Breach Puzzle: A Window on the Future of International Trade Conflicts' (2015) 40 Yale J Int'l L 95, 98, 101–07; Rachel Brewster, 'The Remedy Gap: Institutional Design, Retaliation, and Trade Law Enforcement' (2011) 80 Geo Wash L Rev 102.

[98] Heinz Hauser and Alexander Roitinger, 'Renegotiation in Transatlantic Trade Disputes' in *Transatlantic Economic Disputes* (n 43) 504. Note that precisely in order to ensure the EU's ability to negotiate a solution—other than withdrawing a measure found by the DSS to violate WTO law—the ECJ has consistently denied 'direct effect' to WTO rulings and rules, including in the context of *EC-Bananas*. That is, the ECJ has denied the possibility of individuals and EU Member states to challenge the validity of EU trade-related policies through an appeal to WTO law or legal rulings. See Case C-149/96 *Portuguese Republic v. Council* [1999] ECR I-8395, paras 38–46; Stefan Griller, 'Judicial Enforceability of WTO Law in the European Union: Annotation to Case C-149/96, Portugal v. Council' (2000) 3 J Int'l Econ L 441; Marco Bronckers, 'From "Direct Effect" to "Muted Dialogue": Recent Developments in the European Courts' Case Law on WTO and Beyond' (2008) 11 J Int'l Econ L 885.

[99] Bryan Mercurio, 'Retaliatory Trade Measures in the WTO Dispute Settlement Understanding: Are There Really Alternatives?' in James C Hartigan (ed), *Trade Disputes and the Dispute Settlement Understanding of the WTO: An Interdisciplinary Assessment* (Emerald Group Publishing Limited 2009) 434.

[100] ibid.

[101] Guth (n 22) 6. See also Taylor (n 80) 82–83.

[102] Smith (n 21) 259, 271.

> Whatever the rationale for Ecuador's decision to forgo sanctions, observers in the WTO and participants in the dispute agree that the pace of negotiations with the EU ... accelerated as the prospects of cross-retaliation approached.... In sum, Ecuador's innovative cross-retaliation gambit—which it undertook alone—appeared to enhance its leverage beyond what WTO remedies would normally provide a small developing country.[103]

Hence, while recourse to WTO retaliation by the United States and Ecuador failed to elicit the EU's compliance with WTO rulings, it nonetheless incentivized the EU's return to the negotiating table and facilitated the adoption of the 2001 Understandings on Bananas, thus profoundly changing the course of the conflict. This sequence of events was summarized by a lawyer involved in *EC-Bananas* in these terms:

> [W]hen the United States decided to retaliate and Ecuador requested retaliation on the IP rights ... that was the beginning of these countries getting together and trying to resolve the matter in an amicable fashion.... [W]ithout ... retaliatory action on the side of the United States or the threat of retaliation by Ecuador ... the EU will have continued as ... it was doing before.... Without retaliation ... the EU, the United States and Ecuador wouldn't have signed the Understanding on [Bananas] ... in 2001 ... [under] which the United States, [like Ecuador,] agreed to withdraw its retaliatory action.... [while] the EU agreed ... to move to a tariff-only regime.... [T]he retaliation at that point served a role.... It didn't really lead to the actual withdrawal of the [EU's WTO-inconsistent] measure, but it ... led to the EU moving to a more ... acceptable scenario for the Latin American suppliers.[104]

This is the place to note that while the economic costs inflicted on the EU during the dispute ceased with the removal of the US trade sanctions in 2001 (as agreed in the Understanding on Bananas), the reputational costs attached to each additional finding of an EU violation of WTO law—within the framework of the arbitration proceedings undertaken in 2005 and the second round of compliance proceedings in 2008—continued mounting up, thus further pressuring the EU to actively move towards resolution of the conflict. As a former EU official involved in the case stated, 'it was quite a pressure on the EU to be continuously losing these cases without being able to comply'.[105] What is more, this official stressed, these WTO cases gave the complainants the 'leverage' necessary to say to the EU '"You're not compliant with the dispute settlement system, you have to do something", and

[103] ibid 273.
[104] Interview with WTO practitioner (Geneva, 19 April 2012).
[105] Interview with former EU official (Geneva, 9 July 2012).

that worked. The EU really felt they had to do something in order to get this off the table'. It gave the EU 'the incentive to say: "Okay, let's find a solution for this". Otherwise, it wouldn't have happened'.[106]

A similar picture was painted by a US official who noted that 'the EU ... never would have done anything to provide additional [market] access on bananas ... if it wasn't for the dispute settlement system.... [T]hat was the entire mechanism that prompted the change, even though the change wasn't ... done' by the respondent revoking the WTO-inconsistent measure, 'which is the standard way for most disputes'. 'But still', this official stressed, 'without the disputes ... there would've been no way that they would have ... accommodated the concerns of any of the other parties'.[107]

Importantly, the series of DSS rulings delivered throughout the *Bananas* dispute did not only place 'very tangible pressure' on the defending Member, the EU, constraining its ability to refuse taking further action on its banana regime and 'bending' its 'negotiating position' in the settlement talks.[108] Those rulings were also used by the EU itself 'to put pressure on the ACPs, to tell them, "Look, we still haven't complied according to the WTO. So, unfortunately, we cannot maintain the kind of ... [tariff-quota and licensing] type solution, we have to go towards an EPA, [i.e. a GATT Article] XXIV-type solution"' in order to secure your preferential access to the EU market in the future.[109]

As for the complainants in *EC-Bananas*, although the controversy had been decided in their favour, they accepted the EU's demand for renegotiation from the outset and 'de facto never abandoned the policy of giving favourable consideration to striking a deal with the EC'.[110] Admittedly, they 'did not alter their readiness to negotiate even after it had become obvious that the EC would not comply'; instead, the complainants used the successive DSS rulings as a means 'to get a more favourable bargaining position' and to drive the settlement negotiations forward.[111] In this spirit, a former Latin American ambassador noted, '[t]he dispute settlement [process] was exactly [designed] to allow our side ... the winners ... to push the negotiations' with the EU towards a mutually agreed solution.[112]

[106] ibid.

[107] Interview with US official (Geneva, 17 July 2012). The same view was shared by other WTO practitioners involved in *EC-Bananas*. See, e.g. interview with WTO official (Geneva, 5 July 2012) ('I'm sure that short of the dispute settlement system this [Geneva] Agreement would not have been reached'); interview with WTO practitioner (Geneva, 27 July 2012); interview with WTO practitioner (Geneva, 19 April 2012).

[108] Interview with private attorney (Brussels, 19 July 2012).

[109] Interview with WTO legal officer (Geneva, 10 July 2012); interview with private attorney (Brussels, 19 July 2012).

[110] Hauser and Roitinger (n 98) 504.

[111] ibid.

[112] Interview with former WTO ambassador (Geneva, 23 July 2012); interview with former official of Guatemala (Geneva, 24 July 2012).

As two commentators have rightly observed, from a rule-oriented perspective, one that is focused on the compliance enforcement goal of the DSS, it is hard to explain this 'readiness of the complainants at various stages [of the *Bananas* dispute] to renegotiate an issue which had already been decided in their favour'.[113] Arguably, from a broad and dynamic goal-based perspective, if we view the DSS as a multifunctional system designed, among other things, to stimulate renegotiation, shape bargaining positions, and facilitate the establishment of a newly agreed balance of concessions in the shadow of the law, such readiness may be better understood.

We should further note at this point that the importance of these specific functions of the DSS cannot be overstated, especially in situations where, as in the *Bananas* case, striking asymmetries in power divide the respondent (the EU) from most of the complainants (the Latin American countries). Along these lines, one Ecuadorian official who worked on the case commented: 'if we wouldn't have this [dispute settlement] system . . . [that is, if we had been] in a purely bilateral relationship [vis-à-vis] . . . the EU. . . . I don't think we would have settled this case because of the huge asymmetry between the EU and Ecuador'.[114] In further clarifying the force of the legal proceedings pursued before the mandatory WTO DSS, a former Guatemalan official stressed why the *Bananas* dispute had to be brought before the DSS:

> [O]therwise we wouldn't have the Bananas Agreement today. Why would the EU negotiate with the Latin American countries in the first place if we don't have this leverage of saying, 'Okay, you are in non-compliance'. I don't see a particular reason, especially if they are protecting the interest of the ACP countries.[115]

For the weaker Latin American countries, then, absent the transition towards a compulsory, more rule-oriented WTO dispute settlement system and the ability to press for successive DSS rulings, 'the stalemate that characterized the conflict under the GATT would have likely continued'.[116]

Yet, it should be made clear, the successive rulings rendered by the DSS in *EC-Bananas* did not merely increase the complainants' bargaining power vis-à-vis the EU; they also substantively assisted the parties in narrowing the scope of their legal controversies and in converging on how an acceptable, more WTO-consistent banana regime might look.[117] As a WTO official involved in the case stated, 'each

[113] Hauser and Roitinger (n 98) 504.

[114] Interview with Ecuadorian official (Geneva, 17 July 2012). For an elaborate discussion of Ecuador's strategic use of the DSS in *EC-Bananas*, see Smith (n 21).

[115] Interview with former official of Guatemala (Geneva, 24 July 2012). See also interview with a lawyer representing one of the Latin American complainants (Geneva, 11 July 2012) ('if there had been no binding dispute settlement system' the EU could have kept on resisting a change, and a negotiated settlement would likely not have been reached to this day); interview with former WTO ambassador (Geneva, 23 July 2012).

[116] Melo (n 3) 395.

[117] Interview with AB member (Geneva, 27 April 2012).

decision helped narrow ... the problem and led to successive modifications of the EU measures'.[118] The initial EU banana regime, another senior WTO official elaborated, incorporated several WTO-inconsistencies pertaining to licensing, quotas, tariffs, and services. The DSS, from the first ruling and throughout its consecutive decisions, 'clarified' the relevant WTO obligations, identified the specific EU violations, and progressively led the latter to eliminate most of them, steps that ultimately reduced the dispute to the issue of the EU tariff rates for banana imports from MFN suppliers (which under GATT Article XXVIII had to be negotiated between the parties).[119] It follows that by clarifying ambiguities in the law and the respective facts, as well as by communicating in favour of specific legal outcomes, the DSS continuously constructed the focal points around which the parties could coordinate.[120] It therefore steered the parties towards a common ground on which an agreement accommodating the interests of all could be reached. A WTO official aptly echoed this point as follows:

> [B]y making successive findings of inconsistencies ... [the DSS] helped [the] parties to negotiate an agreement.... [T]his [dispute] was so political that it had to be done through negotiation. But [following] ... each of the [WTO] cases ... the successive negotiations brought [the] parties closer to a better solution, one which guaranteed [the Latin American countries] better conditions of access to the European market, less discrimination, and more development assistance for the [ACP] countries which were affected.[121]

Against this backdrop, a WTO legal officer summarized the goals pursued and roles played by the DSS in *EC-Bananas* in these words, while pointing to the shift away from compliance that characterized this case:

> *[EC]-Bananas* ... showed that ... WTO dispute settlement is a tool to achieve something ... that might not necessarily be full legal compliance.... *Bananas* had shown that the Latin Americans and all of the constituents involved in this dispute wanted to achieve something. The EU wanted to maintain some privileges for [the] ACPs, it was politically taboo not to maintain something. The Latin Americans wanted to improve the standing of their exports [in the EU market], the US too, and they tried various ways.... also political [avenues] outside of the WTO dispute settlement [system]. And the WTO dispute settlement [system]

118 Interview with WTO official (Geneva, 28 March 2012).

119 Interview with senior WTO official (Geneva, 5 July 2012).

120 On the role of international courts, and courts more generally, in creating focal points that facilitate dispute resolution, see Ginsburg and McAdams (n 85); Richard H McAdams and Janice Nadler, 'Coordinating in the Shadow of the Law: Two Contextualized Tests of the Focal Point Theory of Legal Compliance' (2008) 42 L & Soc'y Rev 865.

121 Interview with WTO legal officer (Geneva, 16 March 2012).

> was . . . a . . . powerful tool, . . . but only part of an arsenal, of other sort of arms that you can use . . . to achieve something.[122]

Within the complicated political and economic context of the *Bananas* dispute, the same WTO official added:

> [The DSS] enhanced cooperation between the Membership. . . . It . . . made the Members more flexible and more exposed to each other. . . . [I]t engaged the Members and . . . gave a certain dynamic to the exchanges between Members. Whether the dynamic was always positive . . . is, of course, another question. But it . . . got people around the table and it got people talking.[123]

In *EC-Bananas*, therefore, as the testimonies of practitioners involved suggest, the legalized WTO DSS did not serve merely as a mechanism to elicit strict legal compliance with WTO rules and to maintain the original distribution of commitments articulated in the WTO agreements. Rather, the mandatory DSS, in line with its 'GATT DNA of pragmatism' and flexibility,[124] served to create the space in which noncompliance with the original WTO commitments could be gradually translated into a discursive process of renegotiation and, eventually, a settlement that accommodates the conflicting interests of the parties while reinstating their reciprocal balance of concessions. *EC-Bananas* thus illustrated, in a sense, the merits of 'going through the stages of the dispute settlement [process], but using it as a tool to find the solution elsewhere'.[125]

Containing the Dispute and Sustaining the Stability of the WTO Regime

At no point during this lengthy process, however, was the role of the DSS limited to these goals alone. Parallel to facilitating a bilateral settlement and re-establishing reciprocity between the disputants, the DSS worked throughout to promote the no less important goal of sustaining the operation of the multilateral trade system as a whole. As previously explained (see Chapter 7), perennial disputes, because of their inherent traits—including the major trade partners involved, the political/economic magnitude of the disputed policy, the complexity of the legislative

[122] Interview with WTO legal officer (Geneva, 10 July 2012).

[123] ibid.

[124] Interview with WTO legal officer (Geneva, 10 July 2012). This interviewee elaborated on this point: '[T]he GATT was operating in a very . . . pragmatic fashion. . . . [T]he WTO started [in 1995] with a blank slate, much more legalized. . . . And there was a genuine . . . conception . . . that this would now be . . . a very sort of orderly organization where you have rules that you follow. . . . [Y]ou finally have . . . [an] organization with a legal personality. Everything is sort of nice and neat. And then suddenly, this thing explodes in your face . . . four years after the WTO entered into force [in *EC-Bananas*]. And then people start to scramble around the place, and the institution strives to . . . provide a solution. And, of course, what works is ad hoc, informal, sometimes even behind the scenes arrangements and flexibility. And [in *EC-Bananas*] it showed the flexibility'.

[125] Interview with former EU official (Geneva, 9 July 2012).

changes required, and the long-standing noncompliance in place—put serious strain on the DSS. They likewise risk spoiling the parties' trade relationships and the stability of the cooperative WTO regime more broadly. The transatlantic conflict over trade in bananas aptly exhibited these pressures from the beginning. William Davey, a former head of the WTO's legal affairs division, therefore noted that a few years into *EC-Bananas*, 'it looked like the system might collapse' and '[i]t was unclear whether the EU and the United States, or both of them, might effectively leave the system'.[126]

In light of such pressures, a WTO legal officer who worked on the *Bananas* case cited one additional prominent goal to be pursued by the DSS in this type of intense and protracted conflicts, that of maintaining the stability and functionality of the multilateral trade regime for as long as the case remains on the DSB agenda.[127] According to the same legal officer, the DSS promotes this regime-maintenance goal, first and foremost, by permitting the disputed issues to be brought to the DSS time and again, a technique that allows it to contain the charged conflict within defined legal parameters while providing the parties with a forum where they can air their differences until the dispute's resolution.[128] Another WTO official, when describing the main roles played by the DSS in *EC-Bananas*, similarly observed that throughout the dispute, the DSS 'has given ... to those who were abused ... the forum to express their frustration.... [T]he system has given a forum and a set of rules that can be used' to manage the dispute as long as it endured.[129]

But beyond providing a forum for recurrently addressing the disputed legal issues and the claimed interstate injustices, another important means by which the DSS worked to preserve the WTO regime and to limit the consequences of the contentious *Bananas* feud was the mechanism of suspension of concessions. Although in this case the two-year US countermeasures failed to induce the EU to comply with the WTO legal prescriptions, these countermeasures did not only serve to increase the EU's demand for renegotiation (as seen above), they also worked to temporarily rebalance the market access conditions between the EU and the United States,[130] and thus to 'correct' in some way 'the grievance caused by the violation'.[131]

126 Interview with William Davey (n 42). See also interview with WTO legal officer (Geneva, 16 March 2012).

127 Interview with WTO legal officer (Geneva, 13 March 2012).

128 ibid.

129 Interview with WTO official (Geneva, 5 July 2012).

130 Bown (n 2) 59. On the rebalancing goal of WTO retaliation see also David Palmeter and Stanimir A Alexandrov, '"Inducing Compliance" in WTO Dispute Settlement' in Daniel L M Kennedy and James D Southwick (eds), *The Political Economy of International Trade Law: Essays in Honor of Robert Hudec* (CUP 2002) 647; Robert Z Lawrence, *Crimes and Punishments? Retaliation under the WTO* (Institute for International Economics 2003) 47; Joost Pauwelyn, 'The Calculation and Design of Trade Retaliation in Context: What is the Goal of Suspending WTO Obligations?' in *The Law, Economics and Politics of Retaliation* (n 19) 34; Michelle Limenta, *WTO Retaliation: Effectiveness and Purposes* (Hart Publishing 2017) 10.

131 Interview with WTO official (Geneva, 4 July 2012). On the compensation goal of WTO retaliation, see, e.g. Pauwelyn (n 130); *United States–Continued Dumping and Subsidy Offset Act of 2000,*

In that sense, the temporary suspension of equivalent concessions to reciprocally rebalance the original bargain 'served to settle the dispute for a period',[132] as a WTO legal officer involved in *EC-Bananas* explained:

> [B]asically, the way to ... reestablish that balance [of concessions] would be for the measure which is found inconsistent to be brought into conformity [with WTO law].... But until you achieve that sometimes you need a crutch.... to rebalance temporarily the situation until the inconsistent measure has been modified or withdrawn.... [S]uspension of concessions ... introduces ... a temporary rebalancing of the rights and obligations ... so that you feel ... as the offended country, that in some way the situation has been temporarily rebalanced ... [by] withdrawing some benefits from the other country.[133]

In the case of *EC-Bananas*, Bown has moved on to stress, this rebalancing of the market access bargain between the parties through proportionate retaliatory measures:

> may have preserved overall U.S.-EC commercial relations by preventing the bilateral friction over bananas from spilling over to something much larger that would have adversely affected substantially other areas of the [WTO] agreement. Although the U.S. retaliation of $191.4 million per year is not trivial, this interim outcome of retaliatory collateral damage to reciprocally rebalance the initial bargain can be interpreted as one that produced less damage than other likely alternatives may have.[134]

The temporary rebalancing of the scales in *EC-Bananas*, as suggested, thus played a critical role in sustaining the US–EU bilateral cooperative relations, as well as in safeguarding the broader WTO regime's stability by preventing escalation of the transatlantic conflict into an uncontrolled trade war and avoiding destabilization of other parts of the multilateral trade system during the dispute's existence.

Yet, it may well be the case that this rebalancing act played a vital function in sustaining the WTO's viability not only in the short-term (while the dispute endured), but also over the long haul, by strengthening the willingness of both sides to continue taking part in the multilateral trading system. As a WTO legal officer explained, the possibility to suspend concessions handed the *complainant* 'an incentive to continue participating [in the system] because you feel that there is ...

Original Complaint by Brazil–Recourse to Arbitration by the United States under Article 22.6 of the DSU, Decision by the Arbitrators, 31 August 2004, DS217/ARB/BRA, para 6.3; Limenta (n 130) 9–10.

132 Bown (n 2) 59.
133 Interview with WTO legal officer (Geneva, 16 March 2012).
134 Bown (n 2) 59.

[some] benefit from the system' in situations where, like the *Bananas* case, the respondent remains recalcitrant. '[I]f you feel cheated, you have less of an incentive to continue participating or to continue complying with the rules'.[135] At the same time, in these kinds of situations, where a Member finds it impossible to comply with WTO rulings and rules because of pressing internal or external political pressures, suspension of concessions enables the *respondent* to deviate, at least temporarily, from WTO law while enduring the costs of noncompliance as defined by the DSS. As several commentators have observed, this accommodation of noncompliance through temporary 'breach and pay',[136] rather than undermining the WTO regime, constitutes a 'systemic safety valve'[137] by which the DSS works to secure the long-term stability of the cooperative regime.[138] This it does by adding a degree of flexibility to the system, namely, by providing WTO Members, in periods of heightened political stress, with the opportunity 'to escape their obligations (at least temporarily until the ... political pressure passes to a more "normal" state of affairs)', bear the economic consequences of WTO noncompliance, but still remain within the community of cooperating nations.[139] This increased flexibility, although temporarily reducing international cooperation, decreases the possibility that the WTO regime might break down entirely whenever Members face intense political pressure for protection, and it ensures that states remain willing to participate in the WTO trade liberalization project and adhere to its legal constraints in the long run.[140]

Evidence from the Jurisprudence

The shift in emphasis in *EC-Bananas* towards the DSS's goals of settlement facilitation, rebalancing through renegotiation, and regime maintenance is apparent not only from the evidence generated through interviews with WTO professionals and the sequence of events as they unfolded during the dispute; this goal shift is also apparent from the distinctive judicial choices, interpretations, and techniques

[135] Interview with WTO legal officer (Geneva, 16 March 2012).

[136] On the functioning of the DSS as a de facto system of 'breach and pay', see, e.g. Warren F Schwartz and Alan O Sykes, 'The Economic Structure of Renegotiation and Dispute Settlement in the World Trade Organization' (2002) 31 J Legal Stud S179; Peter B Rosendorff, 'Stability and Rigidity: Politics and Design of the WTO's Dispute Settlement Procedures' (2005) 99 Am Pol Sci Rev 389; Joel P Trachtman, 'The WTO Cathedral' (2007) 43 Stan J Int'l L 127; Eric A Posner and Alan O Sykes, 'Efficient Breach of International Law: Optimal Remedies, "Legalized Noncompliance," and Related Issues' (2011) 110 Mich L Rev 243, 276–78; Judith Bello, 'The WTO Dispute Settlement Understanding: Less is More' (1996) 90 AJIL 416.

[137] Claus D Zimmermann, 'Toleration of Temporary Non-Compliance: The Systemic Safety Valve of WTO Dispute Settlement Revisited' (2011) 3 Trade L & Dev 382.

[138] Rosendorff (n 136).

[139] ibid 389–90.

[140] Zimmermann (n 137); Rosendorff (n 136).

used by WTO adjudicators themselves throughout. One notable illustration of this trend can be observed in the overt and discrete attempts by the adjudicators in *EC-Bananas* to actively encourage a mutually agreed settlement between the parties. Thus, for example, in the DSU Article 22.6 proceedings between the EU and the United States, the three arbitrators, former members of the original *Bananas* panel, chose to open their arbitral award by urging 'the parties to continue in their efforts to reach a mutually acceptable solution to this matter promptly', noting that 'the suspension of concessions is not in the economic interest of either of them'.[141] Later on, in the DSU Article 22.6 proceedings between the EU and Ecuador, the same arbitrators, after having recognized the difficulties Ecuador might encounter in exercising its retaliation rights, concluded their award by manifesting their 'trust that in this eventuality the parties to this dispute will find a mutually satisfactory solution'.[142] Such pronouncements, it should be noted, are rather rare in the landscape of WTO jurisprudence. Indeed, as Porges has remarked, although '[i]n theory, WTO panels may actively encourage settlement ... in practice none do'.[143]

An even more conspicuous illustration of the enhanced settlement facilitation and renegotiation roles played by the DSS in the *Bananas* case is reflected in the striking willingness of the same three panellists to provide the parties with concrete suggestions on how to move forward in the negotiations towards resolution of the dispute—a willingness that clearly contrasts with the general practice of WTO adjudicators of avoiding any such suggestions despite being authorized to do so under DSU Article 19.1.[144] Thus, mindful of the fact that panels have rarely 'made suggestions pursuant to Article 19.1', the first compliance panel in *EC-Bananas* did find it appropriate on this occasion to propose specific steps to the EU '*with a view toward promptly bringing the dispute to an end*'.[145] Consequently, at the end of its report, the compliance panel outlined three possible routes to be taken by the EU with respect to its banana regime. Among these was the move to a tariff-only system for banana imports, accompanied by a tariff or tariff-quota preference for the ACP countries that would be covered by a suitable WTO waiver or an FTA consistent with GATT Article XXIV.[146]

Beyond this notable departure of the compliance panel from the prevailing WTO judicial practice, particularly important for the purposes of the present discussion is the nature and content of the policy recommendations put forward. First, the panel's suggestions to the EU were of the kind that required *all* the parties involved in *EC-Bananas* to cooperate and engage in further negotiations for the

141 Article 22.6 Arbitration (US) (n 18) para 2.13.
142 Article 22.6 Arbitration (Ecuador) (n 20) para 177.
143 Amelia Porges, 'Settling WTO Disputes: What Do Litigation Models Tell Us?' (2004) 19 Ohio St J on Disp Resol 141, 167.
144 Joseph Pelzman and Amir Shoham, 'WTO DSU-Enforcement Issues' in *Trade Disputes and the Dispute Settlement Understanding* (n 99) 376–77.
145 First Compliance Panel Report (Ecuador) (n 15) para 6.154 (emphasis added).
146 ibid, paras 6.154–6.158.

purpose of settling the dispute. Thus, the move to a tariff-only regime as suggested by the panel required all the relevant parties to renegotiate the EU's MFN tariff for banana imports under GATT Article XXVIII. In like manner, a suitable WTO waiver that would allow the EU to maintain its WTO-inconsistent trade preferences for the ACP countries could only be granted through a designated political-diplomatic process coming under Article IX of the WTO Agreement. Finally, the conclusion of FTAs that would exempt the preferential treatment accorded by the EU to the ACP countries similarly required these two groups of states to enter into mutual negotiations.

Second, and no less significantly, the panel's suggestions manifested a good measure of sensitivity to the complexities of the case at hand. Thus, the panel's suggestions did not simply call for the elimination of the discriminatory trade effects of the violative EU banana regime. Rather, the suggestions highlighted several ways by which the EU's trade preferences for the ACP countries could be maintained, but in a manner potentially alleviating some of the WTO-inconsistencies pertaining to the EU banana policy while improving the standing of the Latin American countries vis-à-vis the European market. In the spirit of this sensitivity, and after having made the aforementioned recommendations, the compliance panel ultimately found it appropriate to close its ruling with the following 'concluding remark':

> We recall that the fundamental principles of the WTO and WTO rules are designed to foster development, not impede it. As illustrated by our suggestions on implementation above, the WTO system is flexible enough to allow … appropriate policy responses in a wide variety of circumstances across countries, including countries that are heavily dependent on the production and commercialization of bananas.[147]

Arguably, had the panel perceived its function in *EC-Bananas* merely as enforcing WTO law and securing compliance with the original WTO trade commitments, it would probably have avoided making such pronouncements and recommendations. Instead, by making these specific judicial choices, the panel essentially laid bare the plurality of considerations—beyond rule compliance—that come into play in WTO adjudication. Perhaps more to the point, it revealed the enhanced role played by the DSS in this case in managing the conflict, facilitating a negotiated settlement, and rebalancing the scales while providing the parties with a concrete, enabling bargaining environment. As it turned out, the suggestions included in the ruling of the first compliance panel substantially informed subsequent deliberations between the parties about the resolution to the *Bananas*

[147] ibid, para 6.164.

problem,[148] and formed a pivotal element of the 2001 Understanding on Bananas. Moreover, the compliance panel's ruling, once joined by the rulings in the second compliance proceedings held in 2008, 'laid the legal basis for the eventual political settlement of the dispute' in the form of the twin Geneva Agreements that came into force in May 2012 and January 2013.[149]

Finally, as part of their goal-attainment endeavours in *EC-Bananas*, WTO adjudicators not only took an uncommonly active role in facilitating the resolution of the dispute, they also went out of their way to develop interpretations that would grant the DSS jurisdiction to address the perennial conflict from beginning to end, what might prevent unilateral actions and destabilizing effects on the WTO regime. Such interpretations may be found in the very first panel and AB rulings in the *Bananas* case, where the EU challenged the legal interest of the United States in bringing the dispute to the WTO DSS inasmuch as it (the United States) was not a banana exporter. In reaffirming the US standing to act as a co-complainant in this case, both the AB and the panel significantly loosened the conditions Members must meet in order to file a WTO complaint, reasoning that no DSU provision requires a Member to have a 'legal interest' in order to have recourse to the DSS.[150] The AB observed, in fact, that the DSU's language suggests that Members have broad discretion in deciding whether to file a complaint before the DSS and 'whether such action would be "fruitful" ',[151] even though, as Ruiz-Fabri rightly indicates, the DSU 'texts call for great discipline' in this respect.[152]

A similar reading of the DSU text, done in such a way as to allow the DSS to contain the perennial dispute and thus sustain the stability of the overarching WTO regime, may be found in the last round of litigation in the *Bananas* saga, where both the panel and the AB rejected the EU's claim that the 2001 Understandings on Bananas, concluded between the EU, the United States, and Ecuador, precluded the latter two from initiating additional Article 21.5 compliance proceedings under the DSU.[153] According to the AB ruling of 2008, unless the parties to a mutually agreed solution explicitly renounce their right to have recourse to the DSU, they may not be precluded from initiating proceedings before the WTO DSS.[154] '[T]he relinquishment of rights granted under the DSU', the AB stressed, 'cannot be lightly assumed'. Rather, the language in the Understandings on Bananas, in this

[148] Josling (n 17) 190.

[149] Bruce Wilson, 'Extending the Scope and Strengthening the Legitimacy of WTO Dispute Settlement and Some Personal Recollections' in Gabrielle Marceau (ed), *A History of Law and Lawyers in the GATT/WTO: The Development of the Rule of Law in the Multilateral Trading System* (CUP 2015) 397.

[150] *EC-Bananas* AB Report (n 14) para 132; *EC-Bananas* Panel Report (n 13) para 7.49.

[151] *EC-Bananas* AB Report (n 14) para 135.

[152] Ruiz-Fabri (n 6) 100.

[153] AB Compliance Reports (n 35) paras 199–228; Compliance Panel Report (US) (n 34) paras 7.164–7.165; Second Compliance Panel Report (Ecuador) (n 34) paras 7.135–7.136.

[154] AB Compliance Reports (n 35) paras 212, 217, 228.

case, or in any similar agreement concluded between WTO Members, 'must reveal clearly that the parties intended to relinquish their rights'.[155]

In so reading the DSU, as a senior WTO official observed, the AB enunciated a fundamental principle whereby the DSS remains the forum to address disputes between WTO Members, and that matters can be brought to the DSS again and again, until their satisfactory resolution, unless this right has been explicitly waived in an agreement between the parties.[156] This interpretation tacitly reveals, in turn, the AB's conception of the DSS's role in perennial disputes not as a forum for simple third-party adjudication, shelved after rendering its original judgment, but rather as a dynamic and 'rolling' mechanism for containing and managing the recurrent conflict throughout its life span. Notably, any other interpretation of the DSU in the second round of compliance proceedings in *EC-Bananas* might have deprived the DSS of the jurisdiction to accommodate this additional episode of the *Bananas* saga, thereby leaving the complainants bereft of legal satisfaction and possibly opening the door for unilateral determinations and actions outside the WTO rules-based system. Cognizant of this possibility and in line with its broader efforts to secure the stability of the cooperative WTO framework in this case, the AB opted for the interpretative alternative that would prevent this eventuality from materializing.

8.4 Noncompliance in Perspective: Goal Conflict, Flexibility, and DSS Effectiveness

Alongside the goal-shifting dynamics identified in *EC-Bananas*, this perennial dispute also brings to the fore one of the most conspicuous tensions underlying the DSS's goals. This is the tension between the will to secure rule compliance and legal predictability, and the desire to preserve Members' reciprocal balance of trade concessions through amicable settlements and flexible rebalancing acts, with a view to sustaining the long-term viability of the WTO. In theory, of course, these goals need not necessarily conflict as the settlement of disputes by eliminating WTO-inconsistent measures may allow the simultaneous achievement of them all. But in reality, political constraints may, in some cases, make such goal conflicts inevitable. As a WTO official involved in *EC-Bananas* stated:

> [O]ne [goal of the DSS] ... is ... to achieve pragmatic solutions for disputes. Another goal would be to have ... security and predictability in the system or to achieve compliance.... Generally speaking, there shouldn't be any tension [between these goals]. But in specific cases, you may find a tension because you may

[155] ibid, para 217.
[156] Interview with WTO official (Geneva, 5 July 2012).

> find that parties are able to find a solution, but that solution is not necessarily, strictly in accordance with the agreements, ... [so,] what should you privilege—the fact that you find a solution to a long-standing dispute, or the fact that there isn't full compliance with the agreement?[157]

The protracted *Bananas* dispute illustrates the materialization of precisely this tension between the goals and, consequently, outcomes of the DSS: on the one hand, a satisfactory negotiated settlement,[158] informed by successive DSS rulings, was found in the form of the Geneva Agreements, which restored the bilateral balance of concessions between the parties. On the other hand, the settlement did not fully rectify the enduring violation of WTO law. Thus, upon conclusion of the Geneva Agreements, bananas originating in ACP countries kept on entering the European market on preferential terms, yet no relevant WTO waiver or exception was available to the EU to absolve its still discriminatory, WTO-inconsistent behaviour. As Eckart Guth, a former EU ambassador, has explained, in order to terminate what remained of the gap in EU noncompliance and make the continued tariff preferences for ACP bananas fully WTO-compatible, all EPAs negotiated since 2003 between the EU and the ACP countries had to be signed and implemented (and thus brought under the exception for FTAs enshrined in GATT Article XXIV).[159] However, by the time the Geneva Agreements were reached and initialled in 2009, only one EPA had been concluded;[160] the situation had not changed much when these agreements came into force in May 2012[161] and January 2013. Ultimately, although the EPA negotiations have seen more progress in recent years, not all EPAs have been concluded as envisaged[162] (whereas doubts have been raised about the WTO-compatibility of the agreements reached).[163]

[157] Interview with WTO legal officer (Geneva, 16 March 2012).

[158] Interviews with WTO practitioners indeed reveal general satisfaction among governments and the private sector with the mutually agreed solution achieved in *EC-Bananas*. See, e.g. interview with Ecuadorian official (Geneva, 17 July 2012); interview with former WTO ambassador (Geneva, 23 July 2012); interview with EU official (Geneva, 9 July 2012); interview with senior WTO official (Geneva, 23 March 2012); interview with ACWL lawyer (Geneva, 19 April 2012).

[159] Guth (n 22) 8.

[160] ibid.

[161] Interview with WTO legal officer (Geneva, 10 July 2012).

[162] Tony Heron and Peg Murray-Evans, 'Limits to Market Power: Strategic Discourse and Institutional Path Dependence in the European Union–African, Caribbean and Pacific Economic Partnership Agreements' (2017) 23 EJIR 341. The authors note that '[t]o date, four out of a possible seven regional EPAs have been concluded (or are close to conclusion) but only one of these—the EU-CARIFORUM EPA of 2008—comes close to matching the original prospectus' (ibid 342). '[T]he remaining members of the ACP have signed or initialled regional or subregional "goods-only" EPAs ... or have chosen not to sign an EPA at all' (ibid 347). See also Keijzer and Bartels (n 29).

[163] See Danielle Robertson, 'EU-ACP Economic Partnership Agreements: Modern Colonialism Disguised in Violation of the WTO' (2017) 50 Vand J Transnat'l L 463. See also interview with private attorney (Brussels, 19 July 2012) ('Now, all the system of the EPAs is not necessarily WTO-consistent. But nobody has complained').

And so, while a negotiated settlement was achieved in one of the most acrimonious international trade disputes, securing the complainants greater market access and reallocating the rights and duties of international economic cooperation between the numerous parties and third-parties involved,[164] the state of EU noncompliance with WTO obligations as originally anchored in the WTO treaty did not end with the *Bananas* settlement, and it has essentially continued long afterwards.

From a perspective that perceives the operation and effectiveness of the WTO DSS through the static lens of compliance, this noncompliant outcome may be portrayed as the final—disappointing yet unsurprising—chapter of a chronicle of noncompliance, and, consequently, as an instance of DSS under-effectiveness. Nourished by the view of the legalized WTO DSS as primarily an enforcement mechanism, designed to elicit strict legal compliance, this common reading of the *Bananas* case, as indicated earlier, remains dominant. As a lawyer involved in the case commented: '[I]t's true that if you see it from an outside view, with the perspective of a lawyer trained to be dealing with a clearly identified judicial power, you have the impression that the effectiveness of the system is at stake'.[165] A former Guatemalan official similarly noted: 'Non-compliance makes us think that the [dispute settlement] system has some weaknesses.... [That] there is a problem with the system'. '[B]ut on the other hand', he stressed, 'the [Geneva] Agreement happened because of the [dispute settlement] system.... [E]ven though there was no compliance in terms of the dispute settlement mechanism, ... [this mechanism] was an important element conducive to the negotiations that ended in the Geneva Agreement'.[166]

Hence, from a multidimensional goal-based perspective that takes into account the range of desired outcomes (or goals) the DSS is expected to deliver and their changing emphasis over time and across disputes, the story of *EC-Bananas* and DSS effectiveness becomes more complex. Seen through this prism, the perennial *Bananas* feud is no longer a binary tale of failure or success but an intricate story of shifts and trade-offs between multiple conflicting organizational goals—compliance and settlement, legal predictability and regime stability, rigidity and flexibility. This idea is clearly presented in this statement by a US official:

> [T]he goal of the system ... is compliance.... But ... the goal of the system is also that disputes are solved to the satisfaction of all the Members. And [in

[164] It should also be recalled in this respect that the new EU tariff rates for banana imports negotiated between the EU and the Latin American countries under the Geneva Agreement were incorporated into the EU's WTO tariff schedules. Consequently, the new EU tariffs apply on an MFN basis, so that the redistributive outcome produced in *EC-Bananas* essentially extends to the entire WTO membership.

[165] Interview with private attorney (Brussels, 19 July 2012).

[166] Interview with former official of Guatemala (Geneva, 24 July 2012).

> *EC-Bananas*, everyone knew] ... that the EU is gonna [sic] have political problems resolving the dispute.... Then, the question [be]comes ... how do you deal with this—... one side having a very legitimate claim and ... a strong economic interest. And the other side saying, 'Well, we really can't do anything'.... [T]hat's a difficult situation and that's when ... you [start] ... coming up with alternative ways. That requires ... both the complaining ... parties to express some flexibility in what can be done, to be a little bit pragmatic, but also for the responding party to realize that ... 'they have a legitimate claim and we actually do need to provide a level of satisfaction'.... [T]hat ... sort of shifted ... the [WTO] legal dispute settlement system [in *EC-Bananas*] into ... old school [dispute settlement].... But in some disputes, it's hard to envision that there's gonna [sic] be ... another way.[167]

Continuing along this path, the US official just cited went on to note the following when alluding to the post-litigation, not fully WTO-compliant settlement ultimately produced in *EC-Bananas*:

> [A]lthough it took a long time, we ... ended up in a place where ... they [i.e. the EU] were basically able to come up ... with something that would give market access to the affected parties in a way that even if they didn't remedy the actual violation ... they were able to ... work it out and move forward.... [T]hat is in fact an entirely satisfactory method of resolving the situation.... [I]f the parties are able to take the dispute [settlement decisions] and turn that into an outcome that everybody can live with ... then that's a successful resolution.[168]

When elaborating on this space effectively left for Members under the current system to use DSS rulings as a focal point around which they can ultimately settle disputes to their satisfaction,[169] a WTO legal officer involved in *EC-Bananas* stated:

> [T]he first and foremost objective of the dispute settlement [system] is dispute settlement, or ... a mutually agreed solution.... [T]his is not like a court where ... panels and the AB deliver something and it needs to be rubber stamped ... by this multilateral political body which is the DSB.... [Rather], you have flexibility as the losing defendant to comply in one way or another....

[167] Interview with US official (Geneva, 17 July 2012).

[168] ibid. A similar view was shared by other interviewees. See, e.g. interview with Ecuadorian official (Geneva, 17 July 2012); interview with EU official (Geneva, 9 July 2012); interview with senior WTO official (Geneva, 23 March 2012); interview with former official of Guatemala (Geneva, 24 July 2012).

[169] On this possibility see also Gregory Shaffer, Manfred Elsig, and Sergio Puig, 'The Extensive (but Fragile) Authority of the WTO Appellate Body' (2016) 79 L & Contemp Probs 237, 246.

> [Y]ou have enormous flexibility compared to a [purely] judicial system as to how you comply, what kind of measure you will adopt. And ultimately, you can come up with a mutually agreed solution, which ... has to be WTO-compliant, but nothing prevents that mutually agreed solution from being outside the box....[170]

And so, although DSU Article 3.5 mandates that all solutions to disputes formally raised under WTO dispute settlement provisions must be WTO-consistent, the 'hybrid' nature of the DSS, ranging between negotiation and adjudication,[171] coupled with its explicit preference for mutually agreed solutions (including at the post-adjudication stage),[172] endows disputants with meaningful flexibility in the settlement outcomes they may reach.[173] Within this framework, as Tallberg and Smith note, disputing governments are effectively 'free to reach settlements that tolerate ongoing violations of WTO rules even after formally binding panel and appellate rulings have entered into force'.[174] Under the present system, as an Ecuadorian legal officer put it:

> if Members are able to work together and find a solution to their problem ... [they can and] should be working to do that. And then, if a third Member believes that whatever these two countries had ... agreed is contrary to the rules, they ... [are] entitled to bring their own case [against any alleged WTO-inconsistencies].[175]

Tellingly, the AB, in the second compliance proceedings in *EC-Bananas*, seems to have implicitly acknowledged this flexibility. By stating that a 'mutually agreed solution may encompass an agreement to forego the right to initiate' further DSU proceedings if such an agreement is made explicitly,[176] the AB essentially recognized the freedom of disputants under the current system to agree not to challenge a measure in violation of a WTO obligation and thereby to 'tacitly accept that violation'.[177] Clearly, the mixed, noncompliant outcomes generated by the DSS in *EC-Bananas*, as well as the more general question of the system's effectiveness in such a case, cannot be assessed decoupled from this flexibility; nor can they be assessed without considering the tension between adjudication and negotiation, between

170 Interview with WTO legal officer (Geneva, 10 July 2012).
171 Wolfgang Alschner, 'Amicable Settlements of WTO Disputes: Bilateral Solution in a Multilateral System' (2014) 13 World Trade Rev 65, 82.
172 See, e.g. DSU arts 4.3, 11, 12.7, and 22.8.
173 Alschner (n 171) 70, 76–78, 82.
174 Jonas Tallberg and James McCall Smith, 'Dispute Settlement in World Politics: States, Supranational Prosecutors, and Compliance' (2014) 20 EJIR 118, 126.
175 Interview with Ecuadorian official (Geneva, 17 July 2012).
176 AB Compliance Reports (n 35) para 212.
177 Alschner (n 171) 88, 94–95.

law and diplomacy that undergirds the DSS and which at times imposes conflicting demands and trade-offs on the system in its goal-attainment endeavours, most notably, between rule compliance and settlement.

8.5 Conclusions

The perennial *Bananas* conflict rambled on in the WTO DSS almost from its establishment, testing every corner of the system until the formal resolution of the dispute in 2012. A close legal-empirical analysis of this seemingly never-ending saga, in which the parties went back and forth from the negotiating table to the courtroom, tells a more complex story of the roles played, the aims pursued, and the outcomes generated by the DSS, somewhat different from the narrative often conveyed from the common compliance-centred perspective. As a WTO legal officer aptly put it:

> The *Banana* case ... is a perfect example that can be used to show either that the [WTO dispute settlement] system is very good, or the system is very bad, depending on which view you take.... [Y]ou hear a lot of observers, they tell you, 'Oh, it is used to show that the system is a disaster'.... It took so long and the EU was not complying, etc..... [I]t clearly took a long time, but that's only because the case was a very complex case, ... when you have a case of that dimension ... you need to go gradually.... You cannot just ... destroy this policy that the EU had in place to benefit these ACP countries and to order its own market ... you need to have gradual changes, which the successive dispute allowed. And if you see it from ... [the point of view of] the complainant[s].... [e]very successive case that they brought ... improved their ... access [to] the EU market.... So even before the last case, they were already increasing their participation ... [in the European] banana market.... And, at the same time, the ACP countries, which find it very hard to compete because they have structural problems, have been able to get some development assistance, which hopefully will help them address the kind of structural problems that they need [to tackle].[178]

To be clear, by bringing these additional layers of the *Bananas* dispute to the fore, the analytical endeavour undertaken in this chapter was not intended to portray this case as an impeccable instance of WTO DSS operation. The EU's noncompliance throughout the conflict clearly put pressure on the DSS and the WTO,[179] whereas any WTO-inconsistencies remaining in the post-settlement period may

[178] Interview with WTO legal officer (Geneva, 16 March 2012).
[179] Interview with former EU official (Geneva, 9 July 2012); interview with private attorney (Geneva, 19 July 2012).

not only taint the DSS's compliance record, they may also hinder promotion of legal predictability and the rule of law in the multilateral trade system. In addition, since many WTO Members are not equally positioned to negotiate and 'buy-out' their WTO compliance obligations, as the EU essentially did in this conflict, such events may sustain imbalances of power and inequalities between Members.[180] What is more, the *Bananas* conflict illuminated some of the more systemic problems featured in DSS operation, such as the famous sequencing issue[181] or the difficulties faced by small developing countries in using the WTO suspension of concessions remedy.[182]

Yet, by putting forth a more complex, goal-based account of the perennial *Bananas* dispute, this chapter sought to disclose the still incomplete picture of the DSS's goal-attainment efforts and outcomes usually unfolded through the lens of the prevalent enforcement-oriented perspective of the system and its effectiveness. More specifically, it strove to expose the tacit shift away from compliance enforcement and the enhanced role played by the DSS in this case at the intersection of law and politics. The chapter thus showed that rather than serving as a means primarily aimed at securing strict legal compliance, in *EC-Bananas*, the DSS (including its retaliation tool) came to play a heightened role in promoting renegotiation and settlement, in reinstating the parties' reciprocal balance of trade benefits, and in keeping the WTO regime operational as long as the dispute endured (even at the expense of compliance).

It therefore appears that 'contrary to fears expressed occasionally during the banana splits', and 'although the conflict at times threatened to discredit' the WTO DSS,[183] the latter managed to adjust itself and its goals to the challenges before it and to consistently contain the intense conflict within its boundaries.[184] These important yet often overlooked dimensions of judicial effectiveness are aptly articulated in the following comment by a WTO legal officer, which closes this chapter:

> [A]nother thing is that in the end, the dispute settlement system ... could adapt to the challenge of *[EC-]Bananas*, which was a very complex process—different tracks at the same time, each testing the limits of the system. And they could sort of still keep together and maintain the system operational ... and avoid ... major

[180] John H Jackson, 'International Law Status of WTO Dispute Settlement Reports: Obligation to Comply or Option to "Buy Out"?' (2004) 98 AJIL 109, 117–18, 120–21.

[181] The sequencing problem relates to the relationship between the DSU procedures of compliance review (under Article 21.5) and suspension of concessions (under Article 22). See Mauricio Salas and John H Jackson, 'Procedural Overview of the WTO EC – Banana Dispute' (2000) 3 J Int'l Econ L 145, 153–61.

[182] See, e.g. Marco Bronckers and Naboth van den Broek, 'Financial Compensation in the WTO: Improving the Remedies of WTO Dispute Settlement' (2005) 8 J Int'l Econ L 101, 104–06.

[183] Cadot and Webber (n 3) 36.

[184] Bernhard Zangl, 'Judicialization Matters! A Comparison of Dispute Settlement Under GATT and the WTO' (2008) 52 Int'l Stud Q 825, 845.

inconsistencies and conflicts within the system. I think that was also a risk, that different parts of the house and different tracks that were tested in the context of *Bananas* would start coming into open and direct conflict with each other. And this was avoided. This is maybe not mentioned amongst the main achievements of the *Banana* saga but I think ... what you cannot see is often also an achievement.... What did not happen and what did not go wrong is also an achievement.[185]

[185] Interview with WTO legal officer (Geneva, 10 July 2012).

9

The Transatlantic Conflict Over Beefed-Up Beef

The *Bananas* conflict arrived at the World Trade Organization (WTO) in time to combine with another 'particularly difficult trade dispute with the EU over hormones in beef'.[1] The dispute, it has been argued, 'showed no promise of resolution and was a high priority and high profile issue' for the complainants,[2] the United States and Canada, as well as for the EU, where public resistance to hormone-treated beef created a political situation in which the respondent would find it impossible to comply with an adverse WTO ruling. It ultimately took two decades—featuring repeated rounds of litigation and negotiations and prolonged noncompliance—to bring the contentious transatlantic *Hormones* conflict to an end. Alongside the *Bananas* case, this conflict thus serves as an instructive site for investigating how the challenges invoked in perennial disputes affect the motivations for and the practice of disputing at the WTO, generate shifts and conflicts between the goals of the WTO Dispute Settlement System (DSS), and shape the outcomes it ultimately yields. The present chapter is devoted to this investigation.

The chapter proceeds in five parts. Section 9.1 lays down the basic facts of the *Hormones* dispute and recounts the conflict's major milestones. Section 9.2 distils the key elements that rendered *EC-Hormones* so resistant to compliance and resolution. Building on these benchmarks, Section 9.3 proceeds with an in-depth qualitative analysis of the dispute from a goal-based perspective. It traces the goal shifting that characterized the DSS's operation in this case and analyses the heightened role the system came to play along the fine line between law and politics, between adjudication and negotiation. Section 9.4 takes a close look at the mixed outcomes that eventually emanated from the dispute settlement process in *EC-Hormones*, while addressing the goal conflicts those outcomes represent and their implications for assessing and thinking about the effectiveness of the WTO DSS. Section 9.5 concludes.

[1] John G Stovall and Dale E Hathaway, 'US Interests in the Banana Trade Controversy' in Tim E Josling and Tim G Taylor (eds), *Banana Wars: The Anatomy of a Trade Dispute* (Cromwell Press 2003) 158.

[2] ibid.

9.1 A Roadmap to a Never-Ending Story

Origins of the Dispute

Growth-promoting hormones are commonly used by farmers around the world to speed up the fattening process in animals. In this way, farm animals reach market weight faster and consume less feed. *EC-Hormones*, the dispute in question, revolved around six natural and synthetic hormones used in livestock production that were licensed for use in North America but which the EU came to disallow during the 1980s because of growing public anxieties over their health effects. At the time, concerns had been raised especially about the carcinogenic influences of these hormones. Furthermore, in the late 1970s and early 1980s, several reports appeared in Europe of children exhibiting signs of premature sexual development, believed to result from eating hormone-treated meat.[3] These widely publicized 'hormone scandals' prompted consumer boycotts of beef products across a number of European countries, and generated a fierce demand to ban the use of growth hormones in cattle production throughout the EU.[4] In response to this public outcry, the EU adopted a series of directives between 1981 and 1988 that banned the administration of any of those six hormones to cattle and prohibited the marketing of domestic and imported meat derived from animals that had received these hormones. The EU fully implemented its ban with respect to imports of hormone-treated beef and beef products in 1989.[5]

The EU's ban had an immediate and dramatic impact on the United States and Canada, two of the world's largest beef producers, where some 90 per cent of all beef cattle are treated with growth hormones.[6] Following implementation of the trade ban, exports of beef products from the United States and Canada to the EU were almost eliminated. While the EU maintained that the ban was motivated by health concerns and that it had the right to adopt a precautionary approach seeking 'zero risk' if it chose to do so, the United States and Canada insisted that ample scientific evidence existed on the safety of the growth hormones in question and that support for their use could be found in international food safety standards. In the absence of scientific grounds for the import ban, the United States and Canada saw the hormone ban as part of the EU's broader restrictive agricultural trade policy and as disguised protectionism, geared at shielding European beef producers from cheaper imports.[7]

[3] Sebastiaan Princen, 'EC Compliance with WTO Law: The Interplay of Law and Politics' (2004) 15 EJIL 555, 566.

[4] Donna Roberts, 'Preliminary Assessment of the Effects of the WTO Agreement on Sanitary and Phytosanitary Trade Regulations' (1998) 1 J Int'l Econ L 377, 386.

[5] Kevin Buterbaugh and Richard Fulton, *The WTO Primer: Tracing Trade's Visible Hand Through Case Studies* (Palgrave Macmillan 2007) 108–09.

[6] ibid 110; Mark A Pollack and Gregory C Shaffer, *When Cooperation Fails: The International Law and Politics of Genetically Modified Foods* (OUP 2009) 150.

[7] Princen (n 3) 567.

The *Hormones* Dispute at the GATT

A legal challenge against the EU hormone ban had already been sought under the previous General Agreement on Tariffs and Trade (GATT) system. In 1987, the United States filed a complaint under the GATT's Technical Barriers to Trade Agreement, but the establishment of a panel to review the legality of the ban was blocked by the EU. Faced with this deadlock in GATT dispute settlement procedures, the United States decided to move forward on unilateral sanctions should the import ban on hormone-fed beef enter into force, which it did by preparing a list of European products to be subjected to retaliatory tariffs.[8] Once the import ban became fully effective in 1989, the United States, in open disregard of GATT dispute settlement procedures, started imposing unilateral retaliatory duties on selected EU products in the amount of US$100 million annually, a figure estimated by the United States as comparable to the value of the market loss for American beef exports resulting from the ban. In response, the EU requested the formation of a GATT panel on the unauthorized US sanctions, which the United States blocked. Escalation continued as the European Commission moved to draw up its own list of counter-retaliatory measures, which was answered by the US warning that such a step would trigger further responses.[9] The EU's counter-retaliation was then postponed, subject to progress in negotiations seeking a solution to the conflict with the United States.[10] Negotiations, however, did not lead to a solution but only to 'partial relief',[11] whereby US producers were allowed to ship hormone-treated beef as pet food and to certify certain shipments of meat as hormone-free for use in human consumption,[12] with exports to the EU remaining limited.[13] This stalemate continued for the next six years, during which unauthorized sanctions by the United States continued.[14]

The *Hormones* Dispute at the WTO

In 1995, the WTO came into existence, bringing with it the Dispute Settlement Understanding (DSU), as well as the Agreement on the Application of Sanitary

[8] Bernhard Zangl, 'Judicialization Matters! A Comparison of Dispute Settlement Under GATT and the WTO' (2008) 52 Int'l Stud Q 825, 839.

[9] Christina L Davis, *Food Fights Over Free Trade: How International Institutions Promote Agricultural Trade Liberalization* (Princeton University Press 2003) 327.

[10] ibid.

[11] Daniel Wüger, 'The Never Ending Story: The Implementation Phase in the Dispute Between the EC and the United States on the Hormone-Treated Beef' (2002) 33 L & Pol'y Int'l Bus 777, 780.

[12] Davis (n 9) 328.

[13] Princen (n 3) 567–68.

[14] Cherie O'Neal Taylor, 'Impossible Cases: Lessons from the First Decade of WTO Dispute Settlement' (2007) 28 U Pa J Int'l L 309, 359.

and Phytosanitary Measures (SPS Agreement),[15] which set out the basic rules for the use and maintenance of trade-restrictive policies motivated at the protection of human, plant, or animal health. The SPS Agreement encourages harmonization of SPS policies on the basis of international standards.[16] However, it recognizes the right of Members to adopt SPS measures that provide a higher level of health protection than would be achieved by the internationally established standards as long as Members abide by three conditions:[17] the SPS measures should be based on a scientific assessment of the risks to health,[18] their application should be nondiscriminatory between domestic and foreign producers, and any interference with trade should be kept to the minimum necessary to maintain the designated health standard. The SPS Agreement further provides that where 'relevant scientific evidence is insufficient', WTO Members may adopt a provisional SPS measure 'on the basis of available pertinent information'. However, in such circumstances, Members 'shall seek to obtain the additional information necessary for a more objective assessment of risk' and review their SPS measure 'accordingly within a reasonable period of time'.[19]

Equipped with these new WTO legal disciplines as well as mandatory dispute settlement procedures, the United States and Canada took legal action against the EU hormone ban before the WTO DSS in 1996, claiming that the ban was inconsistent with the SPS Agreement since it was not based on scientific evidence, risk assessment, or international standards. In August 1997, the panel issued its ruling, in favour of the complainants;[20] the Appellate Body (AB) similarly sided with the United States and Canada in its decision of January 1998.[21] Throughout its elaborated decision, the AB reversed many of the panel's legal interpretations and findings, thereby narrowing the operative scope of the latter's decision[22] and suggesting a looser interpretation of the SPS Agreement's provisions.[23] Yet, the AB did uphold the panel's ultimate finding that the EU ban violated WTO law because it was not based on a risk assessment showing convincing scientific evidence that beef treated

[15] Agreement on the Application of Sanitary and Phytosanitary Measures, 15 April 1994, 1867 UNTS 493.

[16] SPS Agreement art 3.1.

[17] SPS Agreement arts 3.1, 3.3, 5.1.

[18] Annex A of the SPS Agreement defines 'risk assessment' as a study reviewing the various harms and the likelihood of each harm to human, animal, and plant health generated by the product or process in question.

[19] SPS Agreement art 5.7.

[20] *European Communities–Measures Concerning Meat and Meat Products (Hormones)*, Report of the Panel, 13 February 1998, WT/DS26/R/USA [*EC-Hormones* Panel Report (US)]; *European Communities–Measures Concerning Meat and Meat Products (Hormones)*, Report of the Panel, 13 February 1998, WT/DS48/R/CAN [*EC-Hormones* Panel Report (Canada)].

[21] *European Communities–Measures Concerning Meat and Meat Products (Hormones)*, Report of the Appellate Body, 13 February 1998, WT/DS26/AB/R, WT/DS48/AB/R.

[22] Pollack and Shaffer (n 6) 151.

[23] Wüger (n 11) 781.

with the six hormones in question posed any risk for human health, as required by Article 5.1 of the SPS Agreement.

Following adoption of the panel's and the AB's rulings, the EU was granted a fifteen-month period to bring its measure into compliance with WTO law, which was to expire in May 1999. However, although the rulings clearly condemned the European ban, the EU took no steps to reverse the WTO-inconsistent measure. Instead, the European Commission announced that it would conduct further risk assessments in order to fill the gap in the ban's scientific foundations as identified by the DSS. Simultaneously, in the wake of the DSS rulings, the EU also entered into negotiations with the complainants in an attempt to reach a mutually agreeable solution to the dispute by exploring several potential alternatives, among them the option of a labelling system for hormone-treated beef, as well as the option of compensation, possibly in the form of an increased quota for hormone-free beef from North America.[24] These preliminary attempts, however, failed,[25] as the EU was unable to persuade either the United States or Canada to accept a compensation package tied to indefinite continuation of the hormone ban.[26]

When the May 1999 deadline expired, the EU had not managed to complete its scientific review. It nonetheless decided to leave its hormone ban in place, stating that the available scientific evidence did not allow it to lift the ban prior to the conduct of additional reviews. In accordance with the DSU, the United States and Canada then moved to request WTO authorization to suspend trade concessions to the EU. Following arbitration proceedings under DSU Article 22.6 over the appropriate level of countermeasures, the United States and Canada were authorized in July 1999 to impose retaliatory tariffs worth US$116.8 million and CDN$11.3 million, respectively, on European goods.[27] With the aim of increasing their leverage, the heaviest share of the North American sanctions fell on Germany, France, Italy, and Denmark, which were viewed as the countries most responsible for the ban.[28] In addition, in an attempt to further pressure the EU into taking action it would find satisfactory, the United States invoked the threat of 'carousel retaliation' in 2000, whereby the EU products subject to retaliation would rotate so as to spread the pain of sanctions across additional industries.[29] Although not utilized, 'this new measure threatened the prospect of more damaging sanctions in the future'.[30] Negotiations between the parties on a compensation agreement that

[24] ibid 812; Princen (n 3) 569.

[25] Princen (n 3) 569.

[26] Wüger (n 11) 812–13; Davis (n 9) 333.

[27] *European Communities–Measures Concerning Meat and Meat Products (Hormones), Recourse to Arbitration by the European Communities under Article 22.6 of the DSU*, Decision by the Arbitrators, 12 July 1999, WT/DS26/ARB; *European Communities–Measures Concerning Meat and Meat Products (Hormones), Recourse to Arbitration by the European Communities under Article 22.6 of the DSU*, Decision by the Arbitrators, 12 April 1999, WT/DS48/ARB.

[28] Buterbaugh and Fulton (n 5) 117–18.

[29] Davis (n 9) 334.

[30] ibid.

could resolve the *Hormones* saga by granting increased market access concessions to the United States and Canada in return for the latter two eliminating their trade sanctions resumed after US and Canadian economic sanctions had been put in place.[31] Disagreements nonetheless remained as to the scope and duration of the concessions to be granted, as well as the schedule for elimination of the sanctions.[32]

As retaliation continued, the EU completed its complementary risk assessments, based on 17 EU-funded studies. The latter concluded that all six hormones have potentially adverse effects on human health, but that evidence is not equally conclusive for them all. On this basis, the EU, in September 2003, replaced its former hormone policy with Directive 2003/74/EC.[33] The new directive maintained a permanent ban on beef treated with oestradiol-17β, which was determined a 'complete carcinogen'.[34] Regarding the other five hormones, the EU noted that the 'current state of knowledge does not make it possible to give a quantitative estimate of the risk to consumers', thus prohibiting their use on a provisional basis in accordance with SPS Article 5.7, pending further scientific information.[35]

In October 2003, the EU notified the WTO Dispute Settlement Body (DSB) of the new directive and the scientific studies, arguing that it had provided risk assessments justifying the import prohibitions under the SPS Agreement.[36] The EU also argued that by adopting the new directive it had fully implemented the DSS rulings in the case and that the US and Canadian retaliatory measures should consequently be lifted.[37] The United States and Canada disagreed. They argued that it was not clear that the EU's implementation measure was WTO-consistent,[38] yet they refused the EU's request that they initiate compliance proceedings under DSU Article 21.5 in order to resolve this disagreement.[39] The EU, for its part, assumed that as the respondent in the *Hormones* dispute, it could not independently seek such proceedings under Article 21.5. Negotiations over this impasse continued until November 2004,[40] when the EU initiated new WTO disputes on the legality of the continued suspension of concessions by the United States and Canada.

On March 2008, the panel issued its report in the *Continued Suspension* disputes.[41] It found that the continued retaliation by the United States and Canada

[31] Wüger (n 11) 813–14.
[32] ibid 814.
[33] Council Directive 2003/74/EC of 22 September 2003 Amending Council Directive 96/22/EC Concerning the Prohibition on the Use in Stockfarming of Certain Substances Having a Hormonal or Thyrostatic Action and of Beta-agonists [2003] OJ L262/17.
[34] ibid.
[35] ibid.
[36] Communication from the European Communities, *European Communities–Measures Concerning Meat and Meat Products (Hormones)* (28 October 2003) WT/DS26/22, WT/DS48/20.
[37] ibid.
[38] DSB, Minutes of Meeting of 7 November 2003 (18 December 2003) WT/DSB/M/157, paras 29–31.
[39] Taylor (n 14) 367.
[40] ibid.
[41] *United States–Continued Suspension of Obligations in the EC–Hormones Dispute,* Report of the Panel, 14 November 2008, WT/DS320/R [*Continued Suspension* Panel Report (US)]; *Canada–Continued*

after notification of the new EU directive in October 2003 was tantamount to unilateral determination and redress of a WTO violation, and was thus prohibited under Article 23 of the DSU. As to the revised EU policy, the panel, after consulting scientific experts, concluded that the policy was inconsistent with SPS Article 5.1 in relation to the permanent ban on oestradiol-17β because the EU had not conducted a risk assessment as appropriate to the circumstances. With respect to the provisional ban on the other five hormones, the panel held that the EU had failed to meet the condition of 'insufficient' scientific evidence under SPS Article 5.7 and thus to justify its provisional restrictions, given that the EU had not demonstrated any 'critical mass' of new evidence that might render the 'relevant, previously sufficient, evidence, now, insufficient'. All three parties appealed.

In its decision of October 2008, the AB rejected the panel's ruling almost in its entirety.[42] First, it overturned the panel's finding that the United States and Canada violated DSU Article 23 by continuing their retaliatory measures after notification of Directive 2003/74/EC. The AB held that where, as in this case, a disagreement arises as to the WTO consistency of an implementing measure, a WTO-authorized suspension of concessions may continue until such time that 'substantive compliance has been confirmed through WTO dispute settlement procedures'. The proper channel for resolving such a disagreement, the AB continued, is through compliance proceedings under DSU Article 21.5, which both the complaining and *defending* parties may initiate. Second, the AB criticized the panel for violating the EU's due process rights, noting that the experts consulted by the panel were prejudiced because they were deeply involved in establishing the international standards (for the Codex Alimentarius) on the hormones at issue, from which the EU's policy deviated. Third, the AB reversed the panel's findings that the EU directive violated SPS Articles 5.1 and 5.7. It held that the panel interpreted these provisions too narrowly, misallocated the burden of proof, and conducted a *de novo* review of the science incompatible with the appropriate standard of review. However, because of flaws in the panel's ruling, the AB was unable to complete the analysis as to whether Directive 2003/74/EC had brought the EU into substantive compliance with WTO law, thus finding that the recommendations and rulings in the *EC-Hormones* case 'remain operative'.[43] In an unusual move, the AB concluded its report by recommending that the DSB request all the parties to initiate Article 21.5 proceedings without delay so as to resolve their disagreement over whether the EU had removed the measure found inconsistent in *EC-Hormones* and whether the

Suspension of Obligations in the EC–Hormones Dispute, Report of the Panel, 14 November 2008, WT/DS321/R [*Continued Suspension* Panel Report (Canada)].

---

[42] *United States–Continued Suspension of Obligations in the EC–Hormones Dispute*, Report of the Appellate Body, 14 November 2008, WT/DS320/AB/R [*Continued Suspension* AB Report (US)]; *Canada–Continued Suspension of Obligations in the EC–Hormones Dispute*, Report of the Appellate Body, 14 November 2008, WT/DS321/AB/R [*Continued Suspension* AB Report (Canada)].

[43] *Continued Suspension* AB Report (US) (n 42) para 737.

continued North American sanctions remained legally valid.[44] The mixed ruling rendered by the AB in *Continued Suspension*, allowing the North American sanctions to continue and the EU to maintain its ban until further DSU proceedings, led all three appellants to declare victory.[45]

Soon after the AB ruling, the perennial *Hormones* dispute took an interesting turn. Allowed to continue suspending concessions against the EU, the United States announced in October 2008 that it was considering changes to the list of EU products subject to increased tariffs under the so-called carousel legislation,[46] a move aimed at intensifying 'pressure for a market access settlement'.[47] Two months later (December 2008), in accordance with the AB's recommendation, the EU requested consultation under DSU Article 21.5 to determine whether its 2003 directive had brought it into compliance with WTO law.[48] Meanwhile, the United States moved forward with its revised retaliatory scheme, declaring in January 2009 the changes to the list of EU exports subject to retaliation that would take effect in March 2009.[49] The EU responded by saying that the US administration's move meant that the EU 'will have no choice but to start preparation in order to take this to the WTO', that is, to request the DSS to rule on the WTO consistency of the revised hormone ban and the legality of the continued US sanctions.[50]

Pending these reciprocal threats of 'carousel retaliation' and a third round of WTO litigation, bilateral talks between the parties gained momentum, leading the United States, in March and April 2009, to delay its modified retaliatory action in order to provide more time for negotiations,[51] as well as to formulate a 'reduced list' of EU products subject to retaliatory duties (bringing the total amount of annual sanctions down from US$116.8 million to US$37.8 million) for the purpose of facilitating a negotiated solution.[52] A Memorandum of Understanding (MOU) was

[44] ibid.

[45] Markus Böckenförde, 'Hormone Ban in Dispute Again: The WTO Refuses to Reject Either the EC Ban or Canadian/US Trade Sanctions' (*ASIL Insights*, 18 December 2008) <http://www.asil.org/insights/volume/12/issue/25/hormone-ban-dispute-again-wto-refuses-reject-either-ec-ban-or-canadianus> accessed 20 December 2018.

[46] Renée Johnson, 'The U.S.-EU Beef Hormone Dispute' (2015) Congressional Research Service Report 7-5700, 12 <https://fas.org/sgp/crs/row/R40449.pdf> accessed 20 December 2018.

[47] Böckenförde (n 45); 'USTR Announces Delay of Trade Action in Beef Hormones Dispute' (*USTR*, 12 March 2009) <https://ustr.gov/about-us/policy-offices/press-office/press-releases/2009/march/ustr-announces-delay-trade-action-beef-hormones-disp> accessed 20 December 2018 [hereinafter USTR Announcement].

[48] *European Communities–Measures Concerning Meat and Meat Products (Hormones), Recourse to Article 21.5 of the DSU by the European Communities*, Request for Consultations by the European Communities, 8 January 2009, WT/DS26/23.

[49] Johnson (n 46) 12–13.

[50] 'EU Prepares WTO Action Over US Trade Sanction Law' (*European Commission*, 15 January 2009) <http://europa.eu/rapid/press-release_IP-09-58_en.htm> accessed 20 December 2018.

[51] Johnson (n 46) 13.

[52] 'Truce Declared in Beef Hormones Dispute' (*ICSTD*, 11 June 2009) <https://www.ictsd.org/bridges-news/bridges/news/11-truce-declared-in-beef-hormones-dispute-on-13-may-us-trade> accessed 20 December 2018.

ultimately signed by the EU and the United States in May 2009.[53] The agreement, establishing the foundations for the resolution of the long-running transatlantic feud over hormone-treated beef, did not affect the EU's decades-old import ban.[54] Instead, it laid out a series of phased-in measures providing for increased access to the EU market for High-Quality Beef (HQB) produced without growth hormones, balanced by a phased reduction in US trade sanctions. In phase 1 (August 2009–August 2012), the EU agreed to expand market access for HQB by opening a duty-free quota of 20,000 metric tonnes in return for a US commitment not to implement its January 2009 revised carousel retaliatory sanctions and to continue applying retaliatory duties on the 'reduced list' of EU products in force since March 2009.[55] In phase 2 (August 2012–August 2013), the EU pledged to further expand market access for HQB by increasing the duty-free quota to 45,000 metric tonnes, while the United States committed to suspending the trade sanctions imposed in connection with the *Hormones* dispute.[56] Phase 3 provided for a possible final resolution of the conflict if the parties agreed that the arrangement was working to their mutual satisfaction. Should that be the case, the EU would make permanent the 45,000-tonne import quota for HQB, and the United States would scrap all retaliatory duties.[57] On 14 April 2014, the EU and the United States notified the DSB of a revised MOU, dated 21 October 2013, wherein the parties agreed to extend phase 2 for two additional years and to enter into negotiations for a definitive solution to the dispute by August 2015.[58] At the time of writing, formal notification to the DSB of a 'mutually agreed solution' has not yet been made.[59] Finally, on 17 March 2011, a similar MOU was concluded between the EU and Canada, in which the latter agreed to immediately suspend (rather than phase out) its respective retaliatory

[53] For the text of the MOU, see Joint Communication from the European Union and the United States, *European Communities–Measures Concerning Meat and Meat Products (Hormones)* (30 September 2009) WT/DS26/28.

[54] Arlo Poletti and Dirk De Bièvre, 'Political Mobilization, Veto Players, and WTO Litigation: Explaining European Union Responses in Trade Disputes' (2014) 21 J Euro Pub Pol'y 1181, 1189.

[55] Johnson (n 46) 13.

[56] ibid 14.

[57] ibid. Note that the issue of hormone-fed beef has also been raised in the framework of the negotiations between the United States and the EU on the Transatlantic Trade and Investment Partnership (TTIP) Agreement. While the negotiations have not seen much progress in recent years, it appears that the EU is not expected to lift its hormone ban within the framework of a future transatlantic deal. See Tim Josling and Stefan Tangermann, 'TTIP and Agriculture: Another Transatlantic Chicken War?' (2016) 31 Choices 1, 6.

[58] See Joint Communication from the European Union and the United States, *European Communities–Measures Concerning Meat and Meat Products (Hormones)* (17 April 2014) WT/DS26/29.

[59] An EU official made an interesting comment when alluding to the fact that the United States and the EU have effectively resolved the *Hormones* dispute but 'have not settled [it] formally', i.e. through the submission of a formal notification of a mutually agreed solution to the DSB. This official noted: 'Whether we will ultimately manage to settle it formally is a difficult [question] … and … a political [one] as well. … There are many cases that are … sort of settled but they are not formally settled. This might end up being one of those [cases]'. Interview with EU official (Geneva, 19 July 2012).

measures.[60] On 28 September 2017, Canada and the EU notified the DSB, in accordance with DSU Article 3.6, that they had reached 'a mutually agreed solution',[61] thereby formally settling their dispute.[62] This development was the last in a series of events effectively bringing the lengthy *Hormones* saga to an end.

9.2 *EC-Hormones*: The Makings of a Perennial Dispute

The agreements concluded between the EU and the United States and Canada 'have drawn to a close a protracted and bitter trade dispute that ranged over two decades and at times threatened the credibility of the entire WTO dispute settlement mechanism'.[63] Underlying this lengthy EU-North American trade row are several controversial, philosophical, social, commercial, and political issues that, in tandem, rendered this dispute exceedingly difficult to resolve and highly resistant to compliance. This section traces these various complicating factors, which shaped in turn the course of the *Hormones* dispute, the motivations and expectations of participants, the challenges faced by the DSS, and the resultant shifts in the roles it played and the goals it pursued throughout the conflict.

Perhaps the most salient factor complicating the *Hormones* dispute was the fact that at its heart, the conflict reflected the fundamentally different cultures and philosophies towards the intersection of technology and food safety cultivated on the two sides of the Atlantic.[64] As is well known, the culture and attitudes of the Europeans have long demonstrated a preference for traditional foods and minimal processing, while exhibiting considerable scepticism towards novel foods and new technologies. In contrast, North Americans have usually been more willing to accept new technologies (e.g. genetic engineering and irradiation), while remaining sceptical towards the safety of traditional methods of food production (e.g. those used for raw milk cheeses and cured meats).[65]

[60] For the text of the MOU, see Joint Communication from the European Union and Canada, *European Communities–Measures Concerning Meat and Meat Products (Hormones)* (22 March 2011) WT/DS48/26.

[61] Notification of a Mutually Agreed Solution, *European Communities–Measures Concerning Meat and Meat Products (Hormones)* (3 October 2017) WT/DS48/27, G/L/91/Add.1, G/SPS/W/71/Add.1, G/TBT/D/7/Add.1, G/AG/W/26/Add.1 [hereinafter EU-Canada Notification of a Mutually Agreed Solution].

[62] Note that the formal settlement of the EU-Canada *Hormones* dispute was also facilitated by the conclusion of the EU-Canada Comprehensive Economic and Trade Agreement (CETA) that came into force on 21 September 2017. See Tom Miles, 'EU and Canada Settle Cattle Battle at the WTO' (*Reuters*, 3 October 2017) <https://www.reuters.com/article/us-canada-eu-wto-meat/eu-and-canada-settle-cattle-battle-at-the-wto-idUSKCN1C81HY> accessed 20 December 2018.

[63] Jill E Hobbs, 'Canada, US-EU Beef Hormone Dispute', *Encyclopedia of Food and Agricultural Ethics* (2014) 273, 276.

[64] ibid 277. See also Isis Amelia Rose Sien, 'Beefing up the Hormones Dispute: Problems in Compliance and Viable Compromise Alternatives' (2007) 95 Geo LJ 565, 575–80.

[65] Marsha A Echols, 'Food Safety Regulation in the European Union and the United States: Different Cultures, Different Laws' (1998) 4 Colum J Eur L 525, 526–30.

These separate cultures and attitudes have found expression in turn in different regulatory approaches at the technology-safety juncture.[66] 'Scientific rationality' has long underpinned the US and Canadian approach to new technologies, while the EU has tended to adhere to 'social rationality'.[67] Resting at the core of scientific rationality in policy-making is a profound 'belief in technological progress, a consideration of both recognized and hypothetical risks', an 'innocent-until-proven-guilty approach to the burden of proof, an acceptance of minimum risk tolerance levels', and a strictly evidence-based interpretation of the precautionary principle.[68] In contrast, at the heart of social rationality as a guide to policy-making are technological precaution, consideration of not only recognized and hypothetical risks but also of 'speculative risks', 'a guilty-until-proven innocent approach' to the burden of proof, a preference for zero risk, and a 'social' (as opposed to science-based) interpretation of the precautionary principle,[69] which together allow for regulatory action in the absence of clear scientific evidence but on the basis of consumer concerns.[70]

These divergent regulatory trajectories and the opposing philosophical beliefs nourishing them have set the scene for different legal determinations of the presence of food safety risks and of how to respond to those risks, as was the case in the *Hormones* dispute. As an EU legal counsel noted in this regard, *EC-Hormones* expressed the collision between different 'philosophical' perspectives, those of the EU and those of its North American trade partners: 'We are more precautionary in the EU. We think that if, scientifically, something is not clear[ly] ... safe, we prefer to be cautious about it'. At the same time, the position adopted by the United States and Canada, as well as some other WTO Members, is that 'if something is not proven to be dangerous ... you can't prevent it. You have to allow trade. And that's ... an underlying, almost ... philosophical difference'.[71] It was this aspect of the *Hormones* dispute that made it so hard for the EU to comply with the WTO rulings and that rendered the case so 'difficult' to resolve.[72] This same EU official elaborated:

> [I]t was ... so difficult because [there was] no way we [in the EU] would accept that we ... have to change the philosophical basis of our society which is ... more cautious.... We are not going to put in jeopardy ... the health of our people ... if we are convinced that we are right, or at least [if] there is sufficient doubt.... That

[66] ibid.
[67] Hobbs (n 63) 277.
[68] ibid.
[69] ibid.
[70] Mark A Pollack, 'The Political Economy of Transatlantic Trade Disputes' in Ernst-Ulrich Petersmann and Mark A Pollack (eds), *Transatlantic Economic Disputes: The EU, the US, and the WTO* (OUP 2003) 75–76.
[71] Interview with EU official (Geneva, 18 July 2012).
[72] ibid.

> was not something that could ever politically fly.... [T]here was no way that we... would... change... the people we are.[73]

As Pollack has noted, this is exactly what makes transatlantic disputes such as *EC-Hormones* 'more bitter and intractable than traditional trade disputes'—the belief of 'both sides ... that they are "doing the right thing"'.[74] An AB member involved in the *Hormones* dispute made a similar observation, while stating that behind the extensive debates over science and experts in this case 'was really the idea of two strong positions on an issue which was considered vital' to both sides:[75]

> *Hormones* inspires strong feelings, very strong feelings because for the Europeans, it is a major issue ... about public health.... And this precautionary principle is... very much on the minds of the Europeans.... And it is exactly the opposite in the United States. They consider that, '... if you are so cautious, you will never do anything'.... This [i.e. the United States] is the land of experimentation, exploration, of conquering new territories.[76]

Yet, as this excerpt further suggests in its reference to the 'strong feelings' inspired by *Hormones*, the opposing philosophical views held by the disputants added another volatile, *emotional* dimension to the conflict. Like the protracted transatlantic dispute over genetically modified organisms (GMOs), an EU official noted, in *EC-Hormones* there was 'a public health concern, which is viewed very differently here than in other countries and that gives the case ... [a] sort of emotional or irrational element', instilling 'a certain impossibility [with respect] to solv[ing] the issue'.[77] A WTO official involved in *EC-Hormones* succinctly summarized this argument: '[W]hy is it a case that you could not legally solve? Because of the emotional dimension in it'. He went on to say:

> You have ... basically ... two categories of cases that are impossible to deal with, the politically overloaded cases and the emotionally overloaded cases.... [In *EC-Hormones*] [t]he EC could not back off its ban for political [and] ... for emotional reasons, the population would not have accepted it.... If they had [lifted the ban],

[73] ibid. See also interview with WTO legal officer (Geneva, 4 April 2012) ('*Hormones* is such a difficult issue in Europe that.... the proposition that we in Europe were going to ... have to eat meat treated with hormones because this is what the WTO has decided, politically this is not something that you can sell... at home'); interview with former WTO and EU official (Geneva, 17 July 2012) ('there are certain things which are impossible in this world in spite of WTO rules, cultural things'); interview with former Canadian official (Geneva, 25 April 2012).

[74] Pollack (n 70) 71.

[75] Interview with former AB member (Geneva, 19 April 2012).

[76] ibid.

[77] Interview with former EU official (Geneva, 9 July 2012). See also Oliver Cadot and Douglas Webber, 'Banana Splits: Policy Process, Particularistic Interests, Political Capture, and Money in Transatlantic Trade Politics' (2002) 4 Bus & Pol 5, 18.

> it would have been impossible to explain [such an action].... So, nothing could have moved.[78]

What is more, *EC-Hormones*, as the last statement implies, did not simply involve a clash between the conflicting, emotionally charged, philosophies of the parties; the dispute and the philosophical clash at its core touched upon an issue—use of growth-promoting hormones in cattle—that was particularly high on the European public agenda. And so, it was the intense public pressure exerted on the EU and the latter's need to relieve consumer fears about food containing hormone residues that led the European legislature to adopt the hormone ban in the first place. Yet in the years following its adoption, public support for the ban only grew stronger. Concerns over food safety intensified in the face of a series of food scandals in Europe in the second half of the 1990s (e.g. the outbreak of 'mad cow disease'[79]), events that 'raised the question of risk regulation to the level of high politics'.[80] Eurobarometer polls conducted at the time repeatedly showed a growing scepticism among citizens 'towards the use of technologies that might endanger food and consumer safety'.[81] European consumer reactions to the panel's and the AB's rulings in 1997 and 1998, declaring the hormone ban WTO-illegal, were consequently fierce and uncompromising. Under these conditions, it has been argued, it would have been 'political suicide' for the EU to lift the ban and allow imports of meat produced from hormone-treated cattle.[82]

Moreover, opening the EU market to imports of North American hormone-fed beef in order to comply with the DSS rulings would have had a negative impact on EU farmers, who had adjusted their production methods to the EU's regulatory framework[83] and who argued that it would be unfair to allow imports of such beef while prohibiting growth hormone use within the EU.[84] Hence, while American farm interests, led by the Farm Bureau Federation, pressured the US government 'to get tough with the EU on beef',[85] European farmers joined consumer organizations in their unyielding support for the hormone ban,[86] thus helping to transform *EC-Hormones* into another intractable quarrel in the tense agricultural trade

[78] Interview with WTO official (Geneva, 28 March 2012). See also interview with WTO official (Geneva, 18 April 2012) (noting that *EC-Hormones* was the 'kind of case where the public is not going to accept whatever you try to tell them' about the disputed policy and the need to change it).
[79] Princen (n 3) 569.
[80] Poletti and De Bièvre (n 54) 1188.
[81] ibid. See also Buterbaugh and Fulton (n 5) 116.
[82] Buterbaugh and Fulton (n 5) 118. See also William A Kerr and Jill E Hobbs, 'Consumers, Cows and Carousels: Why the Dispute Over Beef Hormones is Far More Important than its Commercial Value' in Nicholas Perdikis and Robert Read (eds), *The WTO and the Regulation of International Trade: Trade Disputes between the European Union and the United States* (Edward Elgar 2005) 201; Princen (n 3) 569.
[83] Poletti and De Bièvre (n 54) 1188.
[84] Princen (n 3) 569.
[85] Stovall and Hathaway (n 1) 158.
[86] Poletti and De Bièvre (n 54) 1188; Princen (n 3) 569–70.

relations between the EU and its North American trading partners. As a US official noted: 'You put those two together', first, the 'very protected agricultural [European] market' and the 'strong … protectionist incentives' that the EU had to maintain the hormone ban in order to 'keep out the competition' and, second, the 'very strong … health community [in Europe] that … believes, although there's no scientific evidence to support them, … that these products should not be allowed in the market for health reasons.… [a]nd those are the cases that … become very difficult for the [WTO dispute settlement] system to deal with'.[87]

Finally, beyond the strong political mobilization by farmers and consumers in favour of the status quo in the EU, what made *EC-Hormones* even more complicated and tainted by obstinate noncompliance with WTO rulings and rules, was the large number of veto players involved in the process of domestic reform.[88] Amendment of the European regulatory status quo in this case called for legislative action requiring *both* a qualified majority vote in the Council of Ministers *and* a majority in the European Parliament, in accordance with the EU's co-decision procedure.[89] Involvement of the European Parliament meant that the consent of a higher number of actors was required for a policy change that would be entirely in conformity with WTO law. It also meant that policy-making would become more susceptible to public sentiments, especially given the intense public interest in the issue at hand.[90] Thus, although policy makers in the European Commission and in some EU Member states believed that the EU should comply with the WTO rulings, there was no backing 'for lifting the ban in the European Parliament and among a significant number of member states, reflecting public opinion's and producers' support for the ban and the widespread belief that hormone-treated beef was not safe'.[91] Moreover, even in the face of continuing North American sanctions against large EU Member states, such as France and Germany, which were deemed capable of changing the state of play in the European Council in favour of lifting the ban, those who balked at the ban's reversal had 'an additional veto point in the form of the European Parliament', where they could forestall a WTO-compliant policy reform.[92] In consequence, for the duration of the dispute, the EU was able to produce only minor policy changes and conduct some complementary risk assessments as a basis for slightly revising its hormone directive; the substance of its policy thus remained more-or-less unvarying.

[87] Interview with US official (Geneva, 17 July 2012).

[88] Poletti and De Bièvre (n 54) 1188–89; Alasdair R Young, 'Effective Multilateralism on Trial: EU Compliance with WTO Law' in Spyros Blavoukos and Dimitris Bourantonis (eds), *The EU Presence in International Organizations* (Routledge 2011) 120.

[89] Carsten Daugbjerg and Alan Swinbank, 'Curbing Agricultural Exceptionalism: The EU's Response to External Challenge' (2008) 31 World Economy 631, 649.

[90] ibid.

[91] Poletti and De Bièvre (n 54) 1189.

[92] ibid 1190.

The *Hormones* conflict, as the above indicates, therefore exhibited all the makings of a case likely to result in sustained noncompliance, to prove highly difficult to resolve,[93] and to exert enormous stress on the WTO and its DSS.[94] The dispute involved powerful states, arrived at the DSS with a weighty prior history, and revolved around an issue of great symbolic importance for the disputants. It also implicated the sensitive agricultural sector as well as politically empowered domestic groups on both sides, well-positioned to commit their governments to a hard-line position throughout the conflict. Lastly, the dispute required the losing party to introduce a major policy change, demanding a large shift in resources and, more importantly, in ideology, in circumstances where withdrawal of the contested measure was regarded as politically untenable because of its pervasive support among domestic producers and consumers. In that sense, to borrow from Hudec, *EC-Hormones* was a paradigmatic example of a 'wrong' case of 'ordinary non-compliance', where particularly high political costs were attached to compliance, meaning that the losing party could not but respond to the intense domestic pressures to flout a WTO rule.[95]

9.3 *EC-Hormones*: A Goal-Based Reading

The Conventional Wisdom

'The beef hormone case', Sebastiaan Princen has noted, 'presents a clear example of the relative ineffectiveness' of WTO law and dispute settlement. 'Despite a series of clear WTO rulings against the European ban, the EC has not been willing to reconsider its ban, let alone reverse it'.[96] Antonello Tancredi has added that the 'effectiveness' of WTO 'dispute settlement procedures has been seriously questioned as a result of the decision taken by the EC in relation to *Bananas* and *Beef Hormones* to face protracted United States retaliation rather than bring its legislation into compliance'.[97]

[93] For the various factors that trigger these types of highly contentious, 'impossible', and perennial disputes, see the discussion in Chapter 7.

[94] As implied above, some of the stress placed on the WTO and its DSS in *EC-Hormones* resulted from the nontrade health-related interests involved. As explained in Chapter 7, n 51, the *Hormones* dispute fits the category of perennial conflicts but also that of trade-and disputes and, as described in Chapter 6 (Section 6.1), it exhibits many of the legitimacy-enhancing techniques characteristic of trade-and disputes such as *US-Shrimp* and *US-Clove Cigarettes*. This duality is not surprising given that a dispute's various characteristics may assign it to different categories of WTO cases. For all the reasons presented above, here, *EC-Hormones* is analysed from the perspective of a perennial dispute, where the tension between trade and health encompasses *one* of the case's complicating elements.

[95] cf Robert E Hudec, 'GATT Dispute Settlement After the Tokyo Round: An Unfinished Business' (1980) 3 Cornell Int'l LJ 145, 159; Taylor (n 14) 318.

[96] Princen (n 3) 570.

[97] Antonello Tancredi, 'EC Practice in the WTO: How Wide is the "Scope for Manoeuvre"?' (2004) 15 EJIL 933, 935.

These are but two examples of the prevalent, rather straightforward depiction of *EC-Hormones*, like the *Bananas* case, as a 'legal failure' that entangled the DSS in a long and abashedly murky incident of noncompliance, an event that seriously called its effectiveness into question.[98] This portrayal of *EC-Hormones* also testifies to the widespread perception of compliance as the unremitting primary goal of the DSS and as the key measure by which its effectiveness is to be judged. However, if one were to look beyond compliance, that is, embrace a broader goal-based perspective and examine the *Hormones* case against the intricate ethical, economic, and political context in which the dispute unfolded, together with the way these contextual factors shifted stakeholder expectations of the DSS and the goals it pursued, a far more complex and nuanced story is likely to emerge.

DSS Goal-Attainment in *EC-Hormones*: Actual Trends

Admittedly, the United States and Canada, when initiating legal proceedings against the EU before the mandatory WTO DSS in 1996, wanted to see the European hormone ban lifted subsequent to a WTO ruling declaring the ban inconsistent with the SPS Agreement. Yet, alongside this aspiration, it seems that from the outset, a rather forthright understanding had emerged in the multilateral trading system as to the low prospects for compliance, let alone full and immediate compliance, in this so politically charged dispute. The reigning consensus among WTO practitioners stated that the case would remain with the DSS for a long while. Thus, for example, a WTO official involved in the case noted that upon arrival of *EC-Hormones* in 1996, the prospects for EU compliance with an adverse DSS ruling were practically 'nil'.[99] Another WTO official stressed that it was rather evident 'that the Europeans would not accept to change' the hormone ban given the public's strong support of the ban,[100] as did a former AB member: 'it was clear that the Europeans are not going to . . . comply. It was very clear'.[101]

Other participants in the case likewise described the early recognition that transpired among actors in the multilateral trade circles that *EC-Hormones*, because of its various complicating factors, was likely to develop into a rather long and recurring conflict. Instructive in this respect is the following statement by a WTO

[98] See also Kerr and Hobbs (n 82) 192; Taylor (n 14) 331–32; Wüger (n 11) 815; Gary Horlick and Judith Coleman, 'A Comment on Compliance with WTO Dispute Settlement Decisions' in Merit E Janow, Victoria Donaldson, and Alan Yanovich (eds), *WTO: Governance, Dispute Settlement & Developing Countries* (Juris Publishing Inc. 2008) 773; Marc L Busch and Eric Reinhardt, 'Transatlantic Trade Conflicts and GATT/WTO Dispute Settlement' in *Transatlantic Economic Disputes* (n 70) 475–78; Benjamin L Brimeyer, 'Banana, Beef, and Compliance in the World Trade Organization: The Inability of the WTO Dispute Settlement Process to Achieve Compliance from Superpower Nations' (2001) 10 Minn J Global Trade 133, 134.

[99] Interview with WTO official (Geneva, 28 March 2012).

[100] Interview with WTO official (Geneva, 18 April 2012).

[101] Interview with former AB member (Geneva, 19 April 2012).

official involved in the panel proceedings: '[M]ost people knew that the EU would lose, including the EU. But at the same time, most people also knew that it would only be one step in bringing about a change here'.[102] A former EU official went still further:

> I don't think that ... anybody expected that the [*Hormones*] problem would go away with just one ruling.... [T]here are other disputes where countries feel ... the pressure of being in litigation, of being the defending party ... that they may have the ambition to solve [the case] and make it go away once the ruling is out, [or] even before the ruling is out.... But in *Hormones* ... that wasn't enough to ... weigh up against what was at stake ... so it had to go to the next round [of WTO litigation].[103]

Finally, another EU official stressed that not only were the prospects for non-compliance visibly high, but that *Hormones* was one of those cases where 'if you force compliance.... if you push too hard, then the risk is that the [whole] system breaks down'.[104]

Nevertheless, here as well, despite the gloomy forecast for a reversal of the EU policy, the complainants—like those in *EC-Bananas* and other perennial WTO disputes—chose to take legal action before the DSS, suggesting that there was more than compliance at stake when seeking WTO adjudication. Indeed, one AB member involved in the *Hormones* saga observed that in this case, 'there was ... a situation where Canada and the US did not necessarily pursue what they considered to be right, because it was foreseeable that there would be a problem on the implementation side'.[105] Concurring with this description, another AB member went on to stress that while the prospects for compliance in *Hormones* were clearly low, this was the case with respect to only 'one outcome, which does not exclude the other outcomes' to be generated by the DSS.[106] As will be seen below, these other desired outcomes (or goals) took on extra salience as the dispute progressed.

And so, in *EC-Hormones*, rather than serving as a mechanism oriented solely towards inducing compliance with WTO rules, the primary effect of the DSS was felt at the interface between the legal and the political spheres. Within this framework, the DSS provided an institutional forum for repeated interaction and cooperation, geared to facilitating the settlement of the dispute and restoring the bilateral balance of concessions between the parties through the reconstruction of bargaining scenes and concrete focal points around which they could more constructively

102 Interview with former WTO official (Geneva, 30 March 2012).
103 Interview with former EU official (Geneva, 9 July 2012).
104 Interview with EU official (Geneva, 18 July 2012).
105 Interview with former AB member (Brussels, 19 July 2012).
106 Interview with former AB member (Geneva, 19 April 2012).

negotiate.[107] Yet, as the perennial *Hormones* dispute placed serious strains on North Atlantic economic relations and threatened the WTO regime's stability,[108] the DSS also played an enhanced role in sustaining the cooperative regime and keeping it operational as long as the dispute endured. This it did by defusing the political aspects of the dispute, containing it within defined legal boundaries, and preventing uncontrolled unilateral actions that could escalate the conflict and project destabilizing effects onto other parts of the multilateral system. As shown below, this shift in emphasis in *EC-Hormones* towards the DSS's settlement, rebalancing, and regime-maintenance goals is reflected in interviewees' testimonies, based on their knowledge and experience, the conflict's sequence of events, as well as the distinctive interpretations and judicial choices of WTO adjudicators.

Evidence from the Field

'[I]n the usual case', a former WTO official involved in *EC-Hormones* stated, 'the goal [of the DSS] is to clarify the rules ... and in most cases, the goal is, ... through that clarification, to seek compliance with the rules'.[109] In certain cases, however, other goals come to play a greater role in the DSS's operation. Thus, this practitioner added:

> [E]specially in very ... hard cases, such as *Hormones* ... or *GMOs*, ... everyone almost knows that at best, the WTO ruling would play a role in pushing the defendant in one or the other direction, [and] that it would be quite hard [for the system] to ... force [the] ... countries to change those fundamental rules. But at the same time ... [the DSS serves] to defuse the whole political dispute, to avoid unilateral retaliation, and then to clarify the situation as to is there a breach? To what extent? [And] how much compensation should follow?[110]

In adjudicating such 'hard' cases, the same interviewee went on, the DSS 'set[s] the line [as to] what is in compliance [with WTO law] and what is not, and ... then ... let[s] the parties settle around that line'.[111] In other words, WTO

[107] For an elaborate discussion of these DSS's roles and goals, see Chapter 3. For relevant literature, see, e.g. Christina L Davis, *Why Adjudicate: Enforcing Trade Rules in the WTO* (Princeton University Press 2012) 246; Andrew T Guzman, 'International Tribunals: A Rational Choice Analysis' (2008) 157 U Pa L Rev 171, 180–83; Michael Gilligan, Leslie Johns, and Peter Rosendorff, 'Strengthening International Courts and the Early Settlement of Disputes' (2010) 54 J Conflict Resol 5, 10–11; Tom Ginsburg and Richard H McAdams, 'Adjudicating in Anarchy: An Expressive Theory of International Dispute Resolution' (2004) 45 William & Mary L Rev 1229.

[108] Pollack (n 70) 66, 69; Kerr and Hobbs (n 82) 191. In this respect one senior WTO official noted that at a certain point in the *Hormones* conflict, it was feared that 'the EC was going to pull out of the WTO'. Interview with senior WTO official (Geneva, 25 April 2012).

[109] Interview with former WTO official (Geneva, 30 March 2012).

[110] ibid.

[111] ibid.

litigation and adjudication in such instances provides a structured, legalized framework for the settlement negotiations that take place in the wake of DSS rulings.[112] This 'renegotiation of the contract' occurs in the context of, and is informed by the legal rulings and represents 'one of the goals' of the DSS.[113] After all, this interviewee stressed, 'the [dispute settlement] system as a whole is out there to achieve some balance, through a settlement or through rule-compliance'.[114]

In a similar spirit, a former WTO and EU official observed that in cases like *EC-Hormones*, where it is 'impossible' to comply with the rules because 'fairly strong ... forces are at work', 'a certain amount of rebalancing [is in order].... [I]n some situations ... you have to be content ... with not restoring the competitive opportunities but with actually compensating or renegotiating'.[115] In consequence, a former EU official added, litigation of such complex and perennial disputes before the DSS does not solve the dispute per se. Instead, it 'opens up other avenues of trying to solve' the case and re-establishing the original terms of the bargain by repeatedly serving as 'the stimulant' needed for renegotiation.[116] Concurring with this assessment, a WTO official involved in *EC-Hormones* stated:

> [Y]ou can see, it is not the [WTO legal] cases that directly solved the [*Hormones*] issue, it is the negotiations. Now, of course, as a US delegate used to say in the old days, what is great about winning the panel is that you can start negotiating.... [T]hat was the idea.... [In *Hormones*], the US tried to get a way to negotiate and to force the EC to change its policy, and the EC ... was also ready to negotiate, but ... it wanted to ... know how far it would have to negotiate.[117]

Notably, while many trade disputes are settled through negotiations in the shadow of WTO adjudication, often before a panel ruling is rendered, in other cases, as Shaffer notes, Members only begin to seriously negotiate after a ruling is issued.[118] This was the case in perennial conflicts such as *EC-Bananas* and *US-FSC*;[119] and the same holds true for *EC-Hormones*. As illustrated below, a close look at the braiding of adjudication and negotiation throughout this conflict recounts

[112] Davis (n 9) 49–51; Joseph A Conti, *Between Law and Diplomacy: The Social Contexts of Disputing at the World Trade Organization* (Stanford University Press 2011) 148.

[113] Interview with former WTO official (Geneva, 30 March 2012).

[114] ibid. For a similar argument, including in the specific context of the perennial *Hormones* dispute, see Heinz Hauser and Alexander Roitinger, 'Renegotiation in Transatlantic Trade Disputes' in *Transatlantic Economic Disputes* (n 70) 487.

[115] Interview with former state and WTO official (Geneva, 17 July 2012).

[116] Interview with former EU official (Geneva, 9 July 2012).

[117] Interview with WTO official (Geneva, 28 March 2012).

[118] Gregory Shaffer, 'Developing Country Use of the WTO Dispute Settlement System: Why it Matters, the Barriers Posed' in James Hartigan (ed), *Trade Disputes and the Dispute Settlement Understanding of the WTO: An Interdisciplinary Assessment* (Emerald Group Publishing Limited 2009) 174.

[119] ibid.

the various ways in which the DSS, from its first ruling and through the successive proceedings, advanced the above-mentioned goals of facilitating settlement and rebalancing the scales by recurrently shifting the political balance between the parties towards cooperation and providing them with new negotiating frameworks.

Thus, after years of stalemate, beginning in the GATT era, the deadlock in the transatlantic row over hormone-treated beef was ultimately broken, but only in the wake of the panel's and the AB's rulings in the first round of WTO litigation. As for the complainants, the United States and Canada, only until they litigated the case were they able to assess the exact strength of their arguments under the multilateral trade rules and, therefore, the scope of their bargaining clout.[120] As for the respondent, under the GATT, as indicated earlier, the EU could effectively block any legal pronouncement on the consistency of its hormone ban with its international trade obligations and thereby avoid the reputation pressures attendant on an adverse legal ruling. In this state of play, the EU could afford to address the complainants' demands by doing little beyond simply refusing to act, which is exactly what it did. The mandatory WTO DSS, in contrast, as a former EU legal counsel involved in *Hormones* noted:

> [P]ut pressure [on the EU] because if you can block the constitution of a panel [as was the case in GATT], then you can basically ... prevent litigation.... And you can prevent the case from being openly discussed and possibly ... decided ... by somebody else. If you can't do that anymore then you have to live with the consequence that this dispute might go ahead even though you know you will not be able to implement an adverse ruling. And then you start looking for other solutions.[121]

The first round of adjudication before the WTO DSS indeed constituted an important step in the search for such solutions in this case. The AB's ruling of 1998, giving 'the EU quite a bit of a leeway' in the interpretation of the SPS Agreement,[122] yet ultimately upholding the panel's finding of a WTO violation, meaningfully affected the reputation balance between the complainants and defendant. This judicial outcome consequently set the framework for a new bargaining situation, where several proposals for the dispute's resolution were raised. Among the proposals explored at this initial stage of the negotiations was the replacement of the disputed hormone ban with a labelling system,[123] based on a suggestion made by the

[120] Interview with WTO official (Geneva, 28 March 2012).

[121] Interview with former EU official (Geneva, 9 July 2012). See also interview with WTO official (Geneva, 5 July 2012); interview with senior WTO official (Geneva, 23 March 2012).

[122] Interview with former WTO official (Geneva, 30 March 2012).

[123] 'EU Offers Interim Compliance Plan in WTO Beef Case' (*Bridges Weekly*, 15 February 1999) <http://ictsd.org/i/news/bridgesweekly/94378/> accessed 20 December 2018 [hereinafter EU Proposals]; 'U.S. Offers Country-of-Origin Label to Resolve Beef Dispute' (*Bridges Weekly*, 22 February 1999) <http://ictsd.org/i/news/bridgesweekly/94413/> accessed 20 December 2018.

panel (discussed further below).[124] Other proposals concerned compensation by the EU, possibly through increased market access for hormone-free beef to Europe in return for keeping the ban in place.[125] These initial negotiations essentially laid the foundations of what a decade later would ripen into the agreement settling the *Hormones* conflict.

It was, however, the subsequent breakdown in these negotiations, together with the EU's failure to comply with the WTO ruling by the end of the implementation period that, in mid-1999, caused the complainants to resort once more to the DSS, this time to seek authorization to suspend trade concessions to the EU. Following proceedings under DSU Article 22.6, the arbitrators ultimately set the level of US and Canadian retaliation at an annual US$116.8 million and CDN$11.3 million, respectively, thus assigning the economic costs to the EU's continuing noncompliance.

Clearly, the economic pressure exerted by the authorized North American sanctions, effective as of July 1999, was insufficient to induce European decision-makers to withdraw the WTO-inconsistent hormone ban. As one EU participant in the proceedings openly admitted:

> [E]ven if you would double the remedies ... it wouldn't make a difference.... You wouldn't have a philosophical change in the attitude of the European Union to science....We would still be protecting our people ... if we think that it's a sufficiently compelling case for that.[126]

And yet, a WTO official noted, although 'the countermeasures ... led nowhere' in terms of compliance, the DSS-authorized sanctions did lead 'to gradual negotiations' between the parties towards the settlement of the dispute.[127] Thus, east of the Atlantic, the retaliatory tariffs against European exports, increasing the economic costs of the EU's noncompliant behaviour, generated a growing demand for renegotiation in the ensuing years and strengthened the EU's interest in finding a solution to the conflict. As a former EU official observed, the imposition of increased retaliatory duties 'built ... pressure back home ... [among] the companies that were affected' and which, under the jurisprudence of the European Court of Justice, were not entitled to compensation from the EU for the damages suffered due to its WTO-inconsistent conduct. Those businesses exerted constant pressure on the European Commission, urging it to 'solve this problem' while arguing that

[124] *EC-Hormones* Panel Report (US) (n 20) para 8.274; *EC-Hormones* Panel Report (Canada) (n 20) para 8.278.

[125] EU Proposals (n 123).

[126] Interview with EU official (Geneva, 18 July 2012).

[127] Interview with WTO official (Geneva, 28 March 2012). See also interview with WTO legal officer (Geneva, 16 March 2012) (noting that 'suspension of concessions ... gives an inducement [to the parties] to ... sit down and negotiate an agreement').

otherwise they were 'going to go bankrupt... [because of] these [retaliatory]... tariffs'. '[T]hat is an enormous pressure and that gets the government going', stressed the same official.[128] Another EU legal officer working on *EC-Hormones* drew a similar picture when alluding to the North American retaliatory actions taken during the dispute:

> You had pressure then from certain Member states, [saying], 'Well ... they are targeting our companies. Please do something about it'. Then you [also] have the threat of the 'carousel'... the mere fact that you have a threat there and... companies that didn't want to operate in these conditions of uncertainty as to whether or not their goods at some point would be subject to much higher duties, that in itself was sufficient for us to be kind of worried about it. And it certainly was a factor, no doubt about it. How strong? That's a matter of judgment....[129]

Finally, a former WTO official involved in *EC-Hormones* stressed that while 'retaliation... really pushed the EU... in the direction' of renegotiation with the complainants, the economic costs inflicted by the North American sanctions were accompanied and reinforced by the mounting reputational costs generated by the EU's obstinate noncompliance.[130] Over the years, this interviewee explained, the *Hormones* case 'was continually discussed at the DSB and a lot of pressure [was put] on the EU to comply, so these kinds of costs kept running as well'. These same reputational costs persuaded the EU to renegotiate and resolve the case no less than the direct economic consequences accruing from the prolonged sanctions.[131]

West of the Atlantic, the United States and Canada, in turn, accepted the EU's increasing demands for renegotiation. In fact, their readiness to negotiate endured even after it had become clear that the EU would not comply.[132] And so, at a rather early stage of the dispute, the complainants began using the favourable DSS legal findings and the resulting retaliatory rights not merely as mechanisms to induce withdrawal of the EU's WTO-inconsistent measure, but as means to ensure improved market access for their beef producers in the negotiations over 'a compensation agreement' with the EU.[133] The complainants persisted in this attitude for the duration of the *Hormones* dispute, drawing on the DSS-authorized sanctions

128 Interview with former EU official (Geneva, 9 July 2012); interview with former EU official (Geneva, 17 July 2012) ('French luxury industry was very upset [about the retaliatory tariffs] and always lobbied the commission to really get it over with').

129 Interview with EU official (Geneva, 18 July 2012).

130 Interview with former WTO official (Geneva, 30 March 2012).

131 ibid.

132 Hauser and Roitinger (n 114) 504–05.

133 Wüger (n 11) 813–14 (describing the Bush administration's efforts already in mid-2001 to negotiate 'a compensation agreement that could resolve the trade dispute following the EC's decision to leave its ban in place', in return for a US commitment to eliminate the retaliatory measures effective of July 1999).

as a lever 'to increase pressure for a market access settlement'.[134] Thus, for example, in a later stage of the dispute, before the US-EU MOU was concluded, the United States openly declared that the 'purpose of the modified' retaliatory tariffs it had announced in January 2009 'was to encourage a resolution of the longstanding *Beef Hormones* dispute that would offer a fair outcome for the U.S. beef industry'.[135]

Similar to *EC-Bananas*, a rule-oriented perspective focusing on the compliance inducement objective of the DSS, including its retaliation tool, may be insufficient to explain the complainants' readiness at various stages of the *Hormones* dispute to renegotiate an issue that had already been decided in their favour and which had basically seen no policy change on the part of the respondent even in the face of rightfully imposed retaliatory measures. In contrast, a broad goal-based perspective of the kind pursued here, which accounts for the multiple and dynamic goals pursued by the DSS and its retaliation mechanism, may better explain this readiness by disclosing the shift away from compliance exhibited towards other DSS objectives, namely, facilitation of renegotiation and achievement of a mutually agreed settlement that would reinstate the parties' reciprocal balance of concessions.[136]

This is the place to note that until that settlement's conclusion, WTO retaliation in *EC-Hormones* appears to have served two additional goals of the DSS. As one US official noted, when a dispute arrives at a point where '[t]he [WTO-inconsistent] practice has not been changed' and no agreement has been reached on how to resolve the situation, 'you [then] need to move to rebalancing' through the temporary withdrawal of equivalent concessions vis-à-vis the defendant.[137] In this respect, the suspension of concessions in *EC-Hormones* thus played an important role in the bilateral relationship between the disputants as a means to maintain reciprocity while the dispute endured.[138] Second and no less significant, however, is the systemic regime-maintenance goal served by the DSS-authorized retaliation, a mechanism that through its temporary rebalancing feature enabled the DSS to contain the dispute for a period and control for the consequences of the EU's continued noncompliance, thereby preventing the skirmish over beef hormones from spilling over to other areas of the cooperative WTO regime.[139]

[134] Böckenförde (n 45).

[135] USTR Announcement (n 47).

[136] For a similar argument, suggesting that the DSS and, in particular, its retaliation mechanism served in *EC-Hormones* the purpose of 'inducing a mutually agreeable solution' that 'restores the balance of concessions and benefits', rather than the purpose of inducing compliance, see Michelle Limenta, *WTO Retaliation: Effectiveness and Purposes* (Hart Publishing 2017) 127, 140.

[137] Interview with US official (Geneva, 17 July 2012).

[138] See 'WTO's Appellate Body Vindicates Continued U.S. Imposition of Sanctions After the EU Claimed Compliance in the EU–Hormones Dispute' (*USTR*, 16 October 2008) <http://www.ustr.gov/archive/assets/Document_Library/Press_Releases/2008/October/asset_upload_file626_15173.pdf> accessed 20 December 2018 (this official statement of the USTR explicitly states that the retaliatory tariffs imposed by the United States on certain EU products since 1999 were 'intended to restore the balance of trade concessions under the WTO ...'); Limenta (n 136) 140–41.

[139] Interview with former WTO official (Geneva, 30 March 2012). On the systemic, stability-enhancing role served by WTO retaliation, see, e.g. Peter B Rosendorff, 'Stability and Rigidity: Politics and Design of the WTO's Dispute Settlement Procedures' (2005) 99 Am Pol Sci Rev 389; Claus D Zimmermann,

The DSS so managed and contained the conflict for some time, even when, as originally expected, the parties were required to endure another full round of WTO litigation before they finally were able to conclude a negotiated agreement. In this second round of litigation, referred to as *Continued Suspension*, it was the EU that initiated legal proceedings against the United States and Canada because of the continuation of the North American sanctions following notification of the revised EU hormone ban and the parties' failed attempts to reach a negotiated solution.[140] Disputing, therefore, remained the 'last or default option when diplomatic channels failed to achieve satisfactory outcomes'.[141] As the evidence below suggests, it was the mixed ruling crafted by the AB in *Continued Suspension*—allowing the United States and Canada to maintain their retaliatory measures, while at the same time allowing the EU to retain its revised hormone ban, leaving open the question of its WTO consistency until further proceedings under DSU Article 21.5—that gave a final push to the settlement negotiations and encouraged the parties to find a trade-liberalizing compromise.

The split decision delivered by the AB at this stage of the conflict, including the legal questions it left open and undecided, was by no means accidental. As an AB member sitting on the bench in *Continued Suspension* commented: '[I]f you find . . . as we did, that the [scientific] expertise on the basis of which' the panel declared the revised EU policy WTO-inconsistent 'was not enough', that the experts the panel relied on were 'wrong, then we have not decided the case. . . . The way we judged the [scientific] expertise opens into question the . . . [panel's] decision'.[142] In the complex context of the *Hormones* saga, I argue, this choice of the AB to leave some of the legal questions open and uncertain represents one of those instances where a court chooses 'to be purposefully unclear when this is useful in . . . bringing parties to the negotiating table'.[143] Consider Carmody's comment:

> Ambiguity can force the parties to debate the meaning of a judicial pronouncement which has narrowed, but not altogether resolved, a dispute. The parties will be compelled to further negotiate, with the prospect that the court may impose a remedy where they fail.[144]

'Toleration of Temporary Non-Compliance: The Systemic Safety Valve of WTO Dispute Settlement Revisited' (2011) 3 Trade L & Dev 382.

[140] As noted by Taylor in this regard, while the North American sanctions did not promote the withdrawal of the contested hormone ban they 'did provoke the EU attempt to resolve the dispute through WTO involvement', i.e. through WTO litigation. See Cherie O'Neal Taylor, 'Beyond Retaliation' (2017) 38 Nw J Int'l L & Bus 55, 76.

[141] Conti (n 112) 148.

[142] Interview with former AB member (Geneva, 19 April 2012).

[143] Chi Carmody, 'Remedies and Conformity Under the WTO Agreement' (2002) 5 J Int'l Econ L 307, 311.

[144] ibid.

The mixed, partially vague ruling of the AB in *Continued Suspension*—giving rise to threats of continued retaliation (by the United States and Canada) and the counter threat of a third round of litigation (by the EU)—verily shifted the political balance between the disputants towards cooperation. It channelled them back to the negotiating table while making it possible for both sides to take advantage of selected parts of the ruling in the final stage of the bargaining. As an EU official involved in the case noted, '[t]he real push to the negotiations came after DS320 and DS321 [i.e. the *Continued Suspension* cases], when the Appellate Body ruling came out'.[145] Although the ruling did not solve the dispute 'in the sense ... [of] sid[ing] with one side or the other', a former EU official added, the AB's ruling, which urged both sides to move forward with proceedings under DSU Article 21.5 in order to determine whether the EU had complied and whether the North American sanctions were still legally valid, 'opened up other avenues for trying to solve this [conflict]'.[146] This same interviewee elaborated:

> The parties wouldn't negotiate for a settlement if they didn't have to lose something in continuing litigation. It costs a lot to litigate and you also run the risk of getting an adverse judgment.... And that was certainly the case in *Hormones*. The other side [namely, the US and Canada] ... realized that with what the Appellate Body had said about hormones [in *Continued Suspension*], the risk of going on and getting this really black and white, as a proper [WTO] ruling, was considerable.... [B]ut if they didn't have that pressure of ... the pending litigation, they wouldn't have sat down to settle the case. So ... that's the stimulant that you need in order to negotiate.[147]

While the EU, in the aftermath of the AB's ruling, moved indeed to threaten the United States and Canada with additional proceedings under DSU Article 21.5, the Europeans were well aware of the risks further WTO litigation presented to themselves. They thus welcomed the AB's decision in *Continued Suspension* as 'a sound basis for finding a solution to the dispute' as soon as the ruling was out.[148] As a former EU official involved in the case explained:

> [The ruling made us realize that] we have an Appellate Body decision out there which is quite favourable. We can build on this to launch a third [litigation] round

[145] Phone interview with EU official (24 April 2013).

[146] Interview with former EU official (Geneva, 9 July 2012).

[147] ibid. See also interview with EU official (Geneva, 18 July 2012) ('the result of the [*Continued Suspension*] case led the original complaining parties to essentially settling the case'. Following the AB's decision 'the original complaining parties realized that, well, the odds now are different').

[148] 'WTO Appeals Body Rejects Claim that EU Hormones Ban Breaks WTO Rules' (16 October 2008) <http://trade.ec.europa.eu/doclib/docs/2008/october/tradoc_141039.pdf> accessed 20 December 2018. See also the EU representative's statement pending the adoption of the AB's *Continued Suspension* report by the DSB: '[T]he Appellate Body's ruling was a big step forward for the parties. The EC hoped that the resolution of this long-standing dispute was now in sight'. DSB, Minutes of Meeting of 14 November 2008 (4 February 2009) WT/DSB/M/258, para 5.

> and get it black and white that this [ban on hormone-treated beef] is scientifically justified ... which the other side will not like.... [Yet], [i]t comes with an enormous cost to go through another few years of litigation to do this. There's always the risk that we get the wrong panel and the wrong Appellate Body members, and that the outcome wouldn't be what we think.... So, if we are faced with the choice of settling this now ... then let's do it.[149]

A WTO official, also involved in the case, quite similarly described the way in which the *Continued Suspension* litigation pushed both sides towards finally settling their long-running dispute:

> [T]he panel ... ruling ... made it very clear to the EU that it would ... be extremely difficult for it to scientifically justify its continued ban.... [T]he Appellate Body threw that out but didn't rule the opposite. So, it just left it very uncertain and one could read it either way. But obviously, both sides felt it was so uncertain that they didn't want to take a chance to ... seek a specific ruling on that in the future.[150]

Against this backdrop, an EU legal counsel described the critical role played by the DSS in the conclusion of the negotiated solutions heralding the end of the *Hormones* saga in these terms:

> [O]f course it's difficult to draw a formal link, but I have absolutely no doubt in my mind that ... what happened in the *Continued Suspension* case and how the Appellate Body ruled ... had an immediate effect on the [negotiations that] follow[ed] ... [and] that we wouldn't have the kind of current ceasefire without the Appellate Body report in that case.[151]

A US official likewise declared that the DSS's contribution to the negotiated solutions found was 'huge ... in the sense that nothing would have been done without it. The EU ... never would have done anything to open their beef market if it wasn't for the dispute settlement system.... [I]t was really the entire mechanism that prompted the change, even though the change wasn't ... done' by the defendant withdrawing its noncompliant measure, 'which is the standard way for most disputes'.[152] Much in line with *EC-Bananas*, then, as the numerous testimonies provided suggest, the DSS did not serve as a mechanism for strictly enforcing

[149] Interview with former EU official (Geneva, 9 July 2012).
[150] Interview with WTO official (Geneva, 18 April 2012).
[151] Interview with EU official (Geneva, 18 July 2012).
[152] Interview with US official (Geneva, 17 July 2012); interview with former WTO ambassador (Geneva, 23 March 2012).

compliance in the perennial *Hormones* dispute; rather, it served as a forum for managing and containing the conflict, a site where noncompliance could be progressively transformed into renegotiation, settlement, and a newly established balance of rights and obligations.

Evidence from the Jurisprudence

The enhanced role played by the DSS in the long-standing *Hormones* conflict as an orderly mechanism for fostering settlement and rebalancing the scales, while simultaneously containing the charged dispute and sustaining the stability of the WTO, is also reflected in DSS jurisprudence and the distinctive judicial choices, interpretations, and techniques used by WTO adjudicators throughout the dispute. Each of these, as shown below, uncovers specific goal-attainment efforts on the part of the adjudicators. A good illustration in this respect can be found already in the first decision of the panel in *EC-Hormones*, where it chose to close its ruling with a specific suggestion to the parties on how to move forward towards resolution of the dispute.[153] What the panel essentially did on this occasion was to suggest 'that a voluntary labelling regime might constitute an acceptable compromise in the hormone dispute, providing information on hormone use to consumers which would allow free choice in the marketplace'.[154] This suggestion was subsequently explored by the parties in the bilateral negotiations held following the first round of WTO litigation.[155] As already noted in the previous chapter, these sorts of suggestions, which WTO adjudicators are authorized to make under Article 19.1 of the DSU, are rather uncommon in WTO jurisprudence.[156] Similar to *EC-Bananas*, this notable departure of the panel from usual WTO judicial practice in *EC-Hormones* exposes the subtle shift in its goal-attainment efforts and the heightened role it sought to play in actively facilitating a solution to this intractable conflict.

Yet the panel was not the only body to pursue this endeavour. A similar move was later envisaged by the AB in *Continued Suspension*, where in an attempt to advance a positive resolution of the protracted trade feud, the AB chose to close its ruling by recommending that the DSB request all participants (i.e. the United States and Canada, as well as the EU) 'to initiate Article 21.5 proceedings without delay in order to resolve their disagreement as to whether' the EU 'has removed the measure found to be inconsistent in *EC-Hormones* and whether the application of the suspension of concessions' by the United States and Canada 'remains legally

[153] *EC-Hormones* Panel Report (US) (n 20) para 8.274; *EC-Hormones* Panel Report (Canada) (n 20) para 8.278.

[154] Roberts (n 4) 395.

[155] See EU Proposals (n 123); Wüger (n 11) 812.

[156] Joseph Pelzman and Amir Shoham, 'WTO DSU-Enforcement Issues' in *Trade Disputes and the Dispute Settlement Understanding* (n 118) 376–77.

valid'.[157] What drove the AB's recommendation, with its implicit goal-attainment efforts, becomes even more apparent when one takes into account the fact that DSU Article 19.1 authorizes WTO adjudicators to make recommendations only in those circumstances where a measure has been found 'inconsistent with a covered agreement'; those recommendations were to be directed at the disputing party whose action is needed with respect to the WTO-inconsistent measure. In *Continued Suspension*, however, the AB reversed the panel's finding that the continued sanctions imposed by the United States and Canada violated the DSU and left open the question of the compatibility of the revised EU hormone directive with the SPS Agreement, thereby concluding in no findings of WTO-inconsistency. The AB nevertheless found it appropriate in this case to make the above-mentioned suggestion and refer it to all the parties involved. To obtain a sense of the exceptional character of this recommendation, we need only look at the reactions it provoked. During the DSB meeting pending adoption of the *Continued Suspension* reports, the US representative, for example, stated that:

> Members had authorized … the Appellate Body to make recommendations in only one place: Article 19.1 of the DSU. That Article provided that … the Appellate Body was authorized to issue a recommendation in one circumstance: where it had concluded that a measure within the terms of reference of the proceeding was inconsistent with a covered agreement. In this appeal, the Appellate Body had not concluded that there was any measure that was inconsistent with a covered agreement. The Appellate Body had no authority, therefore, to make any Article 19.1 recommendation in this appeal.[158]

However, the AB did more than stretch the bounds of its mandate in an attempt to bring the parties closer to a resolution in *Continued Suspension*. In parallel, it also went a long distance in developing interpretations that would secure the DSS's jurisdiction to continually manage the recurrent *Hormones* dispute and, in this way, prevent unilateral actions and other effects that might destabilize the DSS and the overarching WTO regime. Thus, by ruling that retaliation under DSU Article 22.8 could continue until the 'final resolution of a dispute', or in case of disagreement as to the WTO-conformity of an implementing measure, until the DSS finds

[157] *Continued Suspension* AB Report (US) (n 42) para 737; *Continued Suspension* AB Report (Canada) (n 42) para 737. Note that the panel in *Continued Suspension* also concluded its report with a suggestion to the respondents in this case (the United States and Canada), that 'in order to implement its findings' under Article 23 of the DSU and 'in order to ensure the prompt settlement of this dispute', they 'should have recourse to the rules and procedures of the DSU without delay'. See *Continued Suspension* Panel Report (US) (n 41) para 8.3; *Continued Suspension* Panel Report (Canada) (n 41) para 8.3.

[158] DSB, Minutes of Meeting of 14 November 2008 (4 February 2009) WT/DSB/M/258, para 12 [hereinafter DSB Minutes of 14 November 2008]. Similar comments were made by other Members, including Canada, Ecuador, Mexico, Japan, Argentina, Australia, and Costa Rica. See ibid, paras 15, 17, 23, 25, 27, 33, 43.

that 'substantive compliance' (a term invented by the AB) has been achieved,[159] the AB worked to entrench the DSS as a forum for handling lengthy disputes such as *Hormones*, for controlling the consequences of sustained WTO noncompliance and, consequently, for reducing the probability of disputants instituting unchecked unilateral measures.

Still, in another novel interpretation of the DSU in *Continued Suspension*, the AB moved to further consolidate the DSS's jurisdiction over this type of recidivist and protracted conflicts. Thus, in contrast to the accepted understanding among WTO Members that only complainants may initiate compliance proceedings under DSU Article 21.5,[160] the AB determined that when a disagreement arises as to whether an implementing measure achieves compliance, complaining and defending parties may *both* launch such proceedings.[161] In fact, the AB went even further, to hold that both parties 'have a duty to engage in WTO dispute settlement' procedures in order to resolve such a disagreement.[162] This interpretation of the DSU not only broadened the scope of the DSS's jurisdiction in perennial disputes, it essentially disclosed the AB's conception of the DSS in these cases as more than a venue for third-party adjudication whose role is completed once a judgment is made; instead, it saw the DSS as a mechanism that 'rolls' along with the dispute as long as it persists.

This yearning of the AB to contain the charged *Hormones* conflict and foster its positive resolution was apparently so strong that it ultimately came at a cost of legal incoherence in its *Continued Suspension* ruling. And so, although the AB stated that disagreements of the kind invoked in *Continued Suspension* should only be addressed through DSU Article 21.5 proceedings, at no point in its decision did the AB find 'that the panel, which was not based on Article 21.5, had no jurisdiction at all to handle this case'.[163] Notably, while such a conclusion was probably more legally sound, it would have deprived the AB of its own jurisdiction over the *Continued Suspension* litigation, thus preventing it from making the legal pronouncements and clarifications it deemed necessary to shape a post-litigation scene conducive to resolution of the *Hormones* saga. In the present case, so it seems, for the AB, the lost legal coherence was a worthy price to pay for advancing these other, highly salient DSS objectives.

159 *Continued Suspension* AB Report (US) (n 42) paras 304–10,

160 See, for example, the view expressed by the EU on this issue. ibid, para 346.

161 ibid, para 368.

162 ibid, paras 310, 336, 340, 355.

163 Böckenförde (n 45). Several WTO Members also alluded to this inconsistency at the DSB meeting pending the adoption of the *Continued Suspension* rulings. The United States, for example, commented: '[T]he Appellate Body had stated that Article 21.5 compliance panel proceedings were the only procedure to be followed for resolving post-suspension disputes – ignoring the fact that this very appeal was from a regular panel proceeding considering a claim under Article 22.8 of the DSU'. DSB Minutes of 14 November 2008 (n 158) paras 9, 19.

9.4 Goal Conflicts, Mixed Outcomes: (Non)Compliance and Effectiveness in Context

> [In] *Hormones* ... the illegal ban on meat from cattle that has received growth hormones ... is still in place, but the dispute is gone because an arrangement was found between the United States and the European Union.... [T]here may be a political reality in which you cannot but accept that this will also sometimes happen.... A query, of course, [is] whether other WTO Members do not pay the price, ... [whether] the compensation that is paid in order to settle one dispute affects the rights of others. But the other [Members] could then, of course, bring a case against the compensation mechanism.
>
> –Interview with AB member (Geneva, 27 April 2012)

After many twists and turns, the parties to *EC-Hormones* ultimately reached negotiated agreements on compensatory measures, restoring their reciprocal balance of concessions under the WTO and putting an end to this lengthy transatlantic trade feud. As noted earlier, the MOUs concluded between the EU and each of the complainants in *EC-Hormones* envisaged the abolition of the North American retaliatory measures in exchange for increased market access for hormone-free 'High-Quality Beef' from the United States, Canada, and elsewhere.[164] As many have observed, however, the policy change brought about by the negotiated settlements 'did not amount to substantial compliance by the EU'.[165] Under both MOUs, the EU got to keep its hormone ban in place even though the legal finding concerning the ban's inconsistency with WTO law remained operative (as the AB indicated in *Continued Suspension*).[166] Furthermore, upon formal notification to the DSB of a 'mutually agreed solution' by the EU and Canada on 28 September 2017, the latter officially renounced its right to retaliate or to initiate further proceedings in relation to the *Hormones* issue, thus effectively relinquishing its right to demand WTO compliance from the EU in this case.[167] The United States might do the same at phase 3 of its agreement with the EU.[168] Yet, DSU Article 3.5 mandates that mutually agreed solutions must be consistent with WTO agreements.[169]

From the prevalent compliance-oriented perspective of DSS effectiveness, the mixed, noncompliant outcomes ultimately produced in *EC-Hormones* are likely

[164] Poletti and De Bièvre (n 54) 1189.

[165] ibid; Limenta (n 136); See also interview with former EU official (Geneva, 17 July 2012); interview with WTO practitioner (Geneva, 19 April 2012); interview with WTO official (Geneva, 18 April 2012).

[166] *Continued Suspension* AB Report (US) (n 42) para 737.

[167] EU-Canada Notification of a Mutually Agreed Solution (n 61). See also Miles (n 62).

[168] Limenta (n 136) 146.

[169] Along these lines, Taylor, for example, has similarly noted that the settlements achieved between the parties to the *Hormones* dispute 'fail the DSU requirement for a legal mutually agreed solution', i.e. 'that any settlement be consistent with WTO agreements'. See Taylor (n 140) 79.

to be considered the final and definitive confirmation of the long-held view of this case as a 'legal failure' for the WTO DSS.[170] Reflecting this view is a comment made by a WTO official: 'I guess the legalistic people' would see the settlements reached in *EC-Hormones* as 'a defect of the system', because amicable settlements 'must be compatible with the obligations of Members' under the WTO agreements.[171]

However, despite its appeal, this enforcement-based approach, using compliance as the key benchmark for assessing the performance of the DSS and the mixed outcomes generated in this case, is bound to be far from inclusive. First, this perspective, predicated on the view of compliance as the highest of DSS goals over time and across disputes, is decoupled from the actual goal-shifting trends exhibited throughout the conflict—in the disputing process, stakeholder expectations, and judicial choices made—towards other DSS goals, most notably, dispute settlement, rebalancing the scales, and maintenance of the WTO regime.

Yet, as the following observations suggest, this narrow, compliance-oriented account is also decoupled from the latent tensions at the foundation of the DSS goal structure and the potential trade-offs to be struck when goal conflicts arise within the DSS framework. This state of tension and fluctuation characterizing DSS goals is captured in the comment of this former WTO official involved in *EC-Hormones*:

> [M]any of those [goals] are a bit in tension. You want to achieve rule-compliance, but at the same time you think some flexibility is needed, or ultimately you want to have some rebalancing, and they don't always meet each other. Or if you want to have ... [legal] predictability, I guess some people are upset when they see [that] the EU is not complying [in *Hormones*] and just compensating. But I think that is, in a way, ... the beauty of the system, you can adapt its goals towards particular cases.[172]

When moving from one category of WTO cases to another, therefore, the list of goals attributed to the DSS yields different emphases and diverse conflicts, the most notable, perhaps, being the conflict just mentioned between securing rule compliance and legal predictability, and promoting positive dispute resolution and preserving pre-existing equilibria through flexible rebalancing acts. Negotiated settlements of the kind achieved in *EC-Hormones*—resolving a long-running conflict amicably while allowing the defaulting party to maintain the WTO-inconsistent measure untouched—faithfully represent the materialization of this

[170] Along these lines, Limenta, for example, notes that 'the contents of the settlements reached' at the non-implementation stage in cases such as *EC-Hormones* and *US-Upland Cotton* 'are often considered disturbing', while alluding to the fact that the settlements reached in these cases 'allow the defaulting parties (the United States and the European Union) to maintain the offending practices and buy out their WTO compliance obligations by offering monetary or other forms of settlement'. See Limenta (n 136) 127.

[171] Interview with WTO official (Geneva, 28 March 2012).

[172] Interview with former WTO legal officer (Geneva, 30 March 2012).

conflict. As an AB member noted, on the one hand, 'the whole purpose of the dispute settlement system is to resolve disputes between Members', preferably through mutually agreed solutions.[173] 'On the other hand':

> the DSU ... indicates that ... [another DSS goal] is to bring security and predictability to the multilateral trading system. Do you really bring security and predictability if a measure ... found to be WTO-inconsistent can then be sort of bought-off by paying compensation? ... What does this mean for all the other Members in their bilateral relations? ... Does it mean that the law is now all of a sudden different? No.[174]

While such instances of 'buy out' by no means imply that the law has changed in any way, they nevertheless illustrate—in line with Trachtman's realistic observation that WTO law 'does not normatively demand compliance at all costs'[175]—the room left under the DSS for Members to trade compliance for settlement when political constraints turn conflict between these goals into an inescapable eventuality. This understanding of the state of play in the present system, which reveals a clear preference for mutually agreed solutions, was expressed quite candidly in an interview with a WTO official: '[In some instances] [t]here is a conflict between achieving compliance and achieving a solution to a trade issue.... And it is clear from the rules that the favor goes to the mutual solution whether it is compliant or not compliant [with WTO law]'.[176] This possibility to reach settlements that effectively tolerate ongoing violations of WTO rules,[177] as seen in the previous chapter, was in some sense recognized by the AB in *EC-Bananas* when it declared that a mutually agreed solution can encompass an explicit agreement of the parties to forgo the right to have further recourse to the DSS.[178] By so stating, the AB implicitly acknowledged Members' freedom to agree not to challenge a measure in violation of WTO law and thus to tacitly accept that violation.[179]

Seen in this light, a WTO practitioner stressed that when judging the outcomes of the DSS in cases like *EC-Hormones*, we must not 'put things in the abstract....

[173] Interview with AB member (Geneva, 27 April 2012).

[174] ibid.

[175] Joel P Trachtman, 'The WTO Cathedral' (2007) 43 Stan J Int'l L 127, 130.

[176] Interview with WTO official (Geneva, 18 April 2012).

[177] For a discussion of this possibility, see Jonas Tallberg and James McCall Smith, 'Dispute Settlement in World Politics: States, Supranational Prosecutors, and Compliance' (2014) 20 EJIR 118, 126; Gregory Shaffer, Manfred Elsig, and Sergio Puig, 'The Extensive (but Fragile) Authority of the WTO Appellate Body' (2016) 79 L & Contemp Probs 237, 246.

[178] *European Communities–Regime for the Importation, Sale and Distribution of Bananas, Second Recourse to Article 21.5 of the DSU by Ecuador/Recourse to Article 21.5 of the DSU by the United States*, Reports of the Appellate Body, 11 and 22 December 2008, WT/DS27/AB/RW2/ECU, WT/DS27/AB/RW/USA, para 212.

[179] Wolfgang Alschner, 'Amicable Settlements of WTO Disputes: Bilateral Solution in a Multilateral System' (2014) 13 World Trade Rev 65, 94–95.

We have to situate [the event] ... into what happens in real life'. And in real life, 'if you compare ... [WTO law] with domestic law', you will find that the system established is not akin to 'criminal law', with 'a super policeman' who monitors violations of WTO law but, rather, to a system more closely resembling 'civil law within countries', where:

> a complainant in a ... case may say, 'I waive my rights against the person who did me wrong'. [And] [t]he state cannot come in and say, 'No, the person who did you wrong must comply'.... WTO law [is] just ... [like] civil law within countries.... [I]f a Member ... accepts that someone is not in compliance but addresses its concerns in a different way, that's fine. If other Members do not agree with that, they are entitled to bring a dispute against the [relevant] Member.[180]

This same practitioner concluded that compliance in the WTO's context, just like in civil law in domestic systems, is not compliance 'in the abstract' but 'compliance to the satisfaction of the complainant'.[181] Under the current system, therefore, if the parties to a dispute are satisfied with the outcomes of the settlement reached and decide to drop the case, the dispute is considered resolved and little can be done unless a third party contests the deal in a new dispute.[182]

We should thus not find surprising the favourable reactions of WTO insiders to the mixed outcomes eventually produced in *EC-Hormones*. Consider this statement, made by a US legal adviser:

> [M]y [position] ... is that if the Members view that they resolved their dispute in a satisfactory manner for both of them, then that's a successful conclusion.... [In] the *Hormones* case ... the US beef exporters are the parties ... being harmed; ... if they can be provided compensation in some other method that gives them an economic benefit ... then the parties basically say, 'Okay [we'll settle]'.... I think that there's no question that if you were to say, would you prefer that they lift the hormone ban or you prefer to get the additional quotas, everybody would say, lift the hormone ban. But there's a certain realistic perspective about, well, that's choice A but we're gonna [sic] have to move to B, and we want B to be at least

[180] Interview with WTO practitioner (Geneva, 25 July 2012). Another WTO official observed, along similar lines, that although mutually agreed solutions should be WTO-consistent and shall not affect the rights of other Members, the WTO DSS is, effectively, 'a system where there is no public prosecutor'. So, in the case of *Hormones*, the 'WTO is not going to go after you because your hormone regime is still illegal. If the United States and Canada are satisfied, that's the end of it'. Of course, if other Members are negatively 'affected by ... [the] deals' struck between the EU, the United States and Canada, they are entitled to bring their own case to the DSS. Interview with WTO official (Geneva, 28 March 2012).

[181] Interview with WTO practitioner (Geneva, 25 July 2012). An AB member similarly opined that what matters in the end is if 'from the point of view of the complaining party there is enough compliance'. Interview with AB Member (Brussels, 19 July 2012).

[182] Limenta (n 136) 146.

sufficiently satisfactory [so] that [we] will let it go. But I think ... if everybody is satisfied ... that's a successful outcome.[183]

As this same official continued:

[I]n a lot of cases, you start in consultations and something is worked out, and that something often isn't 100% in compliance [with WTO rules].... and everybody says, 'Okay, we're satisfied'.... And I think ... everybody would say that at the consultation stage ... that is a successful outcome. And I think that I would say that the same thing is going to be true no matter when that outcome is reached.[184]

A former Canadian official similarly observed:

[I]f it's satisfactory, and Canada decides on a dotted line, then I think that's fine.... It's perfectly legitimate ... for the European Union to negotiate a deal even if it's not exactly what ... the panel or the Appellate Body had said they should do. I think if you have an agreement, the system should say 'fine' and put its hands up.... I don't think there should be any sense on the part of a [WTO] Secretariat official or a government official that the system doesn't work. Clearly, the system has worked.... they've got a deal, a mutually ... acceptable solution. Don't mind how they got it.... it's fine.[185]

The same view was shared not only by US and Canadian representatives but also by WTO Secretariat staff members, as one senior WTO official commented:

[I]f you look at the design of the system ... [it is not] a court of law.... The purpose of the system is not to produce justice. The purpose of the system is to assist the parties in solving a dispute. So, the proof of the pudding lies [in] – has the dispute been solved or not? ... You have to admit that maybe in some cases, for one party it may be politically impossible to move.... I [hear] ... from many Europeans, 'For Europe, it was impossible to move on *Hormones*. It would've caused such a political uproar'. And that's why Europe was subject to sanctions and for such a long period of time. Well they got settled, haven't they? I wouldn't call that exactly a failure.... It took a long time ... but it was finally settled because there was some compensation given, understanding that for one party it became almost impossible to move politically and meet that standard which was required by the findings of the panel and the Appellate Body.[186]

183 Interview with US official (Geneva, 17 July 2012).
184 ibid.
185 Interview with former Canadian official (Geneva, 25 April 2012).
186 Interview with senior WTO official (Geneva, 23 March 2012).

While many other WTO officials expressed a similar position,[187] some still went further to highlight the vitality of the leeway left under the present system for disputants not to comply in certain instances but to compensate and settle instead. In the words of one senior WTO legal officer when alluding to the results achieved in the *Hormones* case and the ability of Members facing 'such a difficult issue' to 'decide not to comply but . . . to pay the price' of the violation:

> [S]ome people would say [about the outcome generated in this case] . . . [that] 'this is not positive, this is negative. It is a deficiency [of the system]' . . . because they would say 'there is no compliance, and the optimal outcome is compliance'. I personally would say . . . it is positive. It is positive for the system to make it possible for countries in certain situations not to comply [but rather to negotiate a settlement and grant compensation].[188]

This possibility (if kept limited, of course) provides some valuable flexibility in the resolution of trade disputes, especially in 'hard cases' such as *EC-Hormones* 'where litigation risks becoming endless . . . [and] compliance is politically impossible',[189] with pressure on the WTO and its DSS exceedingly high. In such instances, 'adaptive institutional flexibility' of this sort enables a Member to deviate locally without putting into question the overall adherence to WTO agreements.[190] This limited flexibility, allowing Members 'to respond to unanticipated shocks or special domestic circumstances', facilitates preservation of the broader institutional framework,[191] prevents exit from the WTO system,[192] and sustains its long-term operation and effectiveness. Limited rule flexibility, in other words, fosters a legitimate and stable normative WTO regime; it does not undermine it.[193] What is more, without this flexibility, it is quite probable that a stronger dispute settlement

[187] See, e.g, interview with WTO official (Geneva, 26 March 2012) (noting with respect to the settlement reached in *EC-Hormones*: 'the lawyer will say that there is a problem that they are not complying with the strict rules, but to me they came to a settlement. . . . [T]he fact that they managed to solve their problem is the essential one'); interview with WTO official (Geneva, 18 April 2012) (noting that although the remaining noncompliance in *EC-Hormones* 'doesn't look good for the WTO', a settlement was achieved that 'is leading to trade' and 'resolving the issue', 'and the priority goes to the settlement . . . that's the way the whole agreement is written, so the priority goes to getting the settlement more than . . . compliance frankly'); interview with WTO official (Geneva, 28 March 2012).

[188] Interview with senior WTO legal officer (Geneva, 4 April 2012).

[189] Alschner (n 179) 66, 97.

[190] See Barbara Koremenos, Charles Lipson, and Duncan Snidal, 'The Rational Design of International Institutions' (2001) 55 Int'l Org 761, 773 (using the notion of 'adaptive institutional flexibility' with respect to those instances where the general goal is to isolate a special trade problem and insulate the broader WTO institution from its impact). For a similar argument see also Hauser and Roitinger (n 114) 494.

[191] Koremenos, Lipson, and Snidal (n 190) 773.

[192] Joost Pauwelyn, 'The Calculation and Design of Trade Retaliation in Context: What is the Goal of Suspending WTO Obligations?' in Chad P Bown and Joost Pauwelyn (eds), *The Law, Economics and Politics of Retaliation in WTO Dispute Settlement* (CUP 2010) 63.

[193] ibid.

system of the kind established in the WTO would not have been possible.[194] This idea is clearly illustrated in the context of the *Hormones* saga, in the following comment by an EU official:

> [*EC-Hormones*] tells you a story that there are certain instances where ... you just can't force compliance because if you ... [do], it might break the system ultimately. If it's politically sensitive and you force a Member to do something that it's just impossible for it to do for technical or some very fundamental political reason, you risk ... then ... charging the whole system.[195]

In contrast, the outcome of noncompliance, if accompanied by agreed compensation to reinstate the distorted balance of concessions, can be 'system-supporting' by allowing the WTO to avoid inordinate pressure on its institutions and rules.[196] Following the lines of this argument, one interviewee concluded that the question of how to assess the effectiveness of the DSS and the noncompliant outcome produced in *EC-Hormones*:

> goes to how you think about the whole system.... I know that some people think of ... [the WTO] as some kind of a human rights treaty that you have to comply with the rules, otherwise the system would fall down.... [But] to me, what they are trying to defend is this balance of concessions that is out there.... [T]hey are trying to detect when you see a violation, and, of course, in most cases you would want to see compliance. But if the violating country is willing to pay the full price of the violation ... [and] you have a settlement, to me that is as good as it gets.... [T]hat is what the DSU says ... they prefer a positive solution. Then my only concern is third parties, and whether they are taken care of.[197]

Hence, as just alluded, the issue remaining in such instances of noncompliance is 'whether other WTO Members do not pay the price, ... [whether] the compensation that is paid in order to settle one dispute affects the rights of others'.[198] This question goes to one of the major rationales underlying the DSU's requirement that mutually agreed solutions be WTO-consistent—ensuring the protection of the rights of third parties participating in the multilateral trade system.[199] In the case of *Hormones*, several meat-exporting Members, such as Argentina, Australia, New Zealand, Brazil, and Uruguay, indeed raised their concerns about the EU–US

[194] ibid.
[195] Interview with EU official (Geneva, 18 July 2012).
[196] Robert Howse and Kalypso Nicolaidis, 'Enhancing WTO Legitimacy: Constitutionalization or Global Subsidiarity?' (2003) 16 Governance 73, 88.
[197] Interview with former WTO official (Geneva, 30 March 2012).
[198] Interview with AB member (Geneva, 27 April 2012).
[199] Interview with WTO official (Geneva, 28 March 2012). See also Alschner (n 179) 96–97.

MOU immediately upon notification of the agreement to the DSB.[200] Troubled especially by the MOU's definition of 'High-Quality Beef' and fearing that it might privilege the kind of meat produced in North America at the expense of that produced elsewhere, these countries sought confirmation that the EU's new tariff-free quota for HQB would provide equal access for all beef exporters in accordance with the most-favoured nation (MFN) rule.[201] Third-party concerns with respect to the *Hormones* deal therefore revolved not so much around the fact that the settlement allowed the EU to retain its WTO-inconsistent ban, than around the potential effects of the deal on their own commercial interests.

In responding to these concerns, the EU stated that the new HQB quota 'would be non-discriminatory' and that its 'definition would be origin-neutral'.[202] When the quota was subsequently opened in August 2009 and then expanded in August 2012, several beef exporters other than the United States and Canada, such as Australia, Uruguay, and New Zealand, managed indeed to gain access to the quota.[203] In June 2013, however, Argentina raised additional concerns about the quota, arguing that although it was 'origin neutral, it was administrated in a way that was tantamount to "de facto" discrimination inconsistent with the MFN principle'.[204] In September 2014, Argentina, too, secured access to the EU's quota.[205] And so, up to the time of writing, no WTO Member has yet brought a formal complaint regarding the arrangement settling the *Hormones* conflict. As a former EU official interestingly observed:

> [T]he experience of *Bananas* and *Hormones* [shows] … that … solutions are found that are acceptable because there is nobody out there who has the desire to go and sue for … [any WTO-inconsistencies allegedly associated with these solutions]…. [The] solutions … [found] suit the two countries who found them…. But so far other countries have not attacked the solutions, right? Look for example at the minutes of the DSB when the *Hormone* settlement was announced, … a few countries … [were] concerned about that settlement and what it does to their own exports of non-hormone treated beef…. but they are not suing for one reason or the other. So, you find solutions that … don't correspond to the letter [of the law]…. [They are] not … necessarily textbook solutions of compliance,

200 See DSB, Minutes of Meeting of 19 June 2009 (28 August 2009) WT/DSB/M/270.
201 ibid, paras 66–75.
202 ibid, para 76.
203 Phone interview with EU official (24 April 2013); Yvan Polet, 'EU HQB Quota Reaches Quota Fill Ceiling as Argentina Secures Access', USDA GAIN Report Number E14051 (*United States Department of Agriculture*, 10 January 2014) <https://gain.fas.usda.gov/Recent%20GAIN%20Publications/EU%20HQB%20Quota%20Reaches%20Quota%20Fill%20Ceiling%20as%20Argentina%20Secures%20Access_Brussels%20USEU_EU-28_10-1-2014.pdf> accessed 18 December 2018.
204 See Limenta (n 136) 143.
205 Polet (n 203).

> but they . . . bring peace . . . and . . . positive feedback . . . [to] the dispute settlement [system, which] is credited for it.[206]

9.5 Conclusions

In the eyes of many, *EC-Hormones* constitutes a paradigmatic 'wrong' case—a case insolvable through adjudication, because highly sensitive domestic political interests were at play, which were deemed likely to prevent the respondent from complying with an adverse WTO ruling.[207] As far as compliance is concerned, *EC-Hormones* was indeed a 'wrong' case, where noncompliance, as initially expected, was a constant feature of the protracted conflict, from beginning to end. Likewise, it was not adjudication that directly solved the case but the agreements reached through bilateral negotiations.

Yet, as the multidimensional goal-based reading of *EC-Hormones* has shown, it was WTO adjudication that played a critical role in establishing the conditions required for the settlement negotiations, providing information and actively shifting the political balance towards collaboration and institution of a new cooperative equilibrium between the disputants. It was also the DSS that, through its legal interpretations, compulsory procedures, and retaliation mechanism, played a systemic role in containing the perennial dispute within defined legal parameters, defusing its political aspects, and forestalling uncontrolled unilateral measures, actions that served to sustain the WTO's operation and stability.

And so, the complex political, economic, and social setting in which the perennial *Hormones* dispute unfolded generated adjustments in the DSS's goal-attainment endeavours, diverting attention away from compliance towards its settlement facilitation, rebalancing, and regime-maintenance goals. While this case clearly demonstrates, in turn, the inherent limits to the effectiveness of the legalized WTO DSS (i.e. the limits placed on the system's ability to concurrently achieve its manifold goals and the need to strike trade-offs between them), it also illustrates the limitations of the prevalent approaches that tend to measure DSS effectiveness through the static, narrow lens of compliance. In particular, and without in any way challenging the general importance of rule compliance as an objective, the goal-based analysis of *EC-Hormones* conducted herein highlights how the state of noncompliance, when processed through the DSS, can, in certain (allegedly 'wrong') cases, serve as a means to achieve other, no-less-important goals assigned to the system.

[206] Interview with former EU official (Geneva, 9 July 2012).
[207] Alschner (n 179) 80.

A former WTO official involved in *EC-Hormones* stated as much in the following concluding remark:

> [From the outset] everyone knew that for the EU to implement [an adverse WTO ruling] or to get rid of the [hormone] ban was just very hard to imagine, and it turned out to be correct and some other settlement had to be found.... [B]ut does that make it a 'wrong' case? ... I think ... at least in the case [before the DSS] you set the line what is in compliance and what is not, and ... then you let the parties settle around that line. So, I think ... [the DSS] still served its purpose.[208]

[208] Interview with former WTO official (Geneva, 30 March 2012).

Conclusions to Part III

An Analytical Overview of Perennial Disputes

> [I]n … *Bananas*, like *Hormones*, after some years of litigation and negotiation … [if] we look beyond the disputes … you get an accommodation [of interests] and you get something which both parties said, 'Okay we're satisfied, this is it, we settle'. So … sometimes for internal, sometimes for external political reasons some cases are more difficult than others to solve, be that as it may, eventually they get settled.
>
> –Interview with WTO official and former state delegate (Geneva, 23 March 2012)

High-stake perennial disputes, involving major powers, a loaded history, and highly sensitive political or economic issues, which begin, proceed, and end as overly controversial and complex cases, have always been part of the multilateral trade system's landscape. 'Even in the old days', as a staff member of the World Trade Organization (WTO) noted, '[t]here have … been difficult cases.… You always have cases that are very difficult for the system to handle'.[1]

Such intractable conflicts, featuring sustained noncompliance and intense resistance to resolution, have constantly formed an integral part of the WTO Dispute Settlement System (DSS) docket, facilitated by the Dispute Settlement Understanding (DSU) reverse consensus rule that effectively abolished the option, previously available under the General Agreement on Tariffs and Trade (GATT), to block such 'impossible' (or 'wrong') cases from entering the system.[2] Inevitably, such cases will probably continue to be part of the DSS's caseload in the future. Furthermore, with the rise of new economic powers and, especially, the growing political and economic competition between the United States and China that has recently seen significant escalation, these types of intense disputes are expected to more frequently transcend the boundaries of the traditional transatlantic rivalries. In fact, the seeds of such disputes may perhaps be identified

[1] Interview with WTO official (Geneva, 4 April 2012).

[2] Cherie O'Neal Taylor, 'Impossible Cases: Lessons from the First Decade of WTO Dispute Settlement' (2007) 28 U Pa J Int'l L 309.

in the looming legal quarrels between the United States and China over alleged Chinese violations in the intellectual property sector[3] and increased US tariffs on Chinese goods,[4] as well as in the series of complaints (and counter-complaints) filed by China, Russia, India, the EU, and others against the recently imposed US tariffs on steel and aluminium products.[5] Such disputes, if they ripen into highly protracted and contentious conflicts, will join the various other perennial disputes that have managed to pave their way to the mandatory WTO DSS over the years. As several observers have aptly stressed, the manner in which the DSS handles these types of 'tough' cases, the long, intense, and highly taxing 'disputes between the major powers', represents a fundamental measure of its effectiveness and ultimate success.[6]

Given my task of developing a broad goal-based framework for assessing the effectiveness of the WTO DSS, this part of the book sought to probe the manner in which the complications inherent in such high-stake perennial disputes and the challenges they pose to the cooperative WTO regime affect the operation of the DSS, shape stakeholders' expectations, shift goal priorities, and stimulate conflicts and trade-offs between the multiple objectives entrusted with the system. This investigation was carried out through a qualitative-empirical, legal analysis of two prominent conflicts falling under this category: *EC-Bananas* and *EC-Hormones*. In exhibiting similar goal-attainment patterns, these two case studies shed clearer light on the actual dynamics of disputing and adjudicating within the framework of perennial WTO conflicts, where the DSS does not seem to be necessarily geared towards securing strict legal compliance; instead, the DSS appears to target its efforts primarily on influencing the intricate nexus of law and politics, of adjudication and negotiation. In such cases, *EC-Bananas* and *EC-Hormones* suggest, the DSS becomes a repeat player in a broader political

[3] *China–Certain Measures Concerning the Protection of Intellectual Property Rights*, Request for Consultations by the United States, 26 March 2018, WT/DS542/1, IP/D/38.

[4] See *United States–Tariff Measures on Certain Goods from China*, Request for Consultations by China, 5 April 2018, WT/DS543/1, G/L/1219.

[5] See, e.g. *United States–Certain Measures on Steel and Aluminium Products*, Request for Consultations by China, 9 April 2018, WT/DS544/1, G/L/1222, G/SG/D50/1; *United States–Certain Measures on Steel and Aluminium Products*, Request for Consultations by India, 23 May 2018, WT/DS547/1, G/L/1238, G/SG/D53/1; *United States–Certain Measures on Steel and Aluminium Products*, Request for Consultations by the European Union, 6 June 2018, WT/DS548/1, G/L/1243, G/SG/D54/1; *United States–Certain Measures on Steel and Aluminium Products*, Request for Consultations by the Russian Federation, 2 July 2018, WT/DS554/1, G/SG/D58/1; *China–Additional Duties on Certain Products from the United States*, Request for Consultations by the United States, 19 July 2018, WT/DS558/1, G/L/1253; *European Union–Additional Duties on Certain Products from the United States*, Request for Consultations by the United States, 19 July 2018, WT/DS559/1, G/L/1254.

[6] See Marc L Busch and Eric Reinhardt, 'Transatlantic Trade Conflicts and GATT/WTO Dispute Settlement' in Ernst-Ulrich Petersmann and Mark A Pollack (eds), *Transatlantic Economic Disputes: The EU, the US, and the WTO* (OUP 2003) 475; William J Davey, 'The WTO and Rules-Based Dispute Settlement: Historical Evolution, Operational Success, and Future Challenges' (2014) J Int'l Econ L 679, 680.

process aimed at the settlement of the dispute, with its prominent functions being, first, to manage and contain the perennial dispute within the rules-based system and thereby sustain the stability and operation of the cooperative WTO regime; and second, whenever faced with breakdowns in the political process, to stimulate renegotiation and construct focal points around which the parties can coordinate towards reaching a settlement and re-establishing their reciprocal balance of concessions.

The analytical exercise conducted in this part of the book brings into view, therefore, critical dimensions of DSS performance and the fluctuating nature of its goals. Where the odds for compliance are low and the pressures on the system high, neither users of the DSS, nor the DSS itself, remain indifferent. Quite the opposite; in response to those odds and the systemic challenges invoked, the goals pursued through WTO adjudication (and retaliation) are recalibrated. Thus, in protracted cases of this type, disputing before the DSS, rather than simply serving to enforce compliance with WTO law, functions as a mechanism by which disputants can harness the law, together with the reputation and economic costs assigned to noncompliance, in pursuit of other organizational goals, particularly settlement facilitation, rebalancing the scales, and maintenance of viable economic relations and sustainable cooperation within the WTO framework.

To be clear, by summarizing the story of the DSS's goal-attainment efforts in *EC-Bananas* and *EC-Hormones* in this way, I do not mean to suggest that the identified DSS goals were the only ones pursued, nor do I suggest that other of the DSS's various objectives did not come into play. I do argue, however, that in the complicated political, legal, historical, and economic environment in which these perennial disputes unfolded, the DSS carried out an enhanced role in promoting specific institutional goals, at times at the expense of its other objectives. Thus, in both *EC-Bananas* and *EC-Hormones*, efforts to facilitate an amicable settlement, ultimately resulting in an agreement at intermediate points convenient to the disputants, came into conflict with the DSS's oft-cited compliance inducement goal, a goal denoting principle-driven adherence to WTO rules, needed to enhance the security and predictability of the multilateral trading system for the benefit of stakeholders beyond the disputants. In terms of outcomes, therefore, in both cases, a negotiated settlement that redistributed Members' trade concessions, granted increased market access rights to the complainants, and promoted long-term cooperative relations outweighed compliance with the originally agreed-upon WTO legal commitments.

While these mixed judicial outcomes clearly suggest limits to the pull of the rule of law and to the ability of the legalized DSS to elicit compliance, they shed light on other variables critical to an effectiveness assessment of this adjudicative system. Prominent in this respect is the way the legalized DSS managed to defuse and contain the intense trade feuds within defined legal boundaries, an outcome preventing the conflicts from 'spoiling broader economic, political or even security relations',[7] as well as from escalating into a spiral of unauthorized retaliation and counter-retaliation as often occurred in such cases during the GATT era.[8] Equally important is the way in which the rule-oriented WTO DSS, through its compulsory procedures, rulings, and retaliation mechanism, continually worked to structure the interaction between the parties and to stimulate renegotiation for the purpose of concluding a mutually agreed solution.

In these senses, it should be noted that in *EC-Hormones* and *EC-Bananas*, the DSS may in fact have achieved the actual goals envisaged by its creators for these types of 'hard cases'. As Alschner notes, the emphasis placed in the DSU on reaching mutually agreed solutions, including at the adjudication stage, 'was a response to pressing concerns among GATT members' during the Tokyo and Uruguay Rounds about 'wrong cases' being brought to a more legalistic DSS—cases that, as explained in Chapter 7, were deemed to be 'irresolvable through adjudication because highly sensitive political or economic interests were at stake that would prevent governments from complying' with an adverse DSS ruling.[9] 'A widespread practice of non-compliance', GATT members feared, 'would undermine the system's prestige and functionality'.[10] Since the GATT contracting parties wanted to avoid this eventuality but, at the same time, also sought to strengthen the access to and efficacy of the multilateral dispute settlement mechanism, Alschner continues, the emphasis placed on mutually agreed solutions at all stages of the dispute settlement process 'was perceived as a way to solve the "wrong case" problem through more negotiation in dispute settlement without foregoing greater legalization elsewhere'.[11] The explicit preference in the DSU for mutually agreed solutions, he thus stresses, was not merely 'a remnant from early GATT diplomacy-only-days … but a solution to a concrete problem facing trade policy makers' in the multilateral trade system's move towards greater legalization.[12]

Seen in this light, the ability of the DSS to manage the *Bananas* and *Hormones* conflicts and to yield an amicable solution by meshing adjudication with negotiation seems to suggest that, at least in these intractable and perennial disputes, the legalized DSS rose to the 'wrong case' challenge. Echoing a somewhat similar thought when addressing the cited cases, a WTO official noted:

> The … [cases] that we hear [about] are those that are basically unmanageable. And they go on and on and on. That doesn't mean that the system doesn't work.

[7] Joost Pauwelyn, 'The WTO 20 Years On: "Global Governance by Judiciary" or, Rather, Member-Driven Settlement of (Some) Trade Disputes between (Some) WTO Members' (2016) 27 EJIL 1119, 1123.

[8] Bernhard Zangl, 'Judicialization Matters! A Comparison of Dispute Settlement Under GATT and the WTO' (2008) 52 Int'l Stud Q 825.

[9] Wolfgang Alschner, 'Amicable Settlements of WTO Disputes: Bilateral Solution in a Multilateral System' (2014) 13 World Trade Rev 65, 80.

[10] ibid.

[11] ibid.

[12] ibid.

> It just means that those cases are irresolvable, that the system is not designed to solve those cases. Or else you could say: 'Yes, they are', because … after … years of dispute … they [i.e. the parties to *EC-Bananas* and *EC-Hormones*] have reached an agreement.[13]

The stories of *EC-Bananas* and *EC-Hormones* unfolded herein reinforce, therefore, the need for a more subtle and nuanced approach to thinking about and studying the effectiveness of the WTO DSS, one that would not capture judicial effectiveness in binary terms of 'wrong' or 'right' cases, 'failure' or 'success', depending on the expected or actual performance of the system in terms of compliance, but which would take into account the system's multiple goals (which extend far beyond compliance) and, no less importantly, their variable and conflicting nature.

Finally, it should be stressed that the same could be said with respect to the question of the goals and effectiveness of the DSS's mechanism of suspension of concessions. As *EC-Bananas* and *EC-Hormones* illustrate, like the broader dispute settlement system in which it is embedded, WTO retaliation serves multiple, varying and competing purposes.[14] While retaliation in its current design may be ineffective in inducing compliance at times, it could nonetheless facilitate a negotiated settlement and, through the temporary rebalancing feature applied, may fulfil a vital stability-enhancing role. In contrast to the tendency to consider compliance inducement as the 'sole aim of WTO retaliation and the primary factor in assessing' its effectiveness,[15] any evaluation of this mechanism or suggestions for its reform should thus be carried out in recognition of the manifold and shifting goals it serves and the ability to carefully recalibrate between them, depending on the circumstances (e.g. the type of conflict at hand, the nature of WTO obligations involved, and so forth).[16] We come back to the issue of reform of the DSS's retaliation mechanism, and its enforcement powers more generally, in the concluding chapter of this book (Chapter 11).

[13] Interview with WTO official (Geneva, 28 March 2012).

[14] See on this matter, Joost Pauwelyn, 'The Calculation and Design of Trade Retaliation in Context: What is the Goal of Suspending WTO Obligations?' in Chad P Bown and Joost Pauwelyn (eds), *The Law, Economics and Politics of Retaliation in WTO Dispute Settlement* (CUP 2010) 34.

[15] For a discussion of this tendency, see Michelle Limenta, *WTO Retaliation: Effectiveness and Purposes* (Hart Publishing 2017) 146.

[16] On the ability to calibrate carefully between the variable goals of WTO retaliation, see Pauwelyn (n 14).

PART IV

WHEN THE MULTILATERAL AND THE REGIONAL INTERSECT

RTA-Related Disputes from a Goal-Based Perspective

10

Extending the Analysis

Multilateral Adjudication in a Regionalizing Economic Order

10.1 Introduction

Parts II and III of the book engaged in a close investigation of two key categories of disputes filed with the World Trade Organization (WTO) Dispute Settlement System (DSS): trade-and and perennial disputes. Through an in-depth analysis of case studies falling into these two categories, Parts II and III sought to understand how the distinct features and challenges associated with each class of disputes shaped the goals pursued by the DSS, generated shifts and conflicts between the multiple objectives it is expected to achieve, and consequently affected this adjudicative body's effectiveness, defined in this book in terms of goal attainment. By revealing the varied goal-attainment efforts exhibited by the DSS in each category, whereby goal priorities fluctuated and trade-offs struck, the examination of trade-and and perennial conflicts illustrated the shifting and contradictory nature of DSS goals and, in the process, the complex dynamics of judicial effectiveness at the WTO.

This is the place to stress that the dynamic reality of judicial effectiveness and goal attainment as it emerges from the analysis in Parts II and III of the book is by no means limited to the specific dispute categories examined therein. One could therefore extend the goal-based research framework applied in the preceding parts to other classes of WTO disputes, which we can expect to disclose somewhat different goal-attainment patterns on the part of the DSS, together with diverse emphases, conflicts, and trade-offs between its various objectives. This fourth part of the book illustrates one possible extension of this research framework by closely looking at an additional category of WTO disputes: those emerging from the growing friction between the WTO's multilateral trade system and the rapidly expanding network of regional trade agreements (RTAs). An analysis of RTA-related disputes, as we shall see, is not only timely in today's changing landscape of global economic governance, it is also useful for exposing crucial variations in the judicial approaches and choices taken by the DSS during its goal-attainment endeavours in this class of cases as compared to those observed in trade-and and perennial conflicts. In that sense, the investigation of cases located at the WTO-RTA nexus, alongside trade-and and perennial disputes, may enable us to capture, through a broader comparative lens, how WTO adjudicators carefully tailor their judicial tools to the dominant organizational goals they pursue in each category of cases before them, and thereby to further hone our understanding of the variable goals steering DSS operation, and which determine its effectiveness.

Note, however, that as opposed to the two previous parts of the book, each of which engaged in a comprehensive, in-depth case study analysis of a pair of WTO disputes, the analysis carried out here takes a broader, more general look at the burgeoning category of RTA-related cases, while addressing the prominent disputes the WTO DSS has been called upon to decide in this area thus far. This analysis is divided, in turn, into two interconnected parts. The first part focuses on issues related to the substantive legal interface between WTO law and RTAs as they surfaced in the series of cases examined, whereas the second part explores questions that emerged out of the jurisdictional intersection between the WTO DSS and regional dispute settlement mechanisms.

In line with this research agenda, the chapter proceeds as follows. Section 10.2 situates the discussion of RTA-related disputes in the broader context of the changing international economic landscape. To this end, this section begins with a short overview of the current state of RTA proliferation, the increasing friction it engenders between multilateralism and regionalism in international economic governance, and the systemic threats it poses to the multilateral trade regime centred in the WTO. This same section then recounts the main challenges raised before the WTO DSS when called upon to address RTA-related disputes, along with the implications they hold for WTO law and institutions, while pointing to the shifts these underlying features seem to be generating among the goals pursued by the DSS in these types of cases. Against this backdrop, Sections 10.3 and 10.4 proceed with a close analysis of the DSS's goal-attainment efforts in RTA-related disputes as manifested in a series of cases implicating *substantive* and *jurisdictional* questions arising in the WTO-RTA context. In so doing, these sections reveal how the challenges posed by regionalism have shaped the goals sought by the DSS in RTA-related cases while highlighting critical points of difference in the judicial practices harnessed to these goal-attainment efforts as compared with those discerned in Parts II and III. Section 10.5 concludes by tying the goal-achievement patterns identified in RTA-related disputes to the broader goal-based effectiveness framework developed in this book.

10.2 RTA-Related Disputes: Context, Challenges, and Goal Shifting

The proliferation of RTAs[1] is a salient feature of today's international economic landscape. Such agreements, however, are by no means a new

[1] An extended version of the analysis conducted in this chapter can be found in Sivan Shlomo Agon, 'Sustaining Multilateralism from the Bench' (2020) 38:1 Berkeley J Int'l L. For the sake of clarity and

phenomenon,[2] nor is the tension between them and the WTO, which has 'dogged' the multilateral trading system 'since its inception in the General Agreement on Tariffs and Trade (GATT) in 1947 and through its institutional transformation into the WTO in 1995'.[3] At the core of this tension, as Lockhart and Mitchell have put it, is the fact that RTAs 'entrench the very discrimination' that the multilateral trade rules 'seek to eliminate'.[4] And so, while RTAs vary widely in nature—in their geographic scope, number of state parties, the trade-related issues subject to regulation, and so forth—common to them all is their reduction of trade barriers between the state parties seeking closer economic integration beyond that of the multilateral trade system, while simultaneously maintaining barriers with states outside the agreement. Nonetheless, although such regional trade arrangements violate the fundamental tenet of nondiscrimination underlying the multilateral trade system as captured in the basic most-favoured nation (MFN) rule, the WTO, like the GATT, has always allowed some space for Members to grant one another more favourable treatment in the framework of RTAs—most notably under Article XXIV of the GATT, subject to the conditions articulated in this provision.[5]

During the last two decades, however, the world has witnessed a sharp rise in the number of RTAs, unparalleled to that envisaged earlier. Whereas the GATT saw 124 notifications of RTAs in the period 1948–1994, more than 290 RTAs were in force between WTO Members as of December 2018, with dozens of other agreements notified to the WTO but not yet in force or currently under negotiation.[6] At present, all WTO Members have reported participation in at least one RTA, and some are party to numerous agreements.[7] In addition, the regulatory coverage of RTAs has also widened and deepened over time, 'moving from the reduction of tariffs to behind-the-border issues such as harmonization of standards, and further, to

consistency, in this chapter I use the term 'Regional Trade Agreements' (RTAs) to refer to both Free Trade Agreements (FTAs) and Customs Unions under GATT Article XXIV, as well as economic integration agreements under Article V of the General Agreement on Trade in Services (GATS). Furthermore, the term 'regional' as used herein does not carry any geographical connotations, meaning that agreements between parties geographically remote from one another are also included.

[2] Simon Lester and Bryan Mercurio, *Bilateral and Regional Trade Agreements* (CUP 2009) 3.

[3] Robert Howse and Joanna Langille, 'Spheres of Commerce: The WTO Legal System and Regional Trading Blocs – A Reconsideration' (2018) 46 Ga J Int'l & Comp L 469, 650.

[4] Nicolas JS Lockhart and Andrew D Mitchell, 'Regional Trade Agreements Under GATT 1994: An Exception and Its Limits' in Andrew D Mitchell (ed), *Challenges and Prospects for the WTO* (Cameron May 2005) 219.

[5] A corresponding provision is embedded in Article V of the GATS. Also of relevance is the 'Enabling Clause', which relaxed the requirements for customs unions and FTAs for developing countries, with a view to facilitating their economic development. See Decision on Differential and More Favourable Treatment, Reciprocity and Fuller Participation of Developing Countries, L/4903, GATT BISD 26S/203 (28 November 1979).

[6] See 'Regional Trade Agreements: Facts and Figures' (*WTO*) <https://www.wto.org/english/tratop_e/region_e/regfac_e.htm> accessed 31 December 2018.

[7] ibid.

so-called "WTO-extra" ... issues such as competition and investment'.[8] Moreover, most if not all RTAs establish some form of dispute settlement procedures, which have likewise 'increasingly shifted from politically-oriented procedures, to more sophisticated, legalistic forms of dispute settlement'.[9]

The so-called 'spaghetti bowl' of multilateral trade rules and proliferating regional trade arrangements, each accompanied by its own dispute settlement mechanism, has inspired extensive debates over the fragmentation of international economic law and the challenges engendered by regime overlap, among them, conflicts of obligations between the WTO and RTAs, jurisdictional competition between their respective dispute settlement fora, and forum shopping.[10] Most notably, the expansion of regionalism, which gained momentum with the failure to break the impasse in the WTO Doha Round of trade negotiations,[11] has been accompanied by vigorous debate about the systemic effects of RTAs on the multilateral trading regime and, particularly, on the latter's role in regulating international trade, what has become a major source of unease for the WTO.[12] As Supachai Panitchpakdi, a former WTO Director General, noted some ten years ago, 'the role of the WTO' in global economic governance is 'being tested by the abundance of regional trade agreements' that continue to spread around the globe, resulting in international trade increasingly being governed by preferential arrangements among selected groups of members, as opposed to trade 'under MFN conditions governed by the WTO'.[13] A decade later, in the face of the continuing regionalization of trade governance and the rise of so-called mega-regionals—RTAs of huge economic size and wide geographical spread (e.g. the EU-Canada Comprehensive Economic and Trade Agreement and the Trans-Pacific Partnership Agreement)—Alan Winters went still further to warn that 'absent a major and conscious change in the value placed by ... countries on multilateralism, we are unlikely to bequeath an effective multilateral trade system to the next generation'.[14]

[8] Claude Chase and others, 'Mapping of Dispute Settlement Mechanisms in Regional Trade Agreements – Innovative or Variations on a Theme?' in Rohini Acharya (ed), *Regional Trade Agreements and the Multilateral Trading System* (CUP 2016) 608.

[9] ibid.

[10] See, e.g. Marc L Busch, 'Overlapping Institutions, Forum Shopping, and Dispute Settlement in International Trade' (2007) 61 Int'l Org 735; Karen Alter and Sophie Meunier, 'The Politics of International Regime Complexity' (2009) 7 Persp on Pol 13.

[11] Lester and Mercurio (n 2) 3; Chad P Bown, 'Mega-Regional Trade Agreements and the Future of the WTO' (2017) 8 Global Pol'y 107.

[12] See, e.g. Todd Allee and Manfred Elsig, 'The Presence of the World Trade Organization Within Preferential Trade Agreements' in Manfred Elsig, Bernard Hoekman, and Joost Pauwelyn (eds), *Assessing the World Trade Organization: Fit for Purpose?* (CUP 2017) 321; Bown (n 11); WTO, *World Trade Report 2011—The WTO and Preferential Trade Agreements: From Co-Existence to Coherence* (WTO 2011) [hereinafter World Trade Report 2011].

[13] Supachai Panitchpakdi, 'The WTO, Global Governance and Development' in Gary P Sampson (ed), *The WTO and Global Governance: Future Directions* (United Nations University Press 2008) 195–96.

[14] Alan L Winters, 'The WTO and Regional Trading Agreements: Is It All Over for Multilateralism?' in *Assessing the World Trade Organization* (n 12) 346.

As the above implies, the shift in trade negotiations away from multilateralism and the continuing surge in regional agreements that accord preferential treatment to some trading partners while excluding others, pose threats to the attainment of those WTO objectives built on nondiscrimination and, more generally, to the viability of the multilateral trading system and the WTO's centrality in the international economic order.[15] What is more, the expanding network of increasingly complex RTAs that parallel and overlap WTO trade disciplines, and which often include their own dispute settlement mechanisms, risk undermining the legal coherence and predictability of the multilateral trade rules.[16] They likewise constitute a source for normative and jurisdictional conflicts with the WTO legal system,[17] as seen in several disputes that have come before the WTO DSS since its creation.[18] As RTAs multiply and mature, more such disputes are expected to reach the DSS's docket.

Such RTA-related disputes demand in turn that the WTO DSS address delicate questions that lie at the heart of the tense relationship between the multilateral and the regional trade regimes, questions pertaining to the interaction between these separate but closely related normative international frameworks, the legal effects of RTA rules on WTO undertakings, and the competing jurisdictions of the judicial bodies established to enforce the distinct sets of trade commitments. As a result, RTA-related disputes impinge in meaningful ways on the integrity of WTO rules, the realization of the multilateral trade liberalization objectives embodied in those rules, and the stature of the WTO as a vehicle for international trade regulation at a time when RTAs flourish as against the stalemate in the WTO's legislative arm. Furthermore, as these RTA-related cases often have a direct bearing on the very jurisdiction of the WTO DSS and its position vis-à-vis other international dispute settlement institutions, these disputes entail critical implications for the authority of the DSS itself and its ability to attain its goals as set forth by WTO Members.

[15] For discussion of these issues, see, e.g. Bown (n 11); Winters (n 14); Marc D Froese, 'Mapping the Scope of Dispute Settlement in Regional Trade Agreements: Implications for the Multilateral Governance of Trade' (2016) 15 World Trade Rev 563; Rafael Leal-Arcas, 'Proliferation of Regional Trade Agreements: Complementing or Supplanting Multilateralism?' (2011) 11 Chi J Int'l L 597; Henry Gao and C L Lim, 'Saving the WTO from the Risk of Irrelevance: The WTO Dispute Settlement Mechanism as a "Common Good" for RTA Disputes' (2008) 11 J Int'l Econ L 899, 900.

[16] See, e.g. WTO, *World Trade Report 2003—Trade and Development* (WTO 2003) 65 (noting that the growing number of overlapping RTAs 'risks undermining the transparency of trading rules' and that 'ubiquitous and highly varied regional arrangements may . . . undermine the integrity and clarity of the multilateral trading system').

[17] See, e.g. Pamela Apaza Lanyi and Armin Steinbach, 'Limiting Jurisdictional Fragmentation in International Trade Disputes' (2014) 5 J Int'l Disp Settlement 372; Gabrielle Marceau and Julian Wyatt, 'Dispute Settlement Regimes Intermingled: Regional Trade Agreements and the WTO' (2010) 1 J Int'l Disp Settlement 67.

[18] For an overview of the various WTO disputes in which the existence of an RTA has been pleaded or argued in one way or another, see Armand C M de Mestral, 'Dispute Settlement Under the WTO and RTAs: An Uneasy Relationship' (2013) 16 J Int'l Econ L 777; Michelle Q Zang, 'When the Multilateral Meets the Regionals: Regional Trade Agreements at WTO Dispute Settlement' (2018) World Trade Rev 1, doi:10.1017/S1474745618000010.

As demonstrated below, DSS awareness of the systemic consequences for WTO rules and institutions embedded in disputes involving RTA-related issues has, from the outset, guided this adjudicative mechanism in attuning its goal-attainment efforts towards specific organizational objectives. Thus, when called upon to decide cases that arise at the WTO-RTA nexus, the DSS—within its strategic judicial space—has deliberately and consistently opted for those interpretive choices that may foster the multilateral trade system's security and predictability, entrench the primacy of the WTO and its norms, as well as sustain the DSS's own authority as a forum for the adjudication of international trade disputes. As one WTO official observed with respect to the line of jurisprudence developed by the DSS in RTA-related cases: '[I]f one were to read all of these cases, the overall assessment is that.... [t]he case law would seem... to preserve the supremacy of... WTO law over other rules'.[19] Going further, the same official added: '[O]ne of the values, ... the normative value, that informs the case law of the Appellate Body and of panellists [in RTA-related cases] is preserving the WTO dispute settlement system and the WTO [regime] and its supremacy over regional trade agreements'.[20]

However, as observed in the disputes previously examined in this book, these DSS's goal-attainment efforts are not asserted outright in RTA-related disputes. Instead, they are often concealed behind a veil of textualism, thus appearing to remain faithful to state consent. And yet, these distinct goal-attainment patterns, as we shall see, are effectively captured not only in the evidence provided by WTO practitioners involved in the operation of the DSS and the RTA-related cases examined; they are also encapsulated in the specific judicial choices made and the legal interpretations developed in these cases, whereby WTO adjudicators have steadily worked along two parallel and mutually reinforcing trajectories to limit the ability of WTO Members to (i) derogate from their substantive WTO obligations through the formation and operation of RTAs, as well as (ii) contract out from the WTO Dispute Settlement Understanding (DSU) through RTAs in a manner compromising the DSS's jurisdiction and thus its power to scrutinize RTA-related deviations from the WTO's substantive legal commitments.[21]

Hence, irrespective of the many pleas made over the years that the WTO DSS 'consider the problems posed by the troubled relationships of RTAs and the WTO from a broad perspective of the unity of international trade law', meaning that it advance a more open policy towards RTA law and dispute settlement,[22] the DSS,

[19] Interview with WTO legal officer (Geneva, 11 July 2012).

[20] ibid.

[21] de Mestral (n 18); Joanna Langille, 'Neither Constitution nor Contract: Understanding the WTO by Examining the Legal Limits on Contracting Out Through Regional Trade Agreements' (2011) 86 NYU L Rev 1482.

[22] de Mestral (n 18) 784. See also Julia Ya Qin, 'Managing Conflicts Between Rulings of the World Trade Organization and Regional Trade Tribunals: Reflections on the *Brazil-Tyres* Case' in Pieter H F Bekker, Rudolf Dozler, and Michael Waible (eds), *Making Transnational Law Work in the Global Economy: Essays in Honour of Detlev Vagts* (CUP 2010) 601; Lanyi and Steinbach (n 17).

under the Appellate Body (AB) leadership, has consciously approached the legal and institutional challenges emerging at the intersection of the WTO and RTAs through a narrow, inward-looking, WTO-centred prism.[23] In contradiction to its own declaration in *US-Gasoline* that WTO agreements are 'not to be read in clinical isolation from public international law',[24] the AB has effectively embraced an 'implicit judicial policy of "clinical isolation" from regionalism'[25] in its uncompromising quest to sustain the multilateral trading system from the bench.

In what follows, the chapter addresses the key jurisprudential milestones established in this quest while unfolding the goal-attainment efforts they marked as the WTO DSS exercised its role as a multilateral adjudicator in an increasingly regionalizing international economic order. In carrying out this goal-based investigation, we first look into the case law developed at the WTO-RTA *substantive* legal nexus (Section 10.3), where conflicts of obligations between the two legal frameworks arose and a range of legal defences were invoked before the DSS as respondents attempted to shield the otherwise WTO-inconsistent measures adopted within the context of their regional agreements. Thereafter, we proceed with a complementary analysis of the DSS's jurisprudence as it emerged at the *jurisdictional* WTO-RTA juncture (Section 10.4), where questions concerning the interaction between the WTO DSS and the overlapping regional dispute settlement fora presented themselves, questions implicating, among others, the very capacity of the DSS as an adjudicative institution to pronounce on international trade law and enforce compliance with the substantive legal norms underlying the multilateral trading system.

10.3 Goal Attainment at the WTO-RTA Substantive Legal Nexus

Embarking on the RTA Challenge: *Turkey-Textiles* and the Reading of the Regional Trade Exception in GATT Article XXIV

As noted above, the positioning of the WTO DSS as a multilateral dispute settlement mechanism in the evolving reality of RTA proliferation has confronted panels and the AB, from their very beginning, with some of the most delicate legal and institutional issues surrounding the intersection of trade multilateralism and regionalism. Included among these issues are several challenging questions related

[23] de Mestral (n 18) 784.

[24] *United States–Standards for Reformulated and Conventional Gasoline*, Report of the Appellate Body, 20 May 1996, WT/DS2/AB/R, 17.

[25] Robert Howse, 'The World Trade Organization 20 Years On: Global Governance by Judiciary' (2016) 27 EJIL 9, 75.

to the substantive legal interaction between WTO law and RTAs, particularly the question of conflicting obligations under the parallel normative frameworks and the legal defences available to justify the WTO-inconsistent measures taken by Members within the framework of their regional trade arrangements. As will be shown, '[t]rue to its mission to bring greater order' to WTO law and the multilateral trading system, 'the AB took on the challenge posed by RTAs as soon as it was offered'.[26] This opportunity came forth in the early *Turkey-Textiles* case,[27] where the AB made its first systemic effort to address the legal relationship between RTAs and the WTO in the context of GATT Article XXIV.[28]

As noted in the previous section, although RTAs deviate from one of the WTO's core principles, the MFN rule, WTO law permits Members to enter into RTAs if certain requirements are met. These requirements are included in Article XXIV of the GATT, Article V of the GATS, and the Enabling Clause—commonly referred to as the 'regional trade exceptions'.[29] Most prominent and debated among these provisions is GATT Article XXIV, which allows Members to form RTAs (both free trade agreements (FTAs) and customs unions) under two main conditions stipulated in subparagraphs (5) and (8). Generally speaking, these conditions include the liberalization of substantially all trade between the parties to the RTA and avoidance of greater trade restrictiveness against WTO Members not party to the agreement. Ultimately, consistency with these conditions is what 'allows WTO Members to deviate from the most-favoured nation obligation that is a cornerstone of the multilateral trading system and to treat other parties to the preferential arrangements better than non-party WTO Members'.[30]

Alongside these substantive conditions, Article XXIV of the GATT also contains a procedural component, requiring notification of every RTA established between WTO Members, with a view to allowing a multilateral review of the agreement and evaluation of its fidelity to the requirements articulated in Article XXIV. As Mavroidis has noted when addressing this requirement, the original intent of the GATT's drafters was to ensure that no RTA 'be consummated absent multilateral clearance'.[31] To this end, during the GATT era, notified RTAs would be reviewed by an ad hoc working party, composed of state delegates, to determine whether they complied with the substantive conditions set out in Article XXIV. After the WTO's creation, in an attempt to bring greater discipline to the review of RTAs, the ad hoc working party system was replaced with a permanent political organ, the

[26] de Mestral (n 18) 790.

[27] *Turkey–Restriction on Imports of Textile and Clothing Products*, Report of the Appellate Body, 19 November 1999, WT/DS34/AB/R.

[28] Howse and Langille (n 3) 661.

[29] Peter Van den Bossche and Werner Zdouc, *The Law and Policy of the World Trade Organization: Law, Text, Cases and Materials* (3rd edn, CUP 2013) 649.

[30] Howse (n 25) 35.

[31] Petros Mavroidis, *The Regulation of International Trade*, vol 1 (MIT Press 2016) 292.

Committee on Regional Trade Agreements (CRTA),[32] which was entrusted with the power to examine RTAs and assess their consistency with the multilateral trade system's law and policy.[33]

Despite its establishment in 1996, the CRTA has proved itself unequal to the task of providing a disciplined review process for the many RTAs since notified to the WTO.[34] Continuing disagreements between Members over ambiguities in the language of GATT Article XXIV, together with the insufficient information submitted by RTA parties and the fact that determinations of WTO-consistency were to be made by all WTO Members, including those whose RTAs were under examination,[35] plagued the CRTA and resulted in its failure to provide a meaningful *ex ante* review of RTAs.[36] At the same time, given that the CRTA was accorded the explicit mandate to review individual regional agreements notified to the WTO, doubts arose as to whether WTO adjudicative bodies could themselves examine the compatibility of such agreements with the substantive requirements of GATT Article XXIV.[37] The AB clarified this and other fundamental questions regarding the application of the regional exception embedded in Article XXIV in the case of *Turkey-Textiles*.

At issue in this case was a complaint brought by India against Turkey regarding quotas imposed by the latter on imports of textile and clothing products from India. According to India, these quantitative restrictions were inconsistent with Turkey's obligations under WTO law, particularly, Articles XI and XIII of the GATT Agreement. Turkey claimed, in response, that these quantitative restrictions were introduced upon the formation of a customs union with the EU and thus were justified under the exception for RTAs embodied in GATT Article XXIV, which, according to Turkey, 'confers on WTO Members a right to enter into a customs union, and to derogate, under certain conditions, from their GATT obligations'.[38]

As noted by Howse, when the case arrived at the WTO DSS, '[i]t was not especially controversial as a matter of judicial competence that the [WTO] dispute settlement organs could review the particular' trade restrictions introduced by Turkey and their link to the customs union with the EU.[39] However, the AB seized the opportunity in this early case to clarify that the judicial competence of WTO adjudicators actually extends beyond examination of the appropriateness of the specific trade-restrictive measures at issue 'to reviewing the overall consistency ... of the customs union with the conditions in GATT Article XXIV'.[40] What

32 de Mestral (n 18) 783.
33 WTO, Committee on Regional Trade Agreements (7 February 1996) WT/L/127.
34 de Mestral (n 18) 783. See also World Trade Report 2011 (n 12) 185.
35 World Trade Report 2011 (n 12) 185.
36 Gao and Lim (n 15) 899; Langille (n 21) 1506, 1508; Howse (n 25) 35.
37 Gao and Lim (n 15) 904.
38 *Turkey-Textiles* (n 27) para 10.
39 Howse (n 25) 35.
40 ibid; Gao and Lim (n 15) 904.

is more, the AB not only made it clear in its ruling that all aspects of Article XXIV were justiciable so that WTO panels *could* examine whether the substantive requirements for an RTA had been fulfilled; it essentially went further, to suggest that panels are *expected* to examine the overall compatibility of an RTA with the requirements of Article XXIV before considering a legal defence contending that a measure related to the formation of an RTA is justified under this provision.[41]

This AB ruling—suggesting that WTO judicial organs 'might have the competence and even the responsibility in certain cases to determine' the consistency of an RTA with Article XXIV,[42] while 'overturning the panel of first instance as well as prior GATT practice' on this issue[43]—was subjected to criticism stating that it upset the institutional balance between the WTO's political and judicial organs.[44] Nevertheless, no 'major revolt' erupted against this AB pronouncement with respect to the application of GATT Article XXIV.[45] As several commentators have noted, while the AB's decision in *Turkey-Textiles* may have intruded upon the authority granted to the WTO's political organs and to the (ineffective) CRTA specifically,[46] it did so with the aim of reinforcing the multilateral trade disciplines and strengthening WTO oversight of the proliferating regional trade arrangements; it was thus 'consistent with the underlying substantive values' and objectives of the WTO community.[47]

And yet, the AB in *Turkey-Textiles* not only 'took a strict or narrow view of the [regional] exception' in Article XXIV in the sense of 'holding that it should be subject to strict judicial scrutiny, not merely diplomatic oversight, in the relevant WTO committee';[48] the AB also went on in its ruling to read the language of Article XXIV itself in a manner that significantly limited Members' ability to use this clause as a shield for WTO-incompatible measures taken within the framework of RTAs. Thus, while the AB in *Turkey-Textiles* acknowledged that GATT Article XXIV may 'justify the adoption' of an RTA-related measure 'which is inconsistent

41 *Turkey-Textiles* (n 27) paras 59–60 (stating that '[w]e would expect a panel, when examining such a measure, to require a party to establish [inter alia, whether the customs union fully meets the relevant requirements of Article XXIV]').

42 Howse and Langille (n 3) 667.

43 Howse (n 25) 35. Note that the first instance panel in *Turkey-Textiles* was uncertain about whether it could assess the compatibility of the RTA between Turkey and the EU with Article XXIV. Exercising judicial economy, the panel thus proceeded in its analysis, assuming *arguendo* that the arrangement between Turkey and the EU is compatible with the requirements of Article XXIV while limiting 'its examination to the question of whether Turkey was permitted to introduce the quantitative restrictions at issue'. See *Turkey-Textiles* (n 27) para 60.

44 See, e.g. Frieder Roessler, 'The Institutional Balance Between the Judicial and Political Organs of the WTO' in Marco Bronckers and Reinhard Quick (eds), *New Directions in International Economic Law* (Kluwer Law International 2000) 325.

45 Howse (n 25) 36.

46 For subsequent developments in the WTO concerning the process of review of RTAs in light of the problems identified with the CRTA, including the adoption of the Transparency Mechanism for Regional Trade Agreements in 2006, see de Mestral (n 18) 783–84; World Trade Report 2011 (n 12) 185.

47 Howse (n 25) 36; Gao and Lim (n 15) 904.

48 Howse (n 25) 73.

with ... GATT provisions, and may be invoked as a ... "defence" to a finding of inconsistency',[49] the AB severely restricted the availability of this defence by introducing a condition that for such a measure to be justified, it must be *necessary* for the formation of the RTA.[50] As a result, according to the AB, a Member claiming the benefit of an Article XXIV defence must comply with two cumulative criteria: First, it must demonstrate that the measure at issue was introduced upon the formation of an RTA that fully meets the conditions of subparagraphs (5) and (8) of Article XXIV, as mentioned above. Second, it 'must demonstrate that the formation' of the RTA 'would be prevented if it were not allowed to introduce the measure at issue'.[51] In inserting this latter criterion to Article XXIV, the AB imposed on Members a severe burden of justification, in the form of the necessity test,[52] thus constraining their ability to derogate from their WTO obligations through an RTA.[53]

We therefore see that in contrast to the expansive interpretative approach envisaged in trade-and disputes (see Part II), where the AB broadly construed the policy exceptions in GATT Article XX so as to better accommodate values 'external' to the WTO regime—such as health or environmental protection—in *Turkey-Textiles*, the AB chose to meaningfully narrow the operative scope of the exception for RTAs embedded in GATT Article XXIV. The message sent by the AB in this case is patent, as are its efforts to achieve its goals of sustaining the integrity of WTO rules and objectives and nurturing a legally predictable multilateral trade system. In Langille's words, according to the AB, the exception for RTAs in Article XXIV 'can only be employed in limited circumstances', whereas 'WTO obligations can only be varied if a measure is necessary for an RTA to be formed'. Stated differently, '[c]reating a preferential arrangement cannot trump the goals of the WTO'.[54]

Fending off Regionalism Under the General Exceptions in GATT Article XX: The Cases of *Mexico-Soft Drinks* and *Brazil-Tyres*

Similar goal-attainment patterns to those envisaged in *Turkey-Textiles*, combined with a conscious attempt to limit Members' ability to derogate from their WTO obligations for RTA-related purposes, can be recognized in cases where Members tried to justify WTO-inconsistent measures adopted in connection with RTAs under the general exceptions provided in GATT Article XX. Illustrative in

[49] *Turkey-Textiles* (n 27) paras 45, 58.
[50] de Mestral (n 18) 791 (noting that 'the AB read into Article XXIV a condition that to be justified any measure must be "necessary" for the formation' of the RTA); Langille (n 21) 1508–09.
[51] *Turkey-Textiles* (n 27) para 58.
[52] Michael Trebilcock, Robert Howse, and Antonia Eliason, *The Regulation of International Trade* (4th edn, Routledge 2012) 117.
[53] Langille (n 21) 1509.
[54] ibid.

this respect is the case of *Mexico-Soft Drinks*.[55] This specific case grew out of a broader dispute between the United States and Mexico concerning the market of sweeteners within the framework of the North American Free Trade Agreement (NAFTA). According to Mexico, US quantitative restrictions imposed on imports of cane sugar from Mexico contradicted a sugar-specific NAFTA annex in which the United States had committed to granting market access to Mexican sugar. When seeking resolution of this dispute, Mexico initially invoked the NAFTA dispute settlement procedures, but the United States nonetheless prevented the establishment of a NAFTA panel by blocking selection of its panellists. In an attempt to induce the United States to comply with its NAFTA obligations and agree to the composition of a NAFTA panel, Mexico decided to retaliate against the United States by imposing an extra 20% tax on soft drinks using sweeteners other than cane sugar, an act favouring Mexico's domestic cane sugar producers. In response, the United States launched dispute settlement proceedings at the WTO rather than NAFTA, while arguing that Mexico's discriminatory tax measures were inconsistent with the national treatment obligation provided for in GATT Article III.

During the WTO proceedings, Mexico claimed that notwithstanding the violation of GATT Article III, its soft drinks tax could be justified under the exception in GATT Article XX(d), which permits WTO Members to impose measures that are 'necessary to secure compliance with laws and regulations which are not inconsistent with the provisions of [GATT]'. According to Mexico, its tax measures were 'necessary to secure compliance' by the United States with the latter's commitments under NAFTA, 'an international agreement that is a law not inconsistent with the provisions of GATT'.[56]

Both the panel and the AB rejected this defence and Mexico's reading of the terms 'laws and regulations' on which it was predicated.[57] In contrast to Mexico's argument that these terms were 'broad enough to include international agreements such as the NAFTA',[58] the AB, like the panel, found that the terms 'laws and regulations' within the context of Article XX(d) narrowly 'refer to the rules that form part of the domestic legal order of the WTO Member invoking the provision and do not include the international obligations of *another* WTO Member',[59] in this case, US commitments under NAFTA. Hence, the AB concluded that Article XX(d) was not available as a justification of WTO-inconsistent measures seeking to secure compliance with a WTO Member's obligations under an international agreement, such as the RTA under discussion.[60]

55 *Mexico–Tax Measures on Soft Drinks and Other Beverages*, Report of the Appellate Body, 24 March 2006, WT/DS308/AB/R [*Mexico-Soft Drinks* AB Report].

56 *Mexico–Tax Measures on Soft Drinks and Other Beverages*, Report of the Panel, 24 March 2006, WT/DS308/R, para 8.162 [*Mexico-Soft Drinks* Panel Report].

57 ibid, paras 8.198, 8.204; *Mexico-Soft Drinks* AB Report (n 55) paras 68–80.

58 *Mexico-Soft Drinks* AB Report (n 55) para 64.

59 ibid, para 75 (emphasis original); *Mexico-Soft Drinks* Panel Report (n 56) paras 8.191–8.197.

60 *Mexico-Soft Drinks* AB Report (n 55) para 79.

Notably, while the AB provided several reasons for why 'laws and regulations' in Article XX(d) refer to rules that form part of a domestic legal system, and while it acknowledged that international obligations could be incorporated into domestic law and in some legal systems with automaticity,[61] the AB, as Davey and Sapir have stressed, 'never explained why the terms ["laws and regulations"] themselves could not also encompass international obligations'.[62] In addition, although the AB provided certain contextual and policy arguments in support of its decision to exclude international agreements from the purview of Article XX(d), those arguments' persuasiveness has been doubted.[63]

For instance, one of the arguments raised by the AB in support of its narrow reading of Article XX(d) can be summarized as follows: If the respective provision were to cover international agreements, a WTO Member could invoke Article XX(d) to justify measures taken *unilaterally* to secure compliance with another Member's obligations under the WTO agreements, in contradiction to the rules detailed in Articles 22 and 23 of the DSU.[64] When elaborating this argument, a WTO official involved in the case began his remarks by alluding to past US practice of 'aggressive unilateralism' and the great attention consequently dedicated to the issue of unilateral measures during the Uruguay Round negotiations when drafting the DSU, which ultimately resulted in a prohibition on unilateral determinations and retaliatory measures in instances of violation of WTO law.[65] This official went on to note that 'a lot of what was in the ... mind' of WTO adjudicators in *Mexico-Soft Drinks* was the threat of such 'unilateral actions' and their potentially negative effect on the stability of the multilateral system and its dispute settlement mechanism.[66] The panel and the AB were both concerned that if they had 'decided differently, people could have read' Article XX(d) as allowing states 'affected by a [WTO] violation of another country, ... [even in the absence of a WTO ruling], ... to impose ... their own countermeasures' unilaterally.[67]

While this argument aptly expresses the desire of WTO adjudicators to secure the stability and predictability of the multilateral trading system by sending 'a signal that ... [Members] cannot take these unilateral measures',[68] it is not entirely convincing. This is particularly so given the fact that the principle of effective treaty interpretation could obviously preclude a Member's attempt to use GATT Article XX(d) to circumvent its obligations under DSU Articles 22 and 23, which forbid

[61] ibid paras 69, 79, fn 148.
[62] William J Davey and André Sapir, 'The *Soft Drinks* Case: The WTO and Regional Agreements' (2009) 8 World Trade Rev 5, 10.
[63] ibid 9–11.
[64] *Mexico-Soft Drinks* AB Report (n 55) para 77.
[65] Interview with WTO legal officer (Geneva, 16 March 2012).
[66] ibid.
[67] ibid.
[68] ibid.

unilateral trade measures and regulate the application of countermeasures within the framework of the WTO.[69]

Another argument invoked by the AB when rejecting the reading of Article XX(d) as covering measures necessary to secure compliance with international agreements was that acceptance of Mexico's position would imply that in order to resolve the case, WTO adjudicators would have to assess whether NAFTA, the regional agreement at issue, had been violated.[70] This, the AB contended, would make WTO panels and the AB 'adjudicators of non-WTO disputes', a function extraneous to their mandate under the DSU.[71] This argument, however, as Davey and Sapir have rightly noted, is not entirely accurate as 'the WTO system would only be taking a view on the other agreement to the extent it was necessary to determine WTO rights and obligations; its view would not constitute adjudication of the dispute under the other agreement'.[72] The cogency of the AB's argument is further undermined by the fact that in other instances, the AB had held that 'it could make determinations about the legal requirements of other legal systems and whether they are met, where needed, in order to apply a WTO legal rule'.[73] Such was the case, for example, regarding the Lomé Convention in *EC-Bananas*, discussed in Chapter 8.[74] On the basis of this earlier case law, Howse has suggested that another route available to the AB in *Mexico-Soft Drinks* was to simply state that 'the operative provision being applied was Article XX(d) of the GATT' and that a finding with respect to a NAFTA violation 'was merely ancillary to determining' whether the Mexican measures were required to secure US compliance, thus making them consistent with the WTO covered agreements.[75]

The AB, like the panel, consciously chose not to pursue this route but to strictly construe GATT Article XX(d) as excluding international agreements, including RTAs, from its scope. This interpretative choice of WTO judicial bodies aptly discloses their 'implicit judicial policy of "clinical isolation" from regionalism',[76] together with their deliberate attempt to control for the negative impacts that RTA proliferation may project onto the WTO legal system. Two messages were therefore made clear in the judicial endeavour undertaken by WTO adjudicators to sustain multilateralism in *Mexico-Soft Drinks*.

First, Article XX(d) was to be interpreted narrowly, meaning that WTO Members may not appeal to this exception in order to justify WTO-inconsistent measures aimed at enforcing compliance with the international obligations adopted under

[69] Davey and Sapir (n 62) 10.
[70] *Mexico-Soft Drinks* AB Report (n 55) para 78.
[71] ibid.
[72] Davey and Sapir (n 62) 10.
[73] Howse (n 25) 74.
[74] *European Communities–Regime for the Importation, Sale and Distribution of Bananas*, Report of the Appellate Body, 25 September 1997, WT/DS27/AB/R.
[75] Howse (n 25) 74.
[76] ibid 75.

the umbrella of regional trade arrangements. Clearly, this narrow interpretative approach is consistent with the strict mode of interpretation embraced by the AB in *Turkey-Textiles* towards the regional trade exception embedded in GATT Article XXIV. At the same time, the narrow approach followed with respect to the same Article XX(d) markedly differs from the broad interpretive stance taken by WTO adjudicators in trade-and disputes towards the exceptions stipulated in Article XX(a), (b), and (g). There, as seen in Chapters 5 and 6, a much more deferential position was manifested towards the interests protected (health and environment, among others), as well as to the non–WTO international law sources of relevance to those interests. When alluding to the non-coincidental variation between the judicial approach taken towards Article XX exceptions in trade-and disputes as compared with the position taken in the RTA-related case of *Mexico-Soft Drinks*, a WTO official working on the case made a highly revealing comment:

> [In *Mexico-Soft Drinks*,] Mexico was saying that... it could invoke [Article] XX(d) to enforce the NAFTA [i.e. a regional trade agreement].... [B]ut if someone were to suggest that they were applying a WTO-inconsistent measure to enforce an international environmental agreement, will they receive more deference than here? Maybe.[77]

This testimony tacitly highlights how the interpretative and judicial policy choices made by WTO adjudicators are shaped by the dominant goals pursued by the DSS in each category of cases, which in RTA-related disputes seem to tilt towards upholding the WTO regime and bolstering the stability and unity of its rules against the threats posed by the expanding regional trading blocs. Indeed, a WTO panellist sitting on the bench in *Mexico-Soft Drinks* suggested as much when he explained the non-deferential approach towards RTAs taken by WTO adjudicators in this case:

> One thing is to show deference [to other international agreements], but ... I see it ... the other way around. There are so many ... free trade agreements that it is very risky to take that road.... It is very dangerous [to show deference to these agreements].... [I]t was [therefore] clear to the panel [in this case] ... that we had ... to establish the limits very clearly.[78]

The second message conveyed by the *Mexico-Soft Drinks* ruling on GATT Article XX(d), particularly by the refusal of WTO adjudicators to look into the relevant legal norms under NAFTA and their assertion that such an act would amount to adjudication of a 'non-WTO dispute', is that the WTO dispute settlement system

[77] Interview with WTO legal officer (Geneva, 18 April 2012).
[78] Interview with WTO panellist (Geneva, 24 July 2012).

'was not available for Members to address gaps and ineffectiveness in regional dispute arrangements'.[79] With respect to this position, a WTO legal officer participating in the case stated:

> The truth is, at the end of the day, that Mexico had a valid complaint that the US is blocking [the operation of the] NAFTA [dispute settlement mechanism]. The question is, should ... it be for the WTO, doomed for being in those situations, to fix their problem or should the WTO stay on the sidelines, like it did....[80]

This same interviewee then added that the AB's ruling on GATT Article XX(d) reflected its 'reluctance to get involved in what was a very messy regional dispute. Not just the [dispute about trade in] sugar, but also this issue about ... the blocking of the [selection] of panellists' by the United States, which prevented the establishment of a NAFTA panel to hear Mexico's claims and resulted in the latter's application of countermeasures.[81] There was some 'concern' among WTO adjudicators at the time 'that the WTO system would be put in a situation in which it would have to resolve regional controversies', a scenario that might undermine its own credibility.[82] The AB, determined to secure the autonomy, stability, and reliability of the WTO legal system, including its dispute settlement apparatus, sought to avoid any such occurrences.

The AB exhibited comparable goal-attainment endeavours in its next case, that of *Brazil-Tyres*,[83] where it essentially held that by following a ruling handed down by a tribunal established in the framework of the Mercado Común del Sur (MERCOSUR)—the RTA created between Brazil and several South American countries—Brazil had acted inconsistently with WTO rules. At issue in this case was an import ban on retreaded tyres, adopted by Brazil in 2000. According to Brazil, the ban was introduced as part of its efforts to reduce the risks to human, animal, and plant life and health associated with waste tyres, the accumulation of which increases the exposure to toxic emissions caused by tyre combustion and facilitates the transmission of diseases by the mosquitos using tyres as breeding grounds. Brazil's 2000 ban had initially been challenged by Uruguay before a MERCOSUR arbitral tribunal in 2001. Siding with Uruguay, the tribunal found Brazil's import prohibition to be 'a new restriction of commerce' in violation of

[79] Howse (n 25) 74.

[80] Interview with WTO legal officer (Geneva, 18 April 2012). A state delegate drew a similar picture when alluding to the AB's decision to reject Mexico's claims in *Mexico-Soft Drinks* and to distance itself from the US-Mexico skirmish under the NAFTA: 'It was clear that it was an unfair situation, but ... the WTO [DSS] can really just say nothing other than "we never said the world is fair and we have our job to reinforce this [WTO Agreement], and we are sorry about what's happening [between the US and Mexico at the regional level]"'. Interview with EU official (Brussels, 20 July 2012).

[81] Interview with WTO legal officer (Geneva, 18 April 2012).

[82] ibid.

[83] *Brazil–Measures Affecting Imports of Retreaded Tyres*, Report of the Appellate Body, 17 December 2007, WT/DS332/AB/R [*Brazil-Tyres* AB Report].

MERCOSUR law, which required MERCOSUR member states not to introduce new trade barriers of any kind between one another. In the wake of this ruling, Brazil adopted a revised regulation in 2004 that instituted an exemption to the import ban for the retreaded tyres originating in fellow members of MERCOSUR ('the MERCOSUR exemption').

This sequence of events led the EU—the primary exporter of retreaded tyres to Brazil prior to the ban[84]—to initiate legal proceedings against Brazil at the WTO. The EU claimed that Brazil's import ban violated the prohibition on quantitative restrictions in GATT Article XI and that the MERCOSUR exemption was inconsistent with Brazil's nondiscrimination obligations under GATT Articles I (MFN) and XIII (nondiscriminatory administration of quantitative restrictions). Brazil defended its position by invoking, inter alia, the exception in GATT Article XX(b), which offers immunity for trade-restrictive measures 'necessary to protect human, animal or plant life or health'.

In addressing this defence, the AB, similar to the strategy it adopted in other environment- and health-related cases, took a rather broad and deferential view of Brazil's regulatory measure at the first stage of the analysis of Article XX, where it examined whether the measure comes under one of the exceptions listed in paragraphs (a) to (j), in this case, the exception in paragraph (b).[85] At this stage, and although retreaded tyres 'contribute only indirectly to the health risks associated with the accumulation of waste tyres',[86] the AB ruled that Brazil's ban on imports of retreaded tyres was indeed 'necessary' to protect 'human, animal and plant life and health', thus upholding the panel's finding that the ban was provisionally justified under Article XX(b).[87] However, things took a different course when the AB turned to the second stage of the analysis under Article XX's chapeau, focusing on the manner in which Brazil's ban was applied, where the AB parted company with the panel and reversed the latter's (relatively RTA-friendly) decision on the MERCOSUR exemption.

And so, in a spirit somewhat different from that displayed by WTO judicial bodies in previous RTA-related disputes, the first-instance panel in *Brazil-Tyres* took a rather accommodating posture towards MERCOSUR, the RTA at issue, when examining the Brazilian import ban under the chapeau of Article XX. The chapeau, it should be recalled, requires WTO adjudicators to ensure that trade-restrictive measures found provisionally justified under one of the exceptions in paragraphs (a)–(j) of Article XX 'are not applied in a manner which would constitute a means

[84] Qin (n 22) 604–05.
[85] Interview with AB member (Jerusalem, 6 June 2012) (noting that the AB 'has given a rather broad interpretation of . . . Article XX' and that its approach has been 'rather broad in admitting an environmental exception' in this case).
[86] Qin (n 22) 622.
[87] *Brazil-Tyres* AB Report (n 83) para 212; *Brazil–Measures Affecting Imports of Retreaded Tyres*, Report of the Panel, 17 December 2007, WT/DS332/R, para 7.215 [*Brazil-Tyres* Panel Report].

of arbitrary or unjustifiable discrimination between countries where the same conditions prevail, or a disguised restriction on international trade'. In *Brazil-Tyres,* the panel found that although the MERCOSUR exemption had resulted in discrimination in the application of the import ban against non-MERCOSUR countries, such discrimination was not 'arbitrary' or 'unjustifiable' within the meaning of the chapeau.[88] First, according to the panel, the discrimination was not 'arbitrary' since the adoption of the MERCOSUR exemption was not 'motivated by capricious or unpredictable reasons' but by Brazil's legal obligation to comply with the MERCOSUR tribunal's ruling. In addition, the said ruling was delivered in the context of a trade liberalizing agreement among MERCOSUR member countries, with such agreements expressly recognized in GATT Article XXIV.[89] Second, the panel held that the discrimination resulting from the MERCOSUR exemption was not 'unjustifiable' because the volume of retreaded tyres imported from MERCOSUR countries, at the time of the panel's examination, had not been significant enough to undermine the import ban's ability to fulfil its intended objectives.[90] As a result, the panel found no violation of the chapeau of Article XX in this respect.[91]

When asked to shed light on the rationale underlying this uncommon deferential approach of the panel towards MERCOSUR and the regional tribunal's ruling that prompted the adoption of the MERCOSUR exemption, one of the WTO panellists sitting on the bench in *Brazil-Tyres* made the following remarks. He noted that in this case, the panel was well aware of the fact that if the MERCOSUR exemption were to be found WTO inconsistent, Brazil might find itself in a legal bind where it would not be able to comply with its obligations under the WTO without violating its obligations under MERCOSUR, pursuant to which the exemption had been adopted.[92] The panel's view was, consequently, that WTO adjudicators should not 'interpret the WTO agreements ... in a way that would put Members in conflict with their obligations under a regional trade agreement' 'if there is an alternative way of' interpreting the WTO agreements.[93] This panellist further stated that in cases where such an alternative interpretation is not available and 'a clear conflict' exists between WTO law and a Member's obligation under the respective RTA, 'all

88 *Brazil-Tyres* Panel Report (n 87) para 7.289.

89 ibid, paras 7.271–7.281.

90 ibid, paras 7.285–7.288.

91 Note, however, that at the end of the day the panel did find the Brazilian import ban to be applied in a manner that failed to meet the requirements of the chapeau of Article XX. This is due to the fact that, despite the existence of the import ban, imports of used tyres to Brazil were in effect allowed through court injunctions and in quite large quantities, what significantly undermined the ban's objectives. For this reason, the panel ultimately concluded that Brazil's ban was applied in a manner that constitutes unjustifiable discrimination and a disguised restriction to trade, and thus could not be justified under GATT Article XX. ibid, paras 7.356–7.357.

92 Interview with WTO panellist (Jerusalem, 6 June 2012).

93 ibid. A WTO legal officer involved in the *Brazil-Tyres* proceedings followed suit, stating: 'The panel's decision implies ... that Brazil, as a member of MERCOSUR, has legal obligations, that it has to obey these obligations, and that the panel recognizes this state of events, and that it is allowed to take that into account'. Interview with WTO legal officer (Geneva, 19 March 2012).

a WTO panel can do ... is to apply WTO law'. Nevertheless, if the issues involved remain cloudy, that is:

> If the conflict [between the RTA and WTO law] is not clear, then there ought to be some recognition given to ... the regional trade agreement, ... recognizing that ... WTO law includes, in fact, regional trade agreements, as Article XXIV says, [and] that they are legitimate parts of the international trading system.[94]

Another WTO official involved in the *Brazil-Tyers* panel proceedings went on to explain that from the panel's perspective, its guiding 'rationale' in the interpretative exercise in this case was to ensure that its decision would not put Brazil in a position impeding its ability to comply with the decisions of both the WTO DSS and the MERCOSUR tribunal:

> [W]hat comes out of the panel report is really that they wanted to make sure that there would not be contradiction [between the rulings of the two fora] ... [thereby] putting Brazil in the situation that they don't know what to do [because] ... [t]hey are basically [forced to act] illegal[ly] ... [with respect to the ruling of] one court ... or the other.[95]

'The AB', however, this same official continued, 'did not seem to worry about' the potential conflict between Brazils' obligations under MERCOSUR and the WTO. Whereas 'the panel was ready to be more flexible on the interpretation of the rules', the AB, as elaborated below, was more concerned with 'the legality of the [panel's] findings'[96] that, as Brink has noted, 'would have allowed WTO Members to circumvent the Article XX chapeau and discriminate in the application of their health and environment policies ... simply on the grounds that they were doing so pursuant to an obligation in *another* international agreement'.[97]

Hence, unlike the panel, whose interpretation of the chapeau indicated a predisposition to avoid any head-on conflict with the MERCOSUR ruling, the AB interpreted the chapeau 'in a way that it knew would require Brazil to breach its treaty obligation under MERCOSUR'.[98] Thus, in rejecting the panel's interpretation, the AB determined, first, that the 'assessment whether discrimination is arbitrary or unjustifiable' within the meaning of the chapeau 'should be made in the light of the objective of the measure' in question.[99] In this case, the AB stressed,

[94] Interview with WTO panellist (Jerusalem, 6 June 2012).
[95] Interview with WTO official (Geneva, 5 April 2012).
[96] ibid.
[97] Tegan Brink, 'Which WTO Rules Can a PTA Lawfully Breach? Completing the Analysis in Brazil-Tyres' (2010) 44 J World Trade 813, 816 (emphasis original).
[98] Qin (n 22) 626.
[99] *Brazil-Tyres* AB Report (n 83) para 227.

the 'discrimination between MERCOSUR countries and other WTO Members in the application of the Import Ban was introduced as a consequence of a ruling by a MERCOUSR tribunal'.[100] This ruling, according to the AB, 'was not an acceptable rationale' for the resulting discrimination because it bore no relationship to the legitimate environment- and health-related objectives pursued by the import ban; it even went against these objectives.[101] Accordingly, the AB concluded, the MERCOSUR exemption resulted in Brazil's import ban being applied in a manner that constitutes arbitrary or unjustifiable discrimination in contrast to the requirements indicated in the chapeau.[102] As a result, the ban could not be justified under Article XX as a whole.[103]

The AB's decision, determining that the MERCOSUR tribunal's ruling could not overcome the discipline of the Article XX chapeau and justify the discriminatory application of the import ban, 'left Brazil in a legal quandary'.[104] 'Brazil could not honour its treaty obligation under the WTO without breaching its obligation under MERCOSUR—and vice versa—unless it agreed to lift the import ban altogether, which was not an option given its declared environmental objective'.[105] The AB, for its part, was well aware of the complex legal situation that Brazil was about to face in the wake of its ruling, as suggested by the following statement of an AB member then sitting on the bench: 'The fact that there ... [was] a [MERCOSUR] decision out there ... meant that ... the [defending] country ... [was] subject to two contradictory injunctions from two different treaties'.[106] In justifying the AB's interpretative exercise, which contributed to this state of conflicting legal obligations at the regional and multilateral levels, the same AB member argued that:

> [W]e had to apply our law.... The judge has ... to exercise his jurisdiction according to the statute and the applicable law before him. He should, of course, not be half blinkered, he should look right and left, but he cannot go against the law that governments [have agreed upon], [or against] his [delegated] functions, simply because of something which is outside his jurisdiction.[107]

Others, however, have argued that the conflict of multilateral and regional obligations faced by Brazil subsequent to the AB's ruling was 'neither inherent nor inevitable'.[108] According to Qin, for example, this conflict arose purely as a result

[100] ibid, para 228.
[101] ibid.
[102] ibid.
[103] ibid, para 252.
[104] Qin (n 22) 609.
[105] ibid. A panellist involved in *Brazil-Tyres* similarly stressed that the AB's ruling 'effectively put Brazil in a position where it could not comply with the WTO obligations and its MERCOSUR obligations at the same time'. Interview with WTO panellist (Jerusalem, 6 June 2012).
[106] Interview with AB member (Geneva, 19 April 2012).
[107] ibid.
[108] Qin (n 22) 609.

of the interpretation adopted by the AB under the Article XX chapeau,[109] which 'showed no interest in facilitating Brazil's compliance with both sets of obligations and with the maintenance of the domestic regulatory scheme' that had already been found provisionally justifiable under Article XX(b).[110] As Howse has added in this regard:

> Had the Appellate Body taken a positive view of the co-existence of regional fora with the WTO dispute settlement system, it could easily have found that Brazil's discrimination in favour of MERCOSUR members was not unjustifiable – there is no definition of 'unjustifiable' in Article XX and no textual basis for confining acceptable justifications to those that pertain to the main purpose of the general regulatory scheme itself.[111]

As seen above, one alternative interpretation of the term 'unjustifiable' in Article XX, different from that adopted by the AB, was developed indeed by the panel.[112] Other interpretations of Article XX, as Qin has demonstrated, were also available.[113] Nevertheless, the AB—despite its reputation for developing new and evolutionary interpretations and for integrating WTO agreements with other areas of international law[114] (see Part II)—consciously chose to reverse the panel's finding on the MERCOSUR exemption and not to explore any interpretation that could avoid a collision with the legal prescriptions under MERCOSUR. When alluding to this choice, a WTO official involved in *Brazil-Tyres* interestingly distinguished the AB's approach to RTAs from its attitude towards other international agreements:

> [T]he AB has been consistently trying ... to build a case law of its own. So, ... there is always a little bit of reluctance to look too much for what's going on elsewhere, especially when what's going on elsewhere is very similar to what is going on in the WTO, ... when it is related to trade. It's a different matter when they are looking at other [international] agreements, for instance, CITES [the Convention on International Trade in Endangered Species, examined] in the *Shrimp* case, where ... they were looking [for] ... an authority on environmental protection. There, I think, they are quite fine to do that.... [The AB's ruling in *Brazil-Tyres*, however,] was meant to ... send a [different] message, that the law, the case law ... to be considered is the case law here, [of the WTO,] and not the trade case law developed by another institution.[115]

109 ibid 609–12.
110 Howse (n 25) 74.
111 ibid.
112 The alternative interpretation developed by the panel was discussed and rejected by the AB. See *Brazil-Tyres* AB Report (n 83) para 229.
113 Qin (n 22) 613–18.
114 ibid 618.
115 Interview with WTO official (Geneva, 5 April 2012).

This message and the low regard the AB held for the MERCOSUR tribunal's ruling and the obligation arising therefrom were not met with surprise in WTO circles; rather, they seemed a natural continuation of the AB's previous rulings in RTA-related cases. As a senior Brazilian official involved in *Brazil-Tyres* commented: 'when the Appellate Body reversed … [the panel's decision on the MERCOSUR exemption], it was not a surprise'. In fact, this official admitted: 'I … was surprised that the panel accepted the arguments' made by Brazil, which relied on the MERCOSUR tribunal's decision.[116]

The picture emerging from this incident, where the AB found that although Brazil was acting pursuant to its MERCOSUR obligations it was still required to meet the requirements of the GATT, particularly, in this case, the chapeau of Article XX,[117] suggests that in *Brazil-Tyres,* the AB was following the same goal-attainment efforts marking its previous RTA-related jurisprudence. That is, the AB was working to preserve the autonomy of the WTO regime and to espouse the supremacy of WTO principles and rules over those of RTAs.[118] For this purpose, the AB further limited the ability of Members to contract out of their WTO obligations and discriminate against other WTO Members by means of an RTA.[119] As a WTO practitioner involved in the case stated, a comparison of the AB's ruling in *Brazil-Tyres* with its rulings in cases such as *Mexico-Soft Drinks* strongly suggests 'that, implicitly, what it is doing, intentionally or unintentionally, is setting the supremacy of WTO law' vis-à-vis RTA law[120] despite the lack of hierarchical relationships between the WTO and RTAs under international law.[121]

When responding to the criticism ultimately levelled at the AB's ruling in *Brazil-Tyres,*[122] urging WTO adjudicators 'to get in dialogue between … courts' so as to avoid such incidents of conflicting obligations, one AB member went on to explain the regime maintenance goal behind this ruling in these words: 'if the WTO [adjudicative] system were to take into account the MERCOSUR, the ASEAN, the African community' or the various other RTAs operating alongside the WTO, 'the [WTO] system then … would be too easy to evade'.[123] Continuing along this path, an EU official made the following comment as he situated the *Brazil-Tyres* ruling in the broader context of increasing regionalism and the threats it poses to the multilateral system of international trade:

[116] Interview with senior Brazilian official (Geneva, 5 July 2012).

[117] Jennifer Hillman, 'Conflicts Between Dispute Settlement Mechanisms in Regional Trade Agreements and the WTO—What Should the WTO Do?' (2009) 42 Cornell Int'l LJ 193, 194–95.

[118] Nikolaos Lavranos, 'The Brazilian Tyres Case: Trade Supersedes Health' (2009) 1 Trade L & Dev 230, 253; Qin (n 22) 622.

[119] Langille (n 21) 1510.

[120] Interview with WTO panellist (Jerusalem, 6 June 2012). See also interview with EU official (Brussels, 20 July 2012).

[121] Qin (n 22) 623.

[122] For relevant criticism, see, for example, Lavranos (n 118); Qin (n 22).

[123] Interview with former AB member (Jerusalem, 6 June 2012).

> [W]hat happened [in this case] is that the Appellate Body realized that in the future, there will be more regional integration ... organizations, and that ... you cannot ... put in danger the WTO system just because ... [those] regional integration organizations [are out there].... [I]t is WTO litigation, so in principle, the WTO Appellate Body should give preference to the GATT [Agreement].[124]

In concluding his observations, this official stressed that 'if a WTO decision can ignore or put aside a domestic measure, why are they not entitled to do the same thing with a regional measure or a regional decision?'[125] As will be seen below, this spirit of isolation from and ascendancy over regionalism, aimed at strengthening the multilateral trade system, was no less prominent in the more recent dispute that arose at the WTO-RTA substantive legal interface, known as *Peru-Agricultural Products*.[126]

The Quest to Sustain Multilateralism Continues: *Peru-Agricultural Products* and the Interpretation or Modification of WTO Law by Means of an RTA

The *Peru-Agricultural Products* case revolved around a complaint brought by Guatemala against Peru's 'Price Range System' (PRS), a tariff regime triggering additional duties on imports of selected agricultural products should their prices fall below a certain floor. According to Guatemala, the PRS constituted a 'variable import levy', incompatible with Article 4.2 of the WTO Agreement on Agriculture, as well as 'other duties or charges', in contradiction to Peru's commitment under Article II of the GATT. However, in an RTA signed by Peru and Guatemala in 2011, the two had agreed that 'Peru may maintain its Price Range System' (so that the PRS, claimed to be in violation of WTO law, was allegedly permissible under the RTA). Guatemala and Peru also agreed in the respective RTA that 'in the event of any inconsistency' between WTO agreements and the RTA, the latter 'shall prevail'. These RTA provisions were later invoked by Peru when defending the WTO violations associated with the PRS before the WTO DSS, thus arousing fundamental questions concerning the interaction between WTO and RTA rules, most notably, the question of whether an RTA concluded between a subset of WTO Members can 'influence or change the interpretation or application of WTO treaty provisions' as they apply between those specific Members.[127]

124 Interview with EU official (Brussels, 20 July 2012).
125 ibid.
126 *Peru–Additional Duty on Imports of Certain Agricultural Products*, Report of the Appellate Body, 31 July 2015, WT/DS457/AB/R [*Peru-Agricultural Products* AB Report].
127 Joost Pauwelyn, 'Interplay between the WTO Treaty and Other International Legal Instruments and Tribunals: Evolution After 20 Years of WTO Jurisprudence' (2016) 17 <https://ssrn.com/

When called upon to decide the case in 2015, the AB could have avoided delving into these intricate, sensitive questions by simply following the panel's finding that the RTA between Guatemala and Peru (ratified by Guatemala only) had not yet entered into force; hence, its provisions were not legally binding on the parties.[128] Instead, the AB took a considerably different approach. After confirming the panel's findings of violation of Article 4.2 of the Agreement on Agriculture and Article II of the GATT,[129] the AB began to tackle head on the issue of the relationship between the respective WTO provisions and the RTA, irrespective of its status. In so doing, as will be explained below, the AB refused to absolve the Peruvian PRS of the WTO violations identified based on any of the RTA-related defences raised by Peru in a judicial exercise that significantly restricted the possible impact RTA rules might have on WTO obligations by means of either interpretation or modification.

The first defence raised by Peru when attempting to exonerate itself of the WTO-inconsistencies associated with its PRS was that under customary rules of interpretation, the WTO provisions at issue should be interpreted in light of the provisions of the RTA between Peru and Guatemala. More specifically, Peru argued that the RTA concluded with Guatemala—which stipulated in paragraph 9 of Annex 2.3 that Peru may maintain the PRS—was pertinent to the interpretation of the WTO provisions applicable to the case as a 'subsequent agreement between the parties', and as other 'relevant rules of international law applicable in the relations between the parties' within the meaning of Article 31(3) of the Vienna Convention on the Law of Treaties (VCLT).[130] The AB dismissed this defence.

First, the AB determined that any interpretation of WTO provisions in light of an RTA—either as a 'subsequent agreement' or as other 'relevant rules' applicable between the parties under VCLT Article 31(3)—cannot go against the explicit text of the WTO treaty, as was the case here, with WTO rules, as previously interpreted by the AB, explicitly prohibiting Peru's PRS.[131] Second, the AB stated that according to its understanding of VCLT Article 31(1), the WTO treaty, as a multilateral treaty, was to be interpreted 'as a whole', in a manner establishing the 'common intentions' of all WTO Members and 'not just the intentions of some of the parties', for example, Peru and Guatemala.[132] To do otherwise 'would suggest that WTO provisions can be interpreted differently, depending on the Members to which they apply and on their rights and obligations under an FTA to which they

abstract=2731144> accessed 22 December 2018. Forthcoming in C E Côté, V Guèvremont, and R Ouellet (eds), *Proceedings of the Québec City Conference on the WTO at 20* (2018).

[128] *Peru-Additional Duty on Imports of Certain Agricultural Products*, Report of the Panel, 31 July 2015, WT/DS457/AB/R, paras 7.526–7.528, 8.1.f [*Peru-Agricultural Products* Panel Report].

[129] *Peru-Agricultural Products* AB Report (n 126) paras 5.61, 5.108. See also paras 6.6(a) and (b).

[130] ibid, paras 5.91, 5.98.

[131] ibid, paras 5.93–5.94.

[132] ibid, para 5.95.

are parties'.[133] Finally, the AB placed further limits on the interpretation of WTO provisions with reference to an RTA's rules by stressing that in order to inform the WTO interpretative process, such 'other rules' must be '*relevant*', that is, 'bearing specifically upon the interpretation' of the WTO provisions at issue.[134] Hence, rather than examining whether the RTA provisions were 'rules applicable in the relations between the parties', the AB chose to focus its examination on whether they could be considered 'relevant' to the interpretation of the WTO articles under discussion.[135] In this respect, the AB found that by stating that Peru 'may maintain its PRS', the RTA between Peru and Guatemala provided no ' "relevant" interpretative guidance' to the construction of Article 4.2 of the Agreement on Agriculture nor to the interpretation of GATT Article II.[136]

Following this line of reasoning, the AB rejected the first RTA-based defence invoked by Peru. In so doing, it significantly raised the bar for a regional trade agreement to be available for the purpose of interpreting WTO provisions[137] in what appears to be a clear attempt of the AB, in its heightened role as the guardian of the WTO legal system, to protect the coherence of the multilateral trade rules and prevent their fragmented application in times of RTA proliferation.

A similar exclusionary approach towards RTAs was exhibited by the AB when it turned to address the second defence implicit in Peru's arguments, according to which the provisions of the RTA permitting it to maintain the WTO-inconsistent PRS modified the WTO provisions at issue inter se, that is, within the bilateral relations of Peru and Guatemala, in accordance with VCLT Article 41 on inter se treaty modifications.[138] Importantly, prior to addressing this defence, the AB concluded, based on its reading of several RTA provisions, that there was an 'ambiguity' as to whether the RTA at all allowed Peru to maintain the WTO-inconsistent PRS.[139] This conclusion, in turn, could have ended the entire discussion. Nevertheless, the AB chose to continue its analysis, 'assuming *arguendo*' that the RTA provisions allowed Peru to maintain the PRS.[140] In following this path, as seen below, the AB seized the opportunity to declare that Peru could not modify its WTO commitments through the RTA and, more generally, that WTO Members' ability to

[133] ibid, para 5.106.

[134] ibid, para 101.

[135] James Mathis, 'WTO Appellate Body, Peru–Additional Duty on Imports of Certain Agricultural Products, WT/DS457/AB/R, 20 July 2015' (2016) 43 Legal Issues Econ Integration 97, 100.

[136] *Peru-Agricultural Products* AB Report (n 126) para 5.103.

[137] Mathis (n 135) 101; Pauwelyn (n 127) 20–21, 26.

[138] Note that this defence was explicitly raised by Peru before the panel (see *Peru-Agricultural Products* AB Report (n 126) para 5.111). However, Peru focused its defence before the AB on the 'interpretation' of WTO provisions, as discussed above. Yet, as the AB rightly observed, on appeal as well Peru implicitly argued that the RTA concluded with Guatemala had 'modified' its obligations towards Guatemala (ibid, paras 5.96–5.97). This defence, as well, was consequently addressed in the AB's ruling.

[139] *Peru-Agricultural Products* AB Report (n 126) paras 5.109–5.110.

[140] ibid, para 5.111.

contract out of their WTO obligations via RTAs was not governed by the general provisions of the VCLT, such as Article 41, but by the terms of WTO law itself.

And so, in rejecting Peru's second defence, the AB found that VCLT Article 41, allowing a subset of members to a multilateral treaty to modify the treaty inter se through a subsequent agreement, could not serve as a basis for two WTO Members to modify WTO rules via an RTA and to permit an otherwise WTO-inconsistent measure to hold between themselves. According to the AB, the WTO contains its own provisions for amendments, waivers, as well as exceptions for RTAs, 'which prevail over the general provisions of the Vienna Convention'.[141] As a result, the AB determined that 'the proper routes' for assessing the lawfulness of RTA provisions departing from certain WTO rules 'are the WTO provisions that permit the formation of regional trade agreements', in this case, GATT Article XXIV, which Peru did not invoke.[142]

At this juncture, and even though Peru did not raise Article XXIV as a defence for its WTO-inconsistent PRS,[143] the AB went still further to reaffirm the strict two-prong test developed in *Turkey-Textiles*, according to which Article XXIV could justify a WTO-inconsistent measure provided that: (i) the measure at issue was introduced upon the formation of an RTA that fully meets the requirements of Article XXIV, and (ii) the formation of the RTA would be prevented if the introduction of the measure was not allowed.[144] In recounting this test, however, the AB did not address the different contexts of the two cases, namely, the fact that in *Turkey-Textiles*, 'the test was applied to set the conditions for validating a measure that violated a *third party's* right in the WTO', whereas in *Peru-Agricultural Products*, the test was applied to a measure that violated WTO law 'only between the *regional members* themselves'.[145] Instead, what the AB did here, when faced with a measure that was not only WTO inconsistent but which raised hurdles to regional trade and placed the party to the RTA in a less favourable position as compared with other WTO Members, was to reinforce its strict reading of Article XXIV by adding that this provision is aimed at 'facilitating trade and closer integration' among RTA parties, and thus cannot be interpreted 'as a broad defence' for measures in RTAs 'that roll back on Members' rights and obligations under the WTO agreements'.[146]

The above judicial move taken by the AB is remarkable. In this interpretative act, the AB suggested, in effect, that 'WTO Members had contracted out of Article 41 of the Vienna Convention through the WTO's own rules on amendments and exceptions',[147] and 'that, *even* where trade with *other* WTO Members is *unaffected*, any

[141] ibid, para 5.112.
[142] ibid, para 5.113.
[143] ibid, para 5.114.
[144] ibid, para 5.115.
[145] Mathis (n 135) 103–04 (emphasis original).
[146] *Peru-Agricultural Products* AB Report (n 126) para 5.116.
[147] Gregory Shaffer and Alan L Winters, 'FTA Law in WTO Dispute Settlement: Peru-Additional Duty and the Fragmentation of Trade Law' (2017) 16 World Trade Rev 303, 320.

attempt by two or more Members to modify WTO obligations among themselves must pass through the relevant WTO legal architecture'.[148] As Howse and Langille have stated when pointing to the systemic goals lurking behind this judicial course of action:

> This arguably goes beyond the obvious purpose of ensuring that . . . [RTAs] do not lead to more restrictive trade with third countries, or to ensuring that they in general result in freer trade, *to assuring the unity and integrity of the WTO as a legal system*. . . . Here the Appellate Body adopts an approach to *preserve the relative autonomy and universality of a multilateral regime under pressure from 'spaghetti-bowl' fragmentation*.[149]

The AB's controversial interpretative exercise,[150] as delineated above, was thus referred to by Pauwelyn, along similar lines, as the AB's 'defensive attempt to shelter the WTO from outside (FTA) attack'.[151] Arguably, since the WTO legal text does not explicitly prohibit inter se modifications, the AB could have opted for other interpretations that do recognize Members' contractual freedom under the general provisions of the VCLT to amend and update the trade rules applying in their bilateral relations.[152] The AB in *Peru-Agricultural Products*, however, 'did not leave any room' for the application of those provisions 'in the WTO legal space with respect to RTAs'.[153] Instead, it made it very clear that while the WTO legal order forms part of international law, it would be misplaced to interpret the question of derogability of WTO law through the lens of the general rules of the VCLT and to assume, in consequence, that WTO commitments 'can seamlessly be amended bilaterally between two WTO members' via an RTA.[154] As Tietje and Lang have noted, any other interpretative approach would have gone 'against the normative duty of the Appellate Body to protect the integrity and coherence of the WTO's legal system'.[155]

Peru-Agricultural Products and the goal-attainment efforts it encompasses thus fit in perfectly with the other RTA-related cases reviewed earlier, all addressing questions that emerge at the substantive legal interface between WTO law and RTAs. Common to all these and other RTA-related disputes (involving safeguard measures, among others)[156] is the attempt to reinforce the stature of the WTO vis-à-vis

[148] Howse and Langille (n 3) 678 (emphasis original). See also Zang (n 18) 21.

[149] Howse and Langille (n 3) 678 (emphasis added).

[150] For a critique of this interpretative move and its legal consequences, see Pauwelyn (n 127) 21–24; Shaffer and Winters (n 147) 320–21; Zang (n 18) 20–23.

[151] Pauwelyn (n 127) 22.

[152] Shaffer and Winters (n 147) 322; Sherzod Shadikhodjaev, 'The "Regionalism vs Multilateralism" Issue in International Trade Law: Revisiting the *Peru-Agricultural Products* Case' (2017) 16 Chinese J Int'l L 109, 120.

[153] Shadikhodjaev (n 152) 120.

[154] Christian Tietje and Andrej Lang, 'Community Interests in World Trade Law' in Eyal Benvenisti and Georg Nolte (eds), *Community Interests Across International Law* (OUP 2018) 207.

[155] ibid.

[156] For a discussion of those cases, see de Mestral (n 18) 791–94; Langille (n 21) 1509–10.

RTAs, uphold its objectives and principles (most notably: nondiscrimination), as well as augment the stability of the multilateral trade rules at a time when regional agreements and negotiations thrive and the WTO political and diplomatic process struggles to overcome its stagnation. In pursuing these goals, we have shown, the DSS, as led by the AB, has consistently worked to secure compliance with WTO obligations and to make deviations therefrom more difficult, not the least by limiting the scope of legal exceptions and defences that may offer shelter to the WTO-inconsistent measures adopted by Members in the context of their RTA-related activities. The DSS has likewise displayed 'no interest in treaty interpretations that could accommodate or facilitate harmonious co-existence with regional regimes',[157] maintaining instead a rather strict separation between the multilateral and regional trading systems despite the fact that the latter are explicitly recognized in WTO agreements.

Similar goal-attainment efforts to those envisioned at the WTO-RTA substantive legal nexus, as we will now see, have been introduced at the complementary WTO-RTA jurisdictional intersection. There, panels, together with the AB, have sought to uphold the WTO DSS's judicial authority and, thereby, the system's ability to enforce WTO substantive legal commitments. With a view to achieving these ends, panels and the AB have not only refused to defer, or refer, to RTA jurisprudence and proceedings, but have significantly constrained the extent to which Members may contract out of the DSU via RTAs in ways compromising the DSS's jurisdiction and the right of Members to WTO adjudication.

10.4 Goal Attainment at the WTO-RTA Jurisdictional Nexus

Woven into the jurisprudence generated at the WTO-RTA substantive legal nexus is another, interrelated strand of jurisprudence, the one dealing with the jurisdictional friction between the WTO and RTAs and the effects of regional dispute settlement mechanisms on the WTO DSS. At this jurisdictional juncture, the co-existence of the WTO DSS alongside multiple RTA dispute settlement fora raises various intricacies, most prominently, perhaps, those relating to the possibility that a dispute will be brought under both the WTO and RTA adjudicative mechanisms.[158] Since considerable overlap is found in the subject matter of the WTO agreements and RTAs, with the latter often referring to the WTO explicitly or even incorporating substantial portions of WTO treaty language,[159] 'a legally and/or

[157] Howse (n 25) 75.

[158] World Trade Report 2011 (n 12) 173; Howse and Langille (n 3) 679.

[159] For an overview, see Todd Allee, Manfred Elsig, and Andrew Lugg, 'The Ties between the World Trade Organization and Preferential Trade Agreements: A Textual Analysis' (2017) 20 J Int'l Econ L 333.

factually identical dispute', or some of its aspects, can be brought before either or both the multilateral and the regional dispute settlement venues.[160] The overlapping and competing jurisdictions of these adjudicative mechanisms may lead, in turn, to forum shopping, waste of resources, loss of predictability, and conflicting decisions, what may ultimately intensify the fragmentation of international trade law.[161]

Awareness of this jurisdictional overlap and the possibility of parallel proceedings at the multilateral and regional levels have prompted RTAs to adopt a number of approaches as to how they regulate the relationship and potential jurisdictional conflicts between their own dispute settlement mechanism and that of the WTO. The most common among these approaches takes the form of a forum exclusion clause (also known as a 'fork-in-the-road' clause), which allows the party initiating the dispute to choose between the multilateral or the RTA forum. However, once that party has initiated the dispute in one forum, the other option (be it the RTA mechanism or the multilateral one) is no longer available to it.[162]

In the WTO, on the other hand, Article 23 of the DSU, entitled 'Strengthening of the Multilateral System', mandates that WTO Members shall have recourse to the rules and procedures of the DSU when seeking redress of a violation of the WTO covered agreements. The AB elaborated that this provision 'lays down a fundamental obligation of WTO Members' to settle disputes under the covered agreements in accordance with the DSU and 'establishes the WTO dispute settlement system as the exclusive forum for the resolution of such disputes'.[163] While DSU Article 23 does not explicitly state that the WTO DSS is hierarchically superior to RTA dispute settlement mechanisms,[164] neither Article 23 nor any other DSU provision sets out rules on how to resolve cases of jurisdictional overlap between the WTO and RTAs, and on whether the WTO DSS should relinquish its jurisdiction on certain occasions in order to overcome the emerging fragmentation issues between the multilateral and regional dispute settlement systems.[165] As an AB member stated in this regard:

> There is nothing ... in the DSU which tells us that you have to take [regional dispute settlement fora] into consideration.... Not only that, but you have a clause of exclusiveness, that any dispute that falls within the [WTO] agreements should be exclusively decided within the system. That is not what states do [however],

[160] Howse and Langille (n 3) 679. See also World Trade Report 2011 (n 12) 173.

[161] Lanyi and Steinbach (n 17).

[162] World Trade Report 2011 (n 12) 173.

[163] *United States–Continued Suspension of Obligations in the EC–Hormones Dispute*, Report of the Appellate Body, 14 November 2008, WT/DS320/AB/R, para 371.

[164] Howse and Langille (n 3) 679.

[165] Songling Yang, 'The Solution for Jurisdictional Conflicts Between the WTO and RTAs: The Forum Choice Clause' (2014) 23 Mich St Int'l L Rev 107, 110; Songling Yang, 'The Key Role of the WTO in Settling its Jurisdictional Conflicts with RTAs' (2012) 11 Chinese J Int'l L 281.

> because all these cases of NAFTA—*Softwood Lumber, Soft Drinks*, etc., ... are played like games of ping-pong between ... NAFTA and [the WTO].... So, in a way, that is the great danger of the free trade areas ... they are ... taking out the substance of the general system. And [in] the general system, we ... have a rule of exclusiveness.[166]

In this state of affairs, and despite the negative effects associated with possible misuses of the overlapping dispute settlement mechanisms, in cases featuring aspects that 'spill over' between a regional forum and the WTO DSS, WTO adjudicators, as demonstrated below, have shifted much of their efforts to assert the autonomy, 'if not a certain kind of supremacy ... of the WTO dispute settlement system'.[167] Thus, seeking to avert potential interference with the integrity of WTO adjudication and rule enforcement against the spread of regional trade arrangements and dispute settlement fora, WTO panels, like the AB, have consistently manifested their unwillingness to engage in a discourse with RTA adjudicative systems, defer to their judgments or suspend proceedings pending the outcome of a related dispute.[168] Rather than pursuing such routes or otherwise applying comity towards international fora with overlapping jurisdictions on trade matters, WTO adjudicators, in all relevant RTA-related cases thus far, have chosen to give precedence to their own jurisdiction, that is, to their power to look into claims, undertake legal analysis and deliver a WTO judgment.[169] While doing so, they have consequently established a distinctively high bar for RTA parties to reach before they can waive their right to WTO judicial review.

As a private attorney and former state delegate put it, the unequivocal 'message' emerging from the WTO cases exhibiting jurisdictional linkage between the WTO and RTAs is that '[i]f there is concurrent jurisdiction, you [should] come here [to the WTO].... Even though you may litigate [your case] ... in a regional tribunal, you are welcome here anytime you want'. In fact, this informant added, the message sent by WTO panels and the AB is far stronger: 'Whenever the coin falls on our table, we're gonna take it. And only in very extreme situations, we're gonna drop the coin to a regional tribunal'.[170]

166 Interview with AB member (Geneva, 19 April 2012). This point was also stressed by other interviewees. See, e.g. interview with EU official (Brussels, 20 July 2012).

167 Howse (n 25) 73, 75.

168 ibid 73–74; Caroline Henckels, 'Overcoming Jurisdictional Isolationism at the WTO-FTA Nexus: A Potential Approach for the WTO' (2008) 19 EJIL 571, 576–79.

169 See Andrew D Mitchell, 'The Legal Basis for Using Principles in WTO Disputes' (2007) 10 J Int'l Econ L 795, 821 (referring to jurisdiction as the power of WTO panels and the AB 'to hear claims and proceedings, examine and determine the facts, interpret and apply the law, ... and declare judgments').

170 Interview with former Mexican official (Geneva, 12 July 2012).

The Case Law: From *Argentina-Poultry* to *Peru-Agricultural Products*, and in Between

The first such dispute to arouse the jurisdictional tension between the WTO and RTAs was *Argentina-Poultry*,[171] where the problem of sequential proceedings (and, consequently, conflicting decisions) with respect to the same measure at the regional and the multilateral fora presented itself. In this case, Brazil brought a WTO complaint against Argentina's anti-dumping duties, which Brazil had previously challenged, unsuccessfully, before a MERCOSUR tribunal. In light of the prior MERCOSUR proceedings, Argentina raised a preliminary objection asking the WTO panel to refrain from ruling on Brazil's claim on the grounds that Brazil had breached its obligation to act in 'good faith' by initiating WTO dispute settlement proceedings against the same anti-dumping measure after having lost the case at the regional level.[172] Argentina also invoked the principle of estoppel, arguing that Brazil, given its actions in MERCOSUR, should be 'estopped' from challenging the same measure before the WTO DSS.[173] Brazil countered by arguing that even if the measure challenged in both cases was the same, the dispute before the MERCOSUR tribunal was grounded on a different legal basis from the dispute before the WTO panel, and that in bringing the case to the WTO it was simply exercising its rights under the DSU.[174] Siding with Brazil, the panel dismissed Argentina's preliminary objection in its entirety.

As to good faith, the panel observed, while citing previous AB jurisprudence, that two conditions must be satisfied before a Member may be found to have failed to act in good faith: First, there must be a violation of a substantive provision of the WTO agreements; second, there must be something 'more than mere violation'[175] (e.g. an egregious breach).[176] However, given that Argentina did not allege a violation of any substantive WTO obligation, there was no basis to conclude that Brazil violated the principle of good faith in initiating the present proceedings.[177]

Similarly, the panel found no room for a plea of estoppel, noting that there was 'no evidence on the record that Brazil made an express statement that it would not bring WTO dispute settlement proceedings in respect of measures previously challenged through MERCOSUR'.[178] In this respect, the panel alluded, inter alia, to the fact that the MERCOSUR choice-of-forum provision to which Argentina

[171] *Argentina–Definitive Anti-Dumping Duties on Poultry from Brazil*, Report of the Panel, 19 May 2003, WT/DS241/R.

[172] ibid, paras 7.17–7.18, 7.34.

[173] ibid, paras 7.18, 7.37.

[174] ibid, paras 7.22–7.24. Note that the dispute before the WTO DSS offered an assessment of Argentina's anti-dumping duties in light of rules under the WTO Agreement on Anti-Dumping that do not exist under MERCOSUR.

[175] *Argentina-Poultry* (n 171) paras 7.35–7.36.

[176] Howse and Langille (n 3) 681.

[177] *Argentina-Poultry* (n 171) para 7.36.

[178] ibid, para 7.38.

referred in its arguments (noting that bringing the dispute to the RTA exhausted WTO options, and vice versa) was not yet in force.[179] The panel further reasoned that the fact that Brazil had chosen not to pursue WTO proceedings after previous MERCOSUR rulings did not mean that Brazil had implicitly waived its right to a judgment under the DSU.[180]

Hence, despite the binding effect of the MERCOSUR ruling on the parties, the WTO panel's 'default reaction', as a former WTO official described it, was that 'unless there is a very clear legal basis, we will not decline jurisdiction'.[181] Having insisted on its jurisdiction, the panel turned to address the alternative argument raised by Argentina in this case. Here Argentina contended that if Brazil were entitled to bring the case to the WTO, then the panel should be 'bound' by the earlier MERCOSUR tribunal's ruling on the measure at issue.[182] According to Argentina, the MERCOSUR ruling formed part of the normative framework to be applied by the panel pursuant to VCLT Article 31(3), which requires that other 'relevant rules of international law applicable in the relations between the parties' be taken into account for the purpose of treaty interpretation.[183] The panel rejected this argument as well, explaining that in raising its claim, Argentina was not asking the panel to 'interpret specific provisions of the WTO agreements in a particular way' but to actually 'rule' in a particular way—something the panel believed it was not authorized to do.[184] Furthermore, in a rather critical tone, the panel concluded by stating that WTO panels 'are not even bound to follow rulings contained in adopted WTO panel reports, so we see no reason at all why we should be bound by the rulings of non-WTO dispute settlement bodies'.[185]

As Langille has noted, '[h]ere the panel asserted the hierarchy of WTO dispute settlement proceedings'.[186] In its effort to entrench the authority of the WTO DSS vis-à-vis regional adjudicative mechanisms, the panel in *Argentina-Poultry* expressed disinterest in mutual accommodation of DSU and RTA proceedings and made it eminently clear that 'if any rule was violated by refusal to take a decision of a MERCOSUR tribunal into account' in WTO proceedings, 'it was that of MERCOSUR' and not the DSU.[187]

The panel ruling in *Argentina-Poultry* resonates with the decision rendered in the later *US-Softwood Lumber* dispute between Canada and the United States,[188]

[179] ibid.
[180] ibid.
[181] Interview with former WTO legal officer (Geneva, 16 July 2012).
[182] *Argentina-Poultry* (n 171) paras 7.17, 7.40.
[183] ibid, paras 7.18, 7.40.
[184] ibid, para 7.41.
[185] ibid.
[186] Langille (n 21) 1512.
[187] de Mestral (n 18) 811.
[188] *United States–Investigation of the International Trade Commission in Softwood Lumber from Canada, Recourse to Article 21.5 of the DSU by Canada*, Report of the Panel, 9 May 2006, WT/DS277/RW [*US-Softwood Lumber* Panel Report].

where the WTO panel again showed 'no sense of ... "judicial comity"' to earlier Canada-US bi-national panels under Chapter 19 of NAFTA, which dealt with essentially the same issues related to anti-dumping and countervailing duties imposed by the United States on Canadian lumber.[189] While Canada sought to use the NAFTA panels' decisions to support its WTO complaint, the WTO panel did 'not make a single reference to the concurrent NAFTA Chapter 19 proceedings',[190] and only agreed to include them in a footnote, where it explained that references to these decisions were inappropriate.[191]

The panel's decision in *Argentina-Poultry* likewise closely corresponds to the spirit of the AB's ruling in *Brazil-Tyres,* discussed earlier in this chapter, where the AB was unwilling to take into account the MERCOSUR tribunal's ruling in its interpretation of the GATT Article XX chapeau and to allow Brazil to premise its actions on this non-WTO legal decision. Rather than applying judicial comity towards the MERCOSUR tribunal, the AB chose to uphold its own authority to interpret and pass judgment on the relevant trade rules.[192] Alluding to the AB's choice and its underlying goals, while situating *Brazil-Tyres* in the broader reality of RTA proliferation, a WTO practitioner involved in the case stated:

> [D]eal[ing] with regional trade arrangements.... is a fundamental issue facing the [WTO dispute settlement] system. And the reason that it hasn't become more of an issue is that we don't have a vibrant dispute settlement process operating under the other systems, but as soon as we have a vibrant dispute settlement process [the problem will intensify].... [So] the Appellate Body [in *Brazil-Tyres*] is looking ahead and ... is setting the primacy [of the WTO DSS] so that they never have to deal with it when it happens.[193]

Elaborating further, this interviewee stressed that the growing friction between RTAs and the WTO is 'an unresolved issue that states ... are not prepared to address ... in the WTO'. The AB, however, 'does have to address it' whenever a dispute in the WTO-RTA context arises, and then it does that 'in a hierarchic way ... "the Appellate Body ... is the boss"'.[194] When later drawing a comparison between the AB and the International Court of Justice (ICJ), this interviewee added: 'Look at the International Court of Justice when other dispute settlement systems were developing, the presidents started to cry out ... "we're the premier, we're the prior one" .... I think it's the nature of a tribunal to assert its jurisdiction'.[195]

[189] Joost Pauwelyn, 'Adding Sweeteners to Softwood Lumber: The WTO-NAFTA "Spaghetti Bowl" is Cooking' (2006) 9 J Int'l Econ L 197, 202; de Mestral (n 18) 798.
[190] Pauwelyn (n 189) 202.
[191] *US-Softwood Lumber* Panel Report (n 188) fn 12.
[192] Langille (n 21) 1511.
[193] Interview with WTO panellist (Jerusalem, 6 June 2012).
[194] ibid.
[195] ibid.

This position was all the more apparent in the *Mexico-Soft Drinks* dispute, where both the panel and the AB affirmed their authority to decide a case even after an RTA's dispute settlement procedures had been invoked.[196] In this case, discussed earlier in the context of the GATT Article XX(d) defence raised by Mexico, the latter argued, as a preliminary matter, that the WTO panel should decline exercising its jurisdiction to hear the present dispute. Mexico reasoned that the case was 'inextricably linked to a broader dispute' over trade in sugar between the parties under NAFTA, where Mexico had already requested a panel, and which formed the appropriate forum for resolving the larger US-Mexico 'sugar war'.[197] Importantly, although the NAFTA includes a fork-in-the-road provision (stating that once dispute settlement procedures have been initiated under the NAFTA or the WTO, that forum is to be used to the exclusion of the other), Mexico did not place this provision before the WTO panel nor did it suggest that there were any other jurisdictional impediments to the panel hearing the case. Instead, it accepted that the panel 'had the authority to rule on the merits' of the US claims but argued that the panel, as an international adjudicative body, possessed the 'implied jurisdictional powers' necessary to refrain from ruling in the circumstances of the present case.[198]

In a preliminary ruling, the panel rejected Mexico's request. Elaborating on this rejection while shedding light on the panel's resolve to exercise jurisdiction in this RTA-related dispute, a panellist sitting on the bench noted:

> [W]e had to respond [to Mexico's request that the panel refrain from exercising jurisdiction] and we had to respond in a clear and sound way. But there was no hesitation.... in the panel as to whether we had jurisdiction or not in this case. They [i.e. the Mexicans] were in breach of a WTO obligation. And ... that is what we were examining. What was behind that is something that we've always tried to separate.[199]

Following this logic, and based on its reading of several DSU provisions, the panel ultimately found that 'under the DSU, it had no discretion to decide whether or not to exercise its jurisdiction in a case properly before it'.[200] The AB, in turn, upheld the panel's finding and the thrust of its legal reasoning. While recognizing that panels do have certain implied powers that are inherent in their adjudicative function, such as the power to determine whether they have jurisdiction in a given case and the scope of that jurisdiction,[201] the AB held that despite these powers, the

196 Langille (n 21) 1512.
197 *Mexico-Soft Drinks* AB Report (n 55) paras 40, 42, 54.
198 ibid, para 44.
199 Interview with WTO panellist (Geneva, 24 July 2012).
200 *Mexico-Soft Drinks* Panel Report (n 56) para 7.1.
201 *Mexico-Soft Drinks* AB Report (n 55) para 45.

relevant text of the DSU *requires* panels to make a ruling on the merits of a dispute once jurisdiction has been validly established.[202] And so, being loath to use the inherent discretionary power of WTO adjudicators to apply comity and co-operate with the regional dispute settlement forum, the AB in *Mexico-Soft Drinks*, as elaborated below, chose to follow a 'strict textual' interpretation of the DSU.[203]

The AB's textual reading of the treaty took the following path. First, the AB reasoned that a panel's refusal to exercise jurisdiction in a case properly before it would breach its obligation under DSU Article 11 to 'make an objective assessment of the matter before it'.[204] Turning to DSU Article 23, the AB then argued for the 'entitlement' of Members to a WTO ruling, derived from WTO Members' obligation to have recourse to the DSS when seeking to resolve a dispute under the WTO covered agreements.[205] According to the AB, as paraphrased by a private attorney, '[n]ot only do you have an obligation to use the [WTO dispute settlement] system, but you are entitled to resolution under this system.... [Y]ou are entitled to that resolution as much as you are obliged to bring the problem to us'.[206] In light of this reading, the AB found that if a panel were to decline jurisdiction over a particular dispute, it would effectively 'diminish the rights' of a WTO Member under the DSU[207] (contrary to the language of DSU Articles 3.2 and 19.2).[208] As a result, the AB concluded by reiterating the panel's statement that 'a WTO panel "would seem ... not to be in a position to choose freely whether or not to exercise its jurisdiction"' in a case properly before it.[209]

Notably, this strict textual interpretation of the DSU differs quite significantly from the flexible and rather expansive interpretative approach to the DSU taken by the AB in other types of cases. Thus, for example, in the trade-and *US-Shrimp* dispute, it was the AB that heavily criticized the panel's interpretation of DSU Article 13 as 'too literal' and 'unnecessarily technical and formal',[210] and which ultimately went beyond the DSU treaty text to allow *amicus curiae* submissions in WTO proceedings.[211] Likewise, in the second round of the perennial *Hormones* dispute, known as *US-Continued Suspension*, the AB did not hesitate to broadly construe Article 21.5 of the DSU as allowing complainants and *defendants* to initiate

202 ibid, paras 48–53.

203 Henckels (n 168) 578.

204 *Mexico-Soft Drinks* AB Report (n 55) paras 50–51. See also *Mexico-Soft Drinks* Panel Report (n 56) paras 7.6–7.8.

205 *Mexico-Soft Drinks* AB Report (n 55) para 52. See also *Mexico-Soft Drinks* Panel Report (n 56) para 7.9.

206 Interview with private attorney (Geneva, 23 April 2012).

207 *Mexico-Soft Drinks* AB Report (n 55) para 53. See also *Mexico-Soft Drinks* Panel Report (n 56) para 7.9.

208 Both Article 3.2 and Article 19.2 of the DSU mandate that panel and AB's rulings 'cannot add to or diminish the rights and obligations provided in the covered agreements'.

209 *Mexico-Soft Drinks* AB Report (n 55) para 53.

210 *United States–Import Prohibition of Certain Shrimp and Shrimp Products*, Report of the Appellate Body, 6 November 1998, WT/DS58/AB/R, para 107.

211 See the discussion in Section 5.2 in Chapter 5.

compliance proceedings,[212] in contrast to the long-standing understanding among WTO Members that only complainants may do so.[213]

Moreover, the interpretative methodology followed by the AB in *Mexico-Soft Drinks*, that of 'rigidly sticking' to the text and 'emphasizing what it perceived to be imperatives in the DSU', contradicts its flexibility in other cases involving non-WTO law, institutions, and values, where the AB was willing to consider linkages between the WTO and other parts of the international legal system, resort to teleological interpretations, and engage in complex normative trade-offs.[214] Thus, in *US-Shrimp* and *US-Clove Cigarettes*, the trade-and disputes discussed in Chapters 5 and 6, the AB went out of its way in order to interpret the relevant WTO provisions in light of the broad 'object and purpose' of the WTO treaty, while introducing a balancing test into the analysis of the competing norms and values at stake. In *Mexico-Soft Drinks*, however, the AB chose not to 'test its interpretation of the text against an overall inquiry into the object and purpose of the DSU or the broader *telos* of state-state dispute settlement'.[215] Nor did the AB explicitly examine or weigh 'the competing norms at issue: textualism and its role in maintaining the integrity of the WTO's adjudicative [system] … '*vis-à-vis* the desirability of flexible accommodation of unanticipated and exceptional circumstances as a means of maintaining the effective administration of justice'.[216] Hence, in *Mexico-Soft Drinks*, the AB, like the panel, simply prioritized the former interest over the latter.

But, as a WTO official involved in the appellate proceedings in *Mexico-Soft Drinks* admitted when alluding to the textual approach taken by WTO adjudicators: 'Of course, … you know, you are never 100% textual, there will always be some of your policy preferences creeping in'.[217] Indeed, as I argue here, the textual approach followed in *Mexico-Soft Drinks* and the interpretative outcomes it yielded attest quite clearly to the policy preferences and objectives pursued by the panel and the AB in this case—most notably, sustaining the operation, credibility, and authority of the WTO and its DSS as the central forum for resolving trade disputes between Members.[218] Along these lines, another WTO official participating in the *Mexico-Soft Drinks* appellate proceedings quite openly stated that the main goal underlying the finding that a WTO panel does not have discretion to decline to rule in a case properly before it was:

[212] *United States–Continued Suspension* (n 163) para 368.

[213] See the discussion in Section 9.3 in Chapter 9.

[214] Henckels (n 168) 591.

[215] ibid.

[216] ibid.

[217] Interview with former WTO official (Geneva, 16 July 2012).

[218] See, e.g. interview with former Mexican official (Geneva, 12 July 2012) (alluding to the will of WTO adjudicators in *Mexico-Soft Drinks* 'to keep [the WTO] working' and to maintain the DSS as 'the main tribunal for addressing state versus state disputes').

> [to] maintain[] the effectiveness of the [WTO dispute settlement] system, sort of protecting the integrity of this system, because otherwise.... if panels were to decline jurisdiction, then ... any type of messy controversy ... at the regional level would certainly paralyze this system. And ... [there was] recognition that one of the reasons why this [dispute settlement] system [in the WTO] gets good reviews, generally, is that it works. It eventually ... delivers a result and doesn't get paralyzed.[219]

Going further to elaborate on the issue of the integrity and credibility of the DSS, the same official stated:

> [A]ny decision in which a panel says, 'We can't decide this case because of x, y, or z' ... may lead to a loss of credibility.... [O]f course, there may be cases in which ... a panel intervenes where it shouldn't intervene, and so there's a loss of credibility for a reason. But there's the risk on the other side as well. If a panel were quick to say, 'Well ... something is happening over there [at the regional level] and maybe we should wait', ... that might hurt the credibility of the [WTO dispute settlement] system because ... the system would not be doing what it was asked to do, which is to resolve disputes.[220]

Against this backdrop, this official concluded, the jurisdictional ruling in *Mexico-Soft Drinks* 'was the safe result'; 'the opposite result would have been potentially ... more problematic, because you ... open a door and you don't know what would ... happen[]'.[221] Continuing along this path, another WTO legal officer who worked on the case commented that if the WTO DSS were to find that a panel having a validly established jurisdiction nevertheless can exercise 'discretion' as to whether to take jurisdiction over a complaint of WTO violation, 'this kind of [discretionary] power would be[come] so open-ended that it would be unpredictable when a panel would ... actually exercise jurisdiction', which is contrary to the DSS's explicit aim of 'providing security and predictability to the multilateral trading

[219] Interview with WTO official (Geneva, 18 April 2012). Echoing a similar view, a former Mexican state delegate involved in *Mexico-Soft Drinks* noted the following when alluding to the goal guiding the AB's and the panel's insistence on the WTO DSS's jurisdiction in this case: '[If you] think about the politics of the WTO, you have three areas—administration of treaties, negotiation, and dispute settlement. Which one is working? Dispute settlement. Which one is having some problems? Negotiations.... So certainly, you don't want to erode the one [area in the WTO] that is working properly'. Interview with former Mexican official (Geneva, 12 July 2012).

[220] Interview with WTO official (Geneva, 18 April 2012). A Brussels-based state official similarly noted that '[t]hrowing a case out is a pretty big thing to do for the Appellate Body' as it may adversely affect its integrity. 'For the Appellate Body ... it is a very big thing because you have a sovereign state who comes there with an international dispute, ... and you are basically sending it home with nothing'. Interview with EU official (Brussels, 20 July 2012).

[221] Interview with WTO official (Geneva, 18 April 2012).

system'.[222] The same interviewee went on to stress that 'any tribunal ... faced with a trade-off like ... [the one faced by the DSS in *Mexico-Soft Drinks*] would probably assert jurisdiction.... [T]hat is the nature of international tribunals, of any tribunal, you don't give up jurisdiction easily'.[223] Offering an additional, related insight, a different WTO legal officer finally stressed: 'If countries continue to bring disputes to this forum, that is what keeps this system going. The system lives only as long as states bring conflicts.... If states ... [took] their trade disputes to competing adjudicating fora, that would affect the relevance of this system'.[224]

These observations aptly reveal the judicial policy informing the interpretative stance taken by WTO adjudicators in *Mexico-Soft Drinks*—a judicial policy that admits the risks posed to the DSS and its overarching WTO regime by RTA proliferation and which recognizes that if the WTO is to remain a dominant actor in the international economic landscape, 'it must provide the central means' of settling trade disputes between states.[225] With the surge in the number of RTAs notified to the WTO and the growing pace of negotiation of even larger regional agreements while WTO negotiations remain stalled, the approach followed by the panel and the AB in *Mexico-Soft Drinks* appears to be geared at maintaining the essential integrity of the WTO as an institution, as a body of trade rules, and as a core platform for settling international trade conflicts that all states, great or small, can rely on.[226]

With a view to achieving these ends, the result of the judicial endeavour carried out in *Mexico-Soft Drinks*, like in previous RTA-related disputes reviewed, is therefore 'greater strength to the multilateral system as opposed to regional ... trade arrangements' in a reality of economic regionalization.[227] That said, it should be noted here that 'the panel and Appellate Body were [both] ... well aware of how big the ... issues [in *Mexico-Soft Drinks*] were and took a fairly cautious approach in addressing them'.[228] While the AB made it clear that it did not accept Mexico's jurisdictional claim in this case, like the panel, it concluded its discussion of the matter by stating that it was expressing 'no view as to whether there may be other circumstances in which legal impediments could exist that would preclude a panel from ruling on the merits of the claims that are before it'.[229]

222 Interview with former WTO legal officer (Geneva, 16 July 2012). Note that China, a third party in *Mexico-Soft Drinks*, had raised a similar argument to which the AB referred twice in its decision. According to China: '[A] WTO panel does not have an implied power to refrain from performing its "statutory function".... [I]f a panel that is "empowered and obligated" to assist the DSB in the settlement of a dispute declines to exercise jurisdiction, such a decision would create legal uncertainty and be contrary to the aim of providing security and predictability to the multilateral trading system as well as the prompt settlement of disputes as provided for in Article 3.3 of the DSU'. See *Mexico-Soft Drinks* AB Report (n 55) paras 34, 43.

223 Interview with former WTO legal officer (Geneva, 16 July 2012).

224 Interview with WTO legal officer (Geneva, 19 March 2012).

225 de Mestral (n 18) 807.

226 ibid.

227 Interview with private attorney (Geneva, 23 April 2012).

228 Interview with WTO legal officer (Geneva, 11 July 2012).

229 *Mexico-Soft Drinks* AB Report (n 55) para 54. See also *Mexico-Soft Drinks* Panel Report (n 56) para 7.10.

After making this statement, the AB briefly noted that no such legal impediments existed in the present case, which was distinct from the case pursued by Mexico under NAFTA in that there was (i) no overlap between the 'subject matter and the respective positions of the parties' in the two cases; (ii) no panel ruling rendered in the 'broader' NAFTA dispute to which Mexico alluded; and (iii) no waiver of jurisdiction, which might ensue from the NAFTA's forum exclusion clause (not 'exercised' by Mexico in this case).[230] Having said that, the AB reiterated its position that it was not expressing 'any view on whether a legal impediment to the exercise of a panel's jurisdiction would exist in the event that features such as those mentioned above were present'.[231] The AB thus left the question open as to whether, for example, a prior RTA ruling deciding the issues raised in the WTO case or, more interestingly, whether an RTA's fork-in-the-road clause (such as the one not exercised by Mexico) or some other type of an RTA provision conceived as a waiver of the right to initiate WTO proceedings could constitute such a 'legal impediment'.[232]

Although speaking informally, a former WTO legal officer involved in *Mexico-Soft Drinks* compensated for the AB's silence by making several interesting observations in reference to the possibility that WTO adjudicators would actually relinquish their jurisdiction based on a waiver or understanding agreed upon by Members within the framework of an RTA. Drawing a parallel to the *EC-Bananas* case,[233] where the AB found that a WTO Member may relinquish, by virtue of a mutually agreed solution in a specific dispute, its right to have recourse to WTO dispute settlement,[234] this interviewee stated that 'the only situation in which the Appellate Body so far has accepted that jurisdiction would be forgone is ... when a Member [explicitly] says, in the WTO, under a mutually agreed solution, "I'm giving up on my right to bring a case"'.[235] Yet, he stressed, 'that is not the same situation you have under an RTA'. The one distinction identified as separating 'the *Bananas* scenario' and an 'RTA-type fork-in-the-road' scenario is grounded in the fact that:

> the [announcement] ... of Members that they are giving up WTO jurisdiction in the *Bananas* [scenario] ... [is confined] ... to ... *a specific dispute*.... It is [a waiver of the right to resort to the DSU] in a particular case, where you know the complainant, you know the defendant, you know ... the subject matter [of the

[230] *Mexico-Soft Drinks* AB Report (n 55) para 54.
[231] ibid.
[232] Davey and Sapir (n 62) 13. See also Howse and Langille (n 3) 687.
[233] *European Communities–Regime for the Importation, Sale and Distribution of Bananas, Second Recourse to Article 21.5 of the DSU by Ecuador/Recourse to Article 21.5 of the DSU by the United States*, Reports of the Appellate Body, 11 and 22 December 2008, WT/DS27/AB/RW2/ECU, WT/DS27/AB/RW/USA.
[234] ibid, paras 212, 217. An elaborate discussion of this ruling may be found in Chapter 8.
[235] Interview with former WTO legal officer (Geneva, 16 July 2012).

> dispute] … and you renounce [your DSU rights] because you have settled [the case]…. It is different if you have a fork-in-the-road provision which was negotiated … 15 years ago on generic terms in an RTA and now you have a dispute. I think it [would be] … harder for … the panel or the Appellate Body to say, 'well, they renounced [their right] … 15 years ago'.[236]

In light of this comparison, the same interviewee assessed that 'it would have to be an extremely clear-cut situation where you, as the WTO panel, would be willing to renounce jurisdiction'.[237] This prognosis, as seen below, including the legal analogy on which it was predicated, turned out to be quite close to the route ultimately taken by the AB in the later *Peru-Agricultural Products* case, where one of the questions left open in *Mexico-Soft Drinks* presented itself: Can WTO Members relinquish their DSU right to WTO dispute settlement proceedings through a waiver or understanding concluded outside the context of a specific WTO dispute, namely, in the framework of an RTA?[238]

In the case of *Peru-Agricultural Products,* discussed earlier, Peru raised a preliminary objection arguing that by agreeing in the RTA to the maintenance of the Peruvian PRS, Guatemala had waived its right to challenge this measure within the framework of WTO dispute settlement. For this reason, according to Peru, Guatemala had acted contrary to its good faith obligations under DSU Articles 3.7 and 3.10 when initiating the present WTO proceedings;[239] it thus requested the panel to refrain from assessing Guatemala's claims. The panel, in response, avoided delving into the fundamental question of whether Guatemala had indeed relinquished its right to bring a WTO complaint in the RTA. Instead, basing its analysis on the 'technical' grounds that the respective RTA had not entered into force, the panel found no evidence for claiming that Guatemala had initiated the WTO proceedings in a manner contrary to its good faith obligations.[240]

While the AB upheld the panel's ultimate finding,[241] it nevertheless took a different judicial course, proving greater willingness to consider the substance of Peru's jurisdictional claim 'under the guise of a potential mutually agreed

[236] ibid (emphasis added).

[237] ibid. The same view was shared by other interviewees. See, e.g. interview with WTO ambassador (Geneva, 5 July 2012); interview with EU official (Brussels, 20 July 2012); interview with private attorney (Geneva, 24 April 2012).

[238] Pauwelyn (n 127) 17.

[239] *Peru-Agricultural Products* AB Report (n 126) para 5.5. DSU Article 3.7, in the relevant section, states that '[b]efore bringing a case, a Member shall exercise its judgement as to whether action under these procedures would be fruitful'. DSU Article 3.10 provides that '[i]t is understood that requests for conciliation and the use of the dispute settlement procedures should not be intended or considered as contentious acts and that, if a dispute arises, all Members will engage in these procedures in good faith in an effort to resolve the dispute'.

[240] *Peru-Agricultural Products* AB Report (n 126) para 5.20; *Peru-Agricultural Products* Panel Report (n 128) paras 7.88, 7.96, 8.1.a.

[241] *Peru-Agricultural Products* AB Report (n 126) para 5.28.

solution'[242] enclosed in the RTA provision in relation to the PRS.[243] In so doing, the AB, while paying little heed to the fact that the RTA was not actually in effect, seized the occasion to reaffirm the fundamental right of Members to initiate WTO legal proceedings and to stipulate the stringent conditions Members must meet in order to waive this right via an RTA.

And so, the AB began its jurisdictional analysis in *Peru-Agricultural Products* by recalling its ruling in *EC-Bananas*, where it had found that a mutually agreed solution to a WTO dispute may contain a waiver by the parties of their right to have recourse to the DSU.[244] Restating its position in the *Bananas* case, the AB stressed that 'the relinquishment of rights granted by the DSU cannot be lightly assumed' and that the parties 'must clearly reveal' that they indeed 'intended to relinquish their rights'.[245] Following a substantive examination of the RTA between Peru and Guatemala, the AB concluded that Guatemala had 'not clearly waived its right to have recourse' to WTO dispute settlement,[246] and, in consequence, had not acted contrary to its good faith obligations under DSU Articles 3.7 and 3.10 when initiating these WTO proceedings.[247] To support this conclusion, the AB found, inter alia, that the RTA did not contain a clear statement of a relinquishment of Guatemala's right to bring a case to the WTO DSS, but in fact provided in Article 15.3 that '[i]n the event of any dispute that may arise under this Treaty ... or the *WTO Agreement*, the complaining Party may choose the forum for settling the dispute'.[248] The AB also found support in one of its findings, mentioned earlier, that there was 'ambiguity as to whether even the ... [RTA] itself, regardless of its legal status', allowed Peru to maintain its PRS.[249] Finally, the AB reasoned that the RTA in question could not constitute a mutually agreed solution because it had been negotiated before the initiation of the present WTO dispute and, as noted earlier, was inconsistent with the WTO covered agreements.[250]

Of crucial importance for future RTA-related disputes,[251] however, is the AB's principled statement in *Peru-Agricultural Products* that it did 'not exclude the

[242] Stephanie Hartmann, 'Recognizing the Limitations of WTO Dispute Settlement—The Peru-Price Band Dispute and Sources of Authority for Applying Non-WTO Law in WTO Disputes' (2016) 48 Geo Wash Int'l L Rev 617, 646.

[243] Referring in a footnote to Peru's appellant's submission, the AB indicated that: 'Peru contends that the parties to the FTA had already reached a "positive solution" within the meaning of Article 3.7 of the DSU when they agreed in the FTA that Peru may maintain its PRS'. See *Peru-Agricultural Products* AB Report (n 126) fn 103.

[244] ibid, para 5.25.

[245] ibid.

[246] ibid, fn 109 and para 5.28, where the AB stated: 'Based on the foregoing discussion, we do not consider that a clear stipulation of a relinquishment of Guatemala's right to have recourse to the WTO dispute settlement system exists in this case'.

[247] ibid, para 5.28.

[248] ibid, para 5.27 (emphasis original).

[249] ibid, para 5.26.

[250] ibid.

[251] Pauwelyn (n 127) 19; Shaffer and Winters (n 147) 318.

possibility of articulating the relinquishment of the right to initiate WTO dispute settlement proceedings in a form *other than a waiver embodied in a mutually agreed solution*'.[252] The AB nonetheless enumerated several conditions to be met for it to recognize such a waiver.[253] First, 'any such relinquishment must be made *clearly*'.[254] Second, the said relinquishment 'should be ascertained ... *in relation to, or within the context of, the rules and procedures of the DSU*'.[255] Third, such relinquishment of DSU rights may not go 'beyond the settlement of *specific disputes*'.[256] It follows from the above that while WTO Members may waive their right to WTO adjudication in actions other than a mutually agreed solution under the DSU, parties to an RTA wishing to close the door to WTO dispute settlement on certain issues must strictly abide by the AB's explicit stipulations,[257] which, as Shaffer and Winters note, 'appear to go beyond the WTO textual requirements'.[258]

These stipulations, in turn, surely require further clarification, yet it is rather patent that they significantly narrow the circumstances under which an RTA-based understanding to relinquish DSU rights would be effective in de facto thwarting a WTO panel's jurisdiction.[259] To begin with, these conditions seem to establish a high burden of proof, requiring demonstration of a Member's 'clear' intent to waive its right to resort to the DSU.[260] In fact, it has been argued, the AB's interpretation is so strict that an RTA provision providing for a waiver of the right to invoke WTO dispute settlement has to be 'absolutely explicit, not subject to any reasonable argument over its interpretation', whereas any resulting contextual ambiguity will be resolved in favour of the complainant and the admission of the case.[261] What is more, for the waiver of the right to initiate WTO legal proceedings to be valid, it must not only meet the textual clarity and explicitness test, it must also apply to 'specific disputes'. While it is unclear what exactly the AB meant by 'specific disputes', this term could be understood as broadly referring to all those disputes falling under both the RTA and the WTO.[262] However, it could also refer to a specific subject or measure regulated in the RTA and subsequently litigated under the DSU.[263] Still, the term 'specific disputes' could be read even more narrowly as referring to a particular WTO complaint,[264] that is, to a dispute 'that has already arisen, thereby excluding

[252] *Peru-Agricultural Products* AB Report (n 126) para 5.25 (emphasis added).
[253] Shaffer and Winters (n 147) 318.
[254] *Peru-Agricultural Products* AB Report (n 126) para 5.25 (emphasis added).
[255] ibid (emphasis added).
[256] ibid, fn 106 (emphasis added). The AB noted that it did not 'consider that Members may relinquish their rights and obligations under the DSU beyond the settlement of specific disputes'.
[257] Pauwelyn (n 127) 20.
[258] Shaffer and Winters (n 147) 318.
[259] See Howse and Langille (n 3) 684; Hartmann (n 242) 648; Gabrielle Marceau, 'The Primacy of the WTO Dispute Settlement System' (2015) 25 Questions Int'l L 3, 7, 13.
[260] Hartmann (n 242) 648.
[261] Mathis (n 135) 104.
[262] Pauwelyn (n 127) fn 68.
[263] Shaffer and Winters (n 147) fn 30.
[264] ibid.

undetermined future disputes'.[265] Should the latter be the case, this might suggest, for example, that even a clearly stipulated, ex ante provision establishing the RTA dispute settlement procedures as the exclusive forum for the resolution of certain or all matters regulated under the RTA would not constitute a sufficient basis for a good faith claim to defeat a WTO panel's jurisdiction. To this, one should add the near impossibility of rebutting the assumption that WTO Members engage in dispute settlement in good faith,[266] and, in the words of the AB, the '"largely self-regulating" nature of a Member's decision to bring' a dispute to the WTO,[267] factors further lowering the odds of a responding Member successfully arguing that an RTA provision contracting out of the DSU constitutes evidence of bad faith and thus the basis for a panel to decline jurisdiction.[268]

We should note at this point, that on other occasions, however, when WTO Members contracted out of the DSU 'within' the WTO framework, the AB exhibited a much more relaxed stance.[269] Thus, for example, in *US-Continued Suspension* (see Chapter 6), the AB did not hesitate to allow the United States and the EU to open the hearings before it to the public through a bilateral agreement (reached 'inside the WTO'),[270] although this agreement effectively contracted out of DSU Article 17.10 (prescribing confidential AB proceedings).[271] In contrast, in *Peru-Agricultural Products*, as Pauwelyn has put it, the AB expressed 'major reservations about Peru and Guatemala bilaterally agreeing "outside the WTO" (in an FTA) to "contract out" of the DSU right to a panel';[272] in fact, it seized the moment to place considerable limits on Members' ability to do so in the future.

If to conclude, the AB's latest ruling in *Peru-Agricultural Products* constitutes a direct continuation of the jurisdictional analysis employed by WTO judicial organs in previous RTA-related cases, an analysis apparently driven by the goal of reinforcing the status of the WTO DSS as the supreme judicial organ in the area of international trade.[273] This it did with a view to not only sustaining the DSS's authority and credibility as an international court but, more systemically, ensuring that the multilateral trade regime remains operational and not undermined by the abundant trade deals concluded at the regional level. The lesson emerging from *Peru-Agricultural Products* echoes and amplifies that emerging from past cases

[265] Pauwelyn (n 127) fn 68.
[266] Marceau (n 259) 12; Hartmann (n 242) 648.
[267] See *Peru-Agricultural Products* AB Report (n 126) para 5.18.
[268] Marceau (n 259) 13 (arguing that following the AB's ruling in *Peru-Agricultural Products*, '[i]t seems difficult to conceive whether and how an RTA can possibly foreclose the use of the WTO DSM for the violation of WTO provisions, unless WTO Members decide to do so in the context of the DSU'). See also Hartmann (n 242) 648.
[269] Pauwelyn (n 127) 29.
[270] *United States-Continued Suspension* (n 163) Annex IV.
[271] Pauwelyn (n 127) 29.
[272] ibid.
[273] Howse and Langille (n 3) 684–85.

along the WTO-RTA jurisdictional nexus. A WTO legal officer phrased this lesson quite succinctly:

> [W]hat we can take from these past cases, is that panels . . . [will not] lightly reach the conclusion that because there is an RTA . . . that relates to the same subject matter, that would . . . , in and of itself, raise the question [of whether] . . . the WTO [jurisdiction is] applicable. No, there has to be the right set of facts and it is clearly. . . . a very high standard that must be met. And in no case to date has that standard been met.[274]

10.5 Conclusions

A long-standing and increasing tension between regionalism and multilateralism in international economic governance, having systemic implications for the WTO as an institution and a legal system, is readily apparent. The analysis throughout this chapter showed how the WTO DSS, in a series of RTA-related cases reaching its docket, has adjusted its goal-attainment efforts so as to face the challenges and threats posed to WTO law and institutions by the ever-intensifying regionalization of international trade relations. In this line of cases, the DSS, 'as guarantor of WTO law'[275] and following the AB's lead, has been engaged in a vehement quest for securing the integrity and functionality of the WTO legal order, facilitating the realization of the multilateral trade objectives, as well as fortifying the authority of the DSS itself.

This heightened quest for sustaining multilateralism at the WTO-RTA nexus has unfolded along two parallel and mutually reinforcing trajectories—the substantive and the jurisdictional. Along the first, substantive legal trajectory, revolving around conflicts of obligations under the multilateral and regional trade systems and raising questions about the effects of RTAs on the substance of WTO rules, the DSS has continually worked to entrench the autonomy and pre-eminence of the WTO legal edifice, from which deviations through RTAs or for RTA-related purposes may be allowed only in limited circumstances and based on the conditions detailed in the WTO's specialized rules. Hence, rather than facilitating greater coherence between WTO agreements and RTA law, WTO adjudicators, when operating along the substantive legal intersection of the two systems, have mainly focused their efforts on deflecting RTAs' destabilizing effects on the multilateral trade regime and its underlying norms.

Along the second, complementary, jurisdictional trajectory, in turn, the DSS has steadily worked to uphold its own authority vis-à-vis regional dispute

[274] Interview with WTO legal officer (Geneva, 11 July 2012).
[275] de Mestral (n 18) 815.

settlement fora and to consolidate its power to review the WTO-compatibility of RTAs, elements vital for sustaining the DSS as an adjudicative institution as well as for ensuring meaningful enforcement of WTO substantive legal norms. With a view to achieving these ends, the DSS has not only asserted, early on, the authority to evaluate the conformity of RTAs to the requirements of GATT Article XXIV, but has gone to establish in WTO jurisprudence a rather high bar before Members can waive their DSU rights and opt out from the DSS's jurisdiction by means of an RTA.

The shift in emphasis marked along these two interrelated trajectories towards the DSS goals of securing the integrity of WTO rules and preserving the authority and viability of the WTO and its adjudicative system has been reflected in the views and experience of WTO insiders; it has likewise been mirrored in the particular judicial choices and interpretative approaches followed by WTO adjudicators in the RTA-related cases examined. Taken together, these factors have exposed a mindful and consistent attempt of the DSS to achieve selected organizational goals in the face of RTA proliferation. As demonstrated throughout the chapter, at any juncture along the RTA-related cases reviewed, other judicial choices could have been made and greater weight ascribed to other DSS objectives. Still, choices have been made that reveal an enhanced emphasis on specific DSS objectives, choices that differ quite significantly from those made by WTO adjudicators in other types of disputes.

Most notably, the strict, textual and exclusionary stance taken by the DSS towards RTAs, maintaining '"clinical isolation" from these other trade fora' and their respective dispute settlement systems,[276] has digressed from the rather integrationist and flexible approach taken by the AB towards general international law in trade-and disputes, where interests such as environmental protection or public health were at stake.[277] This variation in the interpretative approaches taken in trade-and disputes as opposed to RTA-related cases, I argue, largely stems from the different goals pursued by the DSS in the two categories of cases. While in trade-and disputes 'the core force pushing the AB to embrace other international law was to legitimize itself'[278] and the overarching WTO regime among expanding circles of national and global stakeholders, in RTA-related cases, the main force motivating resistance to other international law was the 'threat' to multilateralism represented by the 'outside rules' set by RTAs, that is, 'the fear' that RTA provisions would disturb the 'uniformity of WTO rules' or that dispute settlement under RTAs would undermine WTO adjudication.[279]

[276] Howse (n 25) 73.
[277] cf Shaffer and Winters (n 147) 324.
[278] Pauwelyn (n 127) 31.
[279] ibid 31–32.

This variation in the motivations and goals pursued by the DSS in trade-and disputes as compared with RTA-related cases may also elucidate how the goal-attainment patterns exhibited in the latter category of cases might ultimately result in conflicts between the DSS's multiple goals themselves. More concretely, it may explain how the quest to uphold multilateralism in RTA-related cases might possibly result in a collision with the legitimacy-oriented objectives of the DSS should the latter come to be portrayed as a judicial body unresponsive to the broader challenges raised by the fragmentation of international economic law—that is, a body that in its adamant prioritization of its regime-support and self-preservation goals fails to address the interaction between the WTO and RTAs in a manner more suitable to today's changed economic landscape.[280] At the same time, RTA-related disputes may also illuminate how other DSS goals complement one another, particularly, how the law clarification aim, together with the compliance-inducement goal sought by the DSS, may foster the determinacy and unity of WTO rules and, more broadly, the stability of the WTO regime at a time when its legislative arm has become dysfunctional, parallel with the unabated growth in trade negotiations in regional fora.

In the broader research framework of this book, RTA-related cases constitute, therefore, another informative site for illustrating the shifting, conflicting, and complementing dynamics of goal attainment and, thereby, of judicial effectiveness at the WTO. The distinct systemic challenges faced by the DSS and the multilateral trade regime in disputes arising in the WTO-RTA context have called for new emphases among the various organizational goals the DSS is expected to achieve. Shifts and trade-offs between those goals are consequently inevitable.

But one more, no less-critical lesson that RTA-related disputes teach is that even in these cases, where the DSS has no doubt placed an enhanced emphasis on its oft-cited compliance-inducement goal, an effectiveness assessment of the DSS that focuses on the outcome of compliance alone is bound to yield a partial account of the system's performance at best. Among other things, an effectiveness analysis focusing on the narrow benchmark of compliance can be expected to leave out of the picture the longer-term, legal predictability and regime-support goals assisted by the promotion of the DSS's compliance objective in RTA-related disputes. Moreover, such a compliance-oriented analysis is also likely to overlook the potential costs that the unyielding quest for WTO compliance in RTA-related cases might entail for the achievement of other DSS objectives, among which we find the maintenance of the DSS's fundamental legitimacy.

[280] In a similar spirit, Shaffer and Winters have recently argued that in the face of the continuing trend of RTA proliferation, for the WTO and its DSS to remain relevant, the latter must interpret WTO rules in a manner more suitable to today's changed economic landscape and find ways to facilitate greater coherence between RTAs and the WTO legal system. See Shaffer and Winters (n 147) 321, 324.

To gain a more accurate and nuanced picture of the effectiveness of the WTO DSS in such cases a broader goal-based perspective is therefore needed. Such a perspective, which goes beyond compliance, is crucial because RTA-related disputes and the challenges they present before the multilateral trading system are not going to disappear any time soon; they may perhaps even grow as the surge in RTAs continues.

11
Conclusion
WTO Judicial Effectiveness and Beyond

This book began with a seemingly simple question: is judicial effectiveness all about compliance? When discussing international courts, as the introduction showed, this question seems to capture the essence of much of the existing research on the effectiveness of these empowered adjudicative institutions. This is especially so in writings on the World Trade Organization (WTO) Dispute Settlement System (DSS), where the focus on compliance has been highly conspicuous, triggered by the juridified nature of the system when compared to its predecessor under the General Agreement on Tariffs and Trade (GATT).

Yet despite its juridification, the WTO DSS, as this book has argued throughout and as recent developments in the global trading system have underscored, is not simply a technocratic mechanism for interpreting and inducing compliance with WTO rules. It is a forum for litigation, struggle, interaction, and re-negotiation, where conflicts are fought not only about adherence to formerly agreed rules—though this is certainly a significant element of the system—but over broader, ever-evolving political, economic, legal, and social interests. It is an adjudicative institution devised by WTO Members to pursue numerous goals, a pursuit constituted in a dynamic environment marked by changing practices, expectations, actors, and constraints, which require the DSS to constantly adapt its goal-attainment efforts, as well as the judicial tools harnessed to support those efforts.

These complex institutional dynamics make perfectly clear the temptation to approach the effectiveness of the WTO DSS through a static and narrow lens such as rule or judgment compliance, abstracting the system and the goals mobilizing its operation from the impact of time and social change. But such a fixed and limited orientation cannot provide the basis for a comprehensive analysis of DSS performance. It overlooks the varying roles and objectives assigned to the system, overshadows the diverse social outcomes it generates, and portrays a world of WTO adjudication that is much simpler than the reality. In consequence, a static, unidimensional perspective of this sort may also stand in the way of appropriate institutional reform. Against this backdrop, the need for a more comprehensive, nuanced, and dynamic framework for studying, thinking, and arguing about the effectiveness of the WTO DSS has emerged. This need triggered the writing of this book. Yet, this need seems to have become even more acute by the time of the manuscript's completion, a period when the WTO DSS has come to face severe trials, posed predominantly by its initiator, the United States, and which threaten to undermine the system's future functioning.[1]

In what follows, this final chapter discusses the main conclusions of the book and considers their implications with a look to the future. It first outlines the key findings of the study while assessing the results emerging from a comparative analysis of the three categories of WTO disputes examined in the book. The chapter then revisits the central arguments previously put forward and articulates the lessons to be learned with respect to the goals, operation, and effectiveness of the WTO DSS (and other international courts). It also offers several insights into current debates on DSS institutional change and reform, with a view to ensuring the system's future effectiveness. The chapter closes with some observations that go beyond effectiveness, pertaining to the unintended consequences of more effective and empowered international adjudication.

11.1 Embracing a Goal-Based Approach to WTO Judicial Effectiveness

Building on the rich social science literature on organizational effectiveness, this book has advanced a goal-based approach for analysing the effectiveness of the WTO DSS. Under this approach, the effectiveness of the WTO's judicial system is defined as the extent to which it achieves the goals (namely, the desired outcomes) set for it by its 'mandate providers'—the WTO and its Member states. The theoretical foundations of the goal-based effectiveness framework as applied to the WTO DSS, including its main analytical concepts, the methodological determinations it requires, and the measurement challenges it presents were laid down in Chapter 1.

While the goal-based approach, as Chapter 1 explained, constitutes only one avenue for conceptualizing judicial effectiveness at the WTO, this approach offers a multifaceted, institution-specific, normative benchmark for assessing the performance of the DSS in terms of its manifold designated goals. What is more, this approach encourages us to look even further, beyond the breadth of DSS goals, to uncover the real-life intricacies underlying the system's operation and, consequently, its effectiveness, as these emerge from the multiple, conflicting, and shifting nature of its objectives. With a view to unravelling these fundamental complexities and enhancing our understanding of the question of WTO judicial

[1] As elaborated later in the chapter, at the time of completing this book project (January 2019), the major source of stress facing the WTO DSS is the attack launched against it and, especially, against its Appellate Body (AB), by the United States in the form of blocking the appointment of AB members, what may deprive this body of the personnel needed to adjudicate cases as of December 2019.

effectiveness, the bulk of this book has therefore been devoted to discerning the defining phenomena of goal multiplicity, goal conflict, and goal shifting marking the world of the WTO DSS.

11.2 Reconstructing the WTO DSS as a System of Multiple and Conflicting Goals

The first step towards discerning the various goal complexities characterizing the WTO DSS was taken in Chapter 3. Seeking to put forward concrete normative benchmarks for the DSS's goal-based effectiveness framework, against which its performance is to be evaluated, the chapter mapped out the broad corpus of goals this adjudicative system is expected to achieve, while highlighting their complementing and contradicting relationships. The chapter began by addressing the system's long-term ultimate ends: providing security and predictability to the multilateral trade system, preserving the balance of rights and obligations between WTO Members ('rebalancing the scales'), sustaining the operation of the WTO and the realization of its goals ('regime maintenance'), and conferring legitimacy upon the WTO and its underlying legal norms. Thereafter, the DSS's more-strategic, intermediate goals were delineated. These include inducing compliance with WTO law, promoting the positive and prompt settlement of disputes, preventing unilateral actions, clarifying WTO law, levelling the playing field between WTO Members, and legitimating the authority of the DSS itself.

Hence, rather than framing the various DSS goals in binary terms (e.g. compliance or settlement), the book has recast these aims as multifaceted constructs that nurture mutually reinforcing and contradictory relationships, and that maintain close ties with the overarching WTO edifice in which the DSS is embedded. Precisely in this multiple-goal account, the need for a multidimensional analysis of DSS effectiveness became patent, as did the fallacy of gauging the performance of this multifunctional institution against the benchmark of compliance alone. Furthermore, it is within this account that the exact locus of compliance in the broad matrix of DSS goals became clearly visible. In contrast to the conventional wisdom viewing compliance inducement as the unchanging primary purpose of the DSS, the analysis in Chapter 3 suggested that this goal generally constitutes an intermediate goal, conducive to the realization of some longer-term ultimate ends (e.g. promoting legal predictability or conferring legitimacy upon the WTO regime and rules). At the same time, as the analysis further showed, the DSS's compliance goal maintains conflictual relations with other objectives, particularly rebalancing the scales and facilitating amicable dispute settlement between WTO Members.

The reconstruction of the WTO DSS as a system of multiple, complementing, yet at times inconsistent goals set the scene for the book's major theoretical contribution, the notion of goal shifting—the idea that DSS goals are not fixed but rather dynamic in nature, fluctuating with time and, no less importantly, across disputes. The goal-shifting phenomenon and the actual operationalization of the various DSS aims on the ground were examined through an in-depth, interview-based analysis of three categories of WTO cases—trade-and disputes, perennial disputes, and disputes related to regional trade agreements (RTAs). A comparative assessment of these distinct dispute categories at this stage, as carried out below, clearly illuminates the incessant processes of goal adaptation in which the DSS is engaged given the changing modalities in which it operates. This analysis likewise exposes the goal conflicts and trade-offs such processes engender.

11.3 Goal Shifting and the Real-Life Dynamics of Judicial Effectiveness at the WTO: A Comparative View of Three Categories of WTO Disputes

When confronting trade-and, perennial, RTA-related, or other categories of WTO disputes, the DSS faces a range of choices and trade-offs concerning its various organizational goals and the judicial efforts invested in their realization. Hence, at each junction of the disputes addressed in Parts II–IV of the book, the DSS could have made other judicial choices in pursuit of its goals. Yet, specific choices were made that ascribed greater weight to some goals than to others in the face of the challenges, constraints, and expectations presented to the system.

Thus, in trade-and disputes—disputes that invoke the persisting tension between the WTO's trade liberalization aim and 'nontrade' values such as health and environmental protection—one could see (Part II) how the intensified legitimacy challenges faced by the WTO and the DSS have prodded the latter to heighten its quest for legitimation in this class of cases. This quest has taken place along two parallel and at times conflicting trajectories: the first concerns the DSS's ultimate end as a 'regime court' meant to confer legitimacy on the WTO among internal and external constituencies; the second concerns the DSS's intermediate goal of legitimizing its own exercise of public authority as an international court amidst relevant audiences outside the WTO while simultaneously sustaining the internal support of WTO Members.

The shift in emphasis towards these two legitimization objectives, as the analysis of *US-Shrimp* and *US-Clove Cigarettes* in Chapters 5 and 6 demonstrated, was echoed in numerous testimonies of WTO practitioners involved in these and other trade-and disputes. Moreover, this goal shifting was apparent in the *ratio decidendi* and *obiter dicta* of the trade-and rulings rendered, manifested in a distinctive collection of substantive, procedural, and rhetorical legitimacy-enhancing strategies uncommon in general WTO jurisprudence. These strategies included the move towards teleological and contextual constructions—by an adjudicatory body that has long been known for its strict textual interpretations—so as to endow the adjudicators with greater interpretative leeway and the ability to embed the interest of free trade into the broader context of societal values; the incorporation of a balancing discourse into the analysis of relevant WTO provisions while reading them as reflecting a fundamental equilibrium between trade liberalization and Members' right to regulate for nontrade values; the deliberate attempt of the DSS to manifest—in expressive and substantive forms—vertical institutional sensitivity towards national governments, as well as horizontal institutional sensitivity towards adjacent international regimes; and lastly, the engagement of WTO adjudicators in a rare justificatory discourse with multiple stakeholders, at times through special 'explanatory paragraphs', aimed at clarifying the limited political implications arising from their ruling for the respondent, and signalling that the trade-and dispute at hand may be solved without eliminating the trade-restrictive policy found to be WTO inconsistent.

The choice of these distinctive judicial strategies as opposed to other options available to the adjudicators, I argue, exposes a conscious prioritization of certain organizational goals over others in an attempt to craft politically palatable rulings in trade-and conflicts that may fortify the internal legitimacy of the WTO and its DSS among Member states, as well as their external legitimacy among stakeholders such as nongovernmental organizations, domestic interest groups, the general public, and other international institutions. Furthermore, the judicial choices made, particularly the conciliatory attitude displayed by WTO adjudicators in trade-and rulings, often to ease the burden of compliance on losing defendants, reflect the adjudicators' tacit acknowledgement of the political constraints placed on the authority and perceived legitimacy of the WTO and the DSS in such cases, as well as their recognition of the resulting need for some 'give' on compliance with WTO trade commitments in order to foster other organizational objectives, most notably, sustaining the very legitimacy of the WTO and its DSS.

Yet, as the evidence emerging from the case studies in Chapters 5 and 6 further reveals, this 'give-and-take' between the DSS's compliance and legitimacy objectives was not the sole type of trade-off struck in trade-and disputes. Occasionally, conflicts arose between the DSS's legitimation objectives themselves, that is, between the aim of conferring legitimacy on the entire WTO edifice among stakeholders outside the multilateral trade system, and the need to sustain the DSS's own legitimacy within the inner circle of WTO Members. Such conflicts, whenever they arose, aptly demonstrated the limits to the DSS's capacity to achieve its manifold goals and, it follows, the inherent limits to its effectiveness.

The goal-based reading of the perennial disputes presented in Part III disclosed, in turn, a somewhat different set of systemic pressures and challenges and, in consequence, the distinctive goal-conflict and goal-attainment patterns established by the DSS for this category of cases. These high-stake, politically charged, and protracted trade conflicts between major economic powers aptly illustrated how, where the prospects for compliance are patently low and the strains on the co-operative WTO regime are exceedingly high, the juridified DSS comes to serve as a forum that enables disputants to harness the law in pursuit of goals other than narrow rule observance. In these types of intense and recidivist conflicts, as the case studies of *EC-Bananas* and *EC-Hormones* showed, the DSS, rather than acting as a mechanism geared primarily to mechanically enforce WTO rules, plays an enhanced role along the thin line between law and politics, with its dominant function revolving around two intertwined tracks. First, through its successive rulings, the DSS serves to facilitate the amicable settlement of the dispute and the re-establishment of the bilateral balance of concessions between the parties, by continually framing renegotiation environments and creating focal points around which the parties can coordinate. Along this first track, then, the compulsory WTO DSS is reconfigured in perennial disputes as a forum for repeated interaction and bargaining, where its legal rulings, findings, and clarifications are used as points of convergence that assist disputants in gradually working out a mutually agreed solution. Second, as long as the protracted conflict endures, the mandatory DSS further plays a systemic role in sustaining the WTO's functioning and stability by channelling the charged dispute into defined legal parameters, defusing its political aspects, inhibiting unilateral actions, and thereby forestalling the dispute's escalation into an uncontrollable trade war. Along this second track, therefore, we find the vital dispute containment and dispute management functions of the DSS, through which the system promotes achievement of its fundamental regime-maintenance goal.

Evidence supporting this shift in emphasis in perennial disputes towards the DSS's settlement, rebalancing, and regime-maintenance objectives, as seen in Chapters 8 and 9, was found at multiple levels: testimonies of WTO practitioners with first-hand knowledge of the *Bananas* and *Hormones* cases, the conflicts' sequence of events, and the web of distinctive judicial choices, interpretations, and techniques used by WTO adjudicators in these cases. Among these judicial methods: providing the disputing parties with concrete and pragmatic suggestions on how to move forward towards the dispute's resolution, in contrast to the DSS's general practice of avoiding any such recommendations; adopting interpretations entrusting the DSS with the jurisdiction to recurrently address these perennial feuds while at the same time recognizing the flexibility left for Members in settling their conflicts; and promulgating mixed judicial outputs that may incentivize both parties to return to the negotiating table and find a mutually agreed solution.

Yet alongside this goal shifting, the protracted *EC-Bananas* and *EC-Hormones* disputes also exemplified one of the most conspicuous tensions underlying DSS goals: the tension between the will to secure rule compliance and legal predictability, and the desire to preserve the parties' reciprocal balance of trade concessions through amicable settlements and flexible rebalancing acts conducive to sustaining the WTO's long-term functioning and stability. In theory, of course, these various institutional goals need not necessarily conflict, as the settlement of disputes by eliminating WTO-inconsistent measures may allow the simultaneous achievement of them all. But in reality, as seen in *EC-Bananas* and *EC-Hormones*, heightened political or economic pressures may make such conflicts between the goals and, consequently, the outcomes of the DSS, inevitable. As a result, while in both acrimonious conflicts a satisfactory negotiated settlement, informed by the DSS's successive rulings, was ultimately found, restoring the bilateral balance of trade benefits between the parties, the settlement achieved in each of the cases still fell short of full compliance with WTO law.

From a perspective that perceives judicial effectiveness through the lens of compliance, the noncompliant outcomes generated in the perennial *Bananas* and *Hormones* disputes may be portrayed, of course, as final chapters in chronicles of enduring noncompliance, and thus as instances of DSS ineffectiveness. As noted in Chapter 7, this is indeed the often-told story of these disputes, as well as of other perennial WTO conflicts, derived from the expectation that the legalized DSS will produce nothing less than compliance. This expectation, however, so the alternative goal-based reading of *Bananas* and *Hormones* suggests, is divorced from the actual practice of disputing at the WTO, as Members mobilize the DSS for a variety of motives and purposes, 'which may or may not include the reasonable expectation of compliance'.[2] It therefore follows that from a broad goal-based effectiveness perspective that considers the multiple, conflicting, and dynamic nature of DSS goals, the stories of *EC-Bananas, EC-Hormones*, and the like become more complex. No longer are these binary tales of failure or success but more intricate ones, entailing shifts and trade-offs between manifold competing institutional goals.

Finally, the third category of RTA-related cases, reviewed in Part IV, provided additional testimony of the variable nature of DSS goals, exposing how the growing friction between multilateralism and regionalism in international trade has steadily penetrated the WTO judicial domain, pushing the DSS's pendulum in the direction of some objectives as opposed to others. The analysis of this dispute category thus portrayed the DSS as the guarantor of WTO law and institutions that, in the face of the enduring proliferation of RTAs and long-lasting stalemate in the WTO's legislative arm, has operated to sustain multilateralism along the substantive, as well as the jurisdictional, nexus between the WTO and RTAs. This it has done by fostering the integrity, predictability (and supremacy) of the multilateral trade rules, supporting the continued operation of the WTO and the realization of its goals, and upholding the authority of the DSS itself as the central forum for adjudication of international trade disputes. As part of these goal-attainment endeavours in RTA-related cases, one could also observe the prominent role played by the

[2] Joseph A Conti, *Between Law and Diplomacy: The Social Contexts of Disputing at the World Trade Organization* (Stanford University Press 2011) 153.

DSS's goal of inducing compliance with WTO law yet as a means to achieving the more systemic, long-term purposes just enumerated.

What is more, in pursuing these various purposes, all with a view to sustaining multilateralism against the surge in RTAs, the DSS exhibited some meaningful variations in the judicial approaches and choices taken as compared to those envisaged for trade-and and perennial disputes. Probably most notable among these differences is the strict, exclusionary, and textual interpretative method applied in RTA-related cases, maintaining 'clinical isolation' between the multilateral and regional trade regimes, an approach standing in sharp contrast to the rather integrative stance taken by the DSS towards general international law in trade-and disputes, where WTO adjudicators did not hesitate to develop flexible teleological interpretations so as to accommodate values, interests and actors 'external' to the WTO. This variation, I argue, exemplifies the DSS's constant adjustment of its judicial tools to the dominant organizational goals it seeks to achieve in the different types of cases coming before it. Whereas in trade-and disputes, legitimation pressures pushed the DSS to account for the interests of external stakeholders and integrate public international law concerns over the environment or public health into its interpretation of the WTO agreements, in RTA-related cases, the vehement attempt of WTO adjudicators to safeguard and preserve the multilateral trading order constituted the main motivation to resist RTA rules and restrict their possible effects on WTO law and institutions.

The goal-shifting hypothesis advanced in the book is thus clearly corroborated by the comparison of the three dispute categories. The juxtaposition of the diverse goal-attainment patterns displayed by the DSS suggests that while in all disputes the system is engaged in the routine legal exercise of law interpretation and application in its pursuit of multiple organizational goals, the diverse features of the different disputes reaching its docket shift the emphasis placed on these goals and affect the judicial choices taken towards their achievement as the DSS moves from one dispute category to the other. Conflicts and trade-offs between the various objectives thus become inevitable; they in turn result in different dimensions of effectiveness and ineffectiveness in the system's operation.

11.4 Lessons for the Study of the WTO DSS (and Other International Courts)

The goal dynamics depicted in this book offer several important lessons for the study of the WTO DSS and international courts more generally. First, in contrast to the conventional view of DSS goals, including its compliance objective, as static elements, the analysis conducted herein exposes a more sophisticated and realistic goal structure, shifting in its nature. In this account, the multiple and conflicting aims steering the operation of the DSS are not fixed; rather, they are variable constructs, meaning that their relative weights shift in time and across different types of disputes, depending on a range of factors, such as the subject of the dispute, the social values at stake, the WTO obligations involved, as well as the systemic challenges and external pressures posed. Such forces, and the dynamic environment in which they come into play, provide a context that influences the expectations and choices facing the DSS and shapes the central goals it strives to attain.

This variable nature of DSS goals as it emerges from the comparative analysis carried out in the book is not only descriptively more accurate, portraying a more realistic and nuanced picture of the complex world of WTO adjudication, it is also normatively desirable. In a reality of multiple, often incompatible organizational purposes and shifting operative scenes, the variability embedded in DSS goals enables the system and those invoking it to carefully calibrate the objectives sought through WTO dispute settlement, depending on the circumstances, and to generate outcomes that better respond to the ever-changing flow of challenges and needs as they arise in real cases in the real world. In a certain sense, if you will, it is thus the variable nature of DSS goals that allows one to take seriously the manifold and competing normative demands placed on this adjudicative system and to give effect to its diverse roles by constantly shifting and balancing between them.

Second, the complex goal dynamics observed in the WTO DSS, especially the goal-shifting phenomenon, highlight a subtle refinement to the classical goal-based effectiveness definition presented at the beginning of this book. Under this fine-tuned conceptualization of judicial effectiveness, an effective international adjudicative system is not simply one that meets its goals but one that, given its multiplicity of objectives and varying operational contexts, knows how to adapt itself and its goal-attainment efforts accordingly.

Third, if indeed, as suggested here, the relative salience of DSS goals shifts in time and context, with the move across distinct dispute categories, it follows that a nuanced effectiveness evaluation of the DSS must account for those shifts and the varied outcomes produced by the system in different types of cases. Whereas in trade-and disputes, as this book has shown, such outcomes may have systemic ramifications for the legitimacy of both the WTO and its DSS, in perennial disputes these outcomes may include prevention of uncontrolled trade wars, conclusion of mutually satisfactory (albeit not fully WTO-compliant) settlements, and assurance of long-term international economic cooperation. Still, in RTA-related cases, the outcomes generated by the DSS may have significant effects on the integrity of the multilateral legal order and the future role of the WTO and its DSS in global economic governance.

Prevalent, static, one-dimensional effectiveness models, which treat all WTO disputes as monolithic and consider compliance as the DSS's key effectiveness benchmark, may not capture this variety of outcomes. Moreover, they may not capture the trade-offs such outcomes represent between the compliance objective and other DSS goals (among them, its traditional dispute settlement goal, or more systemic aims such as sustaining the legitimacy and viability of the WTO regime as a whole). In contrast to such models, a goal-based approach of the kind advanced in this book offers an avenue for a more complex understanding of DSS goals, outcomes, and effectiveness.

The richer and more nuanced understanding promised by the goal-based approach entails, to be sure, a more complex analytical process. Such an approach requires assessment of the DSS performance against multiple benchmarks. Also, whereas some DSS goals, such as promoting compliance and prompt settlement of disputes, contain quantitative aspects that are more amenable to measurement, others, especially open-ended ultimate ends such as conferring legitimacy on the WTO regime, may be more difficult to evaluate and may necessitate recourse to qualitative research to elicit information about goal-attainment perceptions. Finally, the tensions underlying DSS goals and goal-shifting trends over time and across disputes may constrain the ability to engage in an overall assessment of the system's effectiveness.

Yet, even if such an all-inclusive evaluation appears too ambitious, the goal-based framework provides fertile ground for a range of more defined and nuanced research projects. Thus, future research into the effectiveness of the system, in its current or any revised form, could draw on the theoretical framework advanced here to examine the DSS functioning with respect to particular organizational goals while exploring how their achievement promotes or hinders the realization of other interrelated or conflicting objectives. Our understanding would also be greatly enhanced by the development of specific structure and process indicators that, in line with the goal-based model, could enable us to better predict the likelihood of attaining respective DSS objectives. In extending the range of indicators that influence DSS goal-achievement capabilities, such future research can throw greater light on the factors that enhance or decrease the system's effectiveness. Lastly, another direction of future inquiry could focus on DSS goal attainment at different stages of the dispute settlement process, along different periods in the DSS's life, or in different categories of WTO disputes, in line with our goal-shifting concept. The findings of this book may contribute to such research efforts by increasing our understanding of the way in which the dynamics of practice, time, and change, from which the work of the DSS cannot be separated, become reflected in the aims pursued and the judicial outcomes generated. The multidimensional goal-based framework and the analytical concepts elaborated throughout the book thus open valuable research horizons for studying judicial effectiveness at the WTO. These horizons may be further extended, in turn, to the study of other international courts and tribunals.

And so, it should be stressed here that the lessons emerging from this book, especially as they relate to the shifting quality of DSS goals, portraying judicial effectiveness as a dynamic and enduring balancing act between multiple objectives, resonate far beyond the WTO domain and may inform theoretical and empirical research of other structures of international adjudication. While the adjudicative system standing at the centre of this book clearly differs in some meaningful respects from other courts currently operating at the international level (e.g. in its design, the subject matter of its jurisdiction, and the nature of the obligations it applies), it is fair to assume that the intertwined elements of goal multiplicity, goal conflict, and goal shifting addressed here are not exclusive to the WTO DSS; rather, these dimensions can be expected to present themselves in varying degrees in other international adjudicative institutions. How exactly do these elements manifest themselves in other international courts? What factors trigger shifts amidst the multiple goals prescribed for those other judicial fora? And how do such shifts shape the judicial outcomes and public goods they ultimately deliver? Those are but a few questions that future research may take up with a view to deepening our understanding of the operation and effectiveness of other sites of the evolving international judiciary.

11.5 Possible Lessons for Institutional Change and Reform

The findings emerging from this book and the analytical concepts developed herein may not only inform future studies on the effectiveness of the WTO DSS along the lines delineated; they may also contribute to the evaluation of future institutional reforms, as well as offer some insights into possible changes that may befall the DSS in wake of the crisis it has recently come to face. And so, while the WTO DSS is currently in high demand, with cases continuing to reach its docket,[3] at the time of wrapping up the writing of this book, the system has become subject to substantial pressure resulting from the increasing number and complexity of cases filed but especially from the United States' continued blocking of appointments to the Appellate Body (AB), a development that may deprive this body of the personnel needed to adjudicate cases as of December 2019.[4] At the core of the recent, unprecedented US attack against the AB—reflected in the former's persistent objection to all motions to nominate or renew the terms of AB members—appears to be what

[3] Thus, during 2018, thirty-nine disputes were filed with the DSS. This is the highest annual total in twenty years. See 'Chronological List of Disputes Cases' (*WTO*) <https://www.wto.org/english/tratop_e/dispu_e/dispu_status_e.htm> accessed 27 December 2018.

[4] The AB is composed of seven members who decide cases in panels of three. As of 1 October 2018, there are only three remaining AB members, and the terms of two of these members expire in December 2019. Hence, unless the United States stops blocking the AB selection process, or some other solution is found to the crisis, the AB will not be able to form panels to hear cases as of December 2019. For discussion of possible solutions to this crisis, see, e.g. Ernst-Ulrich Petersmann, 'How Should WTO Members Respond to the WTO Appellate Body Crisis?' (*International Economic Law and Policy Blog*, 13 December 2018) <https://worldtradelaw.typepad.com/ielpblog/2018/12/ulli-petersmann-on-how-should-wto-members-respond-to-the-wto-appellate-body-crisis.html> accessed 20 December 2018.

Washington views as 'the judicialization of WTO dispute settlement, where the AB has been operating as if it is an international court building a jurisprudence, rather than a modest body that issues ad hoc decisions to help WTO Members resolve discrete disputes'.[5] The recent US obstruction of the AB nomination process, as Rachel Brewster has put it, is thus 'a direct assault on the idea that disputes should be resolved through a neutral interpretation of trade law rather than [a] more negotiated, economic-power-based solution'.[6]

It is unclear at this stage what changes, if any, will be introduced to the WTO DSS and what future course the system will take in the wake of this stalemate. While some WTO Members and commentators have advanced proposals for overcoming the current deadlock by amending the WTO Dispute Settlement Understanding in a manner that may accommodate the AB-related concerns raised by the United States,[7] the latter, for its part, has (for the time being) not delivered any formal proposal for reform.[8] Some have nonetheless submitted that, according to existing indications, what officials in the Trump administration actually want to achieve by pursuing the chosen course of action is 'to revert' the WTO dispute settlement system 'to its less judicialized roots in the GATT'.[9]

[5] Gregory Shaffer, 'A Tragedy in the Making? The Decline of Law and the Return of Power in International Trade Relations' (2019) 44 Yale J Int'l L (forthcoming). For details of the US claims, see 'The President's 2018 Trade Policy Agenda' (*USTR*, 2018) 22–28 <https://ustr.gov/sites/default/files/files/Press/Reports/2018/AR/2018%20Annual%20Report%20I.pdf> accessed 16 December 2018.

[6] Rachel Brewster, 'The Trump Administration and the Future of the WTO' (2019) 44 Yale J Int'l L (forthcoming).

[7] For the various reform proposals raised in an attempt to stave off paralysis of the WTO DSS by unblocking the process for the appointment of new AB members, see Communication from Canada, 'Strengthening and Modernizing the WTO: Discussion Paper' (21 September 2018) JOB/GC/201 [hereinafter Communication from Canada]; Communication from the European Union, China, Canada, India, Norway, New Zealand, Switzerland, Australia, Republic of Korea, Singapore, and Mexico to the General Council (11 December 2018) WT/GC/W/752/Rev.2; Communication from the European Union, China and India to the General Council (11 December 2018) WT/GC/W/753/Rev.1. For a discussion of these proposals, see, e.g. Bryce Baschuk, 'EU Proposes New WTO Reform to Safeguard Dispute Settlement Body' (*Bloomberg*, 26 November 2018) <https://www.bloomberg.com/news/articles/2018-11-26/eu-proposes-new-wto-reform-to-safeguard-dispute-settlement-body> accessed 25 December 2018; Terence P Stewart, 'Proposals for WTO Dispute Settlement Reform – A First Step but not Enough' (2018) Washington International Trade Association Research Paper <https://wita.org/blogs/proposals-for-wto-dispute-settlement-reform-a-first-step-but-not-enough/> accessed 25 December 2018; Jennifer Hillman, 'Three Approaches to Fixing the World Trade Organization's Appellate Body: The Good, the Bad and the Ugly?' (2018) Institute of International Economic Law Research Paper <https://www.allnews.ch/sites/default/files/files/20181212_Georgetown-Hillman_Good_Bad_Ugly_Fix-to_WTO_AB.pdf> accessed 25 December 2018.

[8] Shaffer (n 5).

[9] ibid. In this respect, Shaffer has referred inter alia to a comment made by Robert Lighthizer, the US Trade Representative, whereby he alluded to the superiority of GATT dispute settlement: '[T]here was a system, it was before 1995, before the WTO, under the GATT, and there was a system where you would bring panels and then you would have a negotiation. And, you know, trade grew and we resolved issues eventually. And, you know, it's a system that, you know, was successful for a long period of time'. See 'U.S. Trade Policy Priorities: Robert Lighthizer, United States Trade Representative' (*Center for Strategic and International Studies*, 18 September 2017) <https://www.csis.org/analysis/us-trade-policy-priorities-robert-lighthizer-united-states-trade-representative> accessed 25 December 2018.

Going down the non-judicialization path would, to be sure, carry significant implications for the multilateral trading system, an analysis of which is beyond the scope of this book. Yet, the insights emerging from this study may nevertheless serve to highlight some of the prominent costs to be exacted should this road be taken. Among other things, reverting back to a power-based dispute resolution system would inevitably entail weakening the role played by the WTO DSS as a means for providing security and predictability to the multilateral trading system, for bestowing legitimacy on WTO governance, as well as for safeguarding the integrity of the WTO regime in the face of RTA-proliferation—all major goals served by the compulsory, rules-based DSS and the legal interpretations it has developed over the past two decades, as evidenced in this book.

Yet, as the evidence provided here further seems to suggest, a return to a less-legalistic DSS may effectively impede achievement of the very dispute settlement goal that the United States allegedly wishes to preserve, not least when disputes between major trading powers are at stake. As the case studies of *EC-Bananas* and *EC-Hormones* have aptly illustrated in this respect, absent the transition towards a more rule-oriented WTO DSS, the stalemate that characterized these transatlantic trade conflicts under the power-oriented GATT DSS would have likely continued. Resolution of these two perennial conflicts would have been much more difficult, so the numerous testimonies provided in the book suggest, if the United States and the other complainants in these trade feuds had been unable to draw on the mandatory WTO DSS as a forum for repeated litigation and interaction by which to facilitate settlement bargaining and arrive at a negotiated solution in the shadow of the law. It thus follows from these cases that in contrast to our basic intuitions, undoing judicialization of the WTO DSS may not simply work to the detriment of the weaker players in international trade by diminishing their right and ability to contest the trading practices of larger economic powers and be granted redress for their trade concerns; rather, it may hinder the very ability of the major economic powers to resolve the high-stake trade conflicts that occasionally erupt between themselves.

That being said, the lessons derived from this book may at the same time serve to highlight some of the risks that may be attendant on further legalization of the WTO DSS, as some have advocated over the years. In particular, the dynamics of WTO judicial effectiveness and the DSS's complex goal structure, unfolded herein, seem to suggest that some of the prominent proposals for DSS reform put forth during the last two decades may not necessarily improve the system's overall effectiveness, nor the functioning of the WTO regime as a whole.

And so, many proposals for amendment of the WTO DSS raised repeatedly since its inception in 1995, have pointed to the need to further improve the system's enforcement powers and sanctions, that is, its ability to elicit compliance from recalcitrant Members.[10] Although the DSS has enjoyed a good judgment-compliance

[10] Juscelino F Colares, 'The Limits of WTO Adjudication: Is Compliance the Problem?' (2011) 14 J Int'l Econ L 403, 404.

record throughout this period, 'mainstream scholars', especially legalists, have argued that 'more is to be done to strengthen the system'.[11] When so arguing, they have often pointed to instances of sustained noncompliance with adverse DSS rulings, which on some occasions (e.g. *EC-Bananas* and *EC-Hormones*) endured even in the face of WTO-authorized retaliatory measures, as illustrations of the ineffectiveness of the DSS and its remedies regime.[12] To address this effectiveness gap, these scholars have suggested a range of reforms, including increasing the level of authorized WTO retaliation (beyond the existing equivalence standard), subjecting respondents to compulsory compensation (in lieu of the currently available yet rarely used remedy of voluntary compensation), allowing for retroactive (and not merely prospective) damages, enabling collective (in addition to bilateral) retaliation, and other reforms such as tightening enforcement deadlines or establishing procedures for monitoring the enforcement of WTO commitments in disputes resolved by mutually agreed solutions, all meant to increase the incentives for compliance with WTO rulings and rules.[13]

These sorts of enforcement-enhancing proposals are premised, first, on the common assumption, flagged in this book, of rule compliance as the fixed primary goal the WTO DSS is expected to achieve. However, as the findings discussed above suggest, as a descriptive matter, it is incorrect to assume that compliance inducement is in fact the ultimate objective sought by the DSS at all times and across disputes. And, as the empirical analysis of *EC-Bananas* and *EC-Hormones* in Part III further illuminates, the same holds for the remedy of suspension of concessions that, like the adjudicative system of which it forms a part, serves multiple, competing, and varying purposes,[14] including but not limited to compliance inducement.[15]

[11] ibid 404.

[12] ibid.

[13] ibid. For a recent overview and discussion of these various reform proposals see Michelle Limenta, *WTO Retaliation: Effectiveness and Purposes* (Hart Publishing 2017) 58–69. For specific works advocating reforms to further strengthen the WTO DSS's enforcement mechanisms and remedies, see, e.g. Cherie O'Neal Taylor, 'Beyond Retaliation' (2017) 38 Nw J Int'l L & Bus 55; Di Hao, 'Compliance Problems Under WTO Disputes Settled by Mutually Agreed Solution' (2018) 49 Geo J Int'l L 887; Marco Bronckers and Freya Baetens, 'Reconsidering Financial Remedies in WTO Dispute Settlement' (2013) 16 J Int'l Econ L 281; Lucas Eduardo FA Spadano, 'Cross-agreement Retaliation in the WTO Dispute Settlement System: An Important Enforcement Mechanism for Developing Countries?' (2008) 7 World Trade Rev 511; Won-Mog Choi, 'To Comply or Not to Comply? Non-Implementation Problems in the WTO Dispute Settlement System' (2007) 41 J World Trade 1043; Yuka Fukunaga, 'Securing Compliance Through the WTO Dispute Settlement System: Implementation of DSB Recommendations' (2006) 9 J Int'l Econ L 383, 415; Marco Bronckers and Naboth van den Broek, 'Financial Compensation in the WTO: Improving the Remedies of WTO Dispute Settlement' (2005) 8 J Int'l Econ L 101; Rafiqul M Islam, 'Recent EU Trade Sanctions on the US to Induce Compliance with the WTO Ruling in the Foreign Sales Corporations Case: Its Policy Contradiction Revisited' (2004) 38 J World Trade 471.

[14] On this matter, see also Joost Pauwelyn, 'The Calculation and Design of Trade Retaliation in Context: What Is the Goal of Suspending WTO Obligations?' in Chad P Bown and Joost Pauwelyn (eds), *The Law, Economics and Politics of Retaliation in WTO Dispute Settlement* (CUP 2010) 34.

[15] For a similar argument, advocating a multipurpose perspective of WTO retaliation, see Limenta (n 13).

Yet, the various proposals advocating rigidifying WTO enforcement and sanctions are not only based on the assumption that compliance is the unremitting prime goal of the DSS and its retaliation mechanism, they are also predicated on a second, no less critical assumption that more compliance is necessarily warranted. Stated differently, underlying these proposals is the belief that instances of noncompliance, let alone sustained noncompliance as observed in *EC-Bananas, EC-Hormones*, and other perennial conflicts, constitute a threat to the effectiveness of the DSS and the overarching WTO legal system, and thus should be met with tougher sanctions.

The findings and analysis provided in this book, however, challenge this second assumption, too, suggesting that as a normative matter as well, it is erroneous to assume that more compliance is always good. In fact, the evidence emerging from the case studies of *EC-Bananas* and *EC-Hormones* suggests that pushing too forcibly on compliance may, rather, undermine the stability of the WTO and its DSS and eliminate a source of flexibility crucial for their long-term institutional effectiveness. The experience gained in these cases, as one state official put it, implies 'that there are certain instances where ... you just can't force compliance, because if you force compliance.... if you push too hard, then the risk is that the [whole] system breaks down'.[16] Going further to stress the importance of affording some space for noncompliance, as was the case in *EC-Bananas* and *EC-Hormones*, and as is effectively enabled under the current design of the WTO DSS,[17] a WTO ambassador added:

> [I]f you don't ... give ... some space ... [some] possibility not to comply, well, we are putting the system in jeopardy.... [N]ot now, but in the long term. So, because we care about the system, we are willing to ... be more flexible.... If there is no flexibility ... the system will break.[18]

As these statements underscore, a measured amount of noncompliance need not necessarily be viewed as a threat to the WTO and its DSS; it may alternatively be seen as a systemic safety valve that increases the flexibility of the DSS and decreases the possibility that the WTO system will break down in the face of exceptional political or economic pressures that make compliance impossible for respondents.[19] As Colares has noted, absent the diplomatic flexibility formerly available to Member states under the GATT regime, in the more legalized WTO DSS, noncompliance forms 'a method of last resort, accommodating Members'

[16] Interview with EU official (Geneva, 18 July 2012).

[17] Gregory Shaffer, Manfred Elsig, and Sergio Puig, 'The Extensive (but Fragile) Authority of the WTO Appellate Body' (2016) 79 L & Contemp Probs 237, 246.

[18] Interview with WTO ambassador (Geneva, 24 July 2012).

[19] Peter B Rosendorff, 'Stability and Rigidity: Politics and Design of the WTO's Dispute Settlement Procedures' (2005) 99 Am Pol Sci Rev 389.

strong political and economic interests' in periods of stress, while ensuring the continued operation of the WTO regime as well as sustaining Members' willingness to remain within its normative community in the future.[20] Moreover, as the evidence presented in Part III suggests, noncompliance, when so contained by the DSS and accompanied by a certain level of economic and reputational costs, enables the intertwining between adjudication and negotiation in the DSS's legal shadow to run its course and, somewhere down the line, to be translated into a negotiated agreement, perhaps not fully WTO-compatible, but beneficial for durable economic relations and a viable WTO system.

To be sure, 'operational noncompliance' of this sort does not fit well with a rule of law approach[21] and should be confined for equally important systemic reasons. Noncompliance with WTO rulings, if it does not occur on a limited basis, may gradually erode the reliability of WTO rules and hinder the legal predictability so vital to world trade.[22] It is also clear that the flexibility embedded in noncompliance is currently not distributed evenly between WTO Members.[23] Small countries risk being denied this flexibility by the implicit threat of more powerful states to impose additional costs on them, inside and outside the WTO domain, if they decide not to comply with an adverse DSS ruling.[24] Yet, even absent such threats, not all WTO Members are well-suited to bear the temporary economic costs of noncompliance in the form of tit-for-tat suspension of concessions, or to permanently buy their way out of compliance through negotiated settlements, as the EU essentially did in the *Bananas* and *Hormones* disputes.

While such considerations are no doubt valid, they do not negate the claim, supported by the book's findings, that in an international setting where law and politics must coexist, some flexibility in the resolution of disputes may be systemically no less valuable, and that less-than-perfect compliance, rather than posing a threat to the WTO and its DSS, may work to sustain their enduring functioning and effectiveness, i.e. their ability to achieve their various policy goals in the long run. For these reasons, a former senior WTO official openly stated: 'I think any enforcement system, sorry to say so, should have some tolerance for lawless behavior. This sounds very crude coming from a lawyer, but ... this is something I say to my first-year WTO students'.[25]

[20] Colares (n 10) 405.

[21] For discussion of this concept of 'operational noncompliance', see Jacob Katz Cogan, 'Noncompliance and the International Rule of Law' (2006) 31 Yale J Int'l L 189.

[22] Claus D Zimmermann, 'Toleration of Temporary Non-Compliance: The Systemic Safety Valve of WTO Dispute Settlement Revisited' (2011) 3 Trade L & Dev 382, 404; Heinz Hauser and Alexander Roitinger, 'Renegotiation in Transatlantic Trade Disputes' in Ernst-Ulrich Petersmann and Mark A Pollack (eds), *Transatlantic Economic Disputes: The EU, the US, and the WTO* (OUP 2003) 500.

[23] Hauser and Roitinger (n 22) 500.

[24] ibid.

[25] Interview with former senior WTO official (Geneva, 17 July 2012).

In this light, any suggestion for reform of the DSS that seeks 'to ratchet up compliance levels with WTO rulings to 100 per cent' should be considered with appropriate caution as it may, rather, not enhance but perhaps harm the system's performance.[26] This is not to say that the current WTO DSS is without problems or that no reforms are needed to further improve its effectiveness. It does mean that any amendment to its structures and processes should not go too far in the direction of raising the costs of WTO violation to the point where the flexibility ingrained in noncompliance is diminished. A former AB member stated as much when stressing that the effectiveness of the WTO's adjudicative system rests, to some extent, on its 'light touch' and inability to strictly enforce compliance on recalcitrant Members:

> [S]tates generally say [that] this is a very good system and it's very efficient and very productive and so [forth]. But ... in my view, the reason of this success does not lie in the procedures.... [W]hat makes it work very well, first, is that you have compulsory jurisdiction.... [Second], what people don't realize, is [that] ... the system really reduces enormously the price of losing. It takes care of the sovereignty of the state.... They don't push the [losing] state to do anything it doesn't want to do. They don't tell you what to do. They leave it to you [to decide how to implement an adverse DSS ruling].

And, the same AB member continued, if by the end of the period set for implementation of the DSS ruling the complainant believes that the losing state has not adequately brought its policy into line with WTO rules:

> You have to go a whole cycle again. And then ... if you still have the same thing, you go and ask the DSB [to take further action].... [T]he [losing] country [may then] say[], 'Oh, my constitution doesn't permit [me] to do anything, so I'll give compensation'. If the other [country] accepts compensation, it's alright. And it's always forward looking, and they don't compensate on injuries already suffered. If they don't accept [compensation] ... we get into sanctions.... And what do you get? You never coerce a country to do anything; ... [instead, you] say, 'Okay, you stay ... with your violative measure, but the other [country] can withdraw concessions', on the condition that the other [country] has some concessions to ... withdraw. So, you see, it's a very light touch. I mean, if you lose, it's not the end of the world. It makes it easier for countries to accept [the system].[27]

[26] Manfred Elsig, Bernard Hoekman, and Joost Pauwelyn, 'Thinking About the Performance of the World Trade Organization: A Discussion Across Disciplines' in Manfred Elsig, Bernard Hoekman, and Joost Pauwelyn (eds), *Assessing the World Trade Organization: Fit for Purpose?* (CUP 2017) 29.

[27] Interview with former AB member (Geneva, 19 April 2012).

The WTO DSS—as this testimony and the broader account provided in this book suggests—is thus a system of 'rule-enforcement with caveats',[28] the effectiveness of which (contrary to our basic legalistic intuitions) depends, in part, on its inability to fully enforce WTO rulings and rules on disobedient Members.

11.6 Beyond Effectiveness: Unintended Consequences and a Look to the Future

Since its establishment in 1995, the WTO DSS has grown to play a central role in the multilateral trade system. This pivotal role has become even more apparent against the enduring deadlock in the WTO's negotiating arm and the latter's struggle to deliver substantive results. As a former EU official openly stated when alluding to the status of the DSS within the WTO edifice as it has evolved: 'with the Doha Round basically dead ... there is not much they [i.e. the WTO] can take pride in. I find it is actually only the dispute settlement system [that] they can take pride in'.[29] A WTO legal officer involved in the working of the DSS echoed similar thoughts: 'These days we are the WTO. We give credibility to the rules. Well nothing else is happening [in the organization].... We are a big part of the WTO'.[30]

Yet, the same interviewee immediately went on to add: 'whether it's a good thing or a bad thing, you are getting ... different views. Some people ... don't like it. Some people think that dispute settlement shouldn't be such a big part of the WTO's functions, and that ... it is not a good development but a bad development'.[31] One of the main criticisms to fuel this latter view, voiced most forcefully by the United States, concerns the claimed 'increasing tendency of the dispute settlement process to displace or erode the negotiation function of the WTO'.[32]

And so, the salient role assumed by the judicialized DSS in the multilateral trade system, as a former AB admitted, may in fact 'hide an irony: members of the WTO may be more reluctant to undertake new binding commitments in ... trade negotiations' conducted in the presence of the DSS as it has developed over the last two decades or so.[33] Another former AB member, though using language that is more cautious, made a similar point:

[28] Interview with former EU official (Geneva, 9 July 2012).
[29] Interview with former EU official (Geneva, 9 July 2012).
[30] Interview with staff member of the AB Secretariat (Geneva, 18 April 2012).
[31] ibid.
[32] Terence P Stewart, 'The Broken Multilateral Dispute System' (2018) Asia Society Policy Institute Research Paper, 1 <https://www.law.berkeley.edu/wp-content/uploads/2018/01/Terence-P.-Stewart-Asia-Society-Paper-re-dispute-settlement-WEB-VERSION-1.pdf> accessed 25 December 2018.
[33] A V Ganesan, 'The Appellate Body in its Formative Years: A Personal Perspective' in Gabrielle Marceau (ed), *A History of Law and Lawyers in the GATT/WTO: The Development of the Rule of Law in the Multilateral Trading System* (CUP 2015) 545.

> Well, it is highly speculative for me to say that, but I have always felt that future agreements ... would be made more complicated through the existence of the dispute settlement system.... The Doha Development Round appears to be dead and dead for other reasons. But I could imagine that the dispute settlement system has contributed to the difficulties to agree.[34]

Other WTO practitioners likewise opined that the presence of a stronger DSS has contributed to the impasse in multilateral negotiations by making states more hesitant to agree on new rules that may expose them to further compulsory judicial scrutiny, thereby leading states to pursue clearer treaty texts (that would leave adjudicators with less interpretative leeway) while restraining the use of constructive ambiguity as a way to move negotiations forward.[35] Illustrative in this respect is the following statement of a senior WTO official:

> [O]ne could make the case that one of the reasons it has been so difficult to negotiate the Doha Round is because ... of this more complete legal regime.... [P]eople worry more about making concessions now because ... the legal regime is so effective. So maybe, in a way, the Europeans were right [back then in the Uruguay Round, and] ... the increased strength of the dispute settlement system has been to the detriment of the negotiating system. I tend to think that eventually the negotiating system will get back in action ... but it is probably a lot harder now.[36]

Still, some have gone further to argue that the strengthened WTO judiciary has not only contributed to the difficulties in negotiating new trade rules, it has also reduced the relevance of multilateral negotiations.[37] That is to say, juridification of the WTO DSS has had 'the *unintended consequence* of undermining the need of Members to negotiate on unresolved matters' by encouraging them 'to seek through dispute settlement that which they historically would have sought through negotiations'.[38] Consequently, it has been argued, some issues that could have been addressed through negotiations have instead been raised by Members in disputes before the DSS 'in the hope that they could obtain their goals through litigation ..., even though they knew what they sought had never been agreed [to] by the other Members'.[39] The concern over this state of affairs, which appears to occupy a central

[34] Interview with former AB member (Brussels, 19 July 2012).
[35] Interview with WTO ambassador (Geneva, 24 July 2012).
[36] Interview with senior WTO official (Geneva, 11 July 2012).
[37] Stewart (n 32) 2–3.
[38] ibid 3 (emphasis added). See also Communication from Canada (n 7) ('Adjudication has taken on a more prominent role in sustaining trade cooperation than originally envisaged, in some cases substituting for negotiation').
[39] ibid.

place in the recent US backlash against the WTO DSS, was articulated by the US Trade Representative at the recent WTO Ministerial Conference in these words:

> [T]he WTO is obviously an important institution. It does an enormous amount of good, and provides a helpful negotiating forum for Contracting Parties.
>
> But, in our opinion, serious challenges exist. . . .
>
> [M]any are concerned that the WTO is losing its essential focus on negotiation and becoming a litigation-centered organization. Too often members seem to believe they can gain concessions through lawsuits that they could never get at the negotiating table. We have to ask ourselves whether this is good for the institution and whether the current litigation structure makes sense.[40]

Whether the juridified WTO DSS has indeed developed in a manner that inadvertently worked to the detriment of the WTO's negotiating function, as the above statements imply, is a question deserving further consideration and investigation. Yet, for the purpose of this conclusion, what these statements, reflective of the perceptions of at least some actors in the WTO setting, essentially suggest is that 'there are trade-offs for having this more . . . binding, effective [judicial] system',[41] which alongside its benefits might also be projecting unintended costs onto its environment. These testimonies thus importantly urge future research to go beyond questions of judicial effectiveness—defined in this book in terms of goal attainment, that is, the attainment of predefined, desired outcomes—to also consider the unintended consequences generated through the operation of international adjudicative institutions like the WTO DSS.

The rise of international courts in recent decades has marked a significant development for international law and international affairs. Critical questions have subsequently arisen: Are international courts effective mechanisms for international governance?[42] Do they in fact fulfil the goals for which they were created and entrusted with enhanced legal powers?[43] Do they, by way of example, resolve disputes peacefully and promptly? Do they bestow legitimacy onto the international regimes in which they are embedded? Do they support the ongoing operation of these regimes and the realization of their policy objectives? Do they improve compliance with their underlying legal norms?

When addressing these effectiveness-related questions, however, accounting for the goals, that is, the desired outcomes promoted by international courts, the

[40] 'Opening Plenary Statement of USTR Robert Lighthizer at the WTO Ministerial Conference' (*US Embassy in Argentina*, 11 December 2017) <https://ustr.gov/about-us/policy-offices/press-office/press-releases/2017/december/opening-plenary-statement-ustr> accessed 25 December 2018.

[41] Interview with senior WTO official (Geneva, 11 July 2012).

[42] Yuval Shany, *Assessing the Effectiveness of International Courts: A Goal-Based Approach* (OUP 2014) 3.

[43] ibid.

unintended costs or consequences associated with their work should not go unnoticed. As explained in Chapter 1 and as further elaborated here, these unintended consequences should form an additional and integral part of any critical assessment of international courts' overall performance. To be clear, this should not be taken as a call to undo the judicialization of international affairs, diminish the power of international courts, or forsake the multiple goals they have been established to promote—many of which have been highlighted in this book. Rather, this is a call for future research and practice to embrace a more comprehensive and critical stance towards the complex phenomenon of international adjudication, one that considers the range of *intended* and *unintended* outcomes it engenders and acknowledges the trade-offs it imposes on the structures of international law and international cooperation.

Index

Note: For the benefit of digital users, indexed terms that span two pages (e.g., 52–53) may, on occasion, appear on only one of those pages.